THE CAMBRIDGE HISTORY OF CLASSICAL LITERATURE

GENERAL EDITORS

Mrs P. E. Easterling *Fellow of Newnham College, Cambridge*
E. J. Kenney *Fellow of Peterhouse, Cambridge*

ADVISORY EDITORS

B. M. W. Knox *The Center for Hellenic Studies, Washington*
W. V. Clausen *Department of the Classics, Harvard University*

VOLUME II PART 1
THE EARLY REPUBLIC

THE CAMBRIDGE HISTORY OF CLASSICAL LITERATURE

VOLUME II: LATIN LITERATURE

THE CAMBRIDGE HISTORY OF CLASSICAL LITERATURE

VOLUME II

PART 1

The Early Republic

EDITED BY

E. J. KENNEY

Fellow of Peterhouse, Cambridge

ADVISORY EDITOR

W. V. CLAUSEN

Professor of Greek and Latin
Harvard University

CAMBRIDGE UNIVERSITY PRESS

CAMBRIDGE

LONDON   NEW YORK   NEW ROCHELLE

MELBOURNE   SYDNEY

Published by the Press Syndicate of the University of Cambridge
The Pitt Building, Trumpington Street, Cambridge CB2 1RP
32 East 57th Street, New York, NY 10022, USA
296 Beaconsfield Parade, Middle Park, Melbourne 3206, Australia

First published 1982 as chapters 1–7 of *The Cambridge History of Classical Literature*, Volume II
First paperback edition 1983

Printed in Great Britain by the University Press, Cambridge

Library of Congress catalogue card number: 82-19780

British Library Cataloguing in Publication Data
The Cambridge history of classical literature.
Vol. 2: Latin literature
The Early republic
1. Classical literature – History and criticism
I. Kenney, E. J. II. Clausen, W. V.
880'.09   PA3001
ISBN 0 521 27375 7

CONTENTS

CONTENTS

PLATES

READERS AND CRITICS

1

BOOKS AND READERS IN
THE ROMAN WORLD

For half a millennium the printed book has been the primary means of communicating ideas in the Western world. Now, with the development of film, radio, and television, together with alternative means of storing and retrieving information, the old empire of the printed word is under threat and has indeed already suffered some erosion. Nevertheless, for contemporary Western man the book, in the shape in which he has known it for centuries, still stands firmly at the centre of his literary and scientific culture. This shape is so familiar that it requires a considerable effort of the imagination to grasp the essential differences between the book as it is now and as it was in classical antiquity. In the following pages an attempt is made to sketch the conditions under which books were composed, copied, circulated, preserved, studied and used during the period covered by this volume. In this way it is hoped that the modern reader – who inevitably approaches this subject with certain preconceptions as to what a 'book' should look like and how it is to be read – may be helped to form an idea of some of the fundamental differences between ancient and modern literary culture, and hence achieve a clearer appreciation of the books and authors discussed in the body of the work. In some respects, as will emerge, the literary life of Greece and Rome retained the characteristics of an oral culture, a fact reflected in much of the literature that has come down to us. The modern reader, who is accustomed to taking in literature through the eye rather than through the ear, cannot be too frequently reminded that nearly all the books discussed in this history were written to be listened to.

Any attempt to discuss this subject must begin with a number of caveats, which arise from the extent and character of the evidence available to us. In the first place, whereas the remains of Greek books written in classical antiquity (dating predominantly from the first to the third centuries A.D.) are reasonably plentiful, few Latin papyri survive, and many of them are non-literary.[1] Inferences from the Greek to the Latin book, though in the circumstances inevitable, must be made with great caution.

Secondly, within the span of time covered by the phrase 'the Roman

[1] Texts at Cavenaile (1958) 7–142. See also Plate III.

3

world' – here taken to embrace the period from the third century B.C. to the early fifth century A.D. – only certain select periods, persons and types of literary activity are illuminated by the surviving evidence. This limitation must be patiently accepted and the temptation to generalize resisted. In the effort, for example, to construct a picture of the Roman book trade, much has been made of the well-documented relationship of Cicero with Atticus; but this procedure can be extremely misleading (see below, section 4). It is admittedly reasonable to assume a good deal of continuity in this, as in many other areas of ancient life, during the period under review: so far as our evidence takes us, it seems true to say that the conditions under which Latin books were written, copied, 'published' and read did not in essentials differ (when the effects of the introduction of the *codex* are allowed for) in the time of St Jerome from what they had been in Cicero's day.[1] Even so, general inferences about authorship or the book trade based, for example, on what Martial says about his own work must be recognized for what they are: hypotheses offered *faute de mieux*.

Thirdly, far too much implicit reliance has in the past been placed on arguments from analogy with modern literary and publishing practice. To style Atticus a 'publisher', as is still done in more than one current treatment, is to import into the reconstruction of his activities an entirely modern and obtrusive concept belonging in the world of the printed book.[2] In so far as analogies in this field are valid at all, they should rather be sought in the Middle Ages, and more especially in the last century of the Renaissance (that is, from about 1350 to 1450), when there recurred for the first time since classical antiquity the phenomenon of a highly developed and intensive literary and scholarly culture (which we can document in considerable detail) propagating itself through the medium of the manuscript book.

In the light of these considerations the evidence relating to specific cases must be interpreted with circumspection and not made the basis for superstructures of speculation which it is unequal to bearing. Much of what at present passes for the history of scholarship in the Roman world needs close and sceptical re-examination.[3] The results of such an analysis would no doubt be a less coherent and indeed in some ways less intelligible picture than that presented by some standard works of reference; but not least among the virtues of a student of this branch of scholarship ought to be, in Quintilian's words (*Inst.* 1.8.21), *aliqua nescire* – to accept the necessity to be ignorant of some things.

[1] Arns (1953) *passim*.
[2] Sommer (1926) 422; cf. for instance the highly tendentious title chosen by Kleberg (1967).
[3] Zetzel (1972); id. (1973) 239–43.

1. GREEK AND ROMAN LITERARY CULTURE

Graecia capta ferum uictorem cepit 'captive Greece led her rough conqueror captive' (Hor. *Epist.* 2.1.156). The history of Roman literature effectively begins with Ennius. Plautus in his comedies had reproduced his Greek models in metres in which the influence of native Latin verse is apparent. Ennius, by choosing to naturalize the Greek hexameter as the metre of his national epic, the *Annales*, declared an allegiance which was never thereafter shaken off. Literary dependence on Greek models was part of a general (if not universal and unquestioning) acceptance of contemporary Greek culture by the Romans of the second century B.C.[1] Thus the nascent Roman literary tradition found itself almost overnight the inheritor, not only of the riches of Greek literature itself, but also of a copious and highly developed body of critical, grammatical and rhetorical theory and practice.

The assimilation of this huge mass of intellectual nourishment was a prodigious undertaking, never completely achieved. To take two examples from the extremities of our period: it seems doubtful whether even Cicero's first-hand knowledge of Greek poetry and philosophy was as considerable as his allusions, taken at their face value, appear to suggest;[2] and Claudian was evidently exceptional among his contemporaries for his erudition in both languages.[3] It may be questioned whether a truly unified Graeco-Roman literary culture ever existed; if it did, it was short-lived and precarious. Juvenal and Lucian (especially in his *De mercede conductis*) illuminate the mutual dislike of Greeks and Romans and, more especially, the one-way nature of the cultural traffic. Ammianus Marcellinus and Claudian, whose native language was Greek but who wrote in Latin, are quite untypical. What can safely be asserted is that the Latin poets from Catullus and Lucretius onwards assumed in their readers an acquaintance with – or at all events an awareness of – a wide range of Greek poetry. The educational curriculum also subscribed, in theory, to a similar ideal (see below, section 2). Moreover the criticism and exegesis of Latin literature was conducted through 'the application and misapplication of Alexandrian methods'.[4] In this sense the Roman consumer of literature may indeed be said to have been the prisoner of Greek culture.

2. EDUCATION

Roman educational institutions, predictably, followed Greek models. Indeed, down to the time of Augustus Roman education essentially *was* Greek: that is to say, it was Greek poetry and Greek oratory that formed the staple of study and imitation. 'Latin poetry came into existence so that teachers should have

[1] Marrou (1956) 243–7; Momigliano (1975) 17–21.
[2] Jocelyn (1973); cf. Marrou (1956) 426–7.
[3] Cameron (1970) 305, 348.   [4] Zetzel (1972) 272.

something to argue about': it was not until there was a native literature that could challenge comparison with Greek that Latin texts could become central in Roman education.[1] Cultivated Romans were conscious of the need for a literature of their own and eager to exploit it as it came into being. In the field of oratory Cicero's speeches were studied as exemplary in his own lifetime (*Att.* 2.1.3, 4.2.2), and his treatises *De oratore*, *Orator* and *Brutus* breathe a conviction of authority, a consciousness that their author had laid the foundations of a truly Latin school of eloquence. In the field of epic the *Aeneid* was acclaimed, even before publication, as a work of classical status (Prop. 2.34.65–6); a fact officially recognized, as it were, by the decision of the grammarian Q. Caecilius Epirota in about 25 B.C. to lecture on 'Virgil and other modern poets'.[2] From now on Latin literature could occupy its rightful place in the scheme of education.

This education was almost entirely linguistic and literary, and it served with almost complete single-mindedness the end of perfecting self-expression. Lip-service is paid by Quintilian to the need to study philosophy, natural science, history and law; but in the grand design of his work these recommendations have all the air of an afterthought.[3] For him the aim of the pre-rhetorical stages of education is summed up in the phrase *recte loquendi scientiam et poetarum enarrationem* 'the understanding of correct speech and the interpretation of the poets' (*Inst.* 1.4.2).[4] The methods used to this end were slow, thorough, and relentlessly pedantic. Under his elementary schoolmaster (*litterator*, *magister ludi litterarii*), from about the age of seven, the child practised writing and reciting the letters of the alphabet in every possible combination before repeating the procedure with syllables and then complete words. No short cuts were permitted. 'There is no short way with syllables', says Quintilian: 'they must be learned thoroughly, and the difficult ones must not (as usually happens) be left until they are encountered in actual words' (1.1.30). That is to say, attention to form is to precede attention to sense; and that is the order of priority expressly commended by the Greek critic Dionysius of Halicarnassus (writing under Augustus) at the beginning of his treatise *On composition*.[5] The whole process was taken over entire from Hellenistic primary education.[6]

---

[1] Marrou (1956) 251–2.

[2] Suet. *Gramm.* 16.2 *primus dicitur . . . Vergilium et alios poetas nouos praelegere coepisse.* The word '*nouos*' here means 'modern'; it does not of itself connote the existence of a particular school of poets.

[3] 12.2–4; cf. also 1.4.4 (music, astronomy, science), 1.10 (music, geometry); Marrou (1956) 281–2. Treatment of these topics in school would be even more perfunctory; Servius' commentary on Virgil indicates the level of instruction provided.

[4] This was taken over from Greek: Dion. Thrax 1 on judging poetry, as the end of grammar; cf. Varro *ap.* Diomed. *GLK* 1 426.

[5] Dion. Hal. *Comp.* 3; cf. Guillemin (1937) 47.

[6] Marrou (1956) 150–3, with examples of school-exercises from the papyri. If the recommendations of Quintilian may be taken to represent general practice, children would seem ordinarily to have begun the systematic grammatical study of Greek before that of Latin (1.1.12). However, it is clear that Quintilian himself was much better read in Latin than in Greek, and it may be guessed that these were counsels of perfection.

The same dependence, and the same emphasis on literal and verbal *minutiae*, were evident in the next stage, under the teacher of literature (*grammaticus*), begun usually at the age of eleven or thereabouts. The reading (*praelectio*) and interpretation (*enarratio*) of texts was conducted on a predominantly technical level. An example of the relentlessly pedantic methods employed may be found in Priscian's *Partitiones* ('Distinctions') on the first twelve verses of the *Aeneid*: they occupy some fifty-five large octavo pages in Keil's edition.[1] Exposition of content (*enarratio historiarum*) formed part of the process but was almost entirely an affair of factual erudition. Literary criticism as it is now understood – concern with larger social and aesthetic values – was virtually unknown at any level of scholarly activity and certainly formed no part of the school curriculum. A paradoxical feature of the system, but one which had important implications for literature, was the concentration in the schools on poetical texts, given that the ultimate aim was to produce the *perfectus orator* – a man consummately well trained in the art of effective extempore speech in prose.[2] On the face of it this emphasis was beneficial. The range of authors recommended by Quintilian for school reading in both Greek and Latin (1.8.5–12) is quite extensive and offers an excellent foundation for a literary education. In point of fact his list (like nearly all such lists) reflects a traditional view of what is ideally desirable rather than current reality.[3] However, even when allowance is made for the normal discrepancy between theory and practice, it seems clear that the choice of authors regarded as classical in the highest sense and so especially suitable to form the basis of the curriculum gradually narrowed during the later Empire. For the late fourth-century grammarian Arusianus Messius four authors had come to represent the preferred sources of classical Latin usage, Virgil, Sallust, Terence and Cicero.[4] Again, of these four it was the two poets who predominated in the school curriculum and who attracted most attention from grammarians and commentators. So it is that Virgil and Terence enjoy the best protected traditions of all Latin writers – that is to say, they have been largely immune from the casual and arbitrary alterations that in varying degrees have affected the texts of other authors (cf. below, section 5). But there was no question of studying them, or any other author, for their own sake. The role of poetry in education was always ancillary to the overriding rhetorical purpose of the system. When Quintilian commends the older poets of Rome (1.8.10–12), it is as a source of authority and embellishment for the orator.

[1] *GLK* III 459–515.

[2] Cf. Quint. *Inst.* 1.4.4, 2.5.1–20, suggesting, rather apologetically, the *praelectio* of orators and historians by the *rhetor* as part of the first elements of rhetorical instruction (*prima rhetorices rudimenta*).

[3] This is even more true of his famous conspectus of the reading of the orator in Book 10: on its sources in Alexandrian and later literary tradition see Peterson (1891) xxviii–xxxix.

[4] *GLK* VII 449–515; Cassiodorus (*Inst.* 1.15.7) refers to 'Messius' foursome', *quadriga Messii*. Cf. Marrou (1956) 277–8.

The formal education of many boys no doubt finished with the *grammaticus*. Some moved on, usually at the age of puberty but in some cases several years earlier, to the third, and for most Romans final, stage of their education under the teacher of rhetoric (*rhetor*). Rhetorical teaching in Latin was comparatively late in developing and did not become securely established until early in the first century B.C.[1] What is significant for literature is that its establishment coincided in time with the rise to power of Octavian, later Augustus, and the gradual disappearance of real political liberty at Rome. The main practical element in the education of the Roman boy who was destined (as all Romans of good family were traditionally destined) for public life was declamation: formal speeches on specified topics. At Rome this exercise may have originally tended to resort more often to real life for its choice of themes – contemporary legal and political issues – than its Greek counterpart.[2] Under the Principate there was, for obvious reasons, a shift away from realistic and contemporary subjects to those founded on premises ranging from the improbable through the romantic to the frankly grotesque. Some of the subjects can be seen to have been derived from literature, especially the New Comedy, rather than from life.

Declamation, which began as a purely private exercise, quickly became a public spectacle in which even accomplished speakers and prominent men of affairs did not think it beneath them to participate. Quintilian (10.5.14) recommends declamation as of practical use for the speaker who is already fully perfect in the art and celebrated in the courts, *consummatus ac iam in foro clarus*. A notable example of the adult practitioner was the Emperor Nero (Suet. *Nero* 10). Two types of exercise were in vogue: the *suasoria*, in which the speaker advised some famous character of history or fable on his proper course of action in a difficult situation; and the *controversia*, in which the speakers argued on opposite sides of a case, usually of a legal or quasi-legal nature. Of these types the *controversia* was in general more popular as being more directly competitive. Given the emphasis on competition and the unreal premises of the arguments, the aim of the adepts was not so much to convince as to astonish their auditors. To this end they employed all possible resources: vivid descriptions, striking turns of phrase, paradox, point, sententious epigram, and emotional extravagances of the most extreme kind. Above all they relied on what were technically known as *colores* 'colours': the ingenious manipulation, often to the point of standing things on their heads, of words and ideas, with the object of putting a new and unexpected complexion on the data of the case. In all this probability was hardly regarded; the aim was less to persuade than to outdo the previous speaker.

[1] For the political background to the process see Gwynn (1926) 60–9, Clarke (1953) 11–15, Marrou (1956) 252–3.

[2] Cf. on the anonymous treatise *Ad Herennium* Marrou loc. cit.; Bonner (1949) 25. Cicero's early *De inventione* may, however, give a more typical picture.

Such were the characteristics of declamation.[1] The danger that these exercises, designed as subordinate to the practical ends of oratory, might become an end in themselves was recognized very soon, and the literature of the first century A.D. abounds in criticisms of the excesses and abuses of the schools. But the thought of any alternative form of training was never seriously entertained; Quintilian's belief in the value of declamation when properly controlled is clearly unshakeable (2.10). For Pliny, Quintilian's star pupil, the cultivation of eloquence was a life-long pursuit; and he in turn instructed his juniors in the pleasure and utility of the exercises on which it depended (*Epist.* 7.9, esp. sections 12–14). Only to Tacitus did it occur to question, and then only implicitly, in his *Dialogus*, the *raison d'être* of this ceaseless activity. For Pliny and his circle, as for most others, its necessity and virtue were self-evident.

The effects on literature of this mass conditioning, as it must be accounted, of writers and public alike can be traced already in the work of Ovid, and it is conspicuous in the poets of the Silver Age. However, one reservation must be made: women, who formed a not inconsiderable part of the literate public, did not go through the whole course of education just described. There is some evidence to show that some girls, probably from less well-to-do families, attended elementary schools;[2] but most of those who received any education at all must have received it at home. There is ample testimony to the existence of cultured women in the poetry of Catullus, Propertius and Ovid, and in Pliny's letters;[3] and Juvenal's tirade against bluestockings must have had some basis in fact to be effective satire. Little literature written by women has survived or is known to have existed;[4] but the purity of the Latin spoken by ladies of good family is remarked by both Cicero and Pliny.[5] In attempting to form an idea of the Roman literary scene, therefore, some allowance should be made for the existence of a class of readers who had not been through the mill of contemporary rhetoric.

The most striking feature of ancient education is its extreme conservatism and effective resistance to change. In essentials the Roman schools of the fifth century A.D. were still patterned after those of Hellenistic Greece; the main difference, language apart, was that the emphasis on rhetoric was even more concentrated. Efforts by Cicero and – such as they were – Quintilian to impart

[1] They are best understood through study of the elder Seneca's *Controversiae* and *Suasoriae*; cf. Bonner (1949) 51–70; Winterbottom (1974) vii–xv.

[2] Guillemin (1937) 85 n. 4, citing Martial 8.3.15–16, 9.68.1–2; Friedländer (1908–28) I 230–1, IV 410–11.

[3] Sherwin-White (1966) 347 on Plin. *Epist.* 5.16.3.

[4] There seems to be no good reason to doubt the authenticity of the poems ascribed to Sulpicia in the Tibullan corpus, though the patronizing remarks of an older generation of critics about 'feminine Latinity' will not bear examination: Smith (1913) 80.

[5] *Brut.* 211, *De or.* 3.45, Plin. *Epist.* 1.16.6; cf. Cameron (1970) 317 n. 1.

a more liberal cast to school studies failed. The emphasis remained verbal, grammatical and rhetorical; and the fact is reflected in the critical and exegetical tradition as well as in the literature itself.[1]

3. AUTHOR AND PUBLIC

No quantitative estimate of the extent of literacy at any period in the Roman world is possible.[2] What can be said with some assurance is that the literature with which this discussion is concerned was from first to last the preserve of the relatively small élite in which high culture flourished. To this rule drama and oratory, which were necessarily directed to the wider public, constitute the only exceptions of importance. The other literary genres, along with Hellenistic standards of technical refinement and curious learning in poetry, took over the assumption that the poet wrote for a select group of readers who shared his ideas of how poetry should be written and were competent to judge his work. From the first Latin literature was an affair of groups and coteries. The fact is intimately connected with the largely informal way in which books were 'published' and circulated (see below, section 4). This situation was not altered by the spread of Roman power and the development of Rome into a cosmopolitan capital. Latin literature took on the characteristics of a world literature: Ovid and Martial purport to be conscious of a public extending from Britain to the Black Sea. But most literary activity was concentrated at Rome, and it was to Rome that provincial writers made their way.[3] In spite of the huge and heterogeneous population of the capital, the literary public must have been relatively small: Martial's epigrams give an impression of a closed society whose members were mostly well known to each other. The analogy of, say, eighteenth-century London suggests that this is what might be expected. Literary circles of course existed in the provinces, such as that at Naples, with which Statius was connected,[4] but it was Rome that offered the best opportunities to writers, whether amateur or professional.

Though the idea of a mass audience was rejected by the poet who was conscious of his traditional status, writers were acutely alive to the need to please if their works – and hence they themselves – were to survive. That this idea of survival through one's works was, in a pagan culture, extremely powerful is shown by such affirmations as Horace's Ode *Exegi monumentum* (3.30) and the conclusion of Ovid's *Metamorphoses*. But before submitting himself to a verdict from which there could be no appeal, an author would often try out

[1] For a good general survey see Bonner (1977).
[2] Cf. Guillemin (1937) 78–84, arguing that literacy was widespread.
[3] Most Roman writers hailed from the provinces; there is no proof that any was born at Rome, though Lucretius and Caesar may have been: Watts (1971) 97.
[4] Vessey (1973) 44–6.

his work on a smaller circle. There were good practical reasons for this, founded in the character of ancient publication. Once a book was in full circulation, there was no effective means of correcting it, let alone recalling it. Second thoughts therefore were likely to be unavailing; a corrected second edition could not be guaranteed to supersede the first. Horace puts the matter in a nutshell when he warns intending authors to show their work to competent critics and to keep it by them for revision for nine years before launching it into the world: *nescit uox missa reuerti* 'the word once uttered cannot be recalled' (*A.P.* 386–90). Some at least of the poets who died leaving their work to be published by their executors – Lucretius, Catullus (?), Virgil, Persius – may have been actuated by a desire to postpone the irrevocable moment as long as possible. The feelings of Virgil on the subject were indeed so acute that he tried to ensure that his uncompleted *Aeneid* should perish with him (*Vit. Donat.* 39).

It was, then, even more important than it is today for a writer to submit his work to the test of critical opinion before publication. For the younger Pliny and his friends – though his circle cannot be taken as entirely representative – this became almost an obsession: 'la précaution a dégénéré en tic'.[1] This is where the coterie might assume considerable importance. Books or portions of books were read aloud to a small audience of friends, who were invited to criticize freely what they heard. The origins of this custom go back at least to Hellenistic Alexandria: the variations on the same themes that we encounter in the epigrams of Callimachus and Asclepiades represent a critical as well as a creative activity, practised for a small audience of cultured friends round the dinner-table. About literary coteries at Rome before the age of Cicero we are ill informed. The so-called 'Scipionic circle' – the literary friends of Scipio Aemilianus Africanus Numantinus (185–129 B.C.), who included Terence and Lucilius – cannot on the basis of the extant evidence be shown to have represented any shared artistic position.[2] Similarly the poets who towards the end of the second century B.C. were writing Latin epigrams on the Hellenistic pattern – Valerius Aedituus, Porcius Licinus, Q. Lutatius Catulus – cannot be proved to have formed a group with common aims.[3] It is with Catullus that we first encounter clear evidence of something like a full-blown literary circle, wedded to the Callimachean idea of a poetic programme and a doctrinaire view of poetry.[4]

Under the Principate the sort of private and informal criticism that must have played a part in shaping many of Catullus' poems and that still flourished among Pliny's acquaintance began to yield pride of place to a more public kind

[1] Guillemin (1937) 37; cf. Burr (1959) 59.
[2] Astin (1967) 294, affirming that the term is 'essentially an invention of modern scholarship'.
[3] Ross (1969) 142.
[4] Guillemin (1937) 36, Clausen (1964) 189. On the possible connexion of the grammarian Valerius Cato with Catullus and the 'Neoterics' cf. Crowther (1971) 108–9.

of occasion. The institution of the *recitatio*, the public or semi-public reading aloud by an author of his work, appears (Sen. *Contr.* 4 *praef.* 2) to be due to the historian Asinius Pollio (76 B.C.–A.D. 4). Virgil, as is well known, read (under some compulsion) Books 2 (1?), 4 and 6 of the *Aeneid* to Augustus and members of his family; and it is also recorded that he would on occasion read to larger audiences passages which he felt might benefit from criticism (*Vit. Donat.* 32–3). In the first century A.D. the *recitatio* became a regular feature of the literary life of Rome, as numerous contemporary references indicate.[1] Some of these occasions were private and were genuinely intended to elicit criticism before final publication. However, for writers who were in any sense professional – i.e. who depended on writing for their living (see below, p. 21) – the *recitatio* was primarily a form of advertisement or puffing.

Preliminary publication of this kind, as the *recitatio* must be accounted, undoubtedly influenced the way in which literature was written. In general it may be taken for granted that throughout antiquity books were written to be read aloud, and that even private reading often took on some of the characteristics of a modulated declamation.[2] It might be said without undue exaggeration that a book of poetry or artistic prose was not simply a text in the modern sense but something like a score for public or private performance. This consideration must have been present from the start to the writer who dictated his work (as many did) as part of the process of composition; the next and logical step was obviously to assess the effect on others by experiment. However, the writer who was more concerned to puff his book than to invite criticism of it was apt to study primarily to please his audience – to carry over into the recitation hall the declaimer's ambition to impress by astonishing. So Cestius, quoted by the elder Seneca (*Contr.* 9.6.12): 'Much of what I say is said, not because it pleases me, but because I know that it will please my hearers.' Many of the characteristics of Seneca's tragedies and Juvenal's satires, to take the two most obvious examples, stem from the writer's consciousness of an audience present and waiting, more eager for immediate gratification than attentive to larger questions of proportion and balance or desirous of food for thought. For this feature of Silver Age Latin literature the *recitatio* must bear considerable responsibility, as contemporary opinion, represented most vividly in the first Satire of Persius, clearly recognized.

Connected with the literary coterie is the role of patronage. In the absence of a developed system of publishing as we now know it an ancient writer could not live on the sale of his books (cf. below, section 4). If he lacked sufficient private means he required financial subvention of some kind; moreover, if he

---

[1] Sherwin-White (1966) 115–16 on Plin. *Epist.* 1.13; Juv. 7.36–47.

[2] Bibliography of the question at Allen (1972) 10 n. 25. It is not true that silent reading was unknown, only that it was unusual: Knox (1968). The Roman ear clearly relished sound and rhythm. For the use of the verb *cantare* 'sing' of reading aloud see Allen (1972) *passim*.

was of humble or non-citizen status he might well need protection in case his writings gave offence. Again, more especially in the period down to the end of the Republic, when literary culture was less unified and organized than it later became, his work would in the first instance make itself known only through the channels of personal recommendation: patron to friends, friends to their friends, and so on. Accordingly it is not surprising to find patronage playing a prominent part in the lives of Republican writers such as Ennius and the dramatists.

Under the centralized and autocratic administration of Augustus it became possible to think of using literary patronage as an effective instrument of policy. To what extent this actually happened is disputed.[1] It certainly cannot be assumed that all 'Augustanism' in Augustan literature represents a 'party line' laid down from above; Livy, who belonged to no coterie and had no patron, wrote a history which in many of its fundamental characteristics is quite as 'Augustan' as the *Aeneid*. However, there are clear signs in the literature of the period that poets such as Virgil, Horace and Propertius were aware of an expectation on the part of the Princeps and his lieutenants that literature had a part to play in the establishment of the new order, whether through straight-forward celebration of the achievements of the Princeps or more subtly by canonizing, so to say, the Augustan myths. The frequency in contemporary poetry of the motif of the *recusatio* – the formal, courtly rejection of certain epic or official themes – is sufficient evidence of these pressures. Among the myths seeking poetical recognition may perhaps be reckoned that of Maecenas as typifying the golden age of liberal and disinterested patronage; but the evidence of Horace's *Satires* and *Epistles* is enough to show that the legend of the 'mécénat', though it was exaggerated and embellished during the Neronian and Flavian periods, had a substantial core of truth.

After Augustus Roman emperors displayed little constructive interest in literature. The most important exception was Nero, under whom there occurred something approaching a minor renaissance of Latin poetry, characterized by a neo-Augustan effusion of pastoral. Private patronage, which under Augustus had still flourished in the 'opposition' circle of writers round M. Valerius Messalla Corvinus, which included Ovid and Tibullus, deteriorated during the first century A.D. into a relationship of dependence and degradation: 'Le "mécénat" fit place à la clientèle.'[2] As seen from the writer's point of view the position is vividly depicted in Juvenal's first, fifth and seventh Satires. The letters of Pliny suggest at first sight a more roseate picture, but they refer in the main to the activities of learned amateurs such as Pliny himself, the motto of whose life might have been Horace's *strenua inertia* 'busy idleness'. Between the worlds of Juvenal and Pliny, though they were contemporaries, there is

[1] André (1967) 102.   [2] Guillemin (1937) 96; cf. Vessey (1973) 16–17.

little sign of contact. The professional writer – the writer, that is, with a genuine vocation and a conception of literature as offering a complete and exclusive career (an idea relatively late in developing at Rome)[1] – received very little encouragement after the Augustan period. What the system of patronage as it existed under the early Empire seems to have been designed to foster was ephemeral, amateur and courtly writing. Notable examples are Martial's epigrams and Statius' *Silvae*, released to entertain the world at large, it would seem, only when they had served their first purpose of engaging favour through recitation or private presentation.[2] That not all the literature of the Silver Age falls into these categories says something for the professional conscience of at least some writers.

Patronage apart, what further pressures were brought to bear on literature and how far they were effective can only be considered in specific cases, and the answer is rarely unambiguous. That the emphasis of the *Aeneid* as actually written was due to the promptings of Augustus rather than to Virgil's own sense of artistic fitness seems highly improbable.[3] Nor is it by any means clear what part Augustus played in the rescue and posthumous publication of the poem in despite of the poet's expressed wishes (*Vit. Donat.* 39). If his intervention on that occasion was really decisive, it was not always so. After banishing Ovid the Princeps banned his work from the public libraries, but his action cannot be shown to have had any effect on their survival. Conversely the attempt of the Emperor Tacitus (if the *Historia Augusta* may be believed) to revive interest in his namesake the historian by placing and renewing copies 'in all the libraries' did not save him from total eclipse in the second and third centuries A.D.[4] Signs of remarkable independence are found in literature produced when the Principate was at its most absolute: the seventh book of Lucan's *De bello civili* contains passages of bitter satire that astonish in a poem dedicated – apparently in all seriousness – to Nero.

That it might be dangerous under the Empire to write tragedies glorifying Brutus or Cato we are reminded by the opening chapters of Tacitus' *Dialogus*; but that same work ends with a passage purporting to show that eloquence, as stemming from political faction, has become redundant, in which it is difficult not to discern irony. The reticences and ambiguities of the surviving evidence interpose an almost impenetrable barrier. Even the best-documented episode of all, the disgrace and exile of Ovid, is still surrounded in mystery. Read with attention the poems of his exile are highly, even bitterly, critical of Augustus. That we still have them shows that they were not suppressed; but how widely they were circulated in Augustus' lifetime we do not know – still less whether Augustus ever saw them. As an instrument for arousing public opinion literature

---

[1] Bardon (1956) 318–19.   [2] White (1974).
[3] Bardon (1940) 71–2.   [4] *Hist. Aug. Tac.* 10.3; cf. Syme (1958) 503, 796.

remained relatively powerless in large centralized societies until the coming of the printing-press. Once again consideration of the effects of literature returns us to the questions of its physical medium: the book itself, and the circumstances under which it was copied and circulated.

4. BOOKS AND PUBLICATION

By 'book' in this section is meant papyrus roll; the change to the *codex* and its implications are considered below, section 5. The manufacture of papyrus and the make-up of the book in roll form have been described in Volume I,[1] and what is said there applies for the most part, *mutatis mutandis*, to Roman books. Something must be added, however, on the subject of terminology. The ordinary Latin word for book, *liber*, originally meant 'bark'. Whether it was used as the equivalent for Greek βιβλίον because it already meant 'book', *sc.* book written on bark (the existence of such books being entirely a matter of inference from the name), or whether because bark was the native substance most closely resembling papyrus (which is not indigenous to western Europe) it is impossible to determine. The specifically Roman word for book, to which Greek offers no analogue, was *uolumen* 'roll'. This remained the term proper to the book as a physical object; whereas *liber* might mean (i) 'roll' (= *uolumen*); or (ii) a 'book' of a work written to occupy more than one roll, e.g. a 'book' of Virgil or Livy; or (iii) a 'book' in the sense of a work of literature, e.g. the *Aeneid*. This last sense is rare, and in most of the passages taken by lexicographers and others to represent it, there is at least a tinge of senses (i) or (ii).[2] For a work consisting of more than one *liber* (sense (ii)) the normal designation would be *libri*, as when Cicero refers to his *De re publica* as his 'books on the Constitution' (*Fin.* 2.59 *in nostris de re publica libris*) or Quintilian to his 'books on the teaching of oratory' (*praef.* 1 *libros quos...de institutione oratoria scripseram*).[3] Use was also made of such variants as *opus* 'work' (Ovid, *Amores epigr.* 2, referring to a work in three or five *libelli*), *charta*, properly 'papyrus, paper' (Lucretius 3.10 *tuis ex...chartis*); and of descriptive terms such as *uersus, carmen, poemata, commentarii, epistulae*; or paraphrases with words such as *scribere, dicere, canere*, and the like. The use of these periphrastic expressions is connected with the lack of a universally accepted convention for the identification of books in the modern manner by title. A convenient alternative to *liber* was its diminutive *libellus*, properly 'small book', used particularly of poetry (Catullus 1.1, Ovid, *Amores epigr.* 1, Martial 1 *praef.*, 1.3, Statius, *Silvae* 1 *praef.*, etc.).

On the continuous strip of papyrus forming the book the text was written

---

[1] *CHCL* I, ch. I.   [2] See below, Excursus 1, p. 30.
[3] Contrast Vitruv. 1 *praef.* 3 *his uoluminibus*.

from left to right in columns, *paginae*. Thus to read a book the user held it in both hands horizontally, rolling it up with the left hand and unrolling with the right as he read. The common terms for this process were *explicare* 'unfold', *euoluere* 'unroll', and variants of these verbs.[1] It seems probable that the ends of the roll were commonly reinforced against wear and secured to wooden rollers, the ends of which were often fitted with ornamental knobs called *umbilici* 'navels', or *cornua* 'horns':[2] hence the expression *ad umbilicos* (or *cornua*) *explicare* (or *uenire*), and the like, meaning 'to read to the end' (Mart. 4.89.2, 11.107.1, *al.*). Books were supposed to be kept rolled with the beginning outwards, and on coming to the end of a book a considerate user would re-roll it for the next reader.[3] This thoughtful action was, we may surmise, frequently neglected; which may help to explain why (so far as the Greek evidence goes, at all events) the author and title (or other identification) of the book were often given at the end of the roll.[4] Titling indeed seems to have been something of a difficulty. There was no place on a papyrus roll corresponding to the fore-edge or spine of a modern book; for quick identification the reader must have had to depend on the tag of parchment (*titulus*) which was glued to the outside of the roll and hung down as it lay on the shelf or projected if the roll was stored upright in a box.[5]

All in all, it will be clear that in comparison with a modern book the papyrus roll was impractical and inconvenient to use and to store. It also called for extravagant use of material, since only the inner, protected side was normally written on. As a measure of economy the back of a roll was sometimes used also ('opisthograph'), but for obvious reasons this was an inconvenient expedient. To read a *uolumen* needed two hands, which made note-taking difficult; and when it was not in use it was liable to be crushed unless protected by such devices as parchment wrappers (*membranae*) or book-boxes (*capsae, capsulae*). To find a given book in a large library, even if all the books were duly equipped with *tituli* (which were apt as a matter of course to come off), must have been a tiresome business; and to verify a reference quickly next to impossible – hence the notorious inaccuracy in citation by ancient authorities, who tended to rely on memory and to cite from the beginnings of books. Nor was the text itself as a rule equipped with much in the way of aids to the reader of the kind that the user of modern books takes for granted. In professionally written copies the writing would be a handsome and regular majuscule; but on the analogy of surviving

[1] This terminology survived the transition from roll to *codex*: cf. esp. the common formula in medieval manuscripts 'Liber I Explicit. Incipit Liber II', where *Explicit* is probably an abbreviation of *Explicitus* '(fully) unrolled'.

[2] But see below, Excursus 2, p. 31.

[3] Mart. 1.66.8, 10.93.6, seem to suggest that during this process one end (?) of the roll was tucked under the chin.

[4] Wendel (1949) 24, Turner (1971) 16.

[5] Examples at Turner (1971) 34. On titling see below, Excursus 3, p. 31.

Greek papyri we should expect that there also existed many privately made copies in cursive or documentary handwriting.[1] There were considerable variations in format as well as in legibility. The width of the columns of writing bore no relationship to the sheets out of which the roll was formed (*chartae, schedae/ scidae*; also, confusingly, *paginae, plagulae*), since the joints between these were carefully smoothed down and offered no obstacle to the pen. Their width therefore varied greatly, though there is some evidence that the average length of a hexameter verse, about 35 letters, might on occasion serve as a norm. There were also wide variations in the number of lines in the column, size of margins, and all other aspects of get-up. In these matters, as in everything else connected with book-production, standards depended on circumstances: whether the copy in question was a regular one produced for trade sale, a *de luxe* exemplar intended for presentation, or an amateur effort for personal use.

The few surviving examples of early papyri, taken together with the evidence of contemporary inscriptions, offer some evidence, by no means conclusive, that down to the second century A.D. the words in Latin books were divided in writing by the use of a conventional sign and that punctuation was in use; though such evidence as does exist is not enough to show that there was any generally accepted system.[2] Seneca notes a difference between Greek and Roman usage in this respect.[3] In the second century, in a curious fit of what seems to have been cultural snobbery, the Romans adopted continuous writing without word-division (*scriptura continua*) on the Greek model; and if punctuation had previously been in common use, it too was rejected. Behind this decision may perhaps be sensed a feeling that to make literature more accessible by providing aids to the reader somehow devalues it; the preservation of certain anomalies in English spelling offers an analogy, though admittedly a very incomplete one. It should however be remembered that the best Latin writers impose the required punctuation on the reader's mind and ear by their phrasing, and it must always have been tacitly accepted that the onus was on the author to do this, whatever aids might or might not be provided in the written text. A writer who neglected this duty would be liable to puzzle his readers: Jerome complains that he cannot tell where Jovinian's sentences begin and end (*Adv. Jovin.* 1.2).

[1] Roberts (1956) xi–xii.

[2] Cavenaile (1958) nos. 20 (Cicero, *Verr.* 2.2.3–4; 20 B.C.)*; 41 (anon. on Servius Tullius; 2nd c. A.D.); 43 (hist. fragment; A.D. 100)*; 45 (philos. fragment; before A.D. 115). Not in Cavenaile: *Carmen de Bello Actiaco*; before A.D. 79*. (* = with punctuation.) Cf. Wingo (1972) 50–63. A few later papyri, e.g. Cavenaile 47 (4th–5th c. A.D.), 65 (2nd–3rd c. A.D.) have word-division with interpuncts.

[3] *Epist. mor.* 40.11; but the word *interpungere* may refer either to word-division or to sense-punctuation or possibly (the distinction between them not being hard-and-fast) to both: Wingo (1972) 15 n. 10. For a different interpretation, denying the existence of punctuation in Latin books, Townend (1969) 330–2.

Whatever the reasons for the change, it threw an added burden of interpretation on the individual reader, especially when confronted with a brand-new copy of a text. In that case he was obliged to divide the words and supply any punctuation that he required for himself.[1] As a rule he would indeed have to do a good deal more, for a newly-copied text would normally be full of copying errors. A reader who took textual accuracy at all seriously had virtually to make his own edition of his book by correcting slips of the pen (and sometimes graver corruptions), where possible by comparison with other, putatively if not actually, more reliable copies (*emendare*); by dividing the words and punctuating (*distinguere*); and – if he chanced to be of a scholarly turn of mind – by equipping his text with critical signs (*adnotare*). These routine operations should not be magnified into genuinely philological procedures. The word *emendo* in practice usually meant no more than to correct obvious minor errors.[2] All users of books would have been habituated to do this from their schooldays, since it seems likely that the texts used in schools were copied and corrected by the pupils themselves from the master's dictation.[3] Since it is a matter of common experience that few men are competent textual critics and that the average reader is all too ready to tolerate nonsense in what he reads, there must have been very many bad copies of literary texts circulating in antiquity.

Papyrus was supplied by the trade in various lengths and widths, but a roll could be as long or short as was required, since papyrus is very easy to cut and join (Plin. *N.H.* 13.78–9; Cic. *Att.* 16.6.4). However, very short or (even more) very long rolls were unmanageable: for Greek books a maximum of about 10·5 metres seems to be established.[4] In certain genres, notably epic, the *uolumen* became an accepted literary unit. Ovid refers to the *Metamorphoses* as a work in fifteen *uolumina* (*Trist.* 3.14.19). Thus the architecture of the *De rerum natura* and the *Aeneid* may be said to have in some sense arisen out of the exigencies of ancient book-production.[5] In these cases an artistic virtue has been made out of necessity – or at all events convenience. From Augustan times onwards the average length of a 'book' of poetry became established as about 700–900 lines; we find Martial (1.16) frankly acknowledging the occasional need for an author to pad so as to eke out his book to the minimum which could decently be offered to the public as a *liber*. Even in the totally different modern context authors are to some extent limited by comparable preconceptions as to propriety of length and format.

[1] Such punctuation as is found in ancient *codices* is generally the work of a second hand; the text was written in *scriptura continua* and without aids to the reader (Wingo (1972) 23 n. 11). Scholiasts not infrequently discuss problems of punctuation: for Servius cf. Mountford–Schultz (1930) 55 s.v. 'distinctio'.

[2] Zetzel (1972) 2 n. 8; cf. on the *subscriptiones* below, p. 28. The word did not have the specifically textual connotations that it has acquired in modern technical usage: Zetzel (1972) 6.

[3] Cf. Marrou (1956) 154–5.　　　　[4] Kenyon (1951) 54.　　　　[5] Cf. Birt (1882) 141–50.

In antiquity there were no copyright laws and no legal safeguards against unauthorized copying and circulation of books: therefore there was no such thing as publication in anything like its modern sense. In practice it was often possible for an author to confine the circulation of his work in the first instance to a limited number of friends;[1] but sooner or later the decision would have to be taken, if it had not already been taken by events,[2] to authorize or at least acquiesce in general circulation. Publication in this sense was less a matter of formal release to the public than a recognition by the author that his work was now, so to speak, on its own in the world: the word usually translated 'publish' (edere = Greek ἐκδιδόναι) connotes the resignation of rights and responsibilities.[3] Publication might on occasion operate as a protection in that it served as a formal claim to authorship and constituted some sort of a safeguard against plagiarism.[4] It did not necessarily connote the making of arrangements for the multiplication of copies. That might happen on occasion, but a work once relinquished by its author was public property, and in that sense published, whether or not a bookseller was employed to copy and put it into circulation. What mattered was the author's intention.

Once a book was released in this way the author had no rights in it whatever (even before publication what rights he had were moral rather than legal), no control over its fate, and no secure prospect of being able to correct it.[5] As Symmachus put it: 'Once a poem has left your hands, you resign all your rights; a speech when published is a free entity' (Epist. 1.31; cf. Hor. Epist. 1.20, Mart. 1.3). Thus it was open to any private individual to make or procure for himself a copy of any text to which he had access; and if he could command the services of a trained scribe the result would be indistinguishable from a copy obtained through trade channels – and, according to the quality of the exemplar used, might well be textually superior. The earliest evidence for the existence of a trade in books at Rome dates from the Ciceronian period;[6] before that time the circulation of books must have been almost exclusively a matter of private enterprise – as indeed it continued in large measure to be down to

---

[1] van Groningen (1963) 9, Dziatzko (1899b) 978; cf. Plin. Epist. 1.8.3, accepting the offer of a friend to read and criticize one of his compositions and remarking that even when he had corrected it he could withhold it or publish it as he pleased: erit... et post emendationem liberum nobis uel publicare uel continere.

[2] As was evidently the case with Cicero's speech In Clodium et Curionem, which he thought he had succeeded in suppressing (Att. 3.12.2), and with his juvenile De inventione (De or. 1.94); similarly with the rhetorical treatises of Quintilian (1 prooem. 7, 3.6.68). Fronto, Epist. pp. 111, 137 N.

[3] van Groningen (1963) 5.

[4] Cf. Plin. Epist. 2.10.3, Mart. 1.29, 1.66, 2.20.

[5] van Groningen (1963) 7. The best expedient was to include the correction in some later work: Quint. 3.6.64.

[6] Cic. Phil. 2.21 refers (incidentally) to a taberna libraria 'bookshop'; and Catullus mentions certain contemporary poets as likely to be found on the shelves of the booksellers, librariorum scrinia (14.17–19). The word librarius meant both 'copyist' and 'bookseller'; for the latter the Greek loan-word bibliopola also occurs.

the end of antiquity and in the Middle Ages. Indeed, as one of Cicero's letters to his brother Quintus (*Q.Fr.* 3.4.5) illustrates, many of the books, especially Greek books, which a scholar or amateur might need for his library, were not commercially available. Many well-to-do Romans must have had in their possession one or two slaves trained as clerks, who could be used as copyists of books when not otherwise employed and so build up the libraries of their employers and on occasion their employers' friends. This was how Atticus assisted Cicero; and his further services in copying and disseminating Cicero's own writings represent an extension of the same activity. His services, however, were given in friendship, not in a commercial way, and the picture of him still to be met with in modern handbooks as a 'publisher' on a large scale is quite wide of the mark, being based on anachronistic presuppositions rather than consideration of the contemporary evidence.[1] What Atticus did on a large scale and in a way that happens to be well documented, many others must have done to the extent that their more limited resources allowed. Essentially, however, there was no difference except one of scale.

That a book trade existed is undeniable. What cannot be established even in the sketchiest way is its extent and its economic basis, let alone the details of distribution, remuneration of authors (if any), and the like. From the time of Augustus we begin to hear of named *librarii*; the Sosii, mentioned by Horace, and Tryphon, to whom Quintilian entrusted the *Institutio oratoria* and who is referred to, along with Atrectus and others, by Martial. Rome was clearly the main entrepôt; in the early second century Pliny appears to be surprised to learn that there was a bookshop at such an important provincial centre as Lyons (*Epist.* 9.11.2). Gellius, writing towards the end of the same century, reports having found Greek books for sale at Brindisi, but he does not say that he found them in a bookshop, and the episode may in any case be a figment of his imagination.[2] In the time of Augustine there were bookshops at Carthage and Hippo (*Retract.* 2.58, *Epist.* 118.2.9). By the time of Pliny and Martial Latin literature was widely disseminated in the Western Empire,[3] but we know almost nothing of the channels through which it travelled. How many bookshops there were at any time, what stock they carried, how they acquired their exemplars for copying, whether nearly all their work was done to order, whether the copying and selling of books was generally a sideline, how large a proportion of the trade was in new books and how large in antiquarian – these and many other pertinent questions are matters of speculation.[4]

---

[1] By (e.g.) Kleberg (1967) 23–5, Burr (1959) 604. See Sommer (1926) for a full discussion and analysis of the evidence of Cicero's letters.

[2] Zetzel (1972) 64. In any case, the inference drawn by Kleberg (1967) 45 that there was a flourishing book trade at Brindisi is far too sweeping.

[3] Sherwin-White (1966) 490.

[4] For a brief and admirably sceptical discussion see Zetzel (1972) 255–7.

We are on slightly, though only slightly, firmer ground when we turn to consider what inducements may have existed for an author to entrust his work to the booksellers. They can hardly have been predominantly financial. When Horace refers to the profits from his writing, it is those likely to accrue to the Sosii, not to himself, that he means (*A.P.* 345). Similarly Martial implies that the rewards earned by his pen are virtually non-existent and that (like Juvenal) he is dependent on the client's daily dole for subsistence (10.74.7; Juv. 1.134). More explicitly he remarks elsewhere that it is nothing to him financially that his books are read in distant Britain. For him and for Juvenal poetry is synonymous with poverty.[1] If he, or any other writer, did receive payment from the booksellers it must have been in the form of a lump sum for an exemplar of which the bookseller was to have exclusive use (for the limited time during which the book was not in general circulation) as source for his trade copies. But Martial illustrates again the danger of generalizing. His work was slight, modish, occasional;[2] it would have been a rash man who dared to prophesy at the time that it would outlive the elegies of Gallus and Ovid's *Medea*. For the booksellers any profit to be made from such writing must have come from a quick sale. Martial is not entirely disinterested, it would appear; he refers satirically to those who read his poetry only if they can do so for nothing (5.16.9–10). His interest may have lain in the fact that he could command a respectable price for the authorial exemplar of his latest *libellus*, for immediate publication in a comparatively large edition, with little or no expectation of a continuing sale, in Rome at all events, once copies were widely available. The success of such an arrangement would naturally have been threatened if free copies were available at the same time. Martial sometimes gives friends his own poems as presents, and there may have been provision for a limited number of author's copies.[3] Here too we are thrown back on speculation.

Martial was a special case. Even for the well-to-do writer, professional or amateur, there were advantages other than financial in using the services of a bookseller. It would have suited Horace, for instance, to arrange for his poems, once released for publication, to be distributed initially by the trade, for more than one reason. (Whether it suited the trade would be very much a financial matter.) It was convenient to have somewhere to refer importunate friends in search of a copy (cf. Mart. 1.117). To provide the bookseller with an authorized exemplar, corrected by the author, offered some sort of safeguard, at all events in the early stages of dissemination, that reasonable textual accuracy would be maintained. Here much would depend on the quality of the bookseller and his staff of copyists. The inaccuracy of trade copies was

---

[1] Mart. 11.3.5–6; 3.38.7–10, Juv. 7.74–97. Cf. Tac. *Dial.* 9.1.
[2] As was that of the poets mentioned by Catullus (above, p. 19, n. 6); cf. Sommer (1926) 392.
[3] Birt (1882) 355.

notorious;[1] probably the Sosii and a handful of other *librarii* had a reputation to lose. For a wealthy amateur like Pliny, with a good conceit of himself, these inducements were probably sufficient in themselves. However, the number and tone of the references to booksellers in Pliny's letters and Martial's epigrams also suggest that by the end of the first century A.D. the book trade in Rome had developed to the point where it was normal for new books to be made available through trade channels, as had certainly not been the case in the days of Cicero and earlier.[2]

The size of editions[3] and the arrangements for distribution are also subjects for speculation. In Cicero's day, before the growth of the book trade, the 'edition' of a book was the handful of copies that passed from the author and his coadjutors, if he had any, into the hands of his friends.[4] Even in the time of Martial and Pliny there was no need for the bookseller to keep a large stock of most books on hand. Access to an exemplar was all that was needed; a short *libellus*, such as a book of Martial or Statius' *Silvae*, could if necessary be copied while the customer waited, and no doubt sometimes was (cf. Mart. 2.8.3–4). For distribution in the provinces (a subject about which nothing is known) a single exemplar for each centre of distribution was all that was needed, to serve as source for the copies to be sold. But the demand for books through trade channels must have been quite haphazard and unpredictable; it would have been absurd to lock up capital in the shape of ready-written books.[5] It is therefore not surprising to find that such information as exists about prices is both scanty and conflicting.[6] It must have been entirely a matter of supply and demand. The inflated prices quoted by Gellius for antiquarian books need not detain us; the subject belongs to the history of forgery and bibliomania.[7]

[1] Cic. *Q.Fr.* 3.5.6; Strabo (writing probably under Augustus) 13.1.54 *fin.*; Mart. 2.8.3–4. Trustworthy copyists were clearly not easy to find: Cic. *Q.Fr.* 3.4.5.

[2] Sherwin-White (1966) 91: 'Pliny indicates. . .that the distribution of his books was entirely in the hands of the *bibliopolae*.' It probably was; but his text does not actually prove the fact.

[3] What Birt (1882) 351–2 has to say on the subject is guesswork pure and simple. The case of Rufus' life of his son (Plin. *Epist.* 4.7.2) throws no light on normal practice.

[4] Cf. Sommer (1926) 412–14.

[5] That booksellers held stocks which sometimes had to be 'wasted' may be suggested by references to the use of discarded books as wrapping paper (e.g. Cat. 95.8, Hor. *Epist.* 2.1.269–70, *al.*); but it is hazardous to press the significance of what was clearly a literary *topos*.

[6] Mart. 13.3: a copy of the *Xenia* (Book 13) for 2 or 4 sesterces; 1.117.15–17: a finely produced copy of Book 1 for 5 denarii. In Martial's time a denarius was the price of a day's labour. Statius, *Silv.* 4.9.9, 21: a book of the *Silvae* (?) for a decussis (10 asses = a denarius, old value), contrasted with Brutus' orations for an as; but the context warns us against taking all this literally. On the tariff for copyists laid down in Diocletian's Edict see Birt (1882) 208–9.

[7] Zetzel (1972) 239–43.

5. THE 'FATA LIBELLORUM'

What has been well described as 'the casual and fluid nature of publication in the ancient world'[1] is just as characteristic of what happened to books after publication. The paucity of our evidence for the activities of the book trade must not be pressed to the point of denying that it played some part in keeping literature alive. But it is inherent in the nature of the manuscript book itself that the propagation of texts in antiquity must have been very largely an affair of private enterprise. The fate of any individual book – in basic terms, its physical survival – depended on a number of factors, among which, with a few outstanding exceptions, systematic scholarly and critical activity played a remarkably small part. Changes of public taste, coupled with the gradual narrowing of the educational focus mentioned above, had considerable effects on survival, but sheer hazard must probably be accounted the most potent force at work. That Gallus died under a cloud did not necessarily entail that his works must have perished with him,[2] any more than the *Ars amatoria* perished with Ovid. It seems reasonable to believe that Quintilian would not have recommended Gallus to the budding orator a century later if his poems were not still available; but his inclusion in the catalogue of best books does not prove that Quintilian himself had ever set eyes on a copy of his *Amores*. The disappearance of the first (five-book) edition of Ovid's *Amores* is not to be ascribed to 'respect for his wishes on the part of those responsible for the transmission'[3] so much as (from the poet's point of view) good luck. Nobody was 'responsible' for anything once the book was published. Nor will it do to explain Cicero's failure to suppress the first edition of the *Academica* by the suggestion that in his day things were less well organized than in Ovid's.[4] In that sense they were never at any time 'organized'.

The main, and perhaps the only, element of stability in the process of transmission and conservation of literature was that contributed by the public libraries; though here too intelligent guesswork must form the basis of discussion. There never existed at Rome any real parallel to the huge royal collections of Pergamum and Alexandria, still less to the scholarly and critical activity associated with the Museum. From the second century B.C. Greek books began to enter Italy in quantity as part of the spoils of war; the transition from looting to collection may be observed in the figure of L. Licinius Lucullus (Plut. *Lucull.* 42). These private collections offered a valuable resource to the scholar, of which we find Cicero and Cato availing themselves.[5] As a national Latin literature grew, it too was collected. Under the Empire it became the normal

---

[1] Reynolds–Wilson (1974) 23.
[2] As suggested by Büchner (1961) 340.
[3] Büchner (1961) 326.
[4] Büchner ibid.
[5] Cic. *Fin.* 3.7–8, *Att.* 4.10.1, 4.14.1; cf. Plut. loc. cit.

thing for rich men to equip their houses with libraries, often less for use than for ostentation.[1] These collections must have been very numerous, and the total number of volumes extant at any one time huge; but they could not provide the permanency and the organization that were necessary to ensure that copies of what was most worth preserving – if possible carefully written and corrected copies made from the best available exemplars – were accessible to all accredited comers in known places. The role of public collections in the preservation of literature, as well as their often precarious existence, is illustrated indirectly by the report that when libraries at Rome were destroyed by fire, Domitian sent to Alexandria to procure fresh copies of the lost books (Suet. *Dom.* 20).

The first public library at Rome was founded by C. Asinius Pollio in 39 B.C., and his example was followed by Augustus and subsequent emperors. By the time of Constantine there appear to have been twenty-eight in the City. That founded by Augustus in the temple of the Palatine Apollo served as a prototype for several later foundations. It was on the Greek model, but the plan was double, since Greek and Latin books were separately housed; this segregation of the two languages was, it would seem, the rule throughout antiquity.[2] The fact is another reminder that Greek and Latin culture were never in any real sense integrated. The annexation of the library to a temple was also a recurrent feature, though some library buildings were purely secular. In the provinces local benefactors often endowed their communities with libraries; the example of Pliny's library at his native Comum is well known, since he took pains to record it himself (Plin. *Epist.* 1.8.2). Evidence as to the financing and staffing of libraries is scanty; at Rome they seem to have come under the supervision of the imperial civil service.[3] The Theodosian Code contains details of the *antiquarii* (in this context not 'antiquarians' but 'scribes') employed in the Constantinople library in A.D. 372 in the care and conservation of books,[4] and it is a reasonable guess (no more) that most libraries had copying departments (*scriptoria*) attached to them, in which new copies were made and – if the librarian were a scholar – existing copies corrected.[5] Generally it may be surmised that readers consulted books in the library, but loans were evidently permitted on occasion.[6]

It was notoriously difficult to get accurate copies of books in antiquity; as has already been remarked, the first task of a reader with a new book was to correct it, *emendare*. The life of a papyrus roll kept in a library under ideal

[1] Sen. *De tranqu. an.* 9, Lucian, *Adv. indoct. passim*; cf. Petron. 48.4.

[2] Suet. *Aug.* 29.3; Ihm (1893) 514–18, Callmer (1944) 159; cf. Petron. 48.4.

[3] Ihm (1893) 522–6.

[4] *Cod. Theod.* 14.9.2; Ihm (1893) 529. Cf. the reference to a MS written 'ab eo...Theodoro antiquario qui nunc Palatinus est' in a *subscriptio* to Book 3 of Boethius' *De syllogismo hypothetico* in MS Orleans 267 fol. 51ʳ (Zetzel (1972) 233).

[5] Wendel (1954) 267–8.

[6] Gell. 11.17.1, 13.20.1, 16.8.2; 19.5.4, Fronto, *Epist.* p. 68 N; cf. Clift (1945) 37.

I Rome, Museo Nazionale Romano. Fragment of Christian sarcophagus of ?third
century A.D. showing philosophers in discussion. These were the ordinary ways of
handling a papyrus *uolumen*, open or rolled. See p. 16.

II Rome, Museo Nuovo Capitolino. Tombstone of Q. Sulpicius Maximus, who distinguished himself at the Capitoline poetry contest (cf. Suet. *Dom.* 4.4) in A.D. 94 with the Greek poem here inscribed and died aged eleven. Shows how an open roll might be managed with one hand, leaving the other free for gesture. By a common convention the writing is incorrectly shown as running across the width of the roll, presumably to make it easier to read. For an example of the same convention in Greek vase-painting see *CHCL* I Plate I*a*.

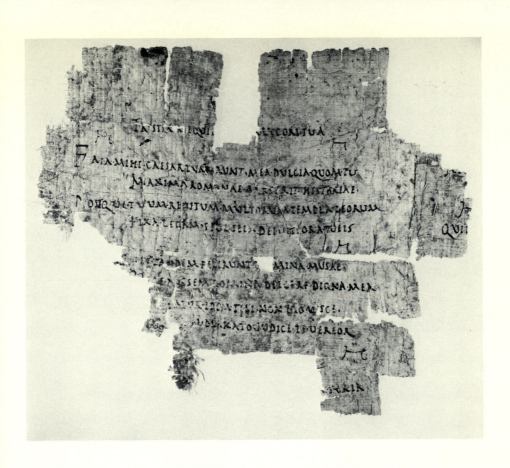

III PQaṣr Ibrîm L 1/2. Part of a papyrus roll written between *c.* 50 and (probably)
c. 20 B.C. containing elegiac verses by Gallus (see *The Age of Augustus*, pp. 114–15).
Before the discovery of this papyrus in 1978 all that survived of Gallus' work was a
single pentameter (*FPL* 99). See Anderson, Parsons and Nisbet (1979).

IV Biblioteca Apostolica Vaticana MS Latinus 3226 (Bembinus), foll. 57ᵛ–58ʳ. A vellum codex written in the fourth or fifth century A.D. containing most of Terence. The photograph shows *Phormio* 179–223. Whereas in the Gallus papyrus (Plate III) the words are separated by dots (interpuncts), the copyist here has followed the fashion that became normal after the second century A.D. of continuous writing without word-division (*scriptura*

conditions – as ideal as might be in the climate of western Europe, which does not really suit papyrus – might be considerably longer than the 200 years mentioned by Pliny or even the 300 mentioned by Galen.[1] Thus if a good copy of a book – ideally one corrected by the author – had been placed in a library soon after publication it might serve as a standing check on the accuracy of current copies, which would have a relatively short life and need replacement at more frequent intervals than library copies. Unfortunately losses by fire were frequent; of all the libraries founded by earlier Roman emperors only Trajan's Bibliotheca Ulpia seems to have survived unscathed down to the fifth century A.D.[2] Nevertheless it seems probable that the transmission of Latin literature as it has come down to us was to some degree dependent on copies conserved in libraries. The textual quality of the average copy in general circulation in antiquity can be inferred from the evidence of surviving papyri and other ancient fragments, citations in grammarians and similar sources, and from the complaints of contemporaries: it was not high. Yet the medieval tradition of many Latin authors is not nearly as corrupt as we should expect if our earliest surviving *codices* are the lineal desendants of such generally current copies.

The simplest way of accounting for this fact is to suppose that the early monastic and cathedral libraries in Italy built up their stocks of books by acquiring or copying from manuscripts in the old pagan public libraries of Rome, some of which might have been of great age and most of which were likely to have been textually superior to copies in general circulation.[3] This hypothesis may also help to account for the survival in corpus form of certain collections of poetry such as the so-called *Corpus Tibullianum*. Individuals would copy or have copied for them Tibullus or 'Lygdamus' in separate rolls according to their own requirements; the collection as we have it was brought together by somebody connected with the literary coterie from which the various poems sprang, soon after the time at which they were written, and lodged in a library as a corpus of separate but related rolls, which was subsequently incorporated in a *codex*, from which our tradition originates.[4]

The other dominant factor, both conservative and destructive, in the transmission of Latin books was the replacement of the roll by the *codex*, the form of book with pages that is in use today. This change was going on at the same time as, though it did not completely coincide with, the replacement of papyrus as the usual writing material for books by parchment or vellum.[5] Parchment had in fact been in use for various purposes since Hellenistic times, and note-

---

[1] Plin. *N.H.* 13.83, Galen 18.630 K; cf. Roberts (1954) 183, Birt (1882) 364–6, Lewis (1974) 59–60.

[2] *Hist. Aug. Aurel.* 1.7, 10, etc., *Prob.* 2.1 – for what this testimony is worth.

[3] Cf. Ihm (1893) 531, Knowles (1958) 139, Callmer (1944) 191.

[4] Cf. Clift (1945) 25–6; Büchner (1961) 324–5; and below, pp. 193–7, on Catullus.

[5] 'There is no essential connexion between format and material' (Roberts (1954) 183); cf. Turner (1968) 8.

books made of it were already common in the first century B.C. It was merely a question of time before this handy combination of format and material was applied to book production. In the event the time was curiously slow in coming. In a well-known group of poems Martial refers to presents in the form of parchment *codices*, evidently miniatures, containing literary texts.[1] It seems a commendable innovation, but it was not generally taken up. The change from roll to *codex*, when it did come, was connected with the eventual triumph of Christianity in the Roman empire. For reasons which are not entirely clear Christian literature, especially the Bible, was from the first, whether written on papyrus or parchment, circulated in *codex*-format.[2] By the middle of the fourth century the *codex* had for all literary purposes ousted the roll and parchment had ousted papyrus. Again the reasons for the general change are neither simple nor entirely clear;[3] though in the light of hindsight it is obvious that for both durability and convenience the old, classical, kind of book could not begin to challenge comparison with the new.[4]

The triumph of the *codex* had important consequences for the transmission and preservation of literary texts. On the credit side the parchment *codex* was a far more robust and durable article than the papyrus *uolumen*, so that a text once transcribed into *codex*-form had a decent chance of survival through the cultural and political collapse of ancient civilization and the subsequent Dark Ages. A text on papyrus had almost none. But survival of a particular text depended on whether it was selected for transcription into *codex*-form. This selection in turn depended on a number of factors. Design and system played little part; no person or agency passed the whole of classical Latin literature in review at this time, allowing some books through the barrier and turning others back. Nor was the whole of classical literature by now available to be reviewed. Substantial losses must have occurred as early as the Silver Age. Already in the first century A.D. the Republican poets were alluded to more often than they were read, and even an actual citation by no means proves first-hand knowledge of the text cited. Gellius' appeal to 'a truly ancient manuscript' of Livius Andronicus 'in the library at Patras' as authority for early Latin spelling must be taken with a pinch of salt.[5] What his testimony does show is that by the end of the second century A.D. it was becoming difficult to find copies of Republican authors; they had to be searched for. Whether Gellius ever visited a library at Patras or found an old manuscript there is less important than the implication that this was the sort of place where at that date an enquirer might be expected

---

[1] Mart. 2.1, 14.184, 186, 188, 190, 192; cf. Roberts (1954) 177–80. Pliny, *N.H.* 7. 85, mentions a complete *Iliad*, small enough to fit into a nutshell, supposed to have been attested by Cicero.

[2] Roberts (1954) 186–91, Turner (1968) 10–12.

[3] Roberts (1954) 203–4.

[4] On the final triumph of parchment in the time of Jerome cf. Arns (1953) 23–5.

[5] Gell. 18.9.5; Zetzel (1972) 65–6.

to look. Even writers such as Macrobius and Servius are unlikely to have taken their citations of early Republican writers direct from the texts themselves. By the time of Augustine texts even of Cicero were hard to come by in Africa (*Epist.* 118.2.9).

For educational and rhetorical purposes epitomes and abstracts were increasingly in vogue; Marcus Aurelius asks Fronto for excerpts from Lucretius and Ennius (Fronto, *Epist.* p. 105 N). Such habits threatened more expecially lengthy works such as Livy's history, but were also generally inimical to the survival of all books not central to the standard school programme. The purpose for which a book was read had an important bearing on its textual fortunes. Literary authors, especially those used as grammatical texts, were respectfully treated. Books which were read for content rather than form – grammars, manuals such as Cato's *De agri cultura* or the cookery book ascribed to Apicius – were abbreviated, expanded, and generally altered at will.

In spite of temporary and local revivals of interest in this or that period or author, as when Juvenal suddenly became popular in the aristocratic circles of Rome in the fourth century – revivals which tended to be offset by a corresponding neglect of other areas[1] – a steady process of attrition had been at work for many years before the roll was finally superseded by the *codex*. *Quod latet, ignotum est* 'what is hidden, is unknown' (Ov. *Ars Am.* 3.397); even those texts which still survived somewhere[2] were effectively lost unless they satisfied two requirements. Their existence had to be known, and they had to be deemed worth the trouble (and expense) of recopying. Texts which failed to pass this double test were doomed to disappearance. Further losses of course were to occur during the Dark and Middle Ages, but they must have been relatively small in comparison with what failed to survive the end of classical antiquity. A text that had been copied into a *codex* and lodged in a monastic or capitular library was by no means out of the wood; but it had a better than sporting chance of coming through.[3]

6. SCHOLARSHIP AND CRITICISM

Roman scholars took over the traditions of Alexandrian literary scholarship along with the rest of Hellenistic culture.[4] An early exercise in the collection and determination of authenticity of texts was conducted by Cicero's contemporary M. Terentius Varro, who established the canon of Plautus' plays

---

[1] Wessner (1929); cf. Cameron (1964) 367–8 on the general neglect of Silver Age literature in the later Empire.

[2] At least one complete text of Ennius' *Annales* was still extant as late as the fifth century: Norden (1915) 78–86.

[3] Cf. Knowles (1958) 143–7.

[4] On Hellenistic scholarship see Pfeiffer (1968) 123–251, Turner (1968) 97–126, Fraser (1972) I 447–79; *CHCL* I.

which became and remained authoritative: only the twenty-one plays (including the fragmentary *Vidularia*) accepted by Varro are transmitted in the medieval tradition.[1] In general, however, there is little evidence for systematic scholarly preoccupation with texts, and to predicate the existence in classical antiquity of textual criticism in anything like its modern sense of orderly recension and emendation is mistaken. Even Probus, whose activities are described in apparently circumstantial detail by Suetonius, was not in any strict sense of the word a critic, and his dealings have left little impression on the texts with which we are told he occupied himself.[2]

In this connexion a recurring and fundamental misconception must be dealt with, concerning the so-called *subscriptiones*. These are notes surviving in the manuscripts of certain authors which testify to the fact that a named individual 'corrected' (the word used is *emendo*) a particular copy of the text in question, with or without the help of a mentor or another copy.[3] Most of these notes can be dated to late antiquity. The *subscriptiones* offer valuable information about particular texts: who was reading such and such a book at such and such a time, where and in association with whom, and so on. Thus the Juvenal *subscriptio* of Nicaeus, who read his text 'at Rome with my master Servius' (the well-known grammarian and commentator on Virgil) helps to illustrate the revival of interest in Juvenal which took place in the fourth century.[4] They are not, as has often been assumed, evidence for the production of critical editions of Latin texts – except in so far as every copy of any text was an edition, being different from every other copy, and in so far as any reader who cared to take the trouble had always been accustomed to correct, punctuate and annotate his own books using whatever resources were open to him. They represent a few documented cases of a practice that went on throughout Roman antiquity. The activity which they represent was essentially a private one and, regarded from the philological point of view, uncontrolled and irresponsible.[5]

The authors of the *subscriptiones* tinkered at their texts for the most part by the light of nature. Scholars such as C. Julius Hyginus, Palatine Librarian under Augustus, and Valerius Probus (end of first century A.D.), as heirs to the Alexandrian tradition, were in theory committed to a code of practice which incorporated stringent safeguards against unauthorized alteration of texts. The text itself was reproduced from the best available copies (however 'best' might be defined); conjectural readings were not admitted. They belonged in the com-

---

[1] Gell. 3.3.3; cf. Zetzel (1972) 19, 76–8. It should be noted that Varro's canon was based, not on an independent appraisal of the evidence, but on the general consensus of existing scholarly opinion.

[2] Suet. *Gramm.* 24; Zetzel (1972) 44–58.

[3] First comprehensively listed by Jahn (1851) 327–72; cf. Büchner (1961) 355–7. A new provisional corrected and augmented list at Zetzel (1972) 225–42, 308–9.

[4] Cf. Cameron (1964) 369–71.

[5] Zetzel (1972) 253. On irresponsible 'correction' of texts by amateurs cf. Quint. *Inst.* 9.4.39.

panion volume of commentary, in which critical and exegetical problems were discussed. A battery of critical signs was used in the text itself to signal the nature and existence of the particular problem.[1] Given the technical limitations of the ancient book and the character of ancient publication, the plan was perfectly sound. In point of fact few traces of the systematic application of these methods have survived, even in Greek papyri;[2] and in the Roman world 'pure' scholarship was hardly known. Such critical discussions as figure in extant Latin commentaries and collections of *scholia* (detached notes of varying age and provenance that have accumulated in the margins of medieval copies) can be seen to represent a by-product of grammatical interpretation rather than a scientific concern with the problem of textual sources and their use.[3]

As to the character of this interpretation, it is of a piece with the educational and rhetorical system which had given it birth and which it existed to serve. There is the same preoccupation with minute, and often absurd, details; there is the same blindness to what we should account the larger issues of literary criticism.[4] Even in the technical sphere of language, metre, and rhetoric, standards are sometimes surprisingly low. Again and again Servius and the other Virgilian commentators betray a fundamental lack of understanding of Virgil's poetry. That the prevailing standard of critical judgement in the face of unquestioned prejudice was low can be seen from the general readiness to accept the ascription of certain poems in what is now called the Virgilian Appendix to the young Virgil.[5] The most striking feature of this situation, which has not received the attention that it deserves, is the discrepancy between the quality of literary appreciation which, on the evidence of the literature itself, the great writers and in particular the learned poets of Rome expected from their readers, and the almost complete failure of the professional exegetes to respond to these standards. This is especially noticeable in the preoccupation with overall economy, balance, symmetry and related questions of structure and scale displayed by (for instance) Lucretius, Virgil, Livy and Tacitus, and the total indifference to these things evident in our critical sources, who almost never allow their attention to stray from the individual word, phrase or verse.

In itself their concentration on details and on rhetorical techniques was by no means misplaced. Again, the literature itself, read with attention and in consciousness of the rhetorical conditioning discussed above, offers ample evidence that it was not only on the large scale that poets and artistic prose-writers took pains. From Virgil onwards Latin poetry was profoundly influenced by rhetoric, and a style of literary criticism that fails to take account of this

---

[1] For these signs, listed in a Paris MS, see *GLK* vii 533–6, Büchner (1961) 329–30.

[2] Reynolds–Wilson (1974) 11; cf. Turner (1968) 116–17.

[3] Cf. on Servius Zetzel (1972) 87–158 *passim*.

[4] Cf. Guillemin (1937) 49–54; and on Fronto's preoccupation with single words Grube (1965) 321.

[5] Cf. *Vit. Donat.* 17–18; and in general Speyer (1971) 112–28.

fact will miss much that is essential to the poetry.[1] But the style of interpretation favoured by most ancient critics and commentators was conditioned by a basic premiss which a modern critic cannot accept, though he must be aware of it, that literary studies were a part of rhetoric and subservient to its social, political and moral ends. Of all the ancient critics whose works have survived the only one who transcended these limitations was the author of the treatise *On the sublime*, who was concerned exclusively with Greek literature.

The student of Latin will find that the most valuable guidance to the appreciation of Latin literature is that which emerges from close study of the texts themselves. The insistence by the poets that they wrote for a restricted and specially qualified readership, mentioned earlier in this discussion, was not a conventional pose. To read Latin literature so as to extract from it the greatest possible profit and enjoyment is a very demanding undertaking. It calls for a combination of detailed knowledge, linguistic and factual, and educated sensibility, that can only come from laborious application. The books in which we read our Latin authors are much more convenient than those which a Roman reader had, and our texts are probably purer than his often were. In other respects, even after allowing for the fact that Latin was his native language, we are not at such a disadvantage as might be thought. Literary Latin was an artificial dialect, quite distinct from the spoken idiom. Moreover a Roman reader must have been to a considerable extent the prisoner of his own age. To a Roman of the second century A.D. the language of Lucretius must have presented many puzzles to which solutions were not easily available even to a scholar with access to a good library. The main advantage that we enjoy, the ready availability of a vast apparatus of accurate scholarship in the shape of commentaries, dictionaries, reference books and other secondary literature, can be attributed directly to the invention of printing and what it made possible in the way of cooperative effort. If we try to imagine ourselves without these aids to understanding of literature we may begin to comprehend something of the situation of the reader in the world of the hand-written papyrus book.

Excursus I. THE SENSE OF 'LIBER' (P. 15)

Sense (iii) of *liber* and also of βιβλίον was denied by Birt (1882) 29–34. Unambiguous examples of this sense are indeed not easy to find. At Gell. 18.9.5, cited both by Dziatzko (1899*a*) 940 and Wendel (1949) 51, the predominant sense is (i), almost = 'copy'. At Juv. 3.41–2 *librum | si malus est, nequeo laudare et poscere* 'I am incapable of praising and asking for a bad book', the sense 'work of literature' is uppermost; but even this passage does not prove that Juvenal would have described (e.g.) the *Thebaid* of Statius as a *liber*. Similar reservations are in order when considering the other examples cited at *OLD* **liber**[4] 2a. Cicero twice refers to his *De gloria*, a work in

[1] Cf. on (e.g.) Lucan's rhetoric Getty (1955) xliv–lxvi.

two books, as a *liber* (*De or.* 2.31; *Att.* 15.27.2, 16.6.4). This however has been explained in the light of 'a last-minute change in the form of the work before publication' (Shackleton Bailey (1965–70) VI 289). The second example cited by Dziatzko, loc. cit., is from the fourth-century grammarian Charisius, who refers to Varro's *De poematis*, a work in three books, as *liber* (1.53, p. 66 Barwick). From these admittedly inconclusive data it seems to emerge that sense (iii) was late in developing and slow to make headway. In this sense *uolumen* is also found: cf. Plin. *N.H.* 3.58, Vell. 1.14.1, 2.131 (Wendel loc. cit.). The definition of a 'book' might be of some legal importance: cf. *Dig.* 32.52, Dziatzko (1899a) 941.

EXCURSUS 2. THE SENSE OF 'CORNUA' (P. 16)

The explanation given in the text is that usually accepted, and analogies such as the use of *cornu* for the tip of a yard-arm seem to lend support to it (*OLD* **cornu** 7e). However, Birt (1882) 299 argued strongly that *cornua* were the ends of the roll itself. In this connexion it is also relevant to consider the meaning of the word *frons* ('front, side, forehead') as applied to a book. The *frontes* are usually taken to be (i) the long edges of the roll (Birt (1882) 365, id. (1913) 304–5, *TLL* VI 1362.84). It has, however, been argued that they were (ii) the ends of the roll (*OLD* **frons**[2] 8b, but 'flat ends' is unclear; Luck (1968) on Ov. *Trist.* 1.1.8 (supporting this as the sense in the singular, sense (i) in the plural); Schubart (1921) 105). The *frons* or *frontes* were smoothed with pumice as part of the process of finishing the book (Ov. *Trist.* 1.1.11, Mart, 1.66.10) and were apparently, with the *titulus*, what showed when the book was shelved (Sen. *De tranqu. an.* 9.6). The emphasis on the appearance of both *frontes* at (e.g.) Mart. 3.2.8 suggests that sense (i) is the more likely, since when the book was properly rolled only the outside end would be visible, whereas both edges would be. The relationship of the *cornua* to the *frons* or *frontes* still remains somewhat obscure, especially since the poets tend to indulge in word-plays of an obvious kind when referring to the external appearance of the *libellus*: cf. Ov. *Trist.* 1.1.8. A much-cited but very difficult verse in this connexion is [Tib.] 3.1.13 *inter geminas pingantur cornua frontes* 'let the *cornua* between the twin *frontes* be coloured'. When the book was rolled, each *cornu*, if taken = knob, would stand out in the centre of its *frons* (sense (i)); but *inter* is not good Latin to express this idea (cf. Luck, loc. cit.; Erath (1971) 29). Ov. *Pont.* 4.13.7 shows that the tag (*titulus*) which identified the book when it stood on the shelf was attached to the *frons*, presumably meaning 'edge' rather than 'beginning of the book' (Erath, loc. cit.). Cf. on these tags Cic. *Att.* 4.4a.1, 8.2 and Shackleton Bailey (1965–70) ad locc.; Turner (1971) 34. On the whole problem see Besslich (1973).

EXCURSUS 3. TITLING (P. 16)

On the analogy of the modern book it might be expected that the author and title of a work would be given at the beginning of the text; the handful of surviving (Greek) rolls in which this is the case are all of late date (Turner (1971) 16). This is not in itself conclusive, since the beginning of a roll is the most vulnerable part of it, and the odds against survival into modern times of a roll complete with its beginning were large. Nor is the indirect evidence clear. Martial writes of the '*Epigramma*' of Book 9 of his poems being placed *extra ordinem paginarum* 'outside the sequence of columns' (9 *praef.*; cf. 2 *praef.*). Since the columns were not numbered, and their *ordo* could begin as close to the beginning of the roll as convention and the taste of the copyist dictated, it is difficult to see what exactly the phrase means. There is more than one possibility: (i) The two passages in Martial (and possibly, for instance, the *Epigramma* to the three-book edition of Ovid's *Amores*) refer to an addition made to the clean copy of the book just before it left the author's hands; it was an easy matter to add another sheet of papyrus to the left-hand end of the roll (cf. above, p. 18). But nothing is specifically said about *adglutinatio*, and in the copies made from the original exemplar peculiarities of this kind would not have been reproduced: the scribe would simply have copied the text as it now stood, starting at the normal place on his clean roll. (ii) The *ordo paginarum* was a matter of scribal differentiation. Martial is distinguishing between the text of the book proper, written in regular columns, and the prefatory matter, set off in some way from the rest and differently treated, thus appearing to stand to the left of a notional line from which the *ordo* began. (iii) The *Epigramma* was written at the beginning of the roll on the *outside*. This last is the solution favoured by (e.g.) Birt (1882) 142, id. (1913) 301, Wendel (1949) 26–7; a few examples of Greek rolls so titled have survived (Turner (1971) 16, 125). Wendel suggests that such matter came to be transferred to the inside of the roll, and then to occupy a separate page in the *codex-*form (ibid. 27, citing Aug. *Epist.* 2.40.2 for the phrase *in liminari pagina* 'on the threshold page'). If Wendel's hypothesis is correct, then both solutions (ii) and (iii) would be correct, but for different periods. Certainly, if an *Epigramma* such as these could stand outside the roll, so *a fortiori* could a shorter inscription, giving merely author and title (or contents: cf. on the question of how books were identified Nachmanson (1941), Koep (1954) 674). But are we to take it that such prefatory matter as (e.g.) Quintilian's letter to Tryphon or the letters introducing the individual books of Statius' *Silvae* (as apparently suggested by Birt (1882) 142 n. 3) regularly stood on the outside of the roll? If so, it is miraculous that they have survived or that their authors expected them to. Indeed it seems unlikely that an *Epigramma* or the like would have been allowed to encroach even on the inside of the roll on the length of papyrus normally left blank for protection at the beginning, for that also would have endangered its survival; the text as a whole, including *Epigrammata* and the like, would start precisely where it normally started, in terms of distance from the left-hand end of the papyrus. It seems preferable to accept solution (ii), i.e. to believe that Martial's reference to the *ordo paginarum* represents a *façon de parler*. This may ultimately go back to a time when identifying details were regularly written outside the roll (Wendel (1949) 24–5); but it strains credulity to think that such a practice can have been followed with textual matter, even when it was of a merely prefatory character.

2

LITERARY CRITICISM

Literary critics today fall into two broad categories. There are the academics, out to impress their colleagues and instruct their pupils. And there are, in the great tradition of Dryden, creative writers meditating on their craft. In the Roman world, academics, or their nearest equivalents, practised on literature something that they called *kritikē* (*iudicium* 'judgement'), but at an infinitely lower level of sophistication than has now been reached. The creative writers might comment on their trades, but they did it less systematically than Dryden or Eliot, and in response, rather, to the feuds and challenges of the moment. Neither teachers nor writers give us anything as abstract and theoretical as Aristotle's *Poetics*, or anything with as perceptive a treatment of cited passages as 'Longinus'. Cicero, Horace and Quintilian, authoritative and influential though they were, not only rank inferior to the best Greek critics: they are not competing in the same field.

I. THE 'ACADEMICS'

Grammatici

Horace, registering the judgement that Ennius was a second Homer, adds *ut critici dicunt* 'as the critics say' (*Epist.* 2.1.51). What, for the Romans, was a *criticus*?

In Greece scholars seem to have been called *kritikoi* before they took over the term *grammatikos*.[1] Even when *grammatikos* was in vogue, the exercise of judgement was regarded as an important part of a scholar's task; and Crates of Mallos, the wheel having come full circle, claimed to be critic rather than, or as well as, grammarian.[2] For Crates a critic was a superior being, 'skilled in the whole science of language'.[3] But we do not know that the great Alexandrians, such as Aristarchus and Aristophanes ('judges of poets', as Quintilian called them: *Inst.* 10.1.54), took their judgements very far. One of their activities was the establishment of an *ordo* or 'ranking' of approved writers in each genre.

---

[1] Pfeiffer (1968) 157. [2] Pfeiffer (1968) 238.
[3] Sext. Emp. *Adv. math.* 1.79.

Another was to decide whether a work, or a portion of a work, was genuine. Both of these functions, of course, involved the making of value judgements; and we know that Aristophanes judged Archilochus' iambi best (Cic. *Att.* 16.11.2), though three writers were 'received' in this genre (Quintilian 10.1.59). But it was the stern textual procedures, as applied especially by Aristarchus to individual lines or passages of poetry, that attracted most lay attention.

It is accordingly a sort of athetesis (diagnosis of spuria) that is most often mentioned in connexion with such Romans as were explicitly called *critici* – which may mean no more than *grammatici* exercising their function of judgement. In his commentary on Virgil, Servius eleven times[1] uses the term, always in a context of blame. Typically, on *Aen.* 8.731 the critics are said to 'censure' (*notant*) the whole verse 'as having been added superfluously'. It is true that this sort of phrase does not seem to carry the implication that Virgil did not actually write the line or word censured: merely that he would have done better not to write it. Thus, very clearly, *Ecl.* 2.65 is 'censured for giving this sentiment to a rustic in contravention of the law of pastoral poetry' (*supra bucolici carminis legem*). Servius' *critici* apply Zenodotus' obelus with realistic regard to the difference between Homer and Virgil. But the grounds for their censure are very similar to Zenodotus'.

Elsewhere we can find close Roman parallels to Greek concern for the genuineness of whole works.[2] Accius' work on the chronology of Roman drama was precursor to the properly 'critical' activity of Varro on Plautus. According to Gellius (*N.A.* 3.3.3) Varro added to the twenty-one comedies commonly attributed to Plautus others that he felt on stylistic grounds – 'swayed by the texture and humour of their language' – to be genuine. And Gellius adds that his own teacher Favorinus employed the same criterion: 'even this one verse can be proof enough that this play is Plautine' (3.3.6).

Nor did Roman scholars shirk the task of establishing, in the wake of the Greeks, an *ordo* of the best Latin writers. The classic case of this, in Quintilian, will have to be discussed further below; but the tendency goes back much earlier. Volcacius Sedigitus' verses ranking the comic authors allude to the many who 'dispute to whom they should award the palm' (Gellius, *N.A.* 15.24). Moreover, Quintilian's concern to match Latin authors with Greek – Virgil with Homer, Livy with Herodotus, and the rest – finds, as we have seen, an earlier counterpart in Horace. It may be Varro who lies behind the docketing of Ennius as a second Homer; in that case, Varronian too will be the succeeding parallels drawn between Afranius and Menander, Plautus and Epicharmus, and the schoolmasterly distinction between the art of Terence and the gravity of Caecilius. Varro certainly extended his interest in literature beyond Plautus,

---

[1] *Ecl.* 2.65; *Aen.* 1.71, 2.668, 8.291 and 731, 9.81, 10.157 and 861, 11.24 and 188, 12.83.

[2] A concern that still weighed with writers on rhetoric: see e.g. Dion. Hal. *Isaeus* 2 and *Dem.* 13.

for we find him assigning Pacuvius, Lucilius and Terence to the three types of style, and incidentally cutting across genres as he did so.[1]

We have seen that in the terminology of the Servian scholia *critici* is used of those who found fault with certain aspects of Virgil's poetry. It has been argued[2] that the phrase refers especially to the early *obtrectatores* or 'disparagers' of the poet, one of whom wrote a distich to make fun of the rusticity of *cuium pecus* in *Ecl.* 3.1[3] Whatever the truth, the Servian *critici* behave little differently from other carpers, who were certainly full-blown *grammatici*. Thus Probus remarked on *Aen.* 4.418 that 'if Virgil had omitted this verse, he would have done better'.[4] And we see the same distinguished grammarian at work in more detail in Gellius (9.9.12–17), who reports his robust discussion of the comparison of Dido with Diana in *Aen.* 1.498–502. The simile, for Probus, is by no means appropriate (*nequaquam conueniens*), Diana's quiver far from functional and her joy far from unconfined. We may well quarrel with the judgement; but the importance of the passage is that it juxtaposes Virgil with his Homeric model (*Od.* 6.102–8) and attempts an aesthetic valuation. This scrap of Probus' scholarship, and others like it, should prevent us from assuming too readily that the Servian commentary, with its reluctance to comment helpfully on, or often even to mention, Virgil's models, is typical of Roman dealings with this most traditional of poets. On the contrary, we can see from the enormous discussion in Macrobius (*Saturnalia* 5–6), where not only tracts of Homer but also many passages of earlier Roman poets are cited *in extenso*, that the ancients took this task as seriously as modern commentators. It did not, fortunately, take long to outgrow the attitude that 'imitation' was no more than 'borrowing' or 'theft'. Where Perellius Faustus 'collected thefts' (*Vita Donati* 44) and drew the pained comment of the poet that it was easier to steal his club from Hercules than a line from Homer, Macrobius regards such transference as a subject for muted congratulation (*Sat.* 5.3.16). Many a Victorian commentator was less sophisticated than that.

But the general run of the scholia on Virgil is less impressive. These commentaries are designed largely to instruct – and to instruct the young; and though their sources are often very learned, they themselves rarely sound very adult. They will (to take examples from a familiar book of the *Aeneid*) identify the Hesperides (4.484), give us a snippet of information on the habits of the planet Mercury (239), put Aulis on the map (426); this is what Quintilian's enthusiasm for knowledge of mythology and astronomy at the grammar school

---

[1] Gell. 6.14.6. Cf. Charisius p. 315, 3 Barwick (= Varro fr. 40 Funaioli), where Caecilius and Terence are contrasted in the matter of the rousing of emotion.

[2] Ribbeck (1866) 102, 107; Georgii (1891) 2.

[3] For him and others see *Vita Donati* 43–5.

[4] Georgii (1891) 560–7 has a helpful table showing the various grounds on which Virgil was criticized in the Servian commentary.

must usually have meant in practice.[1] Then, because grammarian and *rhetor* had always overlapped and tended more and more to fuse,[2] there are rhetorical analyses of speeches, usually very sketchy; the remarks on Anna's speech at 31 as a *suasoria* are fuller than most. There are portentous pronouncements on religious practice, with Aeneas and Dido forced into a mould of priest and priestess (374, etc.). There are occasional hints at allegory (so at 114), a common fate for poetry from Crates to Tiberius Claudius Donatus. Figures are occasionally identified (276, etc.), riddles propounded and solved (262: why did Aeneas wear a bejewelled sword to supervise the building of Carthage?). This, with the pabulum of explication, leaves little room for anything we should regard as literary criticism.

But that is perhaps too hasty a judgement. The occasional condescending pat on the back for Virgil – *bene...* – sometimes prefaces a shrewd point. Thus at 403 the commentator remarks on the 'sublimity' lent by military metaphor to the description of ants. There are modern critics who would be proud to have connected the wounded stag in the Dictaean woods (73) with the herb dittany (*dictamnum*) that was reputed to heal the wounds of wild beasts, as we know that Virgil knew (*Aen.* 12.414). And suggestive recent work on 'multiple-correspondence' similes in Virgil[3] finds firm roots in the remarks of the commentator at 442–5.

We should bring this sort of balance to our judgement on Macrobius, who after all makes Servius participate in the conversation that forms the *Saturnalia*, and who was clearly drawing on largely grammatical or antiquarian sources. There are the same weaknesses. Where *grammatici* are criticized, it is for failing to raise a *quaestio* of their own kind (as at 5.18.3). To prove his own enthusiasm for the fray, one speaker proudly produces the recondite information that Euripides was reproved by Aristotle for saying it was the left foot rather than the right that Aetolians kept unshod (5.18.16–20). And there is a tendency to see Virgil as always right: 'there is another way of *defending* the use of the word *inlaudatus*', someone significantly remarks (6.7.16). At the same time, Macrobius had a certain feel for the relativity of critical judgements: 'let no one think old poets worthless just because their verses seem rough (*scabri*) to us' (6.3.9) – and this at a day when men did not care for the archaic (6.4.1; cf. 6.9.9). There is nothing to be ashamed of in the appraisal of Homer as a poet who showed 'not only grandeur but also simplicity, vividness (*praesentiam*) of language, and silent dignity' (5.13.40). And when it came to detailed assessment, modern studies of the catalogue in *Aeneid* 7[4] do not go far beyond the remarks in 5.15–16, where Homer's catalogue is compared, with due comment

---

[1] Quintilian 1.8.18 (with Colson's note) and 1.10.46–8.
[2] For early instances, Suet. *Gramm.* 4.6, 7.3. For later, Marrou (1958) 10 n. 2.
[3] West (1969).
[4] E.g. Williams (1961). Macrobius doubtless had his sources, here as elsewhere.

on the prominence of the Boeotians, and where the variety of Virgil is contrasted with Homer's repetitiousness which 'somehow supremely suits him, is appropriate to the genius of an ancient poet, and is the right way of conducting an enumeration' (5.15.16). At their best, the *grammatici* did look carefully at passages, not just as strings of words to be glossed but as wholes with literary predecessors, and make judgements on them that have stood the test of time.

Parallel to commentaries on Virgil were similar works on other distinguished poets. Thus Aelius Donatus commented on Terence as well as on Virgil, Acron on Terence and Horace. Asconius Pedianus, author of a lost work 'Against the disparagers of Virgil', bridged the gap between commentators on prose and poetry; for he produced impressive historical comments on speeches of Cicero. He elucidates allusions with economically phrased erudition, and explains in elaborate prefaces the circumstances of each speech. This is one side of what Quintilian was later to call for; he was to point out the desirability of teachers of rhetoric providing *enarratio* for the great orators as the grammarians did for the poets (2.5.1), stressing the need to give details of the case a speech is written for (ibid. 7).[1] But the rest of what Quintilian looked for (ibid. 7–9), close observation of the use made by great masters of rhetorical devices of all kinds, is lacking in Asconius and rarely apparent elsewhere. It was a matter, perhaps, that fell between the stools of *grammaticus* and *rhetor*. The Bobbio scholia on Cicero give an idea of the possibilities in this direction. Yet here, though great attention is properly devoted to detail, there is neglect of the equally vital view of the speech as a whole. The monograph rather than the commentary, or a combination of the two, would have been, then as now, the right vehicle.

Declamation

When he stepped over the frontier dividing grammarian from rhetorician, the Roman school-boy was faced by declamation rather than by oratory; and Quintilian gives the impression of fighting a losing battle in an attempt to widen the syllabus to include constant and detailed reading of prose masters at this stage (2.5.1–2). Declamation looms large, too, in first-century criticism. But much of what is said of it is generalized and polemical. There is the view put by Petronius at the (present) start of the *Satyricon* (1–2), and less vividly but equally forcefully in a mutilated chapter of the *Dialogus* of Tacitus (35), that declamation, with its parade of stepmothers and pirates and plagues, is too divorced from reality to make a satisfactory training for the lawcourts; and that when the unfortunate pupil arrives in the real world of interdicts and ancient lights he is thoroughly out of his depth. There is the balanced reply of

---

[1] Cf. Asconius 54, on the desirability of reading Cominius' prosecution speech as well as Cicero's defence of Cornelius, with Quintilian 10.1.22–3.

Quintilian (2.10). On the one hand, declamation did need some reform: it would help to introduce real names and jokes, and avoid the more unreal sort of theme. On the other hand, declamation was, in its way, a form of display oratory and could hardly avoid excursions into territory more agreeable and fanciful than the average law suit. Quintilian clearly was not prepared to envisage the abolition of declamation; and those who made fun of it seem to have had no alternative to offer. Nor indeed was it abolished; it was still going strong in the time of Ennodius, on the very verge of the early Middle Ages.

Alongside this generalized debate, we do have an occasional glimpse into the detail of declamation. It is here most profitable, perhaps, to study the *sermones* of the pseudo-Quintilian, the introductory remarks of a schoolmaster prefaced to model treatments of the themes he set. The form militates against anything very much like criticism; but there is at least an attempt to guide declamation into practical and useful paths, to show what the aims of a speaker in a given speech were, and how they were best pursued. Look, for instance, at the *sermo* to *Decl.* 270. 'It is easy to argue the case of this old man as far as emotion and equity are concerned. But unless he is also defended with legal arguments, there is danger that he may be condemned by the judges for all his tears.' And there follows a polemic on those who leave out the tougher parts of a speech, leaving flesh lacking bone and sinew. There are certain points to be proved. Only when we have proved them can we proceed to say the things to which most declaimers nowadays restrict themselves. This is in Quintilian's tradition, perhaps even his actual teaching. It shows us a rhetorician conscientiously trying to make the best of his educational tool. It is not unimpressive: more impressive, in a way, than the bitty and anecdotal treatment of the elder Seneca. In his collection of *Controversiae* and *Suasoriae* we have a vast array of fragments of declamation; from Seneca, more than from any other ancient author, derives the surely exaggerated view that declamations consisted of little but epigram. It is true that Seneca normally gives us the 'division' that Latro or some other declaimer applied to a case (e.g. *Contr.* 1.1.13), but he only once (2.7) set himself to give a declamation in full, so enabling us to judge how a speech related to its bare scheme; and on that one occasion, by an irony of fate, a lacuna in our manuscripts cuts the speech short (and deprives us of the division). But in general Seneca was interested in detail, and especially in the epigrams and 'colours', the more or less ingenious slants put on a case. And Seneca's own comments on these matters will hardly be thought of as serious criticism. He ridicules Junius Otho for over-using dreams to supply colours (2.1.33). Epigrams are on occasion – and rather arbitrarily, one feels – picked off as 'very stupid' (5.2) or 'nicely put' (7.1.26), or 'with its own kind of insanity' (9.2.28). Style is characterized as corrupt, Asianic, *kakozelos* ('in bad taste'). The prefaces to individual books attempt a more rounded view of some distinguished declaimers, and include more penetrating assessments of their styles. As for the practice of declamation[1] in general, Seneca's standpoint is sane, and he recounts with some relish the vigorous protests of Cassius Severus against the whole system (3 *praef.*). But he is a magpie rather than a critic; he makes no attempt to see declamation, or even any individual declamation, as a whole. No need to dwell on the incidental judgements on other authors that are scattered through the book. It is in the manner of the *grammaticus* that a description of Cestius' is placed alongside two lines of Virgil and their model in Varro of Atax (7.1.27). And Cicero is declaimed about, not assessed (*Contr.* 7.2; *Suas.* 6 and 7).

Quintilian

Seneca was not himself, it would seem, a practising rhetorician, merely an old man recalling past glories to enthusiastic sons. With Quintilian we come to a professional *rhetor*, well qualified, as well as inclined, to assess Cicero as well as praise him. Yet the part of the *Institutio* that is most widely read, perhaps the most familiar example of ancient literary criticism, is markedly in the tradition of the grammarian. In Alexandria, as we have seen, scholars established lists of selected writers, and laid down orders of merit within genres. Quintilian's famous survey of Greek literature (10.1.46–84) draws on listing of this kind,[2] and his treatment of Roman authors (85–131) provides a rival list for the rival language. Thus on the one hand he tells us that among the elegists Callimachus is 'regarded as leader, while most agree that Philetas took second place' (58); and on the other Virgil is placed first among Roman writers of hexameters (85–6), while Cornelius Severus 'could lay good claim to the second place if he had completed his *Sicilian War* to the standard of his first book' (89). The whole treatment of the Latin authors is consciously modelled on that of the Greeks: 'I must keep to the same order in dealing with Roman writers also' (85). Further, every effort is made to pit Roman against Greek. Virgil is praised as second only to Homer (85); 'I should not be afraid to match Sallust with Thucydides, and Herodotus should not be angry to find Livy put on a par with him' (101). We have seen the same tendency earlier. And where Cicero had in the *Brutus* constructed a 'canon' of Roman orators culminating in himself, in conscious rivalry with the Greeks, Quintilian takes equally open pride in the Roman achievement. 'And perhaps *we* make up by Virgil's good general level for the inferiority our champion shows to Homer's heights' (86). *We* – that is Cicero as opposed to Demosthenes – are victorious in wit and pathos (107). 'As for satire, it is completely ours' (93).

---

[1] Which, thought Seneca (*Contr.* 2 *praef.* 3), 'equips even those whom it does not train for its own ends'.　　[2] Explicitly enough: see sections 52, 54, 58–9, 72–3.

All the same, reminiscent of the *grammaticus* though Quintilian's list is, it is quite clearly directed towards the training of the orator. The reading of all these authors is part of the process of producing a *hexis*, a soundly based ability to speak (10.1.1). 'I am not talking here about how an orator should be trained (I have already expressed myself on that topic enough – or at least as well as I could); now I am dealing with an athlete who has already learnt all the tricks from his teacher: by what kind of exercise is he to be prepared for combat?' (4). Just as in Lucian (*Lexiph*. 22) a progression is envisaged from the best poets through the orators to the heights of Plato and Thucydides, so Quintilian has given a graded course of reading: Homer and Virgil, tragedy, and selections from lyric at the school of the *grammaticus* (1.8.5), Cicero and Livy in the early stages of the *rhetor's* education (2.5.19–20), and then finally, in the last years of the rhetorical training, a whole range of Latin and Greek literature. The list may seem optimistically long; but the intention is to point to the authors available, and to suggest as briefly as possible what elements in them should be imitated and can contribute to the 'strengthening of the faculty of oratory' (10.1.44). And Quintilian is not all-inclusive: 'if I miss people out, that does not mean I have not heard of them...But to those lesser poets we shall return once our strength is complete and established' (57–8). Pisandros, Nicander, Euphorion, Tyrtaeus can wait; meanwhile 'we must get used to the best; our minds must be formed, our style developed, by much reading rather than the exploration of many authors' (59). Only when real maturity is reached can we safely read Seneca, one of whose virtues is that he can exercise the reader's judgement – for him and against him (131).

'Few, perhaps none, can be found, among those who have worn well, who would not have something useful to offer to readers prepared to exercise judgement' (40). And even though Quintilian claims to pick out only the most eminent (45), his list remains long. This fits in closely with Quintilian's view of imitation. Even if there were a supreme model for an orator – and Cicero comes close to being that – our human weakness would prevent us being able in practice to reproduce him whole (10.2.25–6). 'A prudent man should, if he can, make his own what he sees to be best in every author...We should put before our eyes the good points of a number of orators, so that one thing may stick from one source, one from another, and so that we can fit each in at the right place' (26). Nor does this apply only to the reading of orators; there is grist for the mill to be found everywhere. The reading of poetry has its advantages for the orator as well as its dangers (10.1.27–30). Hence the attention Quintilian pays to poets in his list, but hence too his constant care to define how far they can be of use to the orator. On the smaller scale, we see Alcaeus as a poet who is 'often similar to an orator'[1] though he 'also wrote trivia, and

---

[1] Similar phrases in 65 (comedy), 74 (Theopompus); cf. 90 on Lucan.

descended to erotica' (63); Euripides (67) is by general consent more useful to the budding advocate[1] than Sophocles – their merits as *poets* are expressly left out of account. So too on the negative side. Propertius is docketed with the remark that some prefer him (93) not because Quintilian disapproves of him but because he sees nothing in him for the student, not even the terseness and elegance he has just attributed to Tibullus. And on the large scale, when Quintilian discusses Homer, he adopts an elaborate series of rhetorical schemata to catalogue his virtues. He is pattern for forensic and deliberative oratory, not to speak of panegyric (47); he is master of emotion, both gentle and violent (48); he knows how to handle proem, narration, argument, and epilogue (48–50). This is not so much an unhistorical attribution to Homer of rhetorical skills of which he was innocent[2] as a careful directing of the pupil towards the aspects of the great poet to which he needs to pay attention.

All this had to be read *carefully*. 'Everything should be scrutinized – but not merely a little at a time; a book should be read right through, and then taken up again from the beginning' (20). Authors should be masticated, for proper digestion (19). This too cohered with Quintilian's view of imitation. The pupil should not be like those misguided persons who 'imagined that they had reproduced the style of the superhuman Cicero beautifully if they had put *esse uideatur* at the end of the sentence' (10.2.18).[3] Imitation is not just a matter of aping verbal mannerisms. The point was not new.[4] Dionysius of Halicarnassus (*Din.* 7) contrasts two sorts of imitation, one which depends on slavish adherence to rules and results in 'something contrived and unnatural', while the superior kind is 'natural and the outcome of prolonged instruction and familiarity'. 'Longinus', as usual, saw it more grandly: imitating is a matter of being taken over by a spirit, so that, like the priestess at Delphi, you give utterance to sublimities not your own (13.2). Quintilian, in his practical way, places his emphasis on a dogged analysis of oratorical texts.

We must concentrate on the sense of fitness that those great men show in adapting themselves to circumstances and personalities; on their strategy, their arrangement, the way in which everything – even things that seem to be put in merely for entertainment – has victory as its aim. We should note what the proem is designed to do; what sort of tactics are adopted in the narration, and how various they are; what powers of proof and refutation are displayed, what skill in arousing all kinds of emotion; how even public popularity is turned to advantage. . . If we see all this clearly, we shall be able truly to imitate. (10.2.27)

---

[1] And Menander would help not only the orator (69) but the declaimer (71).

[2] As Quintilian observes (49), 'even writers of rhetorical handbooks look to this poet for very many of their examples': an instance (like the Servian commentary) of the cross-fertilization of rhetorical and grammatical precept; Cicero and Quintilian, too, mix prose and verse examples.

[3] Cf. Tac. *Dial.* 23.1, where Cicero's love of this version of a favourite clausula is maliciously exaggerated. For similar remarks on purely verbal imitation, see Seneca, *Epist.* 114.17–19.

[4] 'The true imitator of Demosthenes is one who speaks in the manner of Demosthenes, not one who speaks words of Demosthenes' ([Dion Hal.] *Ars Rhet.* 10.19).

It is clear from this passage, and from that in 10.1.22–4 on the need to acquaint oneself with the historical background of a speech, that Quintilian knew how literary criticism of oratory should be conducted; and it is a mark of his sophistication that only recently have scholars approached Cicero in this wide and unprejudiced way.[1] Quintilian saw that orators did not write in slavish compliance with rhetorical precept,[2] and that they should not be judged by using those precepts as a Procrustean bed to limit them. The pity is that the scope of the *Institutio* did not require him to put these principles into practice. We have seen them applied to some effect by Asconius on the historical side, and by the Cicero scholia on the rhetorical side. But we can only judge the quality of Quintilian's analysis by scattered comments; the sophistication of the *enarratio* by which he had hoped (2.5.1–2) to guide his pupils' reading of their oratorical texts can only be glimpsed.

We may take as an example Quintilian's treatment of a speech he much admired and frequently cited, Cicero's for Milo. Much of what he has to say about it is merely classificatory. *Facere enim probus adulescens periculose quam perpeti turpiter maluit*[3] (*Mil.* 9) is an example of *epiphonema* or exclamation (Quint. 8.5.11). The emotional appeal to the hills and groves of Alba (*Mil.* 85) is used five times, to illustrate apostrophe (9.2.38), luxuriance of style (11.1.34) and grandness (12.10.62), and to comment on the gestures (11.3.115) and tone of voice (11.3.167) that must have accompanied the words. But far more perceptive than these are the passages where Quintilian remarks on the 'design' (*consilium*) of the orator: 'He refused to give his narration before freeing the defendant from the effect of all preceding verdicts. He turned the invidious charge of ambushing against Clodius, even though in fact the fight had been fortuitous. He praised the deed – and yet at the same time denied that Milo intended it. He would not put prayers into Milo's mouth, but took them upon himself' (6.5.10). It is with a similar alertness that Quintilian analyses the technique of narrative that makes Clodius rather than Milo seem the aggressor: the celebrated description of Milo getting ready to leave Rome, pottering about while his wife dressed, is seen for what it is, a careful manipulation of the hearer's reactions: 'Milo seems to have done nothing in a hurry or of set purpose. The great orator produced this effect not only by the content – his stress on the delay and the detail of the prolonged setting forth – but by his common-or-garden, everyday wording and by hiding his art' (4.2.58). And Quintilian sees as a virtue what others might have felt to be a defect, Cicero's bending of the rhetorical rules: usually narrative should directly follow upon the proem, but Cicero was quite right to delay the narrative of the *Pro Milone* by placing

---

[1] I think especially of Neumeister (1964), to whom this account owes much. Compare the remarks of Douglas (1973) 99.

[2] See especially his sane comments on rhetorical precept in 2.13.

[3] 'The upright young man preferred dangerous activity to disgraceful passivity.'

before it three preliminary questions which had to be settled in the defendant's favour before the exposition of the facts could profitably be undertaken (4.2.25). Quintilian anticipated the best modern work on Cicero's speeches by seeing them as instruments of persuasion where every touch might have its effect. The orator, for Quintilian, had to be a good man (12.1.1), and the very definition of rhetoric had to stress moral values rather than persuasiveness (2.15.38:[1] contrast 2.15.3); but when it came to analysing a speech, Quintilian knew, from practical experience (for he was lawyer as well as teacher), that technique is what gets results, and that, as his despised predecessor Celsus remarked, 'the reward is not a good conscience but victory for one's client' (2.15.32).

2. THE CRAFTSMEN ON THEIR CRAFTS

Oratory

Cicero himself only gives us tantalizing scraps of comment on his own speeches, and there in the vaguest of terms. Thus on the *Milo*:

> but as for those who think that it would have been fitting for the speech for Milo to have been made (at a time when the army was in position in the forum and all the temples round about) in the same tone as if I had been speaking about a private case before a single judge: such people are measuring the force of eloquence by their own capabilities, not by its potentialities. (*Opt. gen.* 10)

And when he quotes it is for technical analysis (thus of rhythm at *Orat.* 225) or with a brief condescending glance at his own juvenile excesses (*Orat.* 107 on *Rosc. Am.* 72). Cicero's enormous practical experience is poured into an abstract form in the great dialogue *De oratore* and in the sketch of a perfect speaker, the *Orator*. He gives us the Greek rhetorical rules, modified not only by the demands of the genres he adopts but also by the restrictions he knew that real life imposed on theory. But in one extended passage of the *De oratore* he brings us into the orator's workshop, and shows vividly how the politician got his effects in the Roman court (2.197–203). The speaker in the dialogue is the great orator Marcus Antonius, who died during the Marian troubles; he is made to tell us of the celebrated speech in which he contrived the acquittal of his former quaestor Gaius Norbanus on a charge of *maiestas* or treason. Everything was in favour of the accuser, Sulpicius. There was need of *ars aliqua*, an element of craft. The rules of rhetoric could supply little more than hints on the arguing of the legal issue: in what did treason consist? Antonius argued that point very briefly, though naturally in such a way as to favour his client. He relied instead on two things 'by no means elaborately treated in the handbooks', the rousing of sympathy and indignation: sympathy by playing on his

---

[1] The whole of the previous discussion makes it clear that *bene* contains a moral element.

own record as an advocate and his obligation to defend his former quaestor, indignation by stirring old emotions in the equestrian jury against the cowardice and ineptness of Caepio, whom Norbanus had had convicted. These emotional arguments, used to back up a specious defence of civil strife as the mother of constitutional improvement, carried the day against the odds. Antonius, who has earlier in the dialogue been represented as distrustful of the wisdom of the handbooks, says slyly: 'You will, if you please, find some place in your theories for my defence of Norbanus.' And indeed this is the sort of *exemplum* that, as Quintilian remarks (10.1.15), is more effective than the textbooks. Together with Sulpicius' wry comments on Antonius' simulated hesitation at the beginning of the speech and his inexorable rise to the heights of emotional appeal, these sections give us a perfect example of the criticism of oratory, cunningly disguised behind the urbanities of Cicero's dialogue.

Cicero brought to the theory of oratory a width that it had never known before and was rarely to know again. He thinks often of an ideal orator, who shall have all the qualities of Cicero himself and more besides. The theories of the handbooks are only a beginning, to be supplemented and modified by the lessons of experience and the exigencies of particular circumstances. Furthermore, the orator must have the widest of educations; not only is a detailed knowledge of law an essential, but philosophy will give him the ability to expound the general principles that lie behind individual cases. He will be master of all the styles, grand, middle and plain, and capable thereby of fulfilling all the duties, to move, to please and to instruct. He will be in the best sense eclectic.

But all this, however admirable, is theory rather than criticism; and it is not often to Cicero's point to pass judgement on orators. When he does so, it is sometimes with a casualness that is reminiscent of the *grammaticus*: labelling[1] rather than analysis. Nor are his discussions of Greek literature improved by their normal tendency to argue a general case.[2] Thus in *De oratore* 2.93–5 the Greek orators are paraded by generations to demonstrate the doubtful proposition that each age had a particular manner of speaking and that this similarity was due to the habit of imitation of a single model. They are paraded again in *Orator* 28–32 to show how different they all are, how various the Attic orators whom modern 'Atticists' wished to force into a single pattern. And even the fullest survey, in *Brutus* 25–51, is over-generalized. There is little feel of personal assessment; instead, metaphors that give bloom and blood to the Attic orators before Demetrius turned aside to cloying sweetness. A similar tendency to label and catalogue is forced upon the *Brutus* as a whole by its vast aim –

[1] A familiar feature of Roman critical writing: see e.g. Quintilian 12.10.11, Tac. *Dial.* 25.4 (poking grave fun?), and, most absurdly, Fronto pp. 113–14 Naber (= II 48 Haines).

[2] The same is true of Ovid's eccentric demonstration in *Trist.* 2.363–470 that all literature can be regarded as erotic.

to survey oratory from its Roman beginnings to the present day. Many of the orators mentioned are only names to us, and what Cicero finds room to say of them cannot bring them to life. Even when he launches, occasionally, into a full-dress portrait, little comes across. Thus his picture of the elder Cato (*Brut.* 61–76) is purposely exaggerated in the interests of the Atticist controversy; Cicero does not mean too seriously his analogy between Cato and Lysias (again the *grammaticus*' trick!), and Atticus duly demolishes it later (293–4). Here as elsewhere Cicero relies on schematism and metaphor. Cato was a little uncouth, yet used figures lavishly; he is nearer a Canachus than a Polyclitus.[1] 'Pick out the passages deserving especial notice and praise: you will find all the qualities of an orator there' (65). That is just what Cicero does *not* do. Doubtless the form of his dialogue made it impossible; and doubtless too Cicero was capable of it. His discussion of the Norbanus case, even without quotation from Antonius' speech, shows us what he could have done in the way of oratorical criticism; it is our loss that he did so little.

In the exciting days of the 50s, when Cicero and Calvus were fighting their unequal battle for the primacy in Roman eloquence (Sen. *Contr.* 7.4.6), it was easy to see oratory as the universal art, the key to political as well as literary eminence. Hence the width of the *De oratore.* Once Caesar came to power, the field narrowed; and its narrowness is reflected in the *Orator*'s preoccupation with a somewhat academic controversy, the quarrel of Atticists and Asianists. Cicero, at the very end of his career, found the presuppositions of his emotional, expansive and rhythmical oratory challenged; and in the grave proem to the *Brutus* (6) he senses further the passing of oratory itself as a means to action: 'if Hortensius lived today...his particular regret would be to see the Roman forum...despoiled of any educated voice, any worthy of Roman or Greek ears'. And in fact, as the Empire was consolidated, political oratory, that had been the lifeblood of Cicero, lost importance; forensic speeches rarely swayed wide emotions, and there was more and more call for flattering panegyric. The consequent loss of prestige sustained by oratory was called its decay and corruption; and the phenomenon aroused widespread speculation.[2] The elder Seneca, for instance, under Tiberius, attributed it to 'some grudge on nature's part' (*Contr.* 1 *praef.* 6): perhaps it was the effect of the luxury of the age, perhaps big business had become more attractive than oratory, perhaps it was just an instance of the rule that 'things that rise to the top sink back to the bottom, faster than they rose' (7).[3]

Something like the first of those views would have been taken by the philosopher Seneca, whose 114th letter is the classic statement of the doctrine

---

[1] The parallel with the fine arts is common in ancient criticism: see Quintilian 12.10.1–9 with Austin's notes.

[2] Texts are conveniently assembled and discussed by Caplan (1970) ch. 8.

[3] Cf. also Velleius 1.17.6.

that 'le style est l'homme même'. 'Licentious speech is a sign of public luxury' (2). Maecenas was a striking case in point: 'Is not his style as lax as the man himself was dissolute?' (4). The man who, as Augustus' deputy in Rome, gave the watchword for the day without bothering to put on a belt was the man who indulged in the wildest extravagance of word order and conceit. And, more generally, styles go by fashions, swinging abruptly from the over-archaic to the over-novel, and 'wherever you see that a corrupt style of speech finds favour, you may be sure that morals too have gone astray' (11).

Seneca was thinking purely of style. 'Corrupt' style for him meant an extreme of verbal manipulation. And that is probably what Quintilian concentrated on in his lost 'On the causes of the corruption of eloquence'. He reserves, ironically enough, his longest and sternest criticisms in his review of literature for Seneca himself:

I am supposed to condemn Seneca, and even hate him. This is the result of my attempt to recall a corrupted style of oratory, enervated by every vice,[1] to more rigorous standards: and at the time when I did this, Seneca was virtually the only reading-matter of young men...If he had not scorned the straightforward and yearned for the corrupt, if he had not loved all his own work, if he had avoided breaking up his weighty pronouncements into the briefest possible epigrams, he would be approved by scholars generally, not merely by enthusiastic youth. (10.1.125, 130: text uncertain)

As to oratory as a whole, Quintilian was not convinced that it was dead. He gives praise to several orators of his own century, and 'later writers on oratory will have great scope for sincere praise of those who flourish today' (122) – men, no doubt, like Quintilian's own pupil Pliny. Furthermore, the whole weight of his twelfth book, and his advocacy of Ciceronian standards of education and aspiration, rested on a conviction that there was a role still available to the 'good man, skilled in speaking' (12.1.1). There was room for improvement in style – Quintilian had laboured that point for twenty years, trying to bring a new sanity to the declamation-schools. But oratory was alive and kicking.

It was just this that was challenged by the *Dialogus*. It is generally accepted nowadays that this was given a 'Ciceronian' style because of its Ciceronian genre. Yet that daring innovator, Tacitus, may not have been so fettered by the *lex operis* as we imagine. It is at least a by-product of the old-tyme manner of the work that the whole topic is made to seem a little remote. Aper and Messala and Maternus talk in the grave cadences of a bygone era – and they talk about an oratory that has had its day. Aper – and even he is hinted to be no more than an *advocatus diaboli*[2] – praises the pleasures and practical rewards of

---

[1] Again the moralizing. Sexual metaphor in pejorative literary criticism was common (e.g. Tac. *Dial.* 18.5 with Gudeman's notes).

[2] See 15.2 and note the general agreement expected at 28.1.

forensic oratory. He says to his friends: 'Go on brightening this age of ours with beauty of speech as you can, and as you do' (23.5). Modern eloquence is brilliant and entertaining; contrast the symptoms of the old manner as seen in, say, Caelius: 'shabby language, disjointed rhythm, and lack of periodic structure' (21.4). Cicero developed his style towards something more flowery and epigrammatic, and in doing so showed the way for what was to come. And when Cassius Severus took the decisive step into a new era, it was with the conscious intention of adapting oratory to the requirements of a new age and more sophisticated audiences. Aper's speech uses Ciceronian arguments to deflate Cicero's claims to supremacy; for the *Brutus* (e.g. 68), like, as we shall see, the critical poems of Horace, has a consistent sense of the inevitability of progress from crude to polished.

Messala proffers an educational viewpoint not unlike that of Quintilian: the old wide education has given way to the absurdities of declamation. At the same time, some of what he says is redolent of the moral outlook of the Senecas; for he contrasts the old austerities with the vices of modern youth and even modern children.[1] The new element comes with the final speech of Maternus. Earlier he had seemed to accept the view of Aper that eloquence had influence in modern Rome, while rejecting all that it stood for. Now, as though moving from the Flavian age in which the dialogue is set to the principate of Trajan during which Tacitus was probably writing, or perhaps rather from forensic to political oratory, Maternus cuts the ground from under modern eloquence. Cicero had had interesting things to say about the influence of audiences on orators. It is for the ordinary listener that the orator speaks as much as for the educated critic – perhaps more (*Brut.* 183–200):[2] and the elegant taste of Athens fostered Attic oratory as surely as the uncultivated Carians attracted Asianic (*Orat.* 24–7). But Cicero did not try to think out the effect of a political system on oratory. He connects the rise of oratory in Sicily, and by implication in Greece as well, with the peace following the removal of the tyrants, not with the rise of democracy (*Brut.* 45–6). And he points out the lack of a Spartan orator to take up the terse tradition of Menelaus without any attempt to explain it (50). Maternus picks up that trick. Great eloquence does not arise in well-ordered communities (those, that is, with a king or aristocracy), and the many Athenian orators were the natural product of a city where 'everything was in the power of the people...everyone, you might almost say, had a hand in everything' (40.3). Conversely the Rome of the Empire, where for better or for worse 'the deliberations of state are not left to the ignorant many – they are the duty of one man, the wisest' (41.4), left no room for great oratory. For Maternus his friends are 'as eloquent as our day requires'

---

[1] Though it is true that Quintilian was strong on this point also (e.g. 1.2.6–8).
[2] Compare the intelligent remarks of Dion. Hal. *Dem.* 15.

(41.5). They would have reached the heights of oratory if they had lived a century before; as it is, they have the blessings of the imperial peace to console them.

Between them, two exponents of the art of oratory, Cicero and Tacitus, said much of what can profitably be said about oratory in general. And Cicero gives us, in the most urbane form possible, the Greek precepts for rhetoric as well. It was rarely to Cicero's point, and never to Tacitus', to apply their insights to the task of criticizing individual speeches. And when we turn finally to Horace and the criticism of poetry, we find ourselves again in the company of one who, reacting to the controversies of the time, gives us memorable labels and influential generalities rather than the particularities of a 'Longinus'.

Horace and poetry

Horace's *Satires* 1.4 and 1.10 together give us the poet's programme for satire. His father's method of moral education had been to point to concrete instances of vice – 'don't be like Scetanus' (1.4.112). Horace therefore does the same in his poetry, acting as the 'frank friend' (132) to whom he says he owes any improvement in his own character during adulthood. Those who criticize him for malicious back-biting are wide of the mark. And Horace implicitly contrasts himself with his great predecessor and model Lucilius, who, in a freer age, pilloried 'anyone worthy of being represented as a bad man and a thief, as an adulterer or murderer or some other type of criminal' (3–5). Horace deals only with minor vices, and in any case he does not publish his satires – he only recites to his friends, when he cannot avoid it.

In the course of these two poems Horace has much to say of Lucilius, whom he represents as a diffuse and disorganized writer, flowing along 'like a muddy river' (1.4.11; cf. 1.10.50), mixing Latin and Greek words with no sense of propriety, and producing verse that stops in artistic pretension at the point of ensuring that each line has its six feet. Horace makes no exaggerated claims for his own poems; with whatever irony, he disclaims the very title of poet in this genre. But he emphasizes the need for a style 'now sad, now gay, keeping up the role sometimes of a declaimer or poet, sometimes of a wit who purposely spares his strength' (1.10.11–14), for care in composition, and for use of the eraser. Lucilius was better than his predecessors, and in his turn, 'if fate had made him a contemporary of ours, he'd be cutting a lot out of his own works, deleting everything that goes on after the point is made' (68–70). Those who regard poets as no more than *personae*, and as portraying lives that bear no relation to anything but books, can see all this as merely the taking up of a literary stance. But Horace represents the poems as being reactions to criticism – of Horace's own satirical malice, and of his claim to improve on Lucilius. And to judge from the pointed hostility he displays towards *grammatici*[1] – among them, it seems, 'the pretty Hermogenes' (1.10.17–18; cf. 1.4.72) and 'the well-known ape whose learning extends only so far as singing Calvus and Catullus' (1.10.18–19) – Horace had been genuinely nettled by academics' attempts to laugh off the new satire as inferior to Lucilius', just as, maybe, they saw the *Odes* as inferior to the Neoterics. And he falls back on the favour of a few friends, Varius, Maecenas, Virgil, and some others ('it's *their* approval I want': 1.10.82) because those who formed literate taste in the schoolroom were unready to be favourable. Poets after all can hardly welcome being read by the few, even if, in face of the fact, they make a virtue of it.

This conclusion is reinforced by the observation that a similar defensiveness underlies the famous letter to Augustus. Unlike Augustus, Horace says, poets are not appreciated till they are dead. The Greeks had launched out, after their wars, into a period of inventiveness and experiment, and it is natural that the Romans, after theirs,[2] should do the same. Yet as far as popular taste goes there is a stubborn reluctance to approve higher standards; if Plautus was of inferior quality, the modern theatre is corrupt beyond redemption. We know that Augustus himself enjoyed the theatre, and we may speculate that he cannot have agreed with all that Horace says here. But Horace was surely casting his net wider. He was trying to influence, even to annoy, the philistine Roman public, whose tastes were formed by having Livius Andronicus and the other antique classics beaten into them, as they were into Horace, at school: the sort of people who formed the juries to which Cicero habitually quoted passages from poetry no more recent than Plautus and Terence, and in front of which he had to spend most of a speech defending Archias for being, purely and simply, a modern poet. Horace pleads that the latest generation should not be left out of account. They are trying to improve on the past, and to introduce new standards of craftsmanship. And in any case, a point Cicero made about Archias, poets have their patriotic uses.

Against this background we can also set the most famous of all Horace's critical pronouncements, the so-called *Ars poetica*. There is perhaps no hope of finding in this poem a structure on which all will agree; here, more than elsewhere, Horace makes transitions of bewildering abruptness or subtlety, circling around points and reverting to them with no apparent plan. Nor, maybe, does the structure matter unduly; more important, rather, to decide where the emphasis should lie.

The celebrated parts of the poem, those that have exercised an almost accidental but nevertheless profound influence on later theory and practice,

---

[1] In *Epist.* 1.19.39–41 Horace attributes his lack of popular acclaim to his refusal to 'canvass the tribes of grammarians' (see also *Epist.* 2.2.103).

[2] This is, I think, the implication. This may be another Aristotelian view; compare Aristotle's doctrine on the rise of oratory, used by Cicero in *Brut.* 45–6 (above, p. 47).

largely concern the theatre. Aristotelian and sub-Aristotelian principles, themselves largely inferences from actual Greek tragedy, are here given enduring expression: there should be no violent action on stage, plays should have five acts, gods should rarely intervene, chorus should sing relevant and morally satisfactory odes; myths should be given new twists rather than be entirely discarded; language should be appropriate to character and to the emotion presented. All this had its relevance to the present day: Horace has already alluded to the current pre-eminence of Fundanius as an exponent of 'New Comedy' and Pollio in tragedy (*Sat.* 1.10.40–3). And presumably Horace concentrates on tragedy[1] partly because the Pisones whom he is addressing were interested in the genre: just as in the Epistle to Augustus he spends much space on the theatre. But just as in that poem Horace's true interests lay elsewhere, or rather in the poet generally, so here, in a way, the parts on drama are not at the core of the poem.

Crucial, surely, is what the *Ars poetica* has in common with the other poems we have examined. The Roman public is over-inclined to praise the old favourites: Accius, Ennius, Plautus have technical imperfections to which licence has been granted for long enough. Moreover, the Romans are too materialistic: though, even judging by practical criteria, poets have always had their uses. But far more important than that is the stress Horace places on the craft of the poet. Not everyone can be a poet, though nowadays everyone writes poetry. One has to be a professional, and that means taking pains. 'If you do write something some day, let it find its way to critic Maecius' ears...and be stored up for eight years in your notebooks at home' (386–9). The poet Quintilius was the ideal critic of his friends' work: no room for flattery there, but an insistence on high standards.[2] 'A wise and good man will censure flabby lines, reprehend harsh ones, put a black line with a stroke of the pen beside unpolished ones, prune pretentious ornaments, force you to shed light on obscurities, convict you of ambiguity, mark down what must be changed. He'll be an Aristarchus' (445–50).

This reminds us that for the Romans literary criticism was practised mostly in private. It was a part of *amicitia* to look at your friends' work and help them to improve it for what we have to call publication.[3] The practice clearly left room for insincerity and flattery, but Quintilius will not have been the only one to bring integrity and thoroughness to the task. The literary productions to which we can properly apply the term 'literary criticism' are very few in Latin. But that critical standards existed is abundantly proved by the craftsmanship that, at their best, Romans demanded of their friends and of themselves.

---

[1] His remarks on satyr plays remain mysterious even on this view.

[2] For less rigorous critics see e.g. *Epist.* 2.2.87–101. A little later in that poem (109–25) Horace gives a truly Roman colour to the critic's task by invoking the office of censor.

[3] References are collected by White (1974) 53–4.

EARLY REPUBLIC

3

THE GENESIS OF POETRY
IN ROME

I. THE PRE-LITERARY BACKGROUND

If blatantly historicizing reconstructions, like that of Livy,[1] are excluded, our knowledge of a literature written in Latin begins abruptly in 240 B.C. with the reported performance of a play (probably a tragedy) by Livius Andronicus.[2] This is curious; for knowledge of the history of the Roman people extends back at least three centuries before that, and, with the help of archaeology, much further. Was there no artistic composition in the Latin language before 240 B.C.? The proposition is incredible. For centuries the Romans had achieved considerable political sophistication, and that involved public debates with carefully composed speeches. Roman religion was a series of highly organized cults, with complicated ritual. Roman law had in the far past been codified, and was continually needing – and receiving – well-considered amendments and additions of great complexity. But of all this, little remains to antedate 240 B.C., and what there is has been carelessly preserved, for ulterior purposes, by late authors (mainly grammarians). Yet it is here that scanty and riddling indications must be sought of the background to the literature which seems suddenly to have sprung full-grown into existence in 240 B.C. This can only be done by a series of different approaches, all of them incomplete and uncertain.

Carmina

The word *carmen* (etymologically related to *canere* 'sing') was adopted by Augustan poets as the generic term for their own compositions. But this meaning of 'poem' and 'poetry' was a specialization imposed on a word whose meaning was originally much wider. An earlier meaning appears when Cicero recalls his schooldays:[3] he and his companions had to study the *Twelve Tables* as a *carmen necessarium* to be learnt by heart. The *Twelve Tables* themselves legislated against the use of 'spells': the word used is *carmen*.[4] An early treaty is described by Livy as a *carmen*;[5] so also a sentence of execution[6] and an oath.[7]

---

[1] 7.2.3–12.   [2] Cicero, *Brutus* 72.   [3] *De legibus* 2.59.   [4] Pliny, *N.H.* 28.18.
[5] 1.24.6.   [6] 1.26.6.   [7] 31.17.9.

Elsewhere the word means a prayer or the words of a covenant. There was clearly no limitation to the content of a *carmen*; its characteristic must have been its form.

Typical of the compositions described as *carmina* is the formula under which the investigating tribunal (*duumuiri*) was set up to try Horatius for murdering his sister:[1] *duumuiri perduellionem iudicent; si a duumuiris prouocarit, prouocatione certato; si uincent, caput obnubito, infelici arbori reste suspendito, uerberato uel intra pomoerium uel extra pomoerium* 'let the tribunal of two judge the issue of treason; if he shall appeal from the tribunal, one must argue the case on appeal; if tribunal shall win, one must cover his head, one must hang him by a rope from a barren tree, one must scourge him either within the city-boundary or without the city-boundary'. The language here is not genuinely archaic; it has been modernized. But its essential accuracy is guaranteed by the similar quotation in Cicero's speech for Gaius Rabirius,[2] and one characteristic is clear which is common to all reports of ancient *carmina*: it is not metrical. It is rhythmical prose, with balanced cola, rhyme and alliteration. It is, to this extent, 'artistic': the composition is deliberate and contrived for a particular purpose. The intention is to produce a solemn and measured formality of language, suitable to a ceremonious occasion. This motive, involving particular interest in the sound of the language, explains the style of all surviving *carmina*.

The most extensive surviving *carmen* is a prayer quoted by the elder Cato (writing about 180 B.C.); it was prescribed for performance at the annual fertility ceremony of *lustratio agri* (purification of the land).[3] Here the rhythmical structure depends on parallelism of clauses which have the two basic patterns of dicolon and tricolon, the latter always in the special form of 'tricolon crescendo' (*mihi domo familiaeque nostrae, agrum terram fundumque meum,* or *prohibessis defendas auerruncesque*). It is especially notable that these structures often depend on pleonasm (a similar pleonasm fulfils a similar rhythmical function in the Psalms). Thus all three verbs in the last quoted tricolon have the same meaning ('ward off'); so also among dicola there are found *precor quaesoque, uolens propitius, uiduertatem uastitudinemque*. Formal devices, like anaphora, alliteration and assonance, are used to link the elements in the cola. It becomes clear on a reading of such a hymn that rhythm and structure were not the only relevant stylistic motives: there was evidently considerable solemnity and literary satisfaction to be won from the exhaustive expression of an idea (this is particularly important in religious utterances). The same motive can be seen also in the use of 'polar' expressions like *uisos inuisosque* 'seen and unseen' and in the very frequent use of *figura etymologica* (e.g. *facinus facere* 'do a deed'), the use of which in later Latin always marks a desire for impressive speech (it is never used in ordinary prose).[4]

---

[1] 1.26.6.   [2] *Pro C. Rab.* 13.   [3] *De agri cultura* 141.2–3.   [4] Cf. Haffter (1934) ch. 1.

The linguistic satisfaction and emphatic solemnity which can be achieved by these methods of expression must be stressed, for it explains their influence on all later artistic writing in Latin, especially in poetry, where their frequent occurrence marks off the style even of a poet like Virgil from that of any of his Greek models. These were devices of expression on which a Roman could draw when he wished to speak (for whatever purpose, in verse or in prose) in an impressive way. The occurrence of the same devices in Umbrian (especially on the *Iguvine Tablets*)[1] suggests that their use was not confined to Latin but may have been common to all speakers of Italic dialects. The style survived intact into the very late period, and easily recognizable *carmina* can be found in the fifth-century medical writer Marcellus.[2]

These *carmina* had clearly been composed in Rome from the earliest times,[3] and the artistic forms of expression which had been devised for them were ready to be used by the earliest literary artists in Rome.

Heroic lays

Early in the nineteenth century, the great German historian Niebuhr, anxious to give a basis to his reconstruction of the early Roman tradition, revived the theory[4] that legends such as that of Horatius or Verginia had been preserved by oral tradition in great families in the form of heroic lays. Cicero reports Cato as describing performances of these *carmina* at banquets; the story is repeated with variations by Varro. But it is clear from Cicero's report that the lays, if they ever existed, had perished long before Cato's time. Their existence was given vigorous and romantic life by Macaulay in the introduction to his *Lays of Ancient Rome*.

Unfortunately the evidence is totally inconclusive[5] as far as Roman sources are concerned. But the widespread evidence for the existence of such lays in human societies at all times and in all places (excellently gathered by Macaulay) makes it attractive to posit their existence in Rome too. The difficulty lies in the fact that Roman historians of the second century B.C., who were responsible for formulating the early traditions of Rome, have successfully obliterated all traces of the sources they used. Furthermore, they were apt to invent a Roman pre-history for literary genres on the basis of Greek models. One fact mitigates scepticism: it was precisely those families that would have preserved the lays who were open to the influx of Greek literary culture in the third century B.C., and the new literary standards might well have bred contempt for the rude balladry of their forefathers; such a chronology would fit well with Cato's reported setting of the custom some generations before his own time.[6]

---

[1] Devoto (1954) and Poultney (1959).
[2] *De medicamentis* 15.11; 20.78.
[3] See the collection of Thulin (1906).
[4] Cf. Momigliano (1957) 104ff.
[5] Cf. Dahlmann (1951) and Momigliano, op. cit.
[6] See also p. 59 below.

Versus quadratus[1]

Porphyrio, commenting on Horace,[2] quotes a children's rhyme:

$$\acute{-}\ \cup\acute{-}\ -\quad \acute{-}\ -\ \cup\cup-\quad \acute{-}\ -\ \cup\cup-\quad \acute{-}\ \cup\acute{-}$$
rex erit qui   recte faciet: qui non faciet   non erit

He shall be king who shall act correctly: who shall not so act, shall not be king.

This is analogous to 'I'm king of this castle: get down you dirty rascal', with its play on the etymology of *rex, regere,* and *rectus.* It has a memorable metrical form: a trochaic septenarius, with coincidence of syntactical units and metra. Petronius (about A.D. 60) quotes a riddle:[3]

$$\acute{-}\ -\acute{-}\ -\quad \acute{-}\ -\ \cup\cup-\quad \acute{-}\ -\ \cup\cup-\quad \acute{-}\ \cup\ \acute{-}$$
qui de nobis   longe uenio   late uenio: solue me

I am one who comes out from us in great length, in great depth: solve me.

(The answer is probably 'hair'.) The pattern is the same, and there are many similar examples belonging to the spheres of popular sayings, witticisms and obscenities; for example:

$$\acute{-}\ -\quad \acute{-}\ -\quad \acute{-}\ \cup\ \acute{-}\ -\quad \acute{-}\ \cup\ \acute{-}\ -\quad \acute{-}\ \cup\ \acute{-}$$
postquam Crassus   carbo factus, Carbo crassus   factus est

After Crassus became a cinder, Carbo became dull,

that is, the enmity between the two men was the only thing that kept them at all sharp.[4]

Both the metrical pattern and the uses to which it was put suggest a pre-literary or non-literary origin. There are many lines of the early Roman dramatists which, without slavishly following it, clearly show the influence of the pattern. The technique is quantitative and related closely to Greek practices. There are, further, quite a few examples of oracular sayings, witticisms and lampoons in Greek which display the same metrical pattern, and it is very significant that these (no less than the Latin analogues) differ in certain precise technical features from the norm established for trochaic septenarii by Archilochus and followed by all later Greek poets and tragedians. The simplest hypothesis is that the metrical form was picked up by Romans in early contacts with Greek culture in Italy at a sub-literary level; this would be just one of very many ways in which Roman culture was indebted to Greek in its earliest stages of growth. A similar hypothesis, which does not involve the assumption of direct imitation at a literary level, would give a satisfactory explanation of certain persistent differences in technique between the iambic senarius and the Greek trimeter[5] which are hard to explain on the hypothesis that Roman dramatists directly imitated the metrical techniques of their Greek models.

[1] Cf. Fraenkel (1927).   [2] *Epist.* 1.1.62.   [3] *Sat.* 58.8.
[4] Sacerdos in *GLK* VI 461.26ff.   [5] Cf. Klotz (1947).

This argument could be followed further, but it establishes at least the possibility of the existence of Greek metrical patterns in Rome at a sub-literary level, ready to be used by literary artists when they arose.

Saturnian verse

What may be the earliest poetry in Latin (if the *carmen Arvale* is excepted) is a pair of epitaphs on L. Cornelius Scipio Barbatus, consul in 298 B.C. and his son L. Cornelius Scipio, consul in 259 B.C.[1] The ancient Roman custom was to set a man's *titulus* (his name and, perhaps, a mention of important offices) over his grave: both Scipios have this, painted in red. But both also have epitaphs in Saturnian verse; these are cut in stone on the sarcophagi and that on the son is distinctly earlier than that on the father. The inscribing of a poem over a tomb represents clear Greek influence, and this origin is underlined by one sentiment in the father's epitaph: *quoius forma uirtutei parisuma fuit* 'his physical perfection was the absolute match of his courage'. This translates into Latin the Athenian ideal of καλοκἀγαθία, and significantly the adjective ἀγαθός is given its early-fifth-century sense of 'brave'.

The name of the metre expresses the view that it was native Italic, but basic uncertainty about its true nature and origin persists as strongly now as in the ancient world. Was it Greek in origin and quantitative? Or was it constructed on syllabic principles or principles of stress quite alien to Greek? No certainty can be reached[2] (largely because of the poor textual state of the surviving lines – preserved mainly in quotations by late grammarians who had not the slightest understanding of, or interest in, the metre). But a Greek origin seems the more coherent hypothesis for three reasons: (*a*) the context in which the metre is first found in the Scipio epitaphs suggests a grecizing milieu; and elements of the metre are also found in the *carmen Arvale* which goes back to the fifth or sixth centuries B.C. and certainly contains recognizable Greek religious elements.[3] (*b*) The two poets, Livius Andronicus and Naevius (the one a Greek slave, the other from a region of Greek culture), who first took up the metre in Rome, were both trained in Greek metrical techniques and wrote their other works with an astonishing mastery of those techniques in Latin. (*c*) The detailed statements of Caesius Bassus about the Greek background to the Saturnian can be verified in Greek,[4] and, in particular, a non-literary Greek cult-hymn, displaying the same metrical form, has been preserved.[5] When these facts are put together with the widespread evidence for Greek cultural influence on Rome from the sixth century B.C. onwards, both in customs and in language (and also in metres), it is hard to see the Saturnian as a purely Italic metre.

[1] *CIL* I 2.6–9. [2] Survey and bibliography in Cole (1972).
[3] Cf. Norden (1939) 109ff., 236–78.
[4] Hephaestion cap. XV; Caesius Bassus in *GLK* VI 265f. [5] Fraenkel (1951*b*).

The various approaches above have tried to examine what can be discovered about elements which might have contributed to a literary culture and which existed in Rome prior to 240 B.C. The evidence is meagre and indicates a practical culture: that is, one of compositions designed for specific public occasions. But there is evidence of a certain stylistic sophistication and certainly of acquaintance with Greek techniques: in both these respects, the earliest literary culture in Rome displays features which characterize all later literature composed in Latin.

2. THE EARLIEST EPIC POETRY

It is symptomatic that the first poem (as distinct from drama) in Latin should have claimed to be a translation of Homer's *Odyssey*. Yet the *Odyssia* of Livius Andronicus[1] was far more than a Latin translation; the word used for 'translate' was *uortere* 'turn', but 'adapt' or 'recast' would more truly represent the fact that, even in the wretched fragments (at most forty-five, of which only four exceed one line in extent and only one reaches three lines),[2] one is conscious of reading a genuinely Latin poem. The genius of Livius lay in finding Roman equivalents for Greek ideas:[3] so *Camenae* (a plurality of fountain-goddesses who had a shrine outside the Porta Capena) for Μοῦσαι (Muses); or for the impossible Homeric concept of (*Od.* 3.237–8) ὁππότε κεν δὴ | μοῖρ' ὀλοὴ καθέλῃσι τανηλεγέος θανάτοιο 'whenever the fatal destiny of death which lays low may destroy him...', he wrote *quando dies adueniet, quem profata Morta est* 'when the day comes which Morta has ordained...', where, in a quite different way, the Roman sense of *dies*[4] and the ancient Italic goddess of Fate[5] catch the tone of solemnity in a moving way that is specifically Roman. Homeric metaphors must have been difficult, and here too Livius has happy touches: for the odd Homeric idea of (5.297) λύτο γούνατα καὶ φίλον ἦτορ 'his knees and heart were loosened' he substituted *cor frixit prae pauore* 'his heart froze for terror', and something of the way in which Livius' genius influenced later writers can be seen in Virgil's combination of both metaphors (*Aen.* 1.92) *soluuntur frigore membra* 'his limbs were loosened by the chill (*sc.* of fear)'. In fact, what Livius most conspicuously seems to have missed was the simplicity and grace and speed of Homeric language; for these he substituted solemnity (to be seen, for instance, in an un-Homeric use of patronymics – e.g. 4.557 νύμφης ἐν μεγάροισι Καλυψοῦς 'in the halls of the nymph Calypso' became *apud nympham Atlantis filiam Calypsonem* 'in the house of the nymph Calypso daughter of Atlas'). He also legislated for all later Latin poetry by the way in which he used archaisms as one element in the creation of a specifically poetic language.

[1] Bibliography in Mariotti (1952).
[2] *FPL* pp. 7–17.
[3] Cf. Mariotti (1952) 14–72.
[4] Cf. Fraenkel (1922) 107–10 = (1960) 101–4.
[5] Cf. Latte (1960) 53.

Despite a larger number of extant lines (about sixty, but no fragment exceeds three lines),[1] it is harder to get a real sense of Naevius' *Bellum Poenicum*.[2] This is largely due to the absence of any such help as the Homeric source gives to the appreciation of the *Odyssia*. But Naevius, writing in his later years,[3] contributed a feature that was to dominate Roman poetry and had already been exploited by Roman dramatists: this was the conflation of Greek and Roman material into a unity that constructed a world of ideas which was neither Greek nor Roman but gave hitherto unknown freedom to the play of poetic imagination. Stylistically Naevius depended much on Livius,[4] but he went beyond him in direct imitation of Homeric compounds. However, since the fragments happen to be largely historical in matter, there is a stronger impression of prosiness in Naevius. But this should not be mistaken: it represents, in contrast with Greek historical epics, the Roman poet's emphasis on factual accuracy in recounting a war in which he himself took part (and said so in the poem[5]). Contemporary history and Greek mythology (chiefly the mythical and pre-historical background to Rome and Carthage) were united for the first time and in an exemplary way in the *Bellum Poenicum*. This was probably accomplished (to some extent following Homeric models) by a series of appropriate digressions from the historical narrative.[6] This was a technique often used by Virgil, on whom this work had a profound influence – an influence which can be traced in a most interesting way even on the evidence of the meagre remaining fragments.[7]

The chief disadvantage under which both Livius and Naevius laboured must have been the Saturnian metre, with its jerky combination of iambic and trochaic rhythms that broke each line into predictable halves; it was no match for the easy flow of the hexameter. The choice of that metre for epic must have been forced on them by Roman conditions – a fact which adds to the evidence for the existence of a type of epic balladry in earlier Rome.

[1] *FPL* pp. 17–27.
[2] Bibliography in Barchiesi (1962).
[3] Cicero, *De senectute* 50.
[4] Fraenkel, *RE* Suppl. B. VI 622ff.
[5] Gellius 17.21.45. Cf. Mariotti (1955) 11–83.
[6] Cf. Strzelecki (1935) and Rowell (1947).
[7] Bibliography in Barchiesi (1962).

4

ENNIUS' *ANNALES*

1. THE SCOPE AND CONTENTS OF THE 'ANNALES'

Ennius went further than Naevius in Hellenizing the form of Latin epic, shaping it in books which were to have aesthetic unity and casting it in Homer's hexameter. (The *Bellum Pœnicum* was divided into seven books not by its author Naevius but by Octavius Lampadio, a contemporary of Accius, whose sense of decorum on this point was learnt from Hellenistic poets in general and Ennius in particular (Suet. *Gramm.* 2).) The scale of the books was between about 1,000 and 1,700 lines each; the fragments amount to barely half such a book, and represent less than a twentieth of a poem which in its final form had eighteen books. Most fragments are assigned to their books, and grammarians and others allude to the contents of some: hence, and also because the subject matter was historical, narrated chronologically (though at very varying pace), attempts at reconstruction are saved from utter futility. Ennius appears to have organized his poem as five triads of books, each covering a coherent period of Rome's story.[1] These fifteen books spanned almost or exactly one thousand years in the contemporary reckoning (1184/3 B.C. – 187/184 B.C.), and this may be relevant to the architecture of the poem; see pp. 63–4. A sixth triad, which circulated separately, was added by Ennius in the last years of his life (d. 169 B.C.).

The first triad covered the mythical era from the fall of Troy to the end of the regal period. As is usual with fragmentary authors, the first book is the best represented. It began with an invocation of the Muses. Ennius narrated a dream, formally recalling famous prooemia of Hesiod (*Theogony*) and Callimachus (*Aetia*),in which he told how Homer's spirit appeared and revealed that he, Homer, was reincarnated in Ennius. This stupendous claim asserted the unique importance of Ennius' theme, but it is not clear how literally Ennius meant it. Allegory, though not yet literary allusion, was familiar to the public through tragedy; at the same time, Ennius himself was seriously interested in sub-Platonic astral mysticism and Pythagorean ideas of reincarnation, beliefs which were enjoying some fashion at Rome in the 180s and 170s B.C.[2] The narrative began with the

---

[1] See F. Skutsch, *RE* v 2610, O. Skutsch (1968) 28 n. 4, Jocelyn (1972) 1005f.
[2] See Boyancé (1955) 172–92.

sack of Troy, Aeneas' escape, his arrival in Italy, his alliance with Latinus, and his death. Thus in less than half of the first book Ennius covered more ground than Virgil in the whole *Aeneid*. Ilia, whom Ennius represented as Aeneas' daughter, had a prominent part in the sequel. She narrated a strange dream presaging her future,[1] and bore to Mars the twins Romulus and Remus, who in this version were therefore Aeneas' grandsons.[2] By telescoping the twins' ancestry, Ennius put Ilia at the centre of the stage, as it were, and he evidently presented her in tragic manner, as if she were one of his dramatic heroines. This emphasis on female character and psychology was typically Hellenistic. The rest of the book told the story of the twins, apparently following the usual version as recorded some years earlier in Greek by Fabius Pictor, and the climax of Book 1 was the foundation of the City. An important fragment ((1) 77–96 V = *ROL* 80–100)[3] describes the taking of the auspices with precise regard for modern Roman ritual, and the silence of the onlookers is strikingly compared to that of the people at the games as they wait with bated breath for the consul to signal the start of the chariot-race.[4] These anachronisms characteristically imply the tradition, continuity, even timelessness of Roman public institutions. Somewhere in this book there was a Council of the Gods in Homeric style, at which the deification of Romulus was discussed as if at a meeting of the Senate. This was later parodied by Lucilius and Seneca. Books 2 and 3 are badly represented. Somehow they narrated and filled out the regal period; but on any view there is a chronological problem. An unassigned fragment makes some orator state that 'it is now more or less seven hundred years since Rome was founded' ((*lib. inc.*) 501f. V = *ROL* 468f.). If 'now' were the poet's own time, the foundation of Rome would fall early in the ninth century B.C.; it is, however, probable that Ennius followed Eratosthenes on the date of the fall of Troy (1184/3 B.C.), and since as we have seen Romulus and Remus are Aeneas' grandsons in this version, this implies a date around 1100 B.C. for the foundation of Rome, coeval that is with the Return of the Sons of Heracles (the Dorian invasion) in mythological history. In this case, the fragment belongs in the mouth of someone like Camillus, and the occasion might be the Gallic invasion (390 or 387 B.C.).[5] On either view, of course, it remains unclear how Ennius reconciled his chronology with the usual story of only seven kings, the last of whom, Tarquin the Proud, fell just when the Athenian democracy was being established (*c.* 510 B.C.).

[1] (1) 35–51 V = *ROL* 32–48; Leo (1913) 178f.; G. W. Williams (1968) 689f.
[2] So also Naevius (Serv. auct. *Aen.* 1.273); Eratosthenes made the twins grandsons of Aeneas through Ascanius, not Ilia (ibid.). These versions contradict Timaeus (cf. Lycophron, *Alex.* 1226ff. with the Scholiast) and Fabius Pictor (Plut. *Rom.* 3), whose account is the dominant one.
[3] References to Ennius' *Annales* are given with the numeration of Vahlen (1928) (= V) and Warmington (= *ROL*). The figure in parentheses indicates the book number.
[4] Williams (1968) 684ff., 698.
[5] Skutsch (1968) 12f.

Book 4 covered events from the foundation of the Republic to the Gallic invasion, Book 5 came to the end of the Samnite Wars (*c.* 295 B.C.). Each therefore covered about a century, and both are badly represented. Book 6 was devoted wholly to the war against Pyrrhus (281–271 B.C.), i.e. only ten years: it will have been here for the first time that Ennius had occasion for a more thoroughgoing 'annalistic' presentation in the manner of Naevius. Pyrrhus was one of the earliest figures about whom there was available relatively copious and reliable information, and Ennius presents him in a very magnanimous light.[1] With Pyrrhus, Ennius had reached a point only just beyond living memory, and it is interesting that the gods still participated in this book in Homeric style; there is no certain sign of them later in the poem ((6) 175f. V = *ROL* 207f.).

In the third triad, the centrepiece of the original poem, Ennius entered the period of living memory. We do not know whether he regarded this second half of his work as a *maius opus* (cf. Virgil, *Aen.* 7.45), but it certainly presented extra problems. There was the question what to do with the gods, and the wider problem of maintaining epic dignity without sounding ridiculous when speaking of the recent past.[2] Besides, there was from here on ever less scope for pure fiction, and ever more need both for the historian's methods and acumen, and the diplomat's tact to avoid giving offence by omission or distortion. On the other hand, the example of Naevius' *Bellum Pœnicum* was available. The seventh book opened with an important introduction (Cic. *Brut.* 76; (7) 213ff. V = *ROL* 231ff.).[3] Ennius proposed not to deal with the First Punic War, since 'others', i.e. Naevius, had done it 'in verses which the Fauns and bards used to chant'. He dissociated himself from the ranting bards (*uates*), with whom he unfairly classed Naevius: Ennius was a *poeta*, a 'maker', and he proclaims that no one before himself had been *dicti studiosus* 'keen on the "word"', a loan-translation of the appellation of the scholar-poets of Alexandria, φιλό-λογος.[4] True, he was an 'inspired' poet, but his *sapientia*/σοφία, 'wisdom', was not like that of the seers, oracular and unaccountable; his was a knowledge of the Muses, a religious γνῶσις which was the hard-won result of practice and lucubration ((7) 218f. V = *ROL* 229f.). Here speaks not Homer reincarnated, but the Latin Callimachus. The narrative of 7 took events to the invasion of Hannibal (218 B.C.), an expansion of scale compared with 6 no doubt due to the summary treatment of the First Punic War (264–241 B.C.). The book included a remarkable description of a Roman commander's 'good companion', a *parasitus* seen favourably,

---

[1] Williams (1968) 254f. Cicero knew what passed as a genuine speech of Ap. Claudius Pulcher dissuading the Romans from making peace with Pyrrhus, and quotes the beginning of Ennius' poetic version (*Sen.* 16; (6) 202f. V = *ROL* 194f.), which is directly copied from Homer (*Il.* 24.401). The prose-speech was probably an amplification of Ennius' fiction.

[2] Cf. Hor. *Sat.* 1.10.54 *uersus Enni grauitate minores.*

[3] Cic. *Brut.* 76, cf. Suerbaum (1968) 249–95, Williams (1968) 253, Jocelyn (1972) 1017f.

[4] Jocelyn (1972) 1013 n. 262; an observation made independently by several scholars.

which was later thought to be a portrait of the artist (Gell. *N.A.* 12.4; Enn. *Ann.* (7) 234–51 V = *ROL* 210–27).[1] Books 8 and 9 described the rest of the Second Punic War (218–201 B.C.), a return to the scale of Book 6.

Very little survives of the remainder. Book 10 began with a fresh invocation of the Muses and described the war against Philip of Macedon (201–196 B.C.); 11 and 12 brought the narrative to the eve of war against Antiochus III of Syria (192/1 B.C.). The narrative was becoming very dense, and it was even slower in the final triad 13–15. This covered the war against Antiochus (13, 191 B.C.), the Scipios' victory at Magnesia and the naval war (14, 190 B.C.), while the last book dealt with the deeds of Ennius' patron M. Fulvius Nobilior in Aetolia, Cephalenia, and Ambracia.[2] It is particularly unfortunate that we know so little of this book, for, as we shall see, its ending has an important bearing on the shape and unity of Ennius' *Annales* as a whole. As for Books 16–18, see below, p. 66.

2. ENNIUS AND THE MUSES: THE UNITY AND COMPOSITION OF THE 'ANNALES'

The cult of the Muses was introduced by M. Fulvius Nobilior, who built a *Templum Herculis Musarum* to house statues of Hercules Musageta and the Nine Sisters taken with much other booty from what had once been Pyrrhus' palace in Ambracia.[3] Nobilior and Ennius saw this institution as a Greek Μουσεῖον, 'house of the Muses', and naturally enough they saw the province of the Muses as it was understood at the most famous 'Museum', the one at Alexandria. There the scholars and poets formed a nominally religious group under the presidency of the 'priest of the Museum', who, however, was never as distinguished for learning or poetry as the Royal Librarian.[4] This post had been occupied by Apollonius and after him Eratosthenes, who died between 196 and 193 B.C., while Ennius was making a name as a teacher and dramatist. The province of the Muses as defined by their activities and interests included not only the writing of poetry and literary studies but also science, geography, and history, rather than philosophy and rhetoric: the name φιλόλογοι which was specially theirs implicitly distinguishes them from φιλόσοφοι.

Nobilior composed and deposited in his Templum a work described as *fasti* which included etymological explanations of the months' names.[5] This was evidently more than a bald chronicle: it was a piece of chronological investi-

---

[1] Leo (1913) 178, Skutsch (1968) 92–4, Williams (1968) 691–3, Joycelyn (1972) 993ff.

[2] Jocelyn (1972) 1006. Macrobius, *Sat.* 6.2.30 and 6.3.1 wrongly assigns some passages of 16 to 15.

[3] Badian (1971) 151–95; Cancik (1969) 323–8, (1970) 7–17; Nash (1961/2) 471 (site of the temple). The statues: E. A. Sydenham, *CRR* nos. 810–23 (silver denarii of Q. Pomponius Musa, *c.* 68–66 B.C.); *CIL* I² 615 (the base of one of them). The *aedicula* of the *Camenae* was transferred to the temple from the temple of Honos and Virtus (Serv. *Aen.* 1.8).

[4] Pfeiffer (1968) 96f.; Fraser (1972) I 312–35.

[5] Macrobius, *Sat.* 1.12.16; 13.21.

gation and as such it is important, for it is the earliest known example of specifically Latin 'research', and it reminds one in its field, if only humbly, of the famous and important *chronographiae* of Eratosthenes. In these Eratosthenes presented in summary form a continuous chronology of the Greek world from the fall of Troy (which he put in the equivalent of 1184/3 B.C.) to the death of Alexander (323 B.C.), and popularized the Olympiad-system for Greek dating. This greatly facilitated the composition of the kind of universal history at which Polybius aimed, and gave a more exact perspective and depth to Greek history as a whole by linking the mythical age to the modern by measured steps. Fabius Pictor's Greek history, composed probably in the 190s, used the Olympiad-reckoning where appropriate (809 F 3b Jacoby).

The title of Ennius' poem looks immediately to the priestly *Annales*, 'year-books', instituted by the Pythagorean king Numa Pompilius and kept by the *pontifices*.[1] But, from a different point of view, here were *chronographiae* of a new kind, indirectly made possible, like Fabius' history, by Alexandrian scholarship. The epic form had been used in modern times in Greek for poems about the foundation of cities (e.g. the 'foundation' poems of Apollonius Rhodius), the chronicles of a people (e.g. Rhianus' *Messeniaca*, Euphorion's *Mopsopia*), and the praise of living kings (e.g. Simonides of Magnesia's poem about Antiochus III, and Leschides' about one of the Attalids of Pergamum: see the Suda under these names). The conception of Ennius' verse-history of the Roman People was on a grander and more consciously ambitious scale than anything before, or, it can be argued, since. His practical debt to Fabius Pictor was probably great, and Ennius was not a scientific historian in our sense or the Alexandrians' or even Cato's. In the prose *Origines* Cato made a point of referring to officers on active service simply as 'the consul', 'the praetor', without naming them: in this, he followed the tradition of the priestly *annales*, and implicitly asserted the subordination of the individual to the community (Nepos 24.3.4, cf. Gell. *N.A.* 3.7).[2] Whether conscious or not, this was a reaction against the individualism of Ennius, who praised not only famous men by name, but also adapted Homer to celebrate the bravery of 'other ranks', e.g. a lone stand by a tribune whose name is now, ironically, corrupt ((15) 401–8 V = *ROL* (16) 409–16; *Iliad* 16.102–11, on Ajax; Macrob. *Sat.* 6.3.1).[3] Ennius receives short measure in accounts of Roman historiography: this is unfair, for two reasons. His poem remained until

[1] Jocelyn (1972), 1008–23; published only in the 120s B.C. by P. Mucius Scaevola Pontifex (Serv. auct. *Aen.* 1.373, Cic. *De or.* 2.52).

[2] See Leo (1913) 292, 296f. It is usually assumed (as by Leo) that Cato did not name the heroic tribune whose story is reported by Gellius, loc. cit., just as Caesar left unnamed the brave *signifer* who led the way on Caesar's first British expedition (*Bell. Gall.* 4.25.3). There must be some doubt about this, however, since Gellius' narrative reads as though he had the name Caedicius from Cato's text, and Nepos (loc. cit.) refers to *bellorum duces* only, which does not necessarily mean that no one was named.

[3] G.W. Williams (1968) 687–9.

Virgil's time a central set-piece in Roman education and as such it was a common store of facts, stories, attitudes, and *exempla*, and deeply affected, indeed defined, the Roman consciousness. Again, by dwelling as *exornator rerum* on moral example, Ennius established an enduring trait of Roman historiography.

It has been suggested that Book 15 of the *Annales* ended with the inauguration of the cult of the Muses at Rome: 'In you my beginning, in you my end.'[1] If this is so, the narrative must have gone beyond 188 B.C. (when Nobilior's campaign ended). Nobilior's right to his booty was disputed by Cato and others, his triumph was postponed until summer 187 B.C., and his votive games took place in summer 186 B.C. Meanwhile Roman confidence had been shaken by internal crises – the disgrace of the Scipios (187 B.C.), the Bacchanalian 'conspiracy' (186 B.C.), and the loss of a consular army in Liguria (186 B.C.). The inauguration of a cult and the erection of a temple take time, and analogy suggests that the cult of the Muses will have been inaugurated in 185–183 B.C. or later, certainly not earlier.[2]

There are two separate considerations affecting the content of 15. Ennius cannot have passed over the great crisis of confidence which succeeded the liberal and optimistic spirit of the censorship of Flamininus and Marcellus (189/8 B.C.) and which brought his old patron Cato to the censorship for 184/3 B.C. Cato was elected at a time when in the opinion of his supporters 'Rome was tottering to her fall', and he 'saved the state by his wise measures', as it said on the base of a statue of Cato later erected in the Temple of Salus (Plut. *Cat. maj.* 19.4). The composition of the *Annales* belongs to the 170s B.C. and it is improbable that Ennius began earlier than the late 180s. In retrospect, Cato's censorship stood out as a memorable moral *exemplum*, which could be seen as marking the end and beginning of epochs in Roman history. Here was an appropriate end for the poem, both on private and public grounds. Nor was it only in retrospect that the censorship of the new Lycurgus might be seen as climacteric. It can hardly have escaped the attention of contemporaries that Cato became censor 1,000 years after the fall of Troy. It may be suggested that the Pythagorean Ennius and others saw some significance in this, and that Ennius' poem covered exactly this millennium. If the cult of the Muses was officially inaugurated in or about 184 B.C., as seems probable, there was another fitting personal as well as public conclusion to the epic which proclaimed Rome a full and equal member of the Hellenistic world. Ennius could thus do honour to both the great men who had helped him in his career, in spite of their political divergences.

These speculations – for that is all they are – about Book 15 at least raise important questions about the unity, composition, and publication of the poem.

[1] Skutsch (1968) 20, going beyond Leo (1913) 170; cf. Jocelyn (1972) 1006 n. 183.
[2] Eumenius, *Pan. Lat.* 5.7.3 appears to suggest 179 B.C., but that is not supported by Livy 40.51.

Lucilius refers to the *Iliad* and the *Annales* as examples of *poesis*, 'poetry', as opposed to *poemata*, 'books' (like Lucilius' own) (Lucil. (9) 340–4 M = *ROL* 403–7); they each have *una* θέσις 'one subject', and make ἔπος *unum*, 'one epic'.[1] There is, however, an obvious difference between the poem which deals with the consequences of Achilles' anger over a few weeks, and the poem which spans a thousand years and has many heroes. Ennius himself treated the *Annales* as extendible. After completing 1–15, he 'added' 16–18, which described events of the Istrian War down to 171 B.C. (Pliny, *N.H.* 7.101). Somewhere in 12 Ennius mentioned that he was 67 years old, i.e. that at the time of writing, or publication, which is not the same thing, it was 172 B.C. (Gell. 17.21.43, quoting Varro). The apparent implication is that Ennius wrote 13–15 and then added 16–18 all after 172 B.C., but before 169 B.C. Scholars have been reluctant to accept that a third of the whole therefore belongs to the last three years of the poet's life. This line of thought, however, begs important questions. We may not assume that the books were simply composed in the order in which they are numbered, nor do we know how they were presented to the public, e.g. whether the books came out singly, in triads, or as a complete work. It is too often assumed that Ennius began at the beginning and went on to the end, publishing as he went along. But Ennius was no Lucilius, and allusions in Augustan poets to what they saw as his lack of polish tell us more about Augustan taste than about Ennius. No doubt he worked faster than Virgil, but it is probable that for years his *scrinia* and notebooks were filled with notes, ideas, and 'bits' which had yet to be integrated or which anticipated the narrative. One among several possibilities is that the first fifteen appeared together in 172 B.C. as a complete work. In this case, the various personal appearances which Ennius makes throughout in his assumed poetical guise as *sacerdos musarum*[2] will be, so to speak, simultaneous, not successive. The composition of the *Annales* belonged to the late 180s and 170s: a fragment of Book 9 refers to Cornelius Cethegus (d. 196 B.C., Livy 33.42.5) as one whom 'those who were then alive' admired for his oratory. 'Then' means 215–200 B.C., and would hardly be intelligible if the poet's 'now' were earlier than 180 B.C. The hexameters of the *Hedyphagetica* (see Appendix) were experimental, and it has been shown that this poem must date from after 188 B.C. (see p. 156).

3. ENNIUS THE HELLENISTIC POET: EPIC DICTION AND VERSE

It is typical of Ennius' authority that after him no one attempted extended composition in Saturnians. The latest public inscriptions in that metre date from

---

[1] Ennius himself refers to the *Annales* as *poemata*, (1) 3–4 V = *ROL* 2–3.

[2] It is arguable, but cannot be proved, that Ennius really was *sacerdos musarum* at Nobilior's temple. Someone must have been; who more appropriate than Ennius? This would give a practical reason for Ennius' registration as a citizen.

the Gracchan era, and the Ennian hexameter and elegiac couplet were being used for public and private dedications and epitaphs within a generation of the poet's death. He may himself have set the fashion:

$$- \; \underline{\prime} \; - \; \smile \; \smile \; - \; \smile \smile - \; - \; \underline{\prime} \smile \smile \; \underline{\prime} -$$
nẹmo mẹ dacrumịs decorẹt neu fụnera flẹtu
$$\underline{\prime} - \; \underline{\prime} \quad \smile \smile - \; \underline{\prime} \smile \; \smile \; \underline{\prime} \smile \; \smile -$$
fạxit. cụr? uolitọ uịuo' per ọra uirụm.

(Epigrams 17–18 V = ROL 9–10)

Let no one honour me with tears or attend my obsequies with weeping. Why? I live flying through the mouths of men.

$$- \; \smile \smile \quad - \; \underline{\prime} - \; \smile \smile \; \underline{\prime} \; \smile \smile \; \underline{\prime} \smile \smile \; \underline{\prime} \; -$$
ạspicit(e) ọ ciuẹs senis Ẹnni imạgini' fọrmam;
$$- \; \underline{\prime} \; - \quad \underline{\prime} - \quad \underline{\prime} \; \smile \smile \; \underline{\prime} \; \smile \; \smile \; -$$
hịc uestrụm panxịt mạxuma fạcta patrụm.

(Epigrams 15–16 V = ROL 7–8)

Behold, fellow-citizens, the form of the image of the aged Ennius: he unfolded the marvellous deeds of your forefathers.

The authenticity of these noble epigrams need not þe doubted. Whether or not they reached their respective destinations, the one was intended for Ennius' tomb, and the other for a statue of Ennius to be set in a prominent public place in Rome. The site of Ennius' tomb was later forgotten, and in Cicero's time there was a tradition that a statue of Ennius had been set up in the tomb of the Scipios.[1] That, however, is hardly a public place, and by rejecting that tradition one does not necessarily disprove the view that the busts and representations of Ennius which existed in Cicero's time represent an authentic iconographical tradition.[2] The natural setting for such a statue, actual or intended, would be the Templum Herculis Musarum, where Accius' likeness was placed within his own lifetime.[3] One notes the proud address *o ciues*, alluding to the fact that Ennius himself had been made a Roman citizen by a special grant through the influence of the Nobiliores in 184/3 B.C., i.e. before Ennius began serious work on the *Annales*, and presumably with the tacit consent of Cato the censor. The *Annales*, then, was the work of a full *ciuis Romanus*, not of an alien or of an entertainer who had acquired second-class citizenship through manumission. The language of the epigram is strikingly simple and unadorned in comparison with the first. In this it is like, say, the epitaph of Scipio Barbatus (*CIL* I² 6–7), whose *gesta*, services, are their own eloquence. Ennius has but one service to record. Others might be censors, consuls, aediles; he, as author of the *Annales*, has performed his service through poetry as an historian. His work mattered not because of its literary qualities, but because it was true and morally important.

---

[1] Suerbaum (1968) 210ff.   [2] See Hafner (1968).
[3] See Cancik (1969, 1970) (Lucil. (28) 794 M = *ROL* 844, Pliny, *N.H.* 34.19).

This to the Roman people as a fellow-citizen. As an individual Ennius makes a different claim in the tomb-epigram. It is personal and pointed. A paradox is stated, the reader's query is made explicit, and the explanation is given, as in Catullus 85 *odi et amo*... The claim that a poet's name and his poetry (all of it, not just the *Annales*) will live, and therefore the poet himself, was later a commonplace in Latin poetry. Here it appears to be new; for, perhaps surprisingly, no Greek poet made this claim or had it made for him. It goes beyond the observation made by Callimachus on the poetry of his friend Heraclitus of Halicarnassus (Callim. *Epigr.* 2). Moreover, in Ennius' case there is the complication that he was a Pythagorean. The tone is engagingly cheerful, and the three strong alliterations are nicely contrasted. This commemorates the private artist rather than the public historian.

The elegiac couplet was introduced by Ennius as an epigrammatic form. It was apparently only towards the end of the second century B.C. that it began to be used, e.g. by Q. Lutatius Catulus, for the amatory subjects with which in Latin it is particularly associated (Gell. 19.9.12, 14; cf. Callim. *Epigr.* 41, *Anth. Pal.* 12.73). When Plautus alluded to lovers' *graffiti* as *elegea* (*Merc.* 409) he had in mind what was as yet a Greek, not a Roman expression of affection (cf. *CIL* IV 585 for a later Latin example). The first line consists of a hexameter of six quantitative feet which must be dactyls ($-\cup\cup$) or spondees ($- -$); in the last foot, only a spondee was admitted, though, as in drama, the final syllable might be heavy or light ($\cap$), and hiatus was permitted between lines. The second line, the 'pentameter', was made of two members of the form $-\;\overline{\cup\cup}\;-\;\overline{\cup\cup}\;-$ and $-\;\cup\cup\;-\;\cup\cup\;\cap$. Problems analogous to those which had been satisfactorily solved for drama (see pp. 86–93) arose with the relation of word-accents and the flow of the verse, the *arses* in this metre being the invariable ($-$) and the *theses* being the variable places ($\cup\cup$). Ennius established for the hexameter what proved to be definitive patterns of normal rhythm:

> Musae quae pedibus magnum pulsatis Olympum...
>
> (*Annales* (1) 1 V = *ROL* 1)

Muses, you who shake great Olympus with your steps...

As in *nemo me dacrumis*..., there is here a clash of movements in the middle of the line, resolved at line-end. Conversely, the preferred cadence for the second colon of the so-called pentameter involved a strong clash at line-end, secured by making the last word a disyllable. Four of Ennius' five extant epigrams have this rhythm, which, as versifiers will know, does not occur with an easy spontaneity. These characteristic rhythms differ significantly from those favoured by Greek poets, for whom the placing of the word-accent in relation to the quantitative movement was an irrelevant consideration (see pp. 86–93).

The rhythm of the Ennian hexameter was quite new in Latin, for although anapaestic lines were used in drama, their technique was quite different. In particular, Ennius did not permit himself to scan words ending with a cretic pattern $(-\cup-)$ as if they ended with dactyls $(-\cup\cup)$, as did Plautus. This severely restricted the available vocabulary: words like *cīuĭtās* or *făcĭnŏră* were automatically ruled out. Iambo-trochaic verse was more accommodating. This imposed and encouraged artifice, particularly in the exploitation of archaic forms drawn from the formulae of ritual and law (e.g. *indŭpĕrātōr* for *impĕrātōr*) and in the coining of more or less bizarre expressions calqued from Homer (e.g. *endo suam do* 'into his house' ~ *Od.* 1.176 ἡμέτερον δῶ). The epic style subsumed all the resources of the tragic, but differed in two ways: as it was still 'grander', it could accommodate archaisms avoided by tragic dramatists; and as it was based on Homer, whose dialect is mixed, anomalies and alternative forms were admissible in a manner not permitted in the more homogeneous and economical language of the stage. Final *-s* after a short vowel might be dropped or kept before an initial consonant not (as in drama) according to linguistic but purely metrical rules. Words like *patrem* might be syllabified as *pāt-rēm* (with Homeric precedent) as well as in the natural Latin way, *pă-trēm*. Some final syllables (*-at, -or*) might be scanned heavy in *arsis* and light in *thesis*. Iambic shortening was given up (see p. 87). Elision and synaloepha were admitted less freely than in drama. Unfortunately, we have no idea how Ennius would 'declaim' his verse; these technicalities all point away from a conversational delivery, and there is only one point in which Ennius seems more 'naturalistic' than the language of drama: he is much less fond of end-stopping his lines, and favours no particular punctuation-points within the line.

In drama, the separation of an epithet and its noun was normally significant, i.e. emphasis was thus laid on either or both words. Ennius was responsible for an important innovation in Latin poetic diction which has no real precedent in either Greek or earlier Latin practice. We frequently find epithets and nouns separated in his hexameters, e.g. *magnum...Olympum, ueter...Priamus, pium...Anchisen, teneras...auras, tremulis...artubus, caerula...templa, calido ...sanguine, miserum...homonem, crudeli...sepulcro, densis...pinnis*, without emphasis falling on either word. The obvious explanation, that this facilitated scansion in this 'difficult' metre, will not suffice; for, as in the examples quoted, it is always the adjective which comes first, whereas when adjectives and nouns stand next to each other, the order is free.

> uulturus in spinis *miserum* mandebat *homonem*;
>
> heu, quam *crudeli* condebat membra *sepulcro*.
>
> (*Ann.* (2) 138f. V = *ROL* 141f.)

A vulture was gobbling a poor wight amidst the thorns; alas, in what a cruel tomb did it lay his limbs!

The epithets are qualitative, emotional, and subjective; a riddle, as it were, is posed in mid-line, which is solved by the corresponding noun at the end. In

hic uestrum panxit maxuma facta patrum

(see above) two adjectives precede two nouns. This is rare in Ennius' *Annales*, but it is simply a duplication of the principle described, an elaboration of a very common Ennian trait. It became a mannerism of the neoteric poets, and remained a very important device in all Latin hexameter poetry. That here too Father Ennius was the ultimate source has not been sufficiently recognized.[1]

While Ennius established the norms of Epic rhythm, diction, and word-order without which there would be no Latin hexameter poetry, he also experimented widely with rhythms and stylistic devices which were later restricted or avoided e.g. the shortening rather than elision of a final long vowel in ... *Ēnnĭ ĭmāgĭnī' fŏrmām* (cf. Hom. *Od.* 1.241), the lengthening in *arsis* of a light syllable (*quōm nĭhĭl hōrrĭdĭŭs ūmquām...*, (5) 170 V = *ROL* 474), and Greek 'epicisms' like *ēndŏ sŭām dō* (see above). Some of these, e.g. *Mēttŏēŏquĕ Fŭfĕtĭŏēō* (Quint. *Inst.* 1.5.12), 'of Mettius Fufetius', modelled on the Homeric genitive -oio, suggest that Ennius thought of Latin as a much-corrupted Greek dialect, and here overstepped the bounds of decorum with a spurious archaism. Others, e.g. (*lib. inc.*) 609 V = *ROL* Enn. *spuria* 13...*saxo cere- comminuit -brum*, an absurdly literal and violent tmesis, seem scarcely credible and may only be schoolmasterly jokes. Ennius sometimes played on words in a manner hardly appropriate to the majesty of the epic form. He 'seems to have been joking', we are told, when he wrote *inde parum* [...] *ulabant* ((*lib. inc.*) 524 V = *ROL* 544); evidently there was a pun on *parum* 'too little' and *Parum* '(to) Paros' or 'Pharos'. Again in a line referring probably to the building of the via Flaminia in 220 B.C. we read ((7) 260 V = *ROL* 255) *sulphureas posuit spiramina Nāris ad undas* 'He set blow-holes by the sulphurous waters of the river Nar'; here the nonce-word *spiramina*, literally 'things by which one breathes', is nothing but a synonym of *nāres* 'nostrils'; the unfortunate pun was presumably meant to imply that the river was so called because of its pungent smell (cf. Vitruv. 7.4).

These and other blemishes offended the taste of the Augustan age. However, it would have pained Ennius to learn that although his *ingenium* was acknowledged by such as Propertius and Ovid, they could not repress an amused smile when contemplating his *ars*, his technique – an aspect of his work in which Ennius took pride. Indeed, the romantic view of Ennius, current in Ovid's time, as an untutored and therefore artistically hirsute genius has still not entirely evaporated. He deserves to be judged more analytically and against less

[1] Patzer (1955) 77–95 cites Euphorion fr. 9.10–15, Hermesianax fr. 7.21–6 Powell in connexion with Catullus' practice. There is nothing similar in Apollonius or Callimachus. Norden (1926) 391f. and Pearce (1966, 1968) are concerned with poets of the first century B.C., not with Ennius.

anachronistic criteria; and it should be borne in mind that where others followed, he led the way. Space prevents more than a cursory survey of his diverse techniques.

In Book 6 Ennius described the felling of trees, probably for a funeral pyre, in the following words:

> Incedunt arbusta per alta, securibu' caedunt.
> percellunt magnas quercus, exciditur ilex;
> fraxinu' frangitur atque abies consternitur alta;
> pinus proceras peruortunt. omne sonabat
> arbustum fremitu siluai frondosai.
>
> (Ann. (6) 187–91 V = ROL 181–5)

They pass among the tall groves, they hew with axes. They hack down great oaks; the holm is chopped; the ash is broken and the tall fir is laid low; they overturn high pines. The whole glade echoed with the noise of the leafy forest.

This recalls the passage in Book 23 of the *Iliad* where Meriones is sent with mules and carts to Mount Ida to cut wood for Patroclus' pyre, in particular lines 118–20:

> αὐτίκ' ἄρα δρῦς ὑψικόμους ταναήκεϊ χαλκῷ
> τάμνον ἐπειγόμενοι · ταὶ δὲ μεγάλα κτυπέουσαι
> πῖπτον.

Then straightway they set to with a will and started cutting the high-leafed oaks with long-edged bronze, and the oaks fell crashing mightily.

The whole passage in Homer is an excellent illustration of his rapid, plain, and elevated narrative-style. Ennius in emphasizing the latter qualities sacrifices the first altogether; his description is massive and slow. He has five variations on the theme δρῦς ὑψικόμους...τάμνον, strung together with bald parataxis and end-stopping. The vocabulary is simple and his expression direct. The only qualitative adjectives are variations on the idea 'tall', all simplifications of ὑψικόμους. The solid strength of each phrase is loudly, even crudely, proclaimed by the contrast of its special alliteration with that of the neighbouring phrase. The only subtlety in the enumeration is the variation of active and passive and of plural and singular. The effect is to focus our attention upwards: we see not the sawyers hard at work but the great trees toppling one after another. Homer's ταὶ δὲ μεγάλα κτυπέουσαι πῖπτον lies behind Ennius' superb *omne sonabat arbustum fremitu siluai frondosai*, but is transmuted; for *fremitus* is not (as in Homer) the sound of the trees crashing to the ground – that would be *crepitu*, *strepitu* – but the more continuous murmuring rustle of the leaves (*frondosai*) of the forest, commenting, as it were, on the destruction of the great lords (*proceras*) of their community. The august character of the ancient forest is implied by the slow, spondaic line-end with its (even for Ennius) archaic

71

genitives in -*āī*, a trick used elsewhere by Ennius to achieve a suitably Homeric *grauitas* and solemnity:

óllī respóndīt réx Albáī longáī (*Ann.* (1) 33 V = *ROL* 31)

To him replied the king of Alba Longa...

olli is also archaic, for *illi*; this is Ennius' version of the much lighter Homeric formula τὸν δ' ἀπαμειβόμενος προσέφη 'X addressed him in answer...'. Ennius was here evidently seeking with his massive spondees and his archaisms to mark the importance and majesty of the king's words to the Trojan exiles.

Virgil imitated Ennius' tree-felling passage twice in the *Aeneid*; on both occasions it is a question of preparing a funeral-pyre.

> Itur in antiquam siluam, stabula alta ferarum.
> procumbunt piceae, sonat icta securibus ilex
> fraxineaeque trabes cuneis et fissile robur
> scinditur; aduoluunt ingentes montibus ornos.   (*Aen.* 6. 179–82)

Progress is made into an ancient forest, the full-grown dens of the wild. Pitch-pines topple, the holm echoes struck with axes, beams of ash and fissile oak are split with wedges; they roll huge rowans from the mountains.

> ferro sonat icta bipenni
> fraxinus, euertunt actas ad sidera pinus
> robora nec cuneis et olentem scindere cedrum
> nec plaustris cessant uectare gementibus ornos.   (*Aen.* 11. 135–8)

The tall ash echoes under the iron axe, they overturn pines aimed at the stars, nor do they cease from splitting oaks and the fragrant cedar with wedges, or from conveying rowans on groaning carts.

Virgil here takes some things directly from Homer – most important, his speed and economy – and he tones down Ennius' alliterative emphases. In Book 6 he uses the same variation of active and passive and of singular and plural as Ennius; in Book 11 *euertunt actas ad sidera pinus* is an exaggerated and therefore not wholly felicitous rendering of Ennius' blunt *pinus proceras peruortunt*. It is instructive to see how Silius Italicus (*Punica* 10.527–34) and Statius (*Thebaid* 6.90–127) elaborate still further the basic Ennian theme.

It would be wrong to infer that Ennius always wrote in this powerful, static style:

> concurrunt ueluti uenti quom spiritus Austri
> imbricitor Aquiloque suo cum flamine contra
> indu mari magno fluctus extollere certant...
>   (*Ann.* (17) 443–5 V = *ROL* 430–2)

They [two warriors or armies] run together as when the breath of Auster the rain-starter [i.e. the South Wind] and Aquilo [the North Wind] with his blast strive in opposition to raise billowing waves on the great sea...

This is inspired by *Iliad* 9.4–7:

ὡς δ᾽ ἄνεμοι δύο πόντον ὀρίνετον ἰχθυόεντα
Βορέης καὶ Ζέφυρος, τώ τε Θρήκηθεν ἄητον
ἐλθόντ᾽ ἐξαπίνης· ἄμυδις δέ τε κῦμα κελαινὸν
κορθύεται...

As when two winds, Boreas and Zephyr, stir up the fish-filled sea; they both come sudden, blowing from Thrace, and at once the dark billow raises its crest... (cf. Virg. *Aen.* 2.416–19).

Here Ennius has achieved the rapidity of Homer by using a mixture of dactyls and spondees quite different from that in his tree-felling passage, and by keeping Homer's enjambments, essential to the impetus of a passage describing great and uncontrolled natural forces at large. But he is essentially un-Homeric in calling the South Wind *spiritus Austri imbricitor*: that is Hellenistic baroque.

Ennius had an ear for effective rhythms, as in:

rēges per regnum statuasque sepulchraque quaerunt:
aedíficant nómen, súmma nitúntur ópum uí...
(Ann. (16) 411f. V = ROL 393f.)

kings through kingship seek statues and sepulchres: they build their names, they strive with all the force of their resources...

The strength of these lines comes from the paradox of the tangible and intangible in *aedificant nomen* and from the rhythm: verse-ictus and word-accent wrestle to the end of the second line without resolution. *Summa nituntur opum ui* is repeated here from *Ann.* (4) 161 V = *ROL* 164, *Romani scalis summa nituntur opum ui* 'the Romans strive on the ladders with all the force of their resources', where 'resources' means 'strength', not 'wealth'. By such judicious repetition and adaptation Ennius created the impression of Homer's formulaic diction; once again Virgil paid him the compliment of imitation at *Aen.* 12.552 *pro se quisque uiri summa nituntur opum ui* 'each for himself the men strive with all the force of their resources'.

A more harmonious exploitation of the hexameter is seen in such lines as these:

póste recúmbite uéstraque péctora péllite tónsis...
(Ann. (7) 230 V = ROL 245)

Lean back and beat your breasts with the blades...

lábitur úncta carína per aéquora cána celócis...
(Ann. (lib. inc.) 478 V = ROL (8/9?) 442)

The oiled keel of the cutter glides through the hoary levels...

The un-Homeric care of the *dicti studiosus* manifests itself in other ways too. The elaborately broken punctuation of Ilia's invocation of Venus is intended to express her breathless agitation:

> te nunc, sancta, precor, Venu', te, genetrix patri' nostri,
> ut me de caelo uisas, cognata, parumper...
>
> (*Ann.* (1) 52f. V = *ROL* 49f.)

Holy one, thee now I pray, Venus, thee, who didst bear my father, that thou look down on me from heaven, kinswoman, a little while...

After the appropriately liturgical language of the first line, *cognata*, though logically prepared for by *genetrix patris nostri*, comes as a mildly prosaic shock. 'Grandmother' would have been absurd; 'kinswoman' is a typically Hellenistic conceit. The passage narrating Ilia's frightening dream begins

> excita quom tremulis anus attulit artubu' lumen...
>
> (*Ann.* (1) 35 V = *ROL* 32)

When the old woman was awoken and had brought a lamp with trembling limbs...

The detail *tremulis* effectively paints the eery scene: the lamp gutters in her unsteady grasp, the shadows leap and flicker. That is the economical precision of Callimachus. Ennius sometimes wrote single lines or couplets in which he used rhetorical figures in epigrammatical comments as editor on individuals who display *uirtus* or deserve sympathy; these are eminently quotable and were clearly intended to be quotable as 'tags'.[1] That is Hellenistic, not Homeric. On the other hand there are harshly 'unpoetic' lines such as

> ...nonis iunis soli luna obstitit, et nox...
>
> (*Ann.* (4) 163 V = *ROL* 166)

On the Nones of June the moon blocked the sun, and night...

Such lines are criticized as tasteless; it would however be prudent to suspend judgement on this, for the contexts are unknown and one cannot tell how the severe, annalistic manner evoked here fitted into the texture of a style which was evidently richly various and avoided a monotony of either Hellenistic elaboration or jejune simplicity.

In his essay *On translating Homer* Matthew Arnold identified four characteristic qualities of Homer – his rapidity; his plainness and directness in evolving and expressing his thought; the plainness and directness of the substance of his thought; and his nobility, i.e. his σεμνότης or *grauitas*. Ennius regularly hits the Homeric mark in two or three but rarely in all four respects at once. The tree-felling fragment is plain and direct and noble, but it is anything but rapid; his

---

[1] *uirtus*: (10) 338 V = *ROL* 330 (Flamininus), (12) 370–2 V = *ROL* 360–2 (Fabius Maximus); (*lib. inc.*) 500 V = *ROL* 467 (the Roman state). Pathos: (*lib. inc.*) 519f. V = *ROL* 499f.; (*lib. inc.*) 472f. V = *ROL* 501f.; (2) 138f. V = *ROL* 141f.

wind-simile is noble and rapid and direct in thought but not in expression (*spiritus Austri imbricitor*); his play on *nares* is ignoble and indirect in expression. But Ennius was not really aiming to translate Homer; he was a highly original and eclectic poet. He may pose as Homer in his claim to be the medium of the Muses, in the general form and texture of his narrative, in the anthropomorphic presentation of the gods, in his touches of formulaic diction,[1] and in his similes drawn from Nature; but these were all common coin current among Hellenistic poets who used the form and expression of Homeric verse for new purposes. Ennius' frequent editorial comments, direct and indirect, his didactic tone, the arbitrary pace of the narrative, his stylistic self-consciousness, his exploitation of pathos and his gratuitous interest in female psychology are all features which emphasize the importance of the *poeta* as the organizer of his material in an un-Homeric way. He is, as it were, a master of ceremonies, the priest of the Muses who has both exoteric and esoteric lore to impart. The first line of the poem (quoted above, p. 68) is constructed of Homeric tags and has as its literal meaning 'Muses, you who shake great Olympus with your steps'; but there is also an allegorical meaning, 'Muses, you who make the great sky vibrate with your steps', an allusion to the theory of the harmony of the spheres. The Hellenistic poet at play would tell a tale perhaps trivial or preposterous with a straight face, and with irony and display. The difference with Ennius is that his subject was of the highest seriousness and he addressed not only the *cognoscenti* who knew Callimachus and Greek philosophy, but also the many.

4. ENNIUS THE ROMAN CITIZEN: HIS VALUES AND APPEAL

The *Annales* cannot have been an imperialistic poem like the *Aeneid*. Ennius died two years before the defeat of Philip of Macedon at Pydna in 167 B.C.; his adult life did not quite span the whole of that period of fifty-three years, from 220 to 167 B.C., during which Rome rose from obscurity to world power. As Polybius noted at the beginning of his *History*, written at Rome in the next generation, this was one of the most remarkable facts in history (Polyb. 1.1.5); Polybius already looked back to that time as an age of heroes. Ennius wrote his *Annales* in the wake of wars which had caused changes more rapid than was comfortable or even comprehensible to the Romans: no one in 202 B.C. could have predicted or looked for the phenomenal successes which Rome had experienced in world-politics by 188 B.C. It was not the intention or policy of the Senate to create new provinces or take on commitments outside Italy, and it was still far from clear during the years when Ennius was writing the *Annales* what Rome's precise relationship to the other Great Powers was to be.

---

[1] E.g. *olli respondit*...(1) 33 V = *ROL* 31, (2) 119 V = *ROL* 124, *caelum...stellis fulgentibus aptum* (1) 29 V = *ROL* 59, (3) 159 V = *ROL* 162 (Macrobius, *Sat.* 6.1.9).

Ennius' view of history was moral, individualistic, and aristocratic: *uirtus* was all; the safety of the common weal depended on individual *uirtus*; and *noblesse oblige*...

> unus homo nobis cunctando restituit rem.
> noenum rumores ponebat ante salutem;
> ergo postque magisque uiri nunc gloria claret...
>
> (*Ann.* (12) 370–2 V = *ROL* 360–2)
>
> *One man restored us the commonwealth by delaying;*
> *he would not put grumbling before our safety;*
> *therefore his fame shines now the more in retrospect...*

These famous lines on Fabius Maximus Cunctator express this attitude. Ennius admired Rome like Polybius, but had no sophisticated analysis of its constitution or society, other than to praise *uirtus* where he saw it, and to honour and emphasize the antiquity of Roman institutions. He did this at a time when society was faced with great internal and external changes. The *Annales* celebrated and defined what the Romans of that time liked to think were the qualities which had made them what they were, explained their place in the world, and implied how they should continue. By linking myth to remote history, remote to recent, and recent to the present, Ennius strengthened the community's sense of continuity, hence its identity and purpose, and provided patterns of excellence to which the young should aspire. The success of the poem was immediate and remarkable. We are told that it was declaimed in public not long after Ennius' death, as rhapsodes performed Homer, and for a century and a half it continued to provide the classic definitions and examples of Roman attitudes and values. It had a central place in the school curriculum. But epics, except Homer's, become superannuated. They lose directness, for tastes in style and assumptions about values change. Virgil displaced Ennius in the classroom, and, although the antiquarians of the second century A.D. read Ennius, his manuscripts must have been very rare by A.D. 500. His fragments were first printed in 1564; Scaliger wrote of him 'Ennius, poeta egregius, magnifico ingenio. utinam hunc haberemus integrum et amisissemus Lucanum, Statium, Silium, et tous ces garçons-là...quamquam interdum alium olet, tamen optime animatus est' 'Ennius, an outstanding poet of great genius. If only we had him [i.e. the *Annales*] whole, and had lost Lucan, Statius, Silius Italicus *et tous ces garçons-là* ...Although he sometimes smells of garlic, he has an excellent spirit.' Without wishing ill to 'all those adolescents', we may agree with Scaliger that the loss of Ennius' *Annales* is the most regrettable in all Latin literature.

5

DRAMA

I. THE ORIGINS OF ROMAN DRAMA

The Hellenistic theatre and Italy

After Menander's death (292 B.C.) the Greek theatrical profession, which had been primarily Athenian, became Panhellenic. Many Greek cities built or renovated theatres on a grand scale, and it is the remains of these, not of theatres of the classical period, that the traveller sees at such sites as Delos or Epidaurus. In the generation during which the scholar-poet Callimachus worked at Ptolemy's new 'Museum' in Alexandria, when the Sicilian Theocritus was composing his pastorals, and when the future father of Roman literature, the Greek Andronicus, was still a boy at Tarentum, the acting profession was acquiring a new prestige, even political power. The actors, musicians, and writers of tragedy and comedy were organized into 'chapels' or 'conventicles', θίασοι or σύνοδοι, and they called themselves οἱ περὶ τὸν Διόνυσον τεχνῖται 'the Artists in the service of Dionysus'. Four 'Guilds' of the Artists emerged, each corresponding to a region of the Greek world; apart from regulating terms and rules for dramatic competitions, these organizations even behaved in some ways like independent states, and would negotiate rights of safe passage for their members with a city or federation. Thus the acting profession came to depend and to thrive on a 'circuit' of musical and dramatic festivals among which Athens was only one of several centres. New plays were still produced, but the emphasis shifted to a repertoire of classics – in comedy, Menander, Philemon, and Diphilus; in tragedy, Sophocles, Euripides, and the latter's imitators.

Our knowledge of these developments of the years 290–250 B.C. is largely due to archaeological discoveries, and, as is the nature of such evidence, it is detailed (e.g. for Delphi and Delos) and patchy (e.g. for Sicily and South Italy).[1] We hear first of the Artists at Rome only in the 180s B.C. (Livy 39.22.2, 10), when a Roman drama based on their repertoire was already two generations old. In spite of the absence of direct evidence, it is likely that the Artists

---

[1] Sifakis (1967), *DFA* (1968).

77

did visit such centres as Syracuse and Tarentum in the third century B.C., and it is certain that their example lies behind the vigorous growth of the Roman theatre after the middle of that century.

However, it is clear that the practice of the Artists and the presentation and style of their Attic repertoire were not the only models on which the earliest Latin drama was based. Unfortunately, even the scholars of the Gracchan period (Aelius Stilo, Accius) and of Cicero's time (Varro) knew very little for certain about the beginnings of Roman drama. They tried to provide a pedigree to match the teleological histories of Greek drama prepared by scholars of the Peripatetic school. Accius seems to have regarded Naevius as the first important Roman dramatist, and gave a chronology for Andronicus which seems impossibly late, in spite of modern attempts to vindicate it.[1] Varro claimed the authority of 'old records' to show that Andronicus was the 'first inventor' of Latin drama, and that he produced a play in 240 B.C. at the end of the First Punic War (Cic. *Brut.* 72f.). The remains of accounts of the early theatre which were current in the first century B.C. are entirely worthless with respect to tragedy, and virtually so for comedy.[2] The objective value of the surviving summaries is only to illustrate the dubious methods of inference, synthesis, and invention which scholars like Accius had learnt from the school of Pergamum rather than Alexandria. As such, and since this is what passed for the truth, it is instructive. A source used by Horace (*Epist.* 2.1.139–63) alleged that the extempore joke-capping of harvest-home, the so-called Fescennine ritual which featured also in the celebrations of Roman weddings and triumphs and which was intended to avert malign spirits, led to an equivalent of the uproarious Old Comedy of Athens; this was curbed by law because of its slanderous content. Another account, summarized by Livy (7.2) and Valerius Maximus (2.4.4), is more speciously historical. According to this, Andronicus was indeed a 'first inventor' in that he was the first to present an entertainment with a story-line; it is very strange, however, that the author of this version did not think it interesting or important that the story was taken from a Greek play. The source refers to a dramatic *satura*, 'medley', before Andronicus; this had a written libretto, a prominent part for the musician (*tibicen*), and was acted by professional *histriones*, 'actors', a word borrowed from the Etruscan name for masked dancers of apotropaic rites, who, in their magic capacity, had been known in Rome since at least the early fourth century. The writer regarded these *histriones* with dislike and disdain, and he contrasts them unfavourably with the amateur performers (apparently young Romans of respectable birth) of an extempore kind of farce, borrowed from Oscan Atellae, and hence known as Atellane. He concludes by alluding in a muddled way to mime in an aetiological

[1] Suerbaum (1968) 2 n. 2, 297–300; Waszink (1972) 873f.
[2] Duckworth (1952) 4–17.

story in which he confuses first-century B.C. forms of that unmasked entertain-ment with the presentation of Andronicus' drama: according to him, Andronicus acted and sang in his own productions, but one day, straining his voice, passed his singing part over to a convenient *puer*, while he himself mimed the appro-priate actions.

Etruscan dancers, Atellane farce, *tibicines*, mime, and Fescennine exchanges are relevant in various ways to Roman drama as we know it, but it is striking that this source and others seem determined to mention nothing Greek in connexion with early Roman drama. Yet the long-established prose- and verse-comedies of Sicily, the vigorous Doric verse-comedies of South Italy, and the farces of Rhinthon (*phlyakes*, *hilarotragoediae*), not to mention the repertoire of the Artists, must have had direct and important influences. Roman drama was an adaptation of Hellenic drama. Why was it adopted at Rome so fruitfully in the middle of the third century B.C., rather than much sooner or much later?

It would be a mistake to oppose Greek and Italian elements in the implicitly chauvinistic manner of the sources reviewed above. Nor is it enough to acknow-ledge the importance of the theatrical traditions of South Italy and Sicily. To answer the question posed, one must look at Italy in its Hellenistic setting. The Roman people had no hermetic or racial self-consciousness. Their foundation-myths showed that they were a mixed people and their unusual law of manu-mission made freed slaves members of the body politic, so that potentially anyone of any race might be a *ciuis Romanus*. They were open to Greek influ-ences in all spheres, and their political and military contacts with the Greeks of Epirus, South Italy, and Sicily, in particular, the war against Pyrrhus and the First Punic War, came at a time when Greeks, for their part, were ceasing to think of 'Hellenism' as racially exclusive. As we have seen, it was at just this time that a particularly vivid expression of Hellenism, the Attic drama, was being disseminated more widely than ever before. Under Eratosthenes, the second generation of scholars at the Alexandrian Library were directing their attention outside the Greek world as traditionally defined, and were translating into Greek law-codes, technical manuals, and records in other languages. The most famous of these is the version of the Hebrew Pentateuch which lies behind the Septuagint.[1] It is a striking accident, if it is only an accident, that Andronicus and Naevius should have embarked in this very generation on what is in a sense the counterpart of this activity at Alexandria. Theirs, however, was the more ambitious and difficult task. The works to which the Alexandrians directed their attention were factual; the contents mattered, not the style. The merely factual content of the *Odyssey*, which Andronicus 'translated', or of an Attic play is less important than its presentation: the form and style of a literary

---

[1] Jellicoe (1968) 47–58; Pfeiffer (1968) 152–70; Fraser (1972) 305–35.

work is part of its meaning. Andronicus is a major figure in the history of literature as the first to tackle the problems of literary translation. His approach was crucial for the subsequent development of Latin literature; it was a matter of adaptation rather than of translation of the letter or even of that chimerical aim, fidelity to the spirit. The *Camena* whom Andronicus invoked at the beginning of his *Odyssey* was not Homer's μοῦσα (Muse) relabelled, but an Italian nymph who could inspire the *uates*, the bard. Homer and the Attic dramatists were the foundation of Greek education, and Andronicus was providing his fellow Roman citizens – he was an ex-slave, therefore a *ciuis* – with the works which, as a Greek, he must have seen as essential for a proper education. That a people might be civilized, even Hellenized, yet not speak Greek was a paradoxical idea, characteristic not of the age of Callimachus, but of his successor in scholarship Eratosthenes; its most striking manifestation was the emergence of Roman literature, in particular the drama, in the years after 240 B.C. For more detail of the manner in which the earliest *poetae*, 'makers', went about the business of adaptation (*uertere*, 'turning', as they called it), and how adaptation and free invention merged, see pp. 84ff. on the form of Roman drama, 93ff., 127ff. on light and serious drama, and pp. 58–76 on epic.

The organization of the acting profession at Rome

There was no permanent theatre at Rome until 55 B.C.; plans afoot in 179 and 174 B.C. failed.[1] The tradition at Rome had always been that the entertainers went to the festival, not the festival to the entertainers. Prefabricated wooden stages, presumably like those depicted on South Italian vases, were erected on the various sites of festivals.[2] These and other paraphernalia belonged to actor-*impresari* like T. Publilius Pellio, associated over a long period with Plautus,[3] and L. Ambivius Turpio, who produced, managed, and acted for Terence and Caecilius. There is a persistent belief that the Roman theatre in its early period was the province of the obscure and poverty-stricken. This is questionable. However Pellio and Turpio came to sport such aristocratic-sounding names,[4] they were men of substance and consequence, acquaintances of the élite in politics through their constant trade with the aediles, the future praetors and consuls. Ambivius presents himself in Terence's prologues (of the 160s B.C.)

[1] Livy 40.51.3, cf. 41.27.5, *periocha* 48. Pompey's theatre (55 B.C.): Tac. *Ann.* 14.20, cf. 13.54.
[2] Beare (1964) 176ff., 256ff., 335ff.; Trendall (1967).
[3] Plaut. *Men.* 404 (*Pellionis*, not *pellionis*); 'Pellio's gear' is the wooden stage. An early play. *Stichus* didascalia (200 B.C.). *Bac.* 215 (Pellio is probably acting Pistoclerus' part), 185/4 B.C.
[4] It was still unusual for any but prominent families to have cognomens of pure Latin attributive (usually derogatory) character, e.g. Balbus, Verrucosus, rather than ethnics (P. Terentius Afer) or foreign personal names (L. Livius Andronicus), which implied servile origin. Most people had just two names (C. Laelius).

not only as a great actor, proud of his craft, but also an artistic patron who can afford to back unpopular work and vindicate it (*prol.* Ter. *Hec. passim*). There was plenty of money in Rome in the years following the Punic and Eastern Wars, and Pellio and Turpio belong to the class of men who became rich by taking state-contracts from the aediles. By the 170s a remarkable 'social season' had developed. The religious festivals were preceded by a number of days devoted to entertainment, financed and run by the aediles. Races (*ludi circenses*) and shows (*ludi scaenici*) might be accompanied by 'fringe' events, e.g. boxing matches or tight-rope-walking. The season opened with the *ludi Megalenses* (*Megalesia*) (early April); there followed the *ludi Cereales* (late April), *Florales* (early May), *Apollinares* (mid-July), *Romani* (mid-September), and *Plebeii* (early November). Thus in theory it ran from spring to autumn. In practice, owing to the omission in the 190s of the biennial intercalations, the calendar was seriously out of step with the seasons – by nearly four months in Plautus' heyday, an error only reduced to two and a half months by Terence's time.[1] Thus in the 180s the *Megalesia* was falling in mid-winter, and the *ludi Plebeii* in high summer. The festivals had been instituted one by one, the *ludi Romani* being by far the oldest. The main period of growth was 230–190 B.C., years of great strain and anxiety, when the Senate saw such entertainments as a useful way to sustain public morale. The drama benefited greatly, and by the 180s it is probable that Plautus and Ennius had about fourteen official days for production, hardly less than the time available at Athens for dramatic competitions. That was not all. There were productions at occasional votive or funeral games given at private expense; and when a defect was noted in the ritual, the whole festival, plays and and all, had to be repeated, until things went right.

The prologues to Plautus' *Poenulus* and Terence's *Hecyra* show that audiences were mixed as to class, age, and sex, and that they could be unruly. From 194 B.C., the best seats were reserved for senators (Livy 34.44.5), a reform not welcomed by the people. The audiences of the Greek Artists at great festivals like the Delphic *Soteria* had read the authors of the repertoire at school and could be expected to be knowledgeable and discriminating. At Rome, although there were apparently revival-performances already in Plautus' time (cf. *Bac.* 214f.), most plays, light or serious, were new, and most of the audience would neither know nor care about the models; if they were bored, they would vote with their feet. The cultural levels of the audiences could hardly be more different.[2] There was a competitive aspect to productions at Roman festivals, but it is unclear what exactly was being judged, or by whom, or how central this element was; nor do we know whether or how strictly tragic and comic

---

[1] For the festivals, see Taylor (1937) 284–304; on the disruption of the calendar, see Michels (1967) 102, 170–1, Derow (1973) 345–56.

[2] See Cèbe (1960) 101–6.

offerings were segregated at a festival. Roman production-notices, unlike Greek, only record whether a play 'pleased' or not, and that only sometimes. A large cash prize awarded to Terence for his *Eunuchus* was unusual (Don. *praef. Eun.* p. 266 W).

The real financial competition came earlier, when the *impresario* approached the aediles with his offering. Whether the aediles paid 'standard' rates, or were permitted to supplement public moneys out of their own purses, is unclear. They would be interested in the political success of their festivals rather than in artistic merit, experiment, or social comment, and one can see that the work of a known success, such as Plautus or Ennius around 190 B.C., might be at a premium, whereas an unknown like Caecilius might experience difficulty without the patronage of a successful manager and friends in the nobility. Indeed, a successful actor or playwright enjoyed a peculiar opportunity to make contacts. Unlike a physician or tutor in the *clientela* of a particular family, which might be in political eclipse, e.g. the Julii Caesares of Plautus' time, the actor-manager's *exclusive* business was with the rising stars of politics. That alone explains why after Naevius Roman drama was usually only indirectly political or controversial. It was in the dramatist's interest to avoid offending families whose younger members might be next year's aediles. Clearly, these are all circumstances far removed from those of the contemporary Artists of Dionysus. By the 180s Rome, unlike any one Greek city, was maintaining her own internal and self-sufficient 'circuit'. The theatre was to the politician a convenient means of winning popular favour; to the entrepreneur it was a lucrative business; and to the public it was part (only part) of an enjoyable day off work. The Artists, by contrast, had long-standing traditions; they travelled far and wide to perform the classics before cultured audiences in fine stone theatres financed out of civic pride; artistic competition was central, and the rules and financial terms were minutely regulated by the Guilds.

The Roman acting-profession differed from the Greek also in several points which emphasize that the Artists' organization and tradition was not the exclusive model (cf. p. 78). In Greece, tragedy and comedy were strictly separate professions. The argument at the end of Plato's *Symposium* whether the same man might not try both genres is as speculative as whether a woman might make a good general. At Rome, Andronicus and Naevius developed a similar dramatic form for both light and serious plays, and they were supposed to have acted in their own productions (Festus p. 448 L, Livy 7.2). Specialization came in gradually. Plautus kept to comedy, though he was technically capable of writing serious drama; Ennius was the last to try both kinds. In Terence's time Q. Minucius Prothymus apparently acted tragic as well as comic parts, as later did Roscius (Don. p. 26 W, p. 266 W; Cic. *Orat.* 109). All kinds of Roman drama were far more musical and 'operatic' than Greek. Roman production-notices regularly record the name of the *tibicen* and technical details of his wind-instrument, the double pipe: the musician never figures in the *didascaliae* of Greek plays. The 'three-actor' rule of Greek drama was unknown to Plautus and Terence; the former sometimes has as many as six full actors simultaneously present in one play (*Poenulus*); the latter has up to four (*Heauton timorumenus*). There is no evidence at all for the doubling of roles which was a necessity and a point of pride in the Greek acting profession. However these radical differences of presentation and technique are to be explained, they clearly have nothing to do with the tradition of the Artists. It is here that the weakness of ancient accounts of the development of Roman drama is specially regrettable.

And yet, the Artists' influence is clear. It was their repertoire that was adapted. The iambo-trochaic quantitative verse of Roman drama represents a compromise between the more divergent styles of Greek tragedy and comedy. Latin plays were from the start presented in the contemporary costume of the Greek theatre. This was considered so characteristic a feature that later at any rate (for the terms cannot be traced earlier than Varro) comedies from the Greek repertoire were called *fabulae palliatae* 'Cloak plays' (from *pallium* = ἱμάτιον, 'cloak') and tragedies were called *fabulae crepidatae* 'Buskin plays', with allusion to the high-soled boot of Hellenistic tragedy. Lastly, although certain evidence on this point is lacking, it is unlikely that women ever acted in Roman productions. After all, these were dramas, not mimes, in spite of the confusion in Livy's source (see above, pp. 78–9).

This brings us to the question of masks. The ancient sources are confused as to whether and when Roman actors began using them. The consensus seems to have been that at first they did not, i.e. that the 'actors' were not really *histriones* but *mimi*, 'imitators'.[1] It is hard to believe this. It is not as if masks were alien to the Romans as they are to us. The Etruscan dancers who gave the name *histriones* were certainly masked; the word *persōna* 'mask' is also probably borrowed from Etruscan (it has nothing to do with *per-sŏnare* 'sound through'); the actors of Atellane farce, professional and amateur, had always used masks for the stock characters Bucco, Pappus, Manducus, etc. It seems incredible that a profession which took the names *histrio* 'masked ritual performer' and *artifex* 'artist' (~ τεχνίτης; see below) could have borrowed the plots, verse-form, and costume of the Greek tradition, but not its masks. Arguments against the Roman use of masks have sometimes been adduced on the basis of allusions to changes of expression in the scripts, e.g. the observation that someone is weeping or pale or blushing. These are of course valueless, since they occur also in Greek scripts; and anyway, who can blush at will? It is true that plays like *Menaechmi*, *Amphitruo*, and *Gemini Lenones*, all involving important parts for 'doubles', could be staged without masks, like *Twelfth*

[1] See Beare (1964) 184–95, 303–9.

Night or *The Comedy of Errors*. One must, however, wonder about the feasibility of an unmasked *Trigemini* (pseudo-Plautus) or *Quadrigemini* (Naevius).

Another sign of the influence of the Greek acting profession on the Roman is that the Romans adopted and characteristically adapted the idea of a 'Guild'. A decree of the Senate passed in 207 B.C. permitted actors and *scribae* 'writers', meaning playwrights and notaries, to belong to a conventicle which, like the Artists' organization, was nominally religious.[1] Actors and writers might meet (*consistere* ~ συνοδεύειν) and make offerings (*dona ponere* ~ δῶρα ἀνατιθέναι) in the temple of Minerva on the Aventine, in honour of Livius Andronicus, not as *poeta*, 'maker', because of his plays or his *Odyssey*, but because as *uates*, 'bard', he could be represented as having appeased Juno's anger by the composition and successful performance of a *carmen*, 'spell', for an expiatory rite. Luckily for Andronicus this took place not long before the Roman victory over the Carthaginians at the Metaurus. Roman actors and writers thus avoided association with Dionysus/Bacchus, whose cult was private and increasingly disreputable, and were associated with Minerva/Athene, the general goddess of the *artes*/τέχναι 'skills'; but since none of the festivals was in her special honour, the association was superficial and the secularization of the profession all but complete. Roman theatre-folk – actors, writers, and all – seem to have been known as *artifices scaenici* 'scenic artists', a partial loan-translation of the Greek appellation τεχνίτης Διονύσου. The association with Minerva was therefore to the logical Roman mind an obvious one.

It is unclear how this 'Athenaeum' on the Aventine related to the more successful 'Museum', the Templum Herculis Musarum founded in the 180s and associated with Ennius. Nor is the position of the *collegium poetarum*, the college of poets, fully clear. This body later at least met in the Templum Herculis Musarum, and is first mentioned as such in an anecdote set *c*. 90 B.C. (Val. Max. 3.7.11). By Terence's time there existed some formal procedure at the scrutiny and sale of plays by which hostile parties might be present and raise objections to another's offering on technical grounds (Ter. *Eun.* 19f.). What is certain is that in Rome the 'guild(s)' of actors and writers were never permitted to enjoy the degree of control and influence that the Greek Guilds exercised. That remained in the hands of the capitalist *impresari* and their clients, the nobility.

The form and verse of Roman drama

(i) *Speech, song, and recitative*. There were three modes of presentation in Greek tragedy. Iambic trimeters

$$\text{–} \ \text{–} \ \cup \ \text{–} | \cup \text{–} \ \cup \ \text{–} | \text{–} \text{–} \ \cup \text{–}$$
ὦ κοινὸν αὐτάδελφον ᾿Ισμήνης κάρα

---

[1] Festus p. 466 L. On this, and the *collegium poetarum*, see Horsfall (1976) 79–95.

declaimed without musical accompaniment, were the normal medium for speeches, dialogue, and debates. Trochaic tetrameters catalectic[1]

$$- \cup - \ | - \quad - \cup - | - \quad - \cup - \ | \cup - \cup -$$
ὦ τέκνον, χαῖρ᾽· ἡ γὰρ ἀρχὴ τοῦ λόγου πρέπουσά μοι

longer lines using the same diction and articulation as iambic trimeters,[2] were 'chanted' in some way to a musical ground, and indicated a rise in the emotional temperature. Lastly there was polymetric song, of two kinds. Choral odes were normally strophic in construction, i.e. written in pairs of 'stanzas' (strophe and antistrophe, 'turn' and 're-turn') which corresponded to the choreography of the dance. One also finds passages of polymetric lyric without strophic construction, a style used for highly emotional monodies, duets, and exchanges between a character and the chorus.

New Comedy was very different. The chorus no longer participated in the action, and there was virtually no lyric song. Only iambic trimeters, freer in structure than those of tragedy, and 'recitative' in trochaic and also iambic tetrameters catalectic, accompanied by the musician, were used. The rhythms and diction of tragedy and comedy were distinct, formal and elevated in tragedy, freer and more prosaic in comedy. In both, especially in comedy, spoken iambic trimeters were the norm.

The earliest Roman dramatists composed both light and serious plays, and they developed a dramatic form and medium for both which in some ways was a compromise between the two Greek styles, and in others was new. In comedy they dropped the chorus altogether; as its only function in New Comedy had been to mark the entr'actes, a consequence of this was to obscure the main aesthetic articulations, the 'acts', normally five. More than two-thirds of Plautus is divided between the equivalent of iambic trimeters (referred to in Latin as senarii 'sixers') and the equivalent of trochaic tetrameters catalectic (trochaic septenarii 'seveners'). The rest consists of iambic tetrameters and anapaests (if they are anapaests) written by the line, and lyric songs for up to four parts, which may be polymetric, or written by the line in cretic ($- \cup -$) or bacchiac ($\cup - -$) tetrameters, or in a mixture. The analysis of these songs is still far from fully understood.[3] Everything except senarii was musically accompanied by the tibicen. This style of presentation involved three basic modes (like Greek Tragedy), which we may denote as S (= speech, the senarii),

[1] 'Cut short by one place.'

[2] Trochaic tetrameters catalectic may be analysed as iambic trimeters with a cretic element $- \cup -$ (bridged or unbridged) at the head: (Sŏcrătēs) bĕātŭs ĭllĕ quī prŏcŭl nĕgōtĭīs..., cf. Marius Victorinus in GLK VI 131.17, Fraenkel (1928) 91. Whether or not it is historically justified, this analysis has the advantages that it works, and that it enables one to use the same terms to describe both metres.

[3] Leo (1897), Lindsay (1922) 274–316, Drexler (1967) 67–78, MacCary and Willcock (1976) 219–32.

R (= 'recitative', the septenarii), and O (= 'Opera', i.e. all the other metres, including iambic septenarii and anapaests). It is immediately striking that Plautine comedy was more musical not only than its model, the prosaic New Comedy, but also than Greek tragedy; for the three styles of presentation are about equally represented overall, so that one cannot call any one of them the norm.

It is supposed that Plautus inherited this presentation from Andronicus and Naevius, who are presumed to have extended to comedy the tripartite manner natural enough for their versions of tragedy; and there are among their fragments lines which appear to be lyric.[1] But even so, there remain severe problems, for the techniques of metre and music established by the early dramatists correspond only very roughly to Greek practice. There is no sign of strophic construction either in Plautus or in Roman tragedy: the chorus of serious drama normally expressed itself in blocks of iambo-trochaic recitative, or in anapaests. This implies a quite different style of choreography. Again, the cretico-bacchiac tetrameters so important in Plautus and attested for Andronicus and Naevius have no obvious counterpart in the astrophic lyrics of Greek tragedy, while, on the other hand, the excited dochmiac rhythms of Greek monody and duet do not figure in Roman drama at all. What songs the Romans sang before Andronicus seems beyond conjecture, and we cannot even offer reasonable guesses as to how strange the early dramatists' music and quantitative polymetric lyrics sounded to audiences familiar with Saturnian verse and the cadences of the *tibicines* whose art was ultimately Etruscan.

Although the three styles are fairly evenly distributed overall in Plautus, the proportions vary greatly between plays. *Epidicus* oscillates between O and R, descending to S for only a fifth of the whole. The musician's stamina was a practical consideration. His first rest in *Epidicus* comes at l. 305. On the other hand *Poenulus* moves between S and R and there are only two complex *cantica mutatis modis* 'songs with altered modes'. The *Miles gloriosus* is written wholly in stichic verses, without polymetric songs. No linear pattern of development can be established either towards or away from a more musical style. The normal sequence, and indeed the main dramatic articulation, in Plautus is $(S)OR(S)OR\ldots$, or $SRSR\ldots$ The modulations SO, SR, RS mark entries and exits; the transition OR is less dramatically important, and OS is very rare.

(ii) *Excursus on the nature and art of Latin quantitative verse* The most important metres were the iambo-trochaic.[2] In many ways these were direct imitations of general

---

[1] Andronicus (?), *TRF* 20–2 = *ROL* 20–2 (*Equos Troianus*), Naevius, *TRF* 5 = *ROL* 10f. (*Danae*), Fraenkel (1960) 327ff., 436, *RE* Suppl. VI 633. Andronicus, *CRF* 4f. = *ROL inc.* 4 *affatim edi bibi lusi* looks more like cretic than iambo-trochaic or Saturnian verse.

[2] General accounts: Lindsay (1922), Nougaret (1943, 1948), Raven (1965), Drexler (1967), Questa (1967). Greek iambo-trochaics: Maas and Lloyd-Jones (1962).

Greek practice. The quantitative principles of both will be examined below. The Romans used the same line-lengths as the Greeks and no others. At line-end a light syllable might do duty for a heavy (marked $\frown$), and hiatus was permitted between lines even when there was enjambment. On the other hand the Romans also imitated (in time, with increasing strictness) the strange Greek convention by which elision or synaloepha was obligatory (at least on paper) even across punctuation and changes of speaker within the line. The same restrictions, purely metrical in character, applied in Latin as in Greek to pairs of light syllables occupying one place of the verse – they might not be split between independent words, nor be constituted by the final pair of a polysyllabic word. In other points Roman dramatic verse looks like a compromise between the more divergent styles of Greek tragedy and comedy. Menander was freer than Euripides, for example, with respect to enjambment and pairs of light syllables. Light and serious Latin dramatic verse is more uniform; it is more like Greek tragedy with respect to enjambment, and more like Greek comedy with respect to pairs of light syllables. Again, the jaunty iambic tetrameter catalectic was a species of verse which occurred in Greek comedy. Its Latin equivalent was also admitted in tragedy. This relative unity of verse-style is usually and plausibly attributed to the earliest dramatists, who developed both light and serious drama; and one might also attribute to them certain innovations in prosody which took account of un-Greek features of Latin pronunciation. In speech, a run of syllables $\ldots \cup - \perp \ldots$ could be heard as $\ldots \cup \cup \perp \ldots$, and this is reflected in versification. Thus *ăpŭd mē* (*me* unemphatic) 'at my house' scans as one would expect, but *ăpŭd mḗ* (*me* emphatic) 'at *my* house', does not; here the necessary conditions for so-called 'iambic shortening' apply.[1]

The Latin word-accent is involved in this merely secondary feature; it was also the key factor in a more radical difference between the Latin and Greek brands of iambo-trochaic verse. The minimal rhythmical characteristic which they shared was the predictable alternation of two kinds of place defined not, as in English, by the presence or absence of stress, but by the quantities of the syllables, light or heavy. The sequence of expectation was a segment from a series of places occupied by syllables conforming to the pattern '...never light, maybe light, never light, maybe light...'; iambic sequence began 'maybe light...', and trochaic 'never light...'. A light syllable has a short vowel and is open (*mă-rĕ, fă-cĕ-rĕ*) or closed by one consonant (*uĭr*); all others were heavy (*sphīnx, prāē, rēs*), including those like *uĭr* when placed before another syllable beginning with a consonant (*uĭr-tūs, uĭr bŏnŭs*). The marks – and $\cup$ are thus used to denote both the length of vowels and the weights of syllables, and versification exploited such differences as there are between *lĭvĭd* and *lĭmpĭd, bĕddĭng* and *bĕd-tīme*, words which having the same stress pattern may be interchanged in English metric.

---

[1] Lindsay (1922) 35ff., Drexler (1969), Allen (1973) 179–85, 191–9. 'Iambic shortening' and '*brevis brevians*' ('short (syllable) shortening (the next)') are misnomers for a sandhi-phenomenon which involves not only a preceding *brevis* but also a following word- or phrase-accent; not merely verse-ictus, which may or may not coincide with the accented syllable. Besides e.g. *uŏlŭptătĕm* one may have *uŏlŭptātĕm* and *uŏlūptātĕm*. Even in an intentionally extreme case such as *ūxŏr mĕă mḗăqu(e) ămḗenĭtās, quĭd tŭ ăgĭs?::ŏb(i) ătqu(e) ăbstĭnĕ mănŭm* (*Cas.* 229), where there are two successive examples, *ăbstĭnĕ* becomes *ăbstĭnĕ* not because of the second-last verse-ictus, but because of the last word-accent. The irregularity here is metrical not prosodical. A true dactyl (e.g. *ābstrăhĕ*) would have been equally ungainly, for a resolved place may not be occupied by the last syllables of a polysyllable. Substituting *ăufĕr mănŭm* one normalizes the rhythm – and ruins the effect.

A light syllable counted as one 'time' (*mora*), a heavy as two. Hence a more positive formulation of the rhythm '...never light, maybe light...' would be 'two *morae*, one *or* two...'. In Latin the first kind of place ('never light' = two *morae*) was called the *arsis* 'rise', and the other ('maybe light' = one or two *morae*) the *thesis* 'fall', by a vocal metaphor;[1] for one might underline the quantitative opposition of these places by what the Roman grammarians called 'raising' and 'lowering' the voice at these places in recitation; in fact, they probably meant 'stressing' and 'relaxing' the voice. Another dynamic expression of the quantitative movement would be tapping the foot or a stick to mark the *arses*. It is important to note that either means of marking the 'beat', the ictus of a line, was extrinsic and adventitious, for it was not *necessary* to tap the foot or stress the voice to provide the rhythm. It is therefore strictly wrong to speak of 'ictus-places' in Latin verse, as if ictus were an essential component of the verse; that is to confuse the phenomenon, quantitative alternation, with its epiphenomenon, stressing or tapping. On the other hand, it is hardly less wrong to deny the existence of ictus altogether, for that is to deny that the phenomenon might have its secondary manifestation.[2]

This movement was shared in essence by Greek and Roman iambo-trochaic verse, but it was only one facet of the rhythm. The molecule of Greek verse was a sequence not of two but of four places, the metron (measure); it is only necessary to consider the iambic version ʊ−ᴗ−, the places of which we denote as A B C D, since the trochaic version (−ᴗ−ʊ B C D A) works the same. In tragic style the *arses*[3] B and D were occupied by heavy syllables *B* and *D* occasionally resolved as pairs of light syllables *bb* and *dd*. Taken by itself, then, − = ᴗᴗ. More rarely, one finds *aa* for the usual *A* or *a* of the first *thesis*. Substitution of *cc* for *c* was a very rare licence permitted in proper names. Comic verse was much freer with these resolutions and substitutions, most strikingly in the case of *cc* for *c*, which is thoroughly current coin. In both genres, there was an essential double aspect to the rhythm with respect to the ear's expectation of true heavy and light syllables:

	A	B	C	D
		Tragedy		
Heavy?	maybe	mostly	never	mostly
Light?	maybe	never	always	never
		Comedy		
Heavy?	maybe	maybe	never	maybe
Light?	maybe	never	maybe	never

Thus there was, as it were, a left hand and a right to the movement, fully described only over recurring sequences of four places. The question arises, why, if the comic

---

[1] There are no accepted alternatives to these terms in English (German *Hebung* = French *temps fort* for *arsis* as defined, *Senkung* = *temps faible* for *thesis*); 'definite' 'indefinite' would serve well. Unfortunately the places where one might 'raise' the voice are also the places where one 'drops' the foot in tapping time, and vice versa; in Greek, it was in this exactly opposite sense that the terms *arsis* and *thesis* had been originally used. See Nougaret (1948) 7; Drexler (1967) 10; Allen (1973) 276–9, 431–6.

[2] Contrast, e.g., the lines taken by Drexler (1967) 9–11, and Questa (1967) xi–xii.

[3] We use the term in its usual Latin sense as defined above; cf. above, n. 1.

poets freely admitted *cc* for *c*, did they not also admit a true heavy syllable *C*? The reason is apparent from the pattern of expectation in comedy with respect to *true* heavy syllables which *in sequence* were not simply equated with pairs of light. If *C* were admitted, the pattern for heavies would have become 'maybe, maybe, maybe, maybe', which is not a rhythm at all; the only quantitative movement would have been the binary expectation of 'maybe, never' with respect to light syllables. This is exactly what Roman dramatists did, both in comedy and in tragedy.

This is a startling and apparently gratuitous discontinuity between Greek and Roman practice, not adequately explained by the observation (true in itself) that Latin is less rich than Greek in light syllables. The derogatory inference has been drawn that Andronicus, or whoever did legislate for Latin iambo-trochaic verse, did not understand the essential double movement of the Greek, and that the Latin version is essentially cruder than its model. This is a mistake. It is here that the Latin word-accent is crucially important. If one takes any number of similarly articulated Greek verses, e.g.

> ...οἰωνὸν ⋮ ἔθετο ⋮ κᾀκέλευσ᾽ ἄλλον ⋮ νέον
> κρατῆρα ⋮ πληροῦν· ⋮ τὰς δὲ πρὶν σπονδὰς ⋮ θεῷ
> δίδωσι ⋮ γαίᾳ ⋮ πᾶσί τ᾽ ἐκσπένδειν ⋮ λέγει...
>
> (Euripides, *Ion* 1191–3)

it is apparent that they will not necessarily have similar patterns of word-accents. In fact, the Greek accent, which was of musical pitch, had nothing to do with the rhythm of the line at all. On the other hand, similarly constructed Latin lines necessarily share a single accentual pattern. We mark *arses* with a point below the line, and accents with an acute above:

> ...exọrat, ạufert; dẹtulịt rectạ domụm...   (Plautus, *Casina* 43)
>
> ...non pọtero fẹrr(e) hoc, Pạrmenọ; periị misẹr...
>
> (Terence, *Hecyra* 133)
>
> ...mi gnạt(e), ut uẹrear ẹloquị porcẹt pudọr...
>
> (Pacuvius 67 R³ (*Atalanta*))

The reason is that in Latin the word-accent was strictly regressive (*récta*, *dómum*) and in long words its place determined by the quantity of the second-last syllable; if heavy, it took the accent (*Parmenónem*); if light, the accent retreated to the third syllable (*Pármĕnō*) or in cases like *fắcĭnŏră*, *Phĭlŏlắchēs* to the fourth-last (cf. cápitalist). In very long words like *Pyrgopolyníces*, *índecorabíliter* there is good reason to suppose that there was a secondary accent on the initial syllable; on the other hand, the case for believing that there was a secondary accent on the last syllables of words like *Pármeno*, *éloqui*, *détulit* is very weak.[1] In Greek the accent was not necessarily regressive, and other factors, grammatical and semantic, might determine its placing.

[1] Lindsay (1922) 56 n. 1, Enk (1953) 97. Drexler's theory (1932/3) of 'cretic accentuation' is based on circular argument.

It is immaterial whether the Latin accent was of stress, musical pitch, or both: its placing was a direct function of quantity, and therefore an audible expression of the arrangement of words in a line; if accents fell on *arses* (or their first elements if resolved), the essential sequence '. . . never light, maybe light, never light, maybe light. . .' was reinforced; if accents fell on *theses*, there was a contradiction. These opposed articulations are respectively represented by the first and second halves of the above lines. Too much of the first articulation would be motonous and flabby, as if the poet were apologizing for using a verse-medium at all; too much of the second would be artificial. It is on the blending of these two opposed articulations that an important aspect of the art of dramatic and indeed all Latin quantitative verse depends. The working hypothesis formulated by Bentley that 'Roman dramatists sought to reconcile ictus and accent as far as possible' is a mistaken inference from the fact that the first articulation is in the majority.[1] On the contrary, the second articulation is the salt to the meat, and attempts to explain away as many as possible of the apparent cases of clash as actual reflections of prose-pronunciation start from a false premiss; not but what there are many cases where a clash is only apparent and a linguistic explanation is right – as, for example, when enclitic particles are involved (*uirúm quidem*, like *uirúmque*).

The vital relationship between word-accentuation and quantitative progression is that the opposed articulations are subject to opposed prosodical treatments which emphasize their characters. In a sequence like *exórat, áufert*. . ., the unaccented *theses* may be light, heavy, or double light (subject to the general rule given above, p. 87), as long as the *thesis* in question is next to an accented *arsis*. This is where Roman metric is fundamentally different from Greek. The freedom is extreme; the verse-form as such yields to the flow of the phrase, and the only quantitative pattern is '. . . maybe light, never light. . .', a binary movement quite properly analysed in 'feet'.

On the other hand, the treatment of *theses* was highly determined in sequences like . . . *détulit*. . ., where an unaccented final syllable falls in *arsis*, and like . . . *récta dómum*, where in addition word-accents are falling in *theses*. To formulate the rule, it is best to regard the senarius as a trimeter A B C D/A B C D/A B C D, since it applies over a sequence of four places: if an unaccented word-end falls in an *arsis* D, the cadence should run . . . *c D*, not . . . *cc D* nor . . . *C D*; conversely, if unaccented word-end falls in the last B-place, the cadence should run . . . *A B* or . . . *aa B*, not . . . *aB*. The latter principle, 'Luchs's law', is a mirror image of the first, and its effect is to impose a strongly quaternary quantitative rhythm at line-end, '. . . never light, never light, : always light, never light'. That is stricter even than in Greek tragedy. Luchs's law does not apply earlier in the line – so lines may begin *a B/* – but the other

a a B / c D   A B / c D   a B/

principle does. Hence lines may begin e.g. *lepido seni*. . . or *duro seni*. . . but not *seni*

c c D   a B / C D

lepido or *seni duro*, unless an enclitic follows (e.g. *quidem*), in which case the word-accent is in harmony with the *arsis*, and we have moved into the 'free' articulation. The principle also applies strongly in the middle of the line; here, however, there is

[1] Bentley (1726) xvii–xviii, cf. Meyer (1886) 10–18. The hypothesis has been fundamental to virtually all Anglo-German study of early dramatic verse, notably Fraenkel (1928), Drexler (1932/3), and is still widely taken to be axiomatic (Allen (1973) 153f.).

a well-defined but unexplained exception: lines might run out with the rhythm
...*plebeio piaculumst*, ...*despiciunt Euripidem*, where a single word follows the
irregularity without breathpause. This 'limping' effect was sometimes deliberately
used to express emotions, as in Pamphilus' lines about his estranged wife:

quae numquam quicqu(am) erga-me commeritast, pater,

quod noll(em), et saepe quod uellem : meritam scio;

amoqu(e) et laud(o) et uementer : desidero.

(Terence, *Hecyra* 488–90)

*She never did anything to displease me, father, and I know that she often did things
in order to please me – I love and praise and oh, so badly miss her.*

This licence is so rare in Terence that two consecutive cases are certainly deliberate.
Statistical tests show that combined with breathpause or change of speaker the licence
is a strong departure from the norm, as in

T. non dat, non debet. D. non debet? : T. ne frit quidem.

(Plautus, *Mostellaria* 595)

TRANIO *He's not paying, he owes nothing.*
MONEYLENDER *He owes nothing?*
TRANIO *Not a bean...*

To 'correct' this by reading *non dabit* ('Won't he pay?') would be to throw away
what is a deliberate dragged rhythm intended to mark the speaker's outrage (cf. Ter.
An. 767 for a similar effect).

Roman dramatists established norms of rhythm for tragedy and comedy the para-
meters of which, as with the diction, overlapped; within the genres, individual playwrights had their own norms and idiosyncrasies,[1] the ground against which their
departures and their irregularities are highlighted. These were delicate matters of
more or less, i.e. of style; we must listen to Plautus, as he would say, *perpurigatis
auribus*, with clean ears. By varying the rhythms between the poles of the harmonious
free style and the dissonant strict style, and by exploiting the quite separate resource
of resolution and contraction, a playwright could render a passage fast, slow, pleasant,
ugly, monotonous, or surprising. Here is Pseudolus at the very moment of *Die
Entführung aus dem Serail*:

---

[1] Clash of word-accent and verse-movement is distributed thus in the senarii of Plautus and
Terence, with negligible mean deviations between plays:

	1st foot	2nd	3rd	4th	5th
Plautus	10%	3%	½%	15%	30%
Terence	10%	7%	½%	8%	25%

These figures denote a basic difference between Plautus' and Terence's styles.

＿ – ∪⌣ – ＿⌣ – ∪ ∪– ∪ –
nunc in metu   sum maxumo,   triplici modo:

– – ＿ – – ＿⌣ – ∪∪– ∪–
prim(um) omnium   i(am) hunc comparem   metuo meum,

– ＿⌣– – – ∪ ＿– ＿⌣–
ne deserat   med atqu(e) ad hostis transeat.

∪∪ ＿ – ∪∪∪ ∪∪– ∪∪ – – ∪–
metu(o) autem, ne eru' redeat etiamd(um) a foro,

– ＿ – ＿ – – ＿ – ∪–
ne capta praeda capti praedones fuant;

– ∪∪– ∪∪– ＿ ＿ ＿ – ＿ ∪ –
qu(om) haec metuo, metuo n(e) ill(e) huc Harpax aduenat,

∪∪ ＿ ＿ ＿ – ∪∪∪– – ∪∪∪⌢
priu' qu(am) hinc hic Harpax abierit cum muliere.

(Plautus, *Pseudolus* 1024ff.)

Now I am in the greatest fear, in a triple way; first of all I fear this accomplice of mine, lest he desert me and cross to the enemy; besides I fear lest Master be even now returning from the market; while I fear these things, I fear lest that [real] Harpax comes here before this [fake] Harpax gets away from here [Ballio's house] with the girl.

This bald version fails to bring out the rhythmical quality of the original. It is spoken verse, yet its movement could be the choreography of the stage-business. The first two and a half verses are written in the strict style, *triplici modo*; the spaces separate the 'metra'. The tension of the verse suits the sense well. Then Plautus changes to the harmonious style (*ad hostis transeat*) without exploiting its freedom; the same quantitative pattern ––∪– ends the third line. The next three and a half lines are in the harmonious style too (except as usual the line-ends); note how the heavy lugubrious line *nē capta...* contrasts with the panicky resolutions of its neighbours. The coda of the passage *abierit cum muliere* returns to the strict style, this time with rapid resolutions. This is virtuoso writing; for much more off-hand Plautine stuff see p. 99; and for Terence, p. 124.

Andronicus is not named by any ancient source as *primus inventor* of Roman iambo-trochaic verse, and if he had a claim, it was forgotten or disputed by the first century B.C. (on the *carmen* attributed to Appius Claudius Caecus, see p. 138). The medium appears fully developed in Andronicus, and because of this, some modern scholars would posit a period of experimental development before 240 B.C.; they suppose, among other things, that one articulation of the trochaic septenarius, the *versus quadratus* ('square verse'), e.g.

＿ ∪＿ – ＿ ∪＿ – ＿ – ＿ – ∪∪ ⌢
uos scelesti,   uos rapaces,   uos praedones:: periimus

(Plautus, *Menaechmi* 1015)

represents an ancient Italian metre, on the ground that in later days it was favoured in the popular songs sung at triumphs, and in children's ditties.[1] It is, however, hazardous to infer that the Fescennine verses and children's songs of the fourth century B.C. were not in Saturnians; and what was the subject matter of the 'experimental' verse,

[1] Immisch (1923) 29–34; Fraenkel (1927) 357–70; Drexler (1967) 29.

and who were its audience? The origin of the Roman brand of iambo-trochaic verse remains a mystery, but whoever did invent the form, and in particular the principles respecting word-accent and prosody, was a genius; for analogous principles were naturally followed in all other forms of quantitative verse borrowed from the Greeks. Perhaps we might understand the matter better if more were known of the Saturnian verse (see p. 57) and if we could trust Livy's allusion to a pre-dramatic 'satura' (see pp. 160–2).

2. LIGHT DRAMA

Andronicus and Naevius

Volcacius Sedigitus did not even mention Andronicus in his list of the ten best (i.e. funniest) comic poets, but gave Naevius third place after Caecilius and Plautus, reversing their chronological order. Cicero did not think Andronicus' plays worth a second reading, and it was his fate even more in comedy than in tragedy to suffer invidious comparisons with his successors. Plautus was later supposed to have borrowed a good deal from Andronicus and there was a tradition that at *Eun.* 426 Terence was satirically quoting a line of Andronicus, *lepus tute es: pulpamentum quaeris?* 'You are a hare: are *you* looking for tasty meat?'[1] This has been compared with a favourite Plautine form of expression in which riddles (not, however, epigrams like this) are posed with a more or less bizarre identification followed by an explanation with no connecting or causal conjunction; e.g. *Pseud.* 747 'What when he's caught red-handed?' *anguillast: elabitur* 'He's an eel: he slips away'; *Mer.* 361 *musca est meus pater: nil potest eum clam haberi* 'My father is a fly: you can't keep anything private from him.'[2] The influence of Naevius on Plautus is very evident from the titles and the style of the fragments. If one early dramatist deserves the credit for establishing the form and stabilizing the diction of Roman comedy, it is he.[3] There is some suggestion that Plautus worked with him or revised some of his scripts.[4] Titles such as *Lampadio, Stalagmus, Stigmatias, Technicus* denote leading slaves; the titles of New Comedy very rarely denote a slave, and hardly ever name him. It seems that Naevius, not Plautus, was responsible for the promotion in Roman comedy of the clever slave. On the other hand plays called *Testicularia, Apella, Triphallus/Tribacelus* imply a more bawdy approach than we find either in New Comedy or Plautus. Naevius freely renamed the plays which he adapted, and added material involving Italian allusions or dramatic ideas suggested more or less specifically by other Greek plays. Plautus followed Naevius in these points and we may draw

[1] Wright (1974) 24–7.
[2] Fraenkel (1960) 35ff.
[3] Wright (1974) 33–85.
[4] *Carbonaria, Colax, Fretum, Nervolaria* are titles rightly or wrongly assigned to both; cf. Ter. *Eun.* 25.

the important inference that they did not invite or expect their audiences to enquire after the originals or measure excellence in terms of fidelity either to the letter or the spirit. The allusions in one fragment to Praeneste and Roman diet (*Ariolus*, *CRF* 22–6) have been taken to show that Naevius invented the *togata* ('Toga-play') on domestic Italian themes;[1] he certainly invented the *praetexta* ('Hem'- or 'Robe-play'), the genre in which Roman themes, ancient and modern, were presented in the form and style of the *fabula crepidata* ('Buskin-play'), as representations of Greek tragedy were known in later times. However, it is at least as likely that the *Ariolus* was a *fabula palliata* ('Cloak-play') representing New Comedy, and that Naevius was already exploiting the essential ambiguity of the genre, that apparent Greeks in a domestic setting should speak orotund and zestful Latin verse, to create a Graeco-Roman setting. This too is a central feature of Plautine comedy. Naevius had a reputation among scholiasts for political outspokenness. He was supposed to have got into trouble with the Metelli by naming them in an ironic line on the stage, but whether others of his extant fragments should be related to this seems questionable.[2]

Contemporary allusions in Plautus are for the historian frustratingly elusive. Nevertheless, it would be wrong to regard his plays as wholly unpolitical; he was simply more careful than Naevius (cf. p. 162). He is supposed to have died in 184 B.C., an inference from the absence of later dated production-records. It is possible that Plautus was one of those who attracted the censor Cato's attention in that year of moral correction. The *Poenulus* of 188/7 B.C., though a slap-dash piece of work, is remarkable for its liberal and cosmopolitan premisses. The lover is a Carthaginian by birth and an Aetolian by adoption; thus he represents the two states most detested and least trusted by contemporary Romans. Yet he is portrayed sympathetically like any other Plautine lover. It is as if a play dealing sympathetically with the Germans *and* Japanese had been staged in Britain in the early fifties. The title-figure, the 'poor Carthaginian' Hanno, is presented with a bizarre mixture of traits, now those of a *senex lepidus*, a gay old dog, now of a *servus callidus*, a crafty slave, and now of one who displays the very virtues of an Aeneas – steadfastness and piety. The portrayal is wholly (if disparately) sympathetic, and there is no trace of xenophobia, although the play was certainly produced within Hannibal's lifetime (d. 183 B.C.). It is difficult to imagine a supporter of Cato's financing this play as aedile; that Plautus should even have envisaged its successful production tells us something of his authority in the theatre and of the openmindedness of his audience.

[1] Leo (1913) 92.
[2] Jocelyn (1969) 32–47; Wright (1974) 33f., 56f.

Plautus

(i) *The authenticity of the plays*. Plautus is represented by the twenty-one so-called *Fabulae Varronianae*; our manuscripts descend from a collected edition assembled *c.* A.D. 100.[1] It is as if a distant posterity were to know Shakespeare from copies made from a folio edition compiled from available acting scripts of the various plays in the 1920s. *Vidularia*, the last, is all but lost, and others have more or less serious gaps (*Cistellaria, Amphitruo, Bacchides, Aulularia*). Some plays were available only in revival-scripts (*Casina*) or incompatible versions (*Poenulus*) or drastically cut (*Curculio*).[2] Any signs used by the editors to clarify the status of interpolations, alternative versions, and dislocations have been lost. The plays are divided into scenes and present a dilettante mixture of archaic and 'modern' spelling. The act-divisions in modern editions derive from mistaken inferences by Renaissance scholars from Horace's prescription at *A.P.* 189f.; the same applies to Terence. The manuscripts in which Plautus became known to the Renaissance and from which he was first printed partly neglected the line-division; hence an academic justification for prose as a medium in Italian and Elizabethan comedy. No canon of Plautus' works existed in or near his own time. In the 160s B.C. Terence could at least plausibly allege that he had not known that a certain play had been 'turned' by Plautus (*Eun.* 25–34), and a generation later Accius even denied the Plautine origin of another comedy which Terence had thought genuine (*Ad.* 7, Gell. 3.3.9). Accius' contemporary Aelius Stilo reckoned only twenty-five scripts authentic out of some 130 going under Plautus' name (Gell. 3.3.11). The so-called *fabulae Varronianae* are the twenty-one which Varro grouped as authentic 'by everyone's agreement' (Gell. 3.3.3), i.e. the plays which no one had impugned, and it is virtually certain that these are the twenty-one which our MSS preserve. The plays which really deserve the title *Varronianae* are those which had been suspected by such as Accius and Stilo but which Varro judged Plautine on stylistic grounds, apparently another nineteen (see Appendix).

In view of the precarious nature of the transmission, doubts might be entertained as to the unity of the corpus and the quality of the text. Statistical analysis shows, however, that we have the work of one hand, and that under the circumstances it is remarkably well preserved. Features such as the normal distribution of clash of ictus and accent or the details of prosody, e.g. the treatment of final -*s* after a short vowel before an initial consonant, reveal distinctive internal regularities. Criteria like these are valuable, because they are unnoticed by the listener or reader and are subconsciously determined by the writer;

[1] Leo (1912) 1ff., right in essentials against Lindsay (1904).
[2] See Leo's note on *Cur.* 454 in his edition.

hence they are more reliable than the features of surface style recognized by Varro and used by him for the vindication of disputed plays. Mythological identifications, typical nonce-formations, characteristic turns of phrase (cf. p. 103), etc., are precisely those features which a careful reader will notice, and which any competent imitator or forger would reproduce.

(ii) *Plautus and his models*. Plautus does not care whether we know the name of an original or its author; we may be told either, neither, or both, and only in one case (*Alaẓon* 'Big talker' = (*Miles*) *gloriosus*) is it certain that the information comes from the original script. Only one or two have translation-titles (*Mercator* = *Emporos* 'Merchant') and most are disguised. Five have *-aria* titles, on a Naevian pattern. Three are named after leading slaves against New Comedy practice: thus Epidicus, Pseudolus, Stichus are implicitly given the status of an Ajax or Agamemnon. Several titles are jocosely misleading or even perverse. *Truculentus* 'Grumpy' has nothing to do with the famous *Dyskolos* of Menander; *Trinummus* 'Threepence' is a *Thesauros* 'Treasure'. The titles of Menander, Philemon, and Diphilus fall into well-defined categories which Plautus following Naevius plays with and explodes. Evidently the plays are to stand in their own right. An important corollary for us is that knowledge of the originals as such is irrelevant to the evaluation of Plautus, for he did not expect it in his spectators; or rather, it would be, if we knew more about the precise circumstances and presentation of Plautine comedy. As it is, we have hardly any first-hand information, and the scholiastic tradition as regards historical matters is the narrowest and feeblest attaching to any ancient dramatist. In the circumstances we cannot afford to ignore the archaeology of the plays. By looking into Plautus' workshop we may illuminate his assessment of his audience's taste and discover terms appropriate for his dramatic criticism. For a most disconcerting aspect of Plautus' drama is that instead of trying to reproduce or emulate the special features of the New Comedy – economical and internally consistent plot-construction, subtle characterization, irony, pathos – he utterly subverts them. This is so pervasive and marked that it cannot be regarded as mere negligence, but as the assertion of a comic style quite alien to the naturalism of a Menander or a Terence and the consequent European tradition of the Comedy of Manners.

Three plays are known for certain to be based on Menander (*Cistellaria* 'The casket comedy' = *Synaristosai* 'Ladies at lunch', *Stichus* 'Sketch' = first *Adelphoi* 'Brothers', *Bacchides* 'The Bacchis girls' = *Dis exapaton* 'The double deceiver'). Two are from Philemon (*Mercator* = *Emporos*; *Trinummus* = *Thesauros*) and three from Diphilus (*Rudens* 'The rope'; *Casina* 'Passion-flower' = *Kleroumenoi* 'The lot-takers'; *Vidularia* 'The hamper comedy' = *Schedia* 'The raft' (?)). One is from Alexis (*Poenulus* 'The poor

Carthaginian' = *Karchedonios* 'The Carthaginian') and another from the otherwise unknown Demophilus (*Asinaria* 'The ass comedy' = *Onagos* 'The muleteer'). Plautus' taste in authors centred on the three who dominated the Artists' repertoire, but was evidently catholic. These plays have a uniform surface-style in which wildly hyperbolical comparisons, nonce-formations, bizarre identifications, asyndetic riddles, military imagery, jokes exploiting formulae and concepts of Roman law, and mythological comparisons are prominent.[1] None of these is particularly characteristic of any New Comedy writer, nor of Terence, and it is rightly inferred that they are specially Plautine traits, though one would like to know how markedly Plautus differed here from Naevius. The plots of all Plautus' plays are distorted considerably by the re-casting of their musical and metrical form and by the running together of act-divisions of the originals; this allowed, the two Philemon plays preserve their plots relatively intact. Other plays like this are *Aulularia* 'The jar comedy' (possibly from Menander), *Captivi* 'Prisoners', and *Menaechmi* (from unknown authors). It is significant that Cicero actually quotes only from *Aulularia* (once) and *Trinummus* (several times), that *Menaechmi* was particularly popular in the Renaissance, and that Lessing thought so highly of the *Captivi* that he called it the best play ever written. In these cases Plautus happens to have kept well-wrought New Comedy plots more or less intact, and the dramatic critic familiar with the theory of comedy as a 'mirror of life' has therefore felt more at home with these plays than with others. Plautus is sometimes praised for the characterization of Euclio in *Aulularia* and for having preserved the well-oiled plot of the *Menaechmi*. This praise is in fact misplaced, for his adjustments of the Euclio-figure were such as to simplify and categorize a complex character, and in the *Menaechmi* he has gone out of his way to upset the formal balance of the original. These plays, which are not necessarily to be associated in date,[2] perhaps represent a treatment of plot more characteristic of Caecilius Statius, whom Varro praises for his *argumenta*, but whom nonetheless Gellius found very wanting by Menandrian standards (Gell. 2.23).

Plautus is usually more actively disruptive. The *Stichus* (from Menander; 200 B.C.) begins with a delicate musical vignette depicting two sisters whose father wishes to have them divorced from their absent husbands. The spectator is invited to expect a complex and various family-drama, and that no doubt was the main theme of the original. He might two or three years earlier have seen the *Cistellaria* (also from Menander), which began with a technically similar operatic tableau for female characters. Plautus was already fully himself in the *Cistellaria*; the story-line was prominent, though stretched here, telescoped

---

[1] A comprehensive account of Plautine style in English remains a *desideratum*. See Lejay (1925), Haffter (1935), Fraenkel (1960), Wright (1974).

[2] Among dating-studies Schutter's (1952) is the best.

there, and lopped at the end. In *Stichus* Plautus all but discards the main action of the *Adelphoi*, and the play turns into a balletic *satura* of joyous home-coming – the Punic War was not long over – in which the opposed fortunes of the resident parasite and of the below-stairs characters amount to a theme, hardly a plot. In *Casina* (from Diphilus; after 186 B.C.) Plautus has cut the return of the young lover, the recognition of Casina, and their betrothal (*Cas.* 65). Papyri published in the late nineteen fifties and sixties provided important direct evidence, previously all but lacking, of the great freedom with which Plautus treated the plots of his models. An extensive fragment of Menander's *Dis exapaton* shows that Plautus has cut a scene of this, the original of his *Bacchides*, and has re-cast dramaturgy radically at an act-break of the original, though not without trace.[1] In the *Poenulus* (from Alexis; 189–187 B.C.) Plautus has seriously distorted the dramatic structure of the original (*Karchedonios*) both by episodic expansions (e.g. 330–409) and more importantly by the insertion of a 'second trick' (1086–110; see below). Terence appeals to the example of Naevius, Plautus, and Ennius when defending himself for making alien additions which are not merely episodic in character (Ter. *An.* 15ff.), and he adds to his version of Menander's second *Adelphoi* a scene of Diphilus' *Synapothneskontes* 'Partners in death' which, he says, Plautus had left out in his version of that play (Ter. *Ad.* 9f.). Another addition of a scene containing a dramatic idea, gravely distorting the structure as a whole, occurs in *Miles gloriosus*.[2] It used to be maintained, on a partial and imperfect statement of the problems of these plays, that here and elsewhere Plautus had taken all or most of two Greek originals, and joined them end to beginning. There is no external evidence for this method of composition, and the internal evidence alone, if correctly stated, proves that it was not used in these two cases, which Léo regarded as certain.[3] As an illustration of Plautus' workmanship, and incidentally of his less flamboyant style, it will be convenient to look in more detail at the case of the *Poenulus*.

The central peculiarity of this play is that it contains two tricks which cause it to fall into unsatisfactory halves. The first three acts are devoted to a deception which is sufficiently comprehensive to put the procurer Lycus in a very difficult position. He has been successfully 'framed' thanks to the slave Milphio's wiles, so that Milphio's master Agorastocles can threaten Lycus: 'Either you allow me access to my beloved Adelphasium, or I shall prosecute you for theft; you will be condemned to pay me compensation so huge that all your property, including the girls, will be mine.' The threat is less immediate than Plautus makes out, since 'today' is a holiday and the courts will only be open 'tomorrow', but Plautus, magnifying Milphio, puts no emphasis on this

---

[1] See Handley (1968), Gaiser (1970) 51–87, Questa (1970) 183–228, Wright (1974) 138–41, Arnott (1975) 38–41.

[2] G. W. Williams (1958) 79–105.   [3] Leo (1912) 170.

(Alexis may have). Lycus' response is adequate for the moment – he absconds (795). Only after this do Milphio and then Agorastocles discover that Adelphasium, and her sister Anterastilis, are freeborn Carthaginians (iv.1, v.2 *init.*). By a cleverly economical stroke, the girls' father Hanno is introduced just as they are discussing the implications of the news (v.1–2). Plautus makes out that it provides a separate way of attacking Lycus: simply prosecute him. The Plautine law provides that whether Lycus is acting in good faith or not, the proof that the girls are *ingenuae*, freeborn, will ensure their release, and that since Lycus knows the truth, he will be punished (963ff., cf. 905ff., 919; 1226ff., 1344ff., 1391ff., 1402). Later on (1086ff.) Hanno is invited by Milphio to pretend that he is their father and prosecute Lycus; this is simply an elaborate means of establishing that Hanno really is the girls' father:

MIL. Nunc hoc consilium capio et hanc fabricam apparo,   1099
    ut te allegemus, filias dicas tuas
    surruptasque esse paruolas Carthagine,
    manu liberali causa ambas adseras,
    quasi filiae tuae sint. iamne intellegis?
HAN. Intellego hercle. nam mi item gnatae duae
    cum nutrice una sunt surruptae paruolae.
MIL. Lepide hercle adsimulas iam in principio: id mihi placet.   1105
HAN. Pol magis quam uellem. MIL. eu hercle mortalem malum,
    ⟨senem⟩ catum crudumque, Aeolidam subdolum!
    ut adflet, quo illud gestu faciat facilius!
    me quoque dolis iam superat architectinem!   1110

MIL. (*Self-importantly*) *Now I commend this counsel and I provide you this patent device: that we commission you to say that they are your daughters kidnapped as children at Carthage, and that you lay hands on both of them in a suit for liberty. Do you get it yet?*
HAN. *Indeed I do: my two daughters were kidnapped just like that along with their nurse when they were children.*
MIL. *That's good acting right at the start! I like it!*
HAN. *More than I would wish.*
MIL. *Aha, here's a crafty cove, a tough old trickster, a shifty Sisyphus! Tears to order, to make his performance the more effective! He even beats me the master-builder in deceit!*

Reflection will show that Plautus' legal assumption cannot possibly have been made in Alexis' original; hence this episode cannot have figured at all. The scene is Calydon, the girls are Carthaginian, Lycus did not kidnap them, he bought them long ago from their abductor in Anactorium. Alexis went out of his way to arrange a situation in which precisely the absence of adequate international law was an important theme. The girls are not even Greeks – they are Hellenized barbarians. The law can provide no redress. The best that the slave might suggest at the place equivalent to 964 in the original would be not 'assert their rights at law', but simply 'seize them'. For it was the dramatic, not the legal situation, that was changed in Alexis. Agorastocles is now required by a well-known convention of New Comedy to marry his beloved, not simply have her as his concubine; that implies finding her family – and, ironically, Father has just arrived and is listening. Secondly, and more urgently, it is now vital to prevent either of the girls from returning to Lycus' house. Earlier in the play we saw them depart for the festival of Venus at which they are to dedicate themselves before beginning their professions as *meretrices*. At the festival an unpleasant soldier has seen and taken a fancy to the younger Anterastilis; he is now in Lycus' house waiting for her to return, and he is an immediate threat to her chastity. As long as Agorastocles and Milphio had thought that the girls were mere slaves, this had not mattered; the truth has changed that. This is the organic reason for the soldier's role in Alexis' play: Plautus' adjustments incidentally render the soldier all but irrelevant.

The dénouement which Alexis had in mind seems clear. First, a recognition-scene between Hanno and Agorastocles; next, as in Plautus, the return of the daughters; then, the emergence and pacification of the disgruntled soldier; finally, the return of Lycus, who capitulates not simply because Father has come offering a ransom, still less threatening a lawsuit, but in virtue of the threat posed by the first trick. This is a well-balanced and unitary action, and its emotional interest lies precisely in the absence of any simple legal remedy. There is no room for the proposal of a second trick such as Plautus includes as an elaboration of the recognition and which will only work on premises which ruin the point of Alexis' play.

On this view, the whole episode in which the 'second trick' occurs must be a Plautine addition, substituting for and expanding on a very brief transition by Hanno to the subject of his daughters after the recognition of Agorastocles: 'What were you saying just now about two Carthaginian girls who have been kidnapped? How old are they? Have they a nurse?' The passage in question is 1086–1110, and examination shows that it presents a number of dramatic and dramaturgic flaws. Most strikingly, Agorastocles has nothing to say or do from 1086 on, and is only brought back at 1136, with what in the circumstances is an ineptly surprised question. In the closely-knit recognition which ends at 1085, Agorastocles has been an excited protagonist: Plautus has simply omitted him in his insertion, the purpose of which is to enhance the dwindling role of Milphio. This alone is insupportable as homogeneous dramatic composition. Next the transitions to and from the inserted episode are abrupt and illogical. The change of subject at 1085/6 from Hanno's liberality and Agorastocles' inheritance to Milphio's 'clever idea' is arbitrary; at 1110/11, Hanno has not been told that the supposititious Carthaginian girls have a nurse, and therefore cannot logically ask about her. Thirdly, Milphio's brief explanation of the dramatic situation (1090ff.) is unsatisfactory: he ought to mention that Lycus had at least been put on the defensive. In fact, the relationships, situation, and language which he uses are calqued straight from the prologue and earlier lines of the play; Plautus is thus guilty of a dramatic anachronism: Milphio's description is out of date. Lastly, by describing the girls to Hanno as *meretrices seruolae* (1094) 'working girls', rather than as *Carthaginienses ingenuae*, 'freeborn Carthaginians', as would now be natural, Milphio makes it seem to Hanno that not only is he to pretend to be their father, but also that it is a fiction that the girls are Carthaginian at all.

The dramatic objection to any second trick in the play, its particular legal absurdity, Agorastocles' abrupt disappearance, and the other technical faults mentioned are characteristic of Plautus' neglect of realism. His intentions were to make his Milphio another Epidicus or Pseudolus, and to present Hanno in his readiness to participate (1086ff.) as a 'crafty Carthaginian'. It is significant that he does not balk at seriously distorting the plot of his original in the attempt, and that 'craftiness' is essentially incompatible with what in the original was undoubtedly a wholly serious and high-minded presentation of the alien.

In the opinion of the present writer, the source of Plautus' insertion was a passage of Menander's *Sikyonioi* 'The Sicyonians' known to us from papyrus fragments first published in 1964. Plautus certainly knew this famous play: he borrowed its hero's name Stratophanes and used it for the soldier in his *Truculentus*, a play produced about the same time as *Poenulus* (189–187 B.C.). It is therefore unreasonable to suppose that the episode in question occurred in other plays and that one of these, and not the *Sikyonioi*, provided the model. In any case, we are not dealing with a simple *locus communis*, like the entrance motif of the soldier who sees his beloved embraced by a brother or father and mistakes the situation (e.g. Menander, *Perikeiromene init.*, *Misoumenos* 208ff., *Poen.* 1280ff.) but with a very specific dramatic situation which (as Plautus shows) cannot easily be transplanted – daughter and faithful retainer taken long ago by pirates; ignoble but well-meant proposal of a legal deception to establish the girl's identity;[1] misinterpretation, praise, tears. Here, then, we have the first documentary example of the kind of 'contaminatio' which Terence practised and which he attributed to Plautus (see above, p. 95):

> ΚΙΧ. οὐκ εἰς τὸν ὄλεθρον — ΘΗΡ. χαλεπὸς ἦσθα.
>
>   ΚΙΣ. — ἀποφθερεῖ
>
> ἀπ' ἐμοῦ; Κιχησίαν σὺ τοιοῦθ' ὑπέλαβες
>
> ἔργον ποήσειν ἢ λαβεῖν ἂν παρά τινος   345
>
> ἀργύριον ἀδίκου πράγματος; ΘΗΡ. †Κιχησίαν

---

[1] In the *Sikyonioi* this makes sense, because it is a question *in Attica* of the rights of an Athenian.

Σκαμβωνίδην γενόμενος† εὖ γὰρ ὑπέλαβες·
τούτου με πρᾶξαι μισθὸν αὐτοῦ, μηκέτι
ὧν ἔλεγον ἄρτι. ΚΙΧ. τοῦ τίνος; ΘΗΡ. Κιχησίας
Σκαμβωνίδης γε πολὺ σὺ βέλτιον λέγεις·   350
ποεῖν τι φαίνει τὸν τύπον τοῦ πράγματος.
οὗτος γενοῦ· καὶ σιμὸς εἶ γὰρ ἀπὸ τύχης
καὶ μικρός, οἶον ἔλεγεν ὁ θεράπων τότε,
γέρων. ΚΙΧ. ὅς εἰμι γέγονα. ΘΗΡ. πρόσθες, θυγάτριον
'Αλῆθεν ἀπολέσας ἑαυτοῦ τετραετὲς   355
Δρόμωνά τ' οἰκέτην. ΚΙΧ. ἀπολέσας; ΘΗΡ. εὖ πάνυ·
ἁρπασθὲν ὑπὸ λῃστῶν. ΚΙΧ. ἀνέμνησας πάθους
τὸν ἄθλιόν με καὶ φθόρας οἰκτρᾶς ἐμοί·
ΘΗΡ. ἄριστα. τοῦτον διαφύλαττε τὸν τρόπον
τό τ' ἐπιδακρύειν. ἀγαθὸς ἄνθρωπος σφόδρα.   360

(Menander, *Sikyonioi* 343–60)

KICHESIAS   To hell with you –
THERON   (*Good!*) *You're being awkward!*
KICHESIAS   – *Damn you! Do you imagine that Kichesias would do such a thing or would take money from anyone for a wicked act?*
THERON   *Yes – You've got Kichesias of Skambonidai exactly! Charge me money for just that, not for what I was saying just now.*
KICHESIAS   *For what?*
THERON   *As Kichesias of Skambonidai you're speaking much better. You seem to have got the hang of the matter. Be that man; for as it happens you are a snub-nosed little old fellow just as the servant said that time.*
KICHESIAS   *I am the person I was born.*
THERON   *Add 'who lost his four year old daughter and Dromon the servant at Halae'.*
KICHESIAS   *Lost?*
THERON   *Very good – 'kidnapped by pirates'?*
KICHESIAS   *You remind me in my sorrow of my tragedy and a spoliation piteous for me.*
THERON   *Excellent! Keep that style going and the accompanying tears. The fellow's really very good!*

There are hardly any verbal echoes in Plautus' version (*adflere* ~ ἐπιδακρύειν; *lepide hercle adsimulas* ~ εὖ πάνυ; *intellegere* ~ νοεῖν τι…); even when turning iambic trimeters into senarii, Plautus seems to work from memory and from the occasional glance at his model rather than from close scrutiny. Menander's old gentleman has been offered money (unlike Hanno, who is implausibly slave-like in his willingness to participate in a good wheeze, 1086ff.): part of his supposed 'acting' is his outrage at the very suggestion. Plautus drops this, as well as the subtle change to tragic tones when Kichesias breaks down (ἀνέμνησας… ἐμοί). The passages of *Bacchides* which correspond to trimeters of the *Dis exapaton* have been inflated into trochaic septenarii with much verbal fol-de-rol: this passage by contrast is in Plautus' most off-hand style, and yet the verse obtrudes as verse far more than in Menander. It is end-stopped, and Menander's excited chopping of phrases (which makes the division of parts uncertain) has been simplified. Yet even in this bald style there are characteristically Plautine touches absent in Menander. Alliteration marks Milphio's self-importance (1099) and admiration. Menander's ἄριστα... σφόδρα (359f.) becomes a triadic phrase (*eu hercle...Aeolidam subdolum*) which (if the emendation *Aeolidam* be accepted)[1] involves a typical Plautine mythological identification: *fabrica* and *architectinem* are metaphors from a favourite Plautine stock; *superare aliquem* is a characteristic Plautine turn of phrase in exaggerated comparisons.

The view of the *Poenulus* sketched above is new. Even if it is wrong, it has (besides economy) two virtues as an *exemplum*. If Menander, *Sik.* 343ff. is not the model which Plautus had in mind at this point, something very like it was, and characteristic Plautine traits are still well shown by the comparison. Again, the arguments used above are a good example of the kind of diagnostic analysis which we have described (p. 96) as the 'archaeology' of Plautus' plays. This is an intricate matter, and concentrates on traits and clues in Plautus' text which the audience is not invited or expected to notice. For that very reason, this approach must not be thought itself to be dramatic criticism of Plautus, yet it is often mistaken for it. While such analysis is itself of interest for the history of New Comedy, it is for Plautus only an indispensable preliminary to dramatic criticism, an indirect method, which, since we cannot intuitively share the values and assumptions of Plautus' audience, helps to define what Plautus thought important. It is, for example, startling to discover that he values imbroglio and deception for its own sake *so* much more than plot-structure, realistic dialogue and characterization. His plays are in an evidently only very attenuated sense 'translations': many critics from Gellius on have felt that a Menander should not be used thus, and condemned this approach to comedy. Plautus is not even trying to capture Menandrian qualities: he positively rejects them, and therefore cannot be any good. But the comparison of chalk and cheese is not profitable. Where then is the grace and charm of Plautine comedy, if any? It lies in quite different aspects of his drama, to which we now turn.

(iii) *Character and presentation.* Plautus has as strong an aversion from the central repertoire of *persona*-names of New Comedy as from their titles.

---

[1] A new suggestion for the corrupt *crudumque est ollidum* of the MSS; *crudumq· ǫolidam* would have been mistaken for *crudumq··e·olidam* (· *e·* = *est*, *ǫ* = *ae*, *q·* = *que*). The allusion is to 'Sisyphos Aiolides, who was the most crafty of men' (*Iliad* 6.153), and specifically the type of the *aged* trickster (see Roscher *s.n.*) as opposed to Odysseus/Ulysses, himself an Aeolid. Hence support for Leo's *senem* at the line-beginning, where there is a separate corruption.

Chrysalus sings

> non mihi isti placent Parmenones Syri
> qui duas aut tris minas   auferunt eris   (*Bacchides* 649f.)

I do not like your Parmenoes and Syruses who steal (a mere) two or three minae *from their masters.*

In the *Dis exapaton*, Chrysalus was himself a Syros. Plautus only rarely kept a name, e.g. Lydus in the same play. His stage-population are given individual names varying in formation from the possible but unattested (Agorastocles) to the absurd (Pyrgopolynices). Only very few are borrowed from New Comedy. The young man Charinus and old men Callicles, Demipho, Charmides, Simo are allowed to appear in two plays each, but that is the extent of Plautine duplication. Some others known in New Comedy appear once each,[1] but most are kept at bay, down the street, in the house, in the past, in imaginary lists (e.g. Davus, Dromo, Chaerea). Most, however, do not receive even that ghostly tribute (Gorgias, Sostratos, Pythias, etc.). Plautus plays many games in naming his *personae*. The aged Laches of New Comedy makes his only appearance as the second element of the young man's name Philolaches. The Menaechmi twins are named after the mathematician of Syracuse (*fl.* 350 B.C.) who had evolved a method for duplicating regular solids by conic sections; the cook is called Cylindrus. Characters whose names end in *-io* (Acanthio, Ballio, Milphio, Olympio, etc.) and *-lus* (Toxilus, Chrysalus, Dordalus, etc.) are slaves or otherwise disreputable: the patterns seem to be Scipio and Attalus.

Most of Plautus' audience will have had only a vague second- or third-hand acquaintance with New Comedy practice as to names, and for them the more striking contrast will have been with the Atellane farce in which the names of the stock-characters were fixed. By giving his characters individual names, Plautus was drawing a sharp line between the extempore farce and his own entertainments with their fixed scripts and complex musical structure. For us, the contrast with New Comedy practice is the more obvious, and we, who are used to the idea (then new) that a dramatist might invent all his characters' names, might draw the conclusion that the pimps Ballio, Dordalus, Lycus, Labrax, and Cappadox for example are intended to be individual characters each with special traits of his own. This would be wrong. For all the apparent individuation by names quirky and fantastical, the same Atellane-type troupe in fact appears in every play. It is a mistake to look for individual characterization in Plautus, or to regret its absence. At the same time, we must not leave the matter there, for aspects of what we mean by characterization are the very essence of Plautine comedy.

[1] Bacchis, Cario, Lydus, Myrrina, Philaenium, Sosia, Strobilus, Stratophanes; not many among about 150 named inhabitants of Plautinopolis.

Characterization is not a category in its own right. It is a function of five others: the plot, the typology, the musical and metrical form, the diction and the dramatic illusion. In New Comedy, a dramatist began with the germ of a dramatic idea; this involved certain roles. The action, as it was worked out in greater detail, determined which of the traditional stock of named masks – the *dramatis personae* 'masks of the action' – would be suitable; Daos, Laches, Myrrina, etc. It was the same in tragedy, and it is in this context that one should understand Aristotle's assertion of the primacy of the 'story' over 'character' (Arist. *Poetics* 1450a20–2). In proceeding thus New Comedy playwrights were like Goldoni writing for masked Italian *commedia* types rather than, say, Jonson or Molière, whose typology was derived not from appearance, the outer shell, but from a theory of humours, the categories of inner disposition. A playwright might commission a special new mask for a particular purpose, for example the grumpy Knemon of *Dyskolos* or the Carthaginian Himilkon of *Karchedonios*, both Menandrian inventions; these might be used by someone else, and, if popular, join the 'stock'. Essentially, however, New Comedy writers began with a plot and selected the necessary chessmen for their game from a simple typology based on appearance, age, and class as denoted by the named masks. Daos appears in at least eight of sixteen better-known Menander-plays. No doubt he looked the same in each and the Athenian audience knew who he was without being told and how he differed in physiognomy from his fellow-slaves Parmenon, Getas, and Tibeios. This, however, did *not* determine his ethos, at least in the hands of a master like Menander. In one play he is deftly sketched and has a tiny role; in another he is drawn more fully and carefully, and quite differently as a 'character'. So the old bottles might be filled with different wines. The importance of plot and typology of the masked drama being defined thus, the other factors, diction, metrical form, and dramatic illusion were developed in New Comedy to sustain a quiet and relatively prosaic naturalism. This was essential for the subtle and realistic depiction of ordinary contemporaries, the 'mirroring of life' which came to be seen as characteristic of the genre, and towards which Terence sought to bring the reluctant form of comedy as inherited from Plautus and Caecilius.

Plautus' approach to characterization will be understood best if we review in turn the five aspects of the term as defined above. First, as to plot. He did not approach his task like a Menander or his own Pseudolus, who, 'like a poet when he has opened his notebook seeks for what is not, yet finds it' (*Pseud.* 401ff.). The plot is given, and is not the real substance of his plays. He cuts, stretches, squashes, and amplifies. Dramaturgically, all Plautus' plays are far simpler than the early yet complex and finely-handled *Dyskolos* of Menander. The comings and goings have been simplified, and with them, the action. The motive for alteration and expansion is generally Plautus' desire to amplify the farcical aspects of the play at the expense of the pathetic, and in particular to increase in volume and apparent importance the role of the leading slave and of his deception. The plays of known derivation are fairly characteristic of the *œuvre* as a whole in this respect. Love is the *primum mobile*, but not married love; a *Hecyra* would not have attracted Plautus as a model. The lover is represented sympathetically, but farcically; the pathos of his frustration or dejection as depicted by a Menander or Theocritus is shunned entirely. If he loves a *meretrix*, she is a delightful gold-digger; if she returns his affection or is a virgin in distress, money must be had by deceiving Father or a wicked *leno* or *lena* who has richer clients in mind. The slave is promoted to be master-builder or general in devising and administering a trick to outwit the blocking character. If the girl is a wronged citizen, the young man does not know this at first; her separation from her family is explained by themes of exposure or kidnapping, and after the recognition – only sometimes played 'straight' for pathos – she will be betrothed to her lover. Plautus is less fond than Terence of sub-plots and exploration of the relationship of father and son except in its farcical aspect when they are rivals in love; but the ludicrous lust of the *senex amans* never prospers, for Mother finds out and produces her rolling-pin. Thus the same broad themes of love, misapprehension, and deception are as central in Plautus as in New Comedy. Comparison of Plautus with Terence and New Comedy, however, show that a very imperfect impression of the themes, tone, variety, and emphases of New Comedy would be had from Plautine comedy alone. He seeks farce, promotes deception, simplifies relationships, categorizes themes, and is not interested in ethos, social commentary, or the exploration of motives. In adjusting a plot he does not mind loose ends, dramatic anachronism, implausibilities, or minor obscurities, and sometimes he omits the expository prologue even in a recognition play (*Epidicus, Curculio*). The plot is treated as an excuse, not as an end in itself. We turn now to the typology.

Plautus simplifies ethos drastically according to the doctrines of a comic catechism, an absurd catalogue of appropriate behaviour. The central members of the troupe are the *adulescens amans* and his clever slave, most characteristically represented in *Bacchides, Epidicus, Miles gloriosus, Mostellaria, Pseudolus*, and (less successfully) *Poenulus*. The slave is unswervingly loyal to his master, though his own definition of the love of *meretrices* is *damnum merum* 'a dead loss'.[1] The volume and apparent importance of his deception are much inflated. He is *doctus* 'clever', *astutus* 'sophisticated', *malus* 'bad', *nequam* 'good for nothing', and is given to self-glorification, arrogating to himself the status and rights of a citizen, reversing roles with his betters and giving the orders, and, as master-builder and military expert, comparing his

---

[1] E.g. *Cur.* 49, *Poen.* 199, *Men.* 133 (where the lover is speaking with the slave's voice: see below, p. 107).

exploits and strategy with those of kings and epic heroes.[1] The slave is the most internally consistent of Plautus' types, and he has the power to address the audience confidentially without disrupting the dramatic illusion. He is at once a member of the audience and of the cast, the director of the action, and the intermediary between us and the more exotic characters. There is, as it were, no actor behind the mask of the slave.

By contrast the lover is the most schizophrenic of Plautus' characters. His ruling humour as lover is *immodestia*, a lack of a sense of proportion (cf., e.g., *Bac.* 612ff.), and *in propria persona* he will dither, rush, express without warning extravagantly incoherent joy or zestfully indulge in a show of despair (Charinus, *Mer.*), speak impiously of his parents or the gods (Calidorus, *Pseud.*) and beat his slave for no offence (Agorastocles, *Poen.*). The reason is that he is in love, a self-sufficient excuse for anything, for love is represented not as Plato's divine madness but plain if amiable lunacy. The sentiment expressed at Plautus, *Mil.* 1252 and *Poen.* 140f. is a travesty of the generous idea reproduced from Menander by Terence at *Eun.* 880f. The nearest that the lover comes to reflection and ratiocination are the immensely prolix and exuberant arias at *Most.* 84ff. and *Trin.* 223ff.; pathos is entirely avoided.[2] The soliloquy of Mnesilochus at *Bac.* 500–25 is characteristic. This represents two speeches of Sostratos in *Dis exapaton*, one before, the other after an interview with his father which Plautus has dropped in his version (*Dis exapaton* 18ff., 89ff. Sandbach). Sostratos is represented as suffering a turmoil of emotions – disappointment in his friend and bitterness towards the *hetaira*; he is of course mistaken on both points. The tone and means of expression are exactly those of Catullus. He uses short phrases and colloquial language; he turns from apostrophe through reflection to self-address, and at the end of his second speech he is inclined to blame the girl rather than his apparently faithless friend. In all these points one is reminded of Demeas' fine speech at Menander, *Samia* 325–56, elements of which Plautus absurdly echoes at *Asin.* 140ff. (cf. *Sam.* 326, 377ff., 390f.). The actual verbal echoes of Menander in Mnesilochus' speech are minimal, as in Caecilius' operatic version of a father's entrance-speech from Menander's *Plokion*.[3] Mnesilochus begins *in propria persona* as if he were to propound a thesis, 'Which is my worse enemy, he or she?', to be worked out in the manner of Hamlet's 'To be or not to be...?' In fact, he decides at once that the girl is to blame, and forgets all about his friend. In what follows (503ff.) we are not listening to a sad lover – there is no such thing in Plautus – but rather to a *servus* addressed as an *amans* who cracks jokes which being in the first person defeat expectation; put in the third person, they are simply the Plautine slave's

---

[1] Fraenkel (1960) 223–41 and *passim*.

[2] Menandrian lovers also fail to know what is appropriate, but the gentle humour of, e.g., Men. *Dysk.* 52ff., 76ff. is different from anything in Plautus – or Terence.

[3] Gell. 2.23; G.W. Williams (1968) 363–6, Wright (1974) 120–6, Traina (1970) 41–53.

axioms about love and lovers' behaviour. This is the other aspect of the lover's personality: the Plautine lover is ever and again presented as really being a Plautine slave *ornatus*, dressed up, and saying those things which he and we agree in this comic world to be ineptly appropriate for lovers to say. Thus there is a certain depth to Plautus' typology: behind the mask of the *amans* there is not simply an actor, but another *servus callidus*. In this way the domination of the stage by the *servus callidus* is rendered even more extreme than it appears; for *non iucundum est nisi amans facit stulte* 'it isn't funny unless the lover acts stupidly' as the lover Calidorus says (*Pseud.* 238). When *servus* and *amans* merge again (*Bac.* 513), it is to express offended pride in a long, weighty sentence; but no pain or regret with respect to the friend Pistoclerus. That is reserved for a long and sententious intrusion of *flosculi* on the nature of friendship which has no counterpart in the swift and laconically eloquent encounter of the two friends in Menander. It could not have been inferred from the Plautine text that this sententiousness had no direct equivalent in Menander, a salutary proof that Plautus can 'look Greek' even in his own embroidery.

Fathers in Plautus are *anxii* rather than *duri* – Caecilius' harsh fathers were famous (Cic. *Cael.* 16.37) – and their comic office is not willingly to part with a penny. Father is no pantaloon: he is a formidable opponent for the slave. The *senex amans*, on the other hand, a Plautine favourite,[1] is a buffoon in whom both aspects of the young lover appear. The *senex lepidus* has escaped marriage and is Epicurean in outlook, without the parasite's selfishness and greed. For him to love is *facere sapienter* 'do act wisely', the counterpart of the normal idea that it is *facere stulte* 'to act foolishly': and he honours Plautus' favourite deities, Venus and Pietas.[2] The *leno* is extravagantly villainous and mercenary. His task is perfidy, his one aim in life is *lucrum*, profit, and he takes pleasure in telling us so.[3] By implicitly exploiting aspects and features of Roman law Plautus makes him more wicked than perhaps intended by the Greek dramatists. For example in the *Pseudolus*, Ballio is represented as breaking a solemn Roman contract (*sponsio*) in accepting a higher offer for his girl from a rival; in Greek custom it was open to a vendor to accept a higher bid even when a deposit had been paid.[4] Most notably in the *Poenulus*, but also in the *Rudens*, *Curculio*, and *Persa* Plautus implies that a *leno* is breaking the law merely by owning girls whom he knows to be 'freeborn' without specification of the girls' origin. Greek dramatists took care to arrange things so that a former citizeness of

---

[1] *Asinaria, Bacchides, Casina, Mercator, Amphitruo* – a quarter of the *corpus* – have *senes amantes*.

[2] *facere sapienter, Amph.* 289. *Poen.* 1092, inverting the usual definition (Publilius Syrus A 15, 22 *amare et sapere uix deo conceditur*). The sympathy (*Mil.* 638), piety (675, 736f.), and liberality of Periplecomenus are the opposites of the *leno*'s qualities (contrast, e.g., *Poen.* 449ff., 746ff. with the passages cited).

[3] E.g. *Pseud.* 264ff., *Poen.* 746ff., *Rud.* 727, *Persa* 689f.

[4] G. W. Williams (1956) 424–55.

City One is, through exposure or kidnapping, in the power of a *leno* in City Two which has no reciprocal arrangement regarding civil rights with One, precisely to prevent the mere demonstration of the truth about the girl's origin from seeming sufficient to ensure her release and her owner's punishment. Like the *amans*, whose arch-enemy he is without the need of detailed motivation, the *leno* sometimes appears to be a character who is being acted by another *servus callidus*, so zestful is his self-incrimination. You cannot really blame him, it is his job to be like that (e.g. *Pers.* 479, 688; *Pseud.* 351–77; *Rud.* 1343ff.). The hungry parasite is the most explicitly Italian of all the types. The most specifically Italian allusions occur in parasite scenes,[1] not only in respect of food;[2] his language and imagery are gaudy;[3] he is an accomplished rhetorician, but he takes no interest in the *res publica*,[4] for all that he may expound his way of life as a philosophy or an honourable ancestral profession.[5] If he is faithless to his patron, his outrageous parody of self-sufficiency leads from initial complacency to frustration and rejection. Technically he is a free man, but is in fact the spiritual slave, the very opposite of the loyal *servus callidus*. For this reason, we rarely hear the voice of the slave-commentator from behind the parasite's mask, his narrow-spirited dedication to food matches that of the *leno* to profit, and he is consequently an ambiguous figure. The helpful parasite Curculio is an important exception: here Plautus has invested the role with the gusto of a Pseudolus or a Pyrgopolynices. The flattering parasite (*colax*) is represented in Plautus only by Artotrogus in the *Miles gloriosus* (*init.*), and, fleetingly, in scenes where other characters don and doff the role as part of Plautus' play with the typology.[6] The professional soldier (Greek, not a Roman) is presented as vainglorious, selfish, and deluded; it is remarkable that Menander's military characters seem to have been presented in a far less formulaic way.[7] Females in Plautus are 'other' and their psychology as women does not interest him. Apart from Alcumena, presented powerfully as a tragic

[1] E.g. *Cap.* 90 (*porta Trigemina*), 158ff. and 877ff. (Italian towns), 489 (*Velabrum*), 492ff. (cf. *Stich.* 193f.) (*mores barbari*), 790ff. (cf. *Cur.* 280ff.) (praetorian edict).

[2] E.g. *Cap.* 818, 847, 901ff., *Men.* 208ff. (the words are the parasite's), *Cur.* 323ff. On butchers and pork-cuts in Plautus, almost absent from the gourmet-lists of fish-dishes and sweet confections of New Comedy, see Fraenkel (1960) 109, 124f., 141, 408–13.

[3] Bizarre imagery: *Cap.* 153 (*edendi exercitus*), 187 *calceatis dentibus* 'teeth with boots on'; Latin puns: *Cur.* 316 (*uentum*), *Persa* 103 (*Essurio*); mixed metaphors: *Cur.* 318 ('teeth full of rheum, blind jaws'), *Cap.* 109 ('inebriated with repletion'), cf. *Boeotia* fr. 1.9 ('parched with starvation'); prosopopoeia: *Cur.* 338ff., *Cap.* 479ff., *Stich.* 185ff., *Mil.* 61–5; rhythmical effects: *Cap.* 309f.; sub-Stoic paradoxes: *Men.* 95.

[4] *Men.* 451ff., *Persa* 75ff.

[5] *Cap.* 69ff., *Men.* 79ff., *Persa* 53ff., *Stich.* 155ff.; Leo (1906) 441–6.

[6] E.g. Mercury (*Amph.* 515ff.), the *aduocati* in *Poen.*, Romans in disguise.

[7] Pyrgopolynices (*Mil.*), Stratophanes (*Tru.*), Cleomachus (*Bac.*), 'Antamoenides' (*Poen.*), Therapontigonus (*Cur.*), Harpax (*Pseud.*) are all treated with the same brush; in boasting of their prowess, they remind one of the *servi gloriosi*. Plautine soldiers are Macedonians, not Romans; see Shipp (1955) 193–52.

heroine in *Amphitruo*, the *matrona* in her housewifely setting is kept behind doors as much as possible, and appears only in plays where her husband is unfaithful (*Men.*, *Asin.*, *Cas.*) and is severely restricted in her musical presentation. The *virgo* is the opposite of the *amans*, being self-consistent, *modesta*, and given to *docta dicta*.[1] The *meretrix* is exotic, extravagant, and amoral rather than immoral. She is presented as the intellectual equal of the clever slave, being *docta, astuta, callida, faceta, mala, nequam*, and taking the same detached view of love as he. He never aims his tricks at her, and she sometimes helps or herself sustains deceptions (*Mil.*, *Tru.*).

When Plautus had to deal with complex characters in his models, he thought in terms of this simple Atellane-style typology, and mixed traits which are strikingly incompatible by Menander's or Terence's standards. Hanno in the *Poenulus* is perhaps the most extreme case, in whom are the violently disparate elements of *pater pius*, *senex lepidus*, and *servus callidus*. In the same play Adelphasium is dressed as a *meretrix* but is in fact a *virgo*; in her first appearance, the mere fact that she is dressed as a *meretrix* is exploited by Plautus in his episodic expansion of the scene to allow her to behave as a *meretrix*, even though this is incompatible with her role as a whole and involves contradictions and loose ends.[2] Euclio in *Aulularia*, Therapontigonus in *Curculio*, Truculentus in his eponymous play, and many others have had their roles simplified in this way. A character will sometimes explicitly adopt another's characteristic role, e.g. Mercury's inept imitation of the *parasitus* at *Amph.* 515ff.

So much for Plautus' treatment of plot and typology. As we have seen (pp. 85f.) there is a particularly violent contrast between the musical and metrical forms of New Comedy and Plautus. Each of the three modes, speech, recitative, and opera affects the presentation of character. The scale of time and space in the spoken parts (iambic senarii) is closest to the audience's real world. Addresses 'on the doorstep', remarks 'aside', and meetings here are usually reasonably brief; but even in this mode Plautus happily offends against plausibility when telescoping acts (*Cist.* 630/1, *Men.* 880/1) or recasting the dramaturgy (*Poen.* 707ff.) or preparing an episodic insertion (*Poen.* 975ff.). The worlds of recitative (trochaic septenarii) and of song (all the other metres) are much more spacious and elastic. A character on stage will fail to notice a lengthy canticum sung by someone entering (*Bac.* 925ff., *Men.* 966ff.). Running slaves deliver long harangues out of all proportion to the size of the stage.[3]

[1] *Persa* 336–89, *Poen.* 284–312.
[2] *Poen.* 210–329 is integral to the action of the play and based on an episode of the original, but the sequel 330–409 is formless Plautine farce intended to promote Milphio's role. Fraenkel (1960) 253ff. wrongly regarded the whole of 210–409 as lifted from another play.
[3] *Bac.* 832 *tris unos passus* implies a stage about fifty feet wide, if we assume three doors and symmetrical arrangement. Vitruvius, the size of theatres of the imperial era, and the lengths of many harangues by running slaves are misleading evidence.

Ballio's entrance in *Pseudolus* is a memorable expansion of a brief doorstep address, introducing the Roman idea that it is his birthday and presents must be given him (*Pseud.* 133ff.). The imbalance of *Men.* 110ff. and 466ff., 603ff. and 700ff. is due to the different musical presentations. Plautus likes to spin out that split second when two people notice each other,[1] and keeps surprising the audience with his variations of musical form.

Female characters (played by boys) are given highly operatic parts in proportion to their charms: the Bacchis sisters, Palaestra and Ampelisca (*Rudens*), Adelphasium and Anterastilis (*Poenulus*), and others such never merely speak senarii. When women do, e.g. the girl in *Persa*, it is because the mode has been established for the scene by an unsympathetic male character. *Matrona* in *Menaechmi* is a significant exception: she has the initiative at 559ff. and 701ff., but she chooses senarii, a formal hint that we are not to feel too sorry for her. The flowery language of Phoenicium's letter (*Pseud.* 46ff.) in senarii is, as it were, a canticum in reported speech. Conversely, villains like Cappadox (*Cur.*) and Lycus (*Poen.*) or unsympathetic characters like the tutor Lydus in *Bacchides* live in the worlds of senarii and septenarii. It is part of Ballio's outrageous charm in *Pseudolus* that, very unconventionally for a *leno*, he bursts on us in song at his first entrance. Even he spends most of his time in the more prosaic modes. Pivotal characters, the lovers and their slaves, are equally at home in all three modes, e.g. Pseudolus and Calidorus, Tranio and Philolaches (*Mostellaria*). It is important that the mere reader be careful to allow for bold, unpredictable changes of mood and pace which are an expression of the musical structure. The plot is not only distorted by truncations and additions, there is a certain variable geometry of space, time, and mood, a more than Elizabethan variety of tone. In *Poen.* iii.3 we may almost be persuaded that we are eavesdropping on an internally stylized but self-consistent representation of a street-scene; there is no question of that in v.4 of the same play, where we are assaulted by a kaleidoscopic mixture of the most varied emotions and impressionistic presentation. The metrical presentation of a *persona* is thus not an insignificant element of his characterization and is a major aspect of the dramatic experience.

Plautine diction, the fourth aspect of characterization, is not intended to sustain the prosaic realism of a Menander. In canticum and recitative Plautus was normally embroidering and filling out trimeters in the prolix and alliterative manner evident at *Bac.* 496–500 ~ *Dis exapaton* 11–16. Even his senarii are by comparison with Menander's trimeters emphatically a verse-diction, not a mere analogue for prose. Here he is like Naevius. End-stopping is the norm; the movement and weight of the verse are elements of the meaning;

---

[1] *Bac.* 534ff. (contrast *Dis exapaton* 101), *Amph.* 292ff. (recitative); *Persa* 13ff. (canticum); *Poen.* 975ff. (senarii).

obsolescent forms are artificially exploited at line-end to facilitate scansion
(e.g. *siem* = *sim, laudarier* = *laudari*). Word-order and syntax however relate
directly to contemporary speech, so that, e.g., hyperbaton is significant when it
occurs. Contrary to a common opinion, Plautus' language is not in any sense
vulgar. In vocabulary, for example, *lumbi* 'bottom' occurs, but not *culus* 'arse',
and words like *fabulari* which disappear from polite diction after Terence but
survive in Romance (> Fr. *faibler*, Sp. *hablar*) were stylistically neutral in
Plautus. Greek borrowings and 'neat' Greek are admitted, the latter (like
obscene jokes) only just enough to make one wonder why there is not more;
this Greek is sub-literary Doric and is attributed almost exclusively to the lower
orders.[1] Here is an example of the internal social differentiation of the stage-
language, and it is a question that would reward investigation whether the
greater variety of Plautine syntax relative to the classical language is also to
some extent socially determined.[2] Plautus was quite capable of writing well-
sustained complex sentences (e.g. *Amph.* 1ff., the longest in Plautus[3]) and
could affect an almost Terentian telegraphic style (*Mer.* 562ff., *Trin.* 1078ff.);
normally, however, when he wishes to express emotion in any of his modes,
he does so not by those means which would convey the impression of real life
overheard, for example, studied brevity, broken utterance, and baldness of
expression, but rather a bludgeoning prolixity, exuberance of imagery, verbal
inventiveness, bizarre identifications, and elevation of the tone to that of tragic
discourse; borrowing elements of archaic and public diction, with festoons of
alliteration and assonance. Lastly, Plautine diction is characterized by its great
variety of resources. Any one of these, e.g. the use of riddle-jokes, of legal
terms and ideas, of particular diminutive or adverb formations, etc., will be
found by itself to be less common overall than anticipated. Terence's three
main alterations of the inherited stage-diction were to loosen the movement of
the verse, to reduce but not eliminate the aural exuberances of a Plautus, and
to exploit a smaller number of resources but with greater internal variety and
absolute frequency.

The last and most remarkable feature of Plautine comedy bearing on the
question of characterization is its setting and dramatic illusion. There was no
point in inviting a Roman audience to 'imagine that this is Phyle in Attica', as
Menander's Pan (*Dysk.* 1ff.); the evocations would be lost. Plautus' plays are
nominally set in 'Athens', 'Epidamnus', even 'Aetolia', but in fact we are
always in the same *ciuitas graecoromana*, a universal city as large as the
civilized world, the contemporary *oecumene*. Celts, Scyths, and Spaniards are

[1] Shipp (1953) 105–12, (1955) 139–52. For example *Pseud.* 483ff. ναὶ γάρ is a combination of
affirmative particles never found in written Greek, and a word like *thermipolium* 'bistro, café' is
borrowed from a Greek word which no doubt existed in southern Italy, but is unrecorded in literature.
[2] Arnott (1972) 58–64 broaches the question of linguistic characterization in Plautus.
[3] A parody of the *exordium* of a magistrate's speech, cf. Cic. *Pro Murena init.*

mentioned as outsiders, but the inhabitants of Plautinopolis have never heard of Rome and Italy, only of *barbari* and *barbaria*. Romans are mentioned explicitly only once in a passage of vigorous Plautine quality but of doubtful authenticity, a jokingly uncomplimentary allusion (*Poen.* 1314), as are all veiled allusions to sections of the audience.[1] There is no praise or celebration of the city as was traditional in Attic comedy. The stage-city is remarkably objective and cosmopolitan. The caricature of a Greek sketched by Curculio (280ff.) is not at all chauvinistic, and characteristically the humour is that a *persona* dressed as a *Graecus palliatus* is made to deliver a parody of a praetorian edict against *Graeci palliati*. We have alluded (p. 94) to the remarkably sympathetic treatment of Carthage and Aetolia in *Poenulus*; Aetolians are again treated with sympathy in *Captivi*.

The dramatic time is the present, and the place is an ambiguous 'here'. Plautus does not mechanically reproduce unintelligible allusions from his models, or simply keep situations which depend on alien assumptions, customs or laws. Either he explains them (*Cas.* 68ff., *Stich.* 446ff.), or, more commonly, he assimilates and adjusts the material to Italian usage. Thus Ballio is supposed to be celebrating his birthday in *Pseudolus*; his demand for gifts gives the opportunity for the famous tableau i.2. But the giving of presents on annual birthdays was a Roman, not a Greek custom. Exotic Greek pastries such as abound in Athenaeus' citations of New Comedy are supplemented and supplanted by Italian hams and pork-cuts. First-cousin marriages do not appear in Plautus or Terence at all, yet marriages of this degree of kin were commonplace in upper-class Athenian society and therefore in New Comedy. Plautus implicitly exploits concepts and formulae of Roman law in jokes of all kinds[2] and sometimes he exploits Roman legal assumptions which may distort the plot of his model (*Poen., Pseud.*). Plautus inflates the Roman law to fill his comic city so that it is a basic rule that a manumitted slave is supposed to become a citizen of 'Athens' by virtue of the manumission. That is Roman law disguised.[3] Plautus similarly represents 'freeborn' persons held as slaves in this city as having an absolute legal right to freedom, if they have been kidnapped; this too is inflation of the Roman law, and thus by accident, for the first time in history, freedom and free birth are represented as legal absolutes which need not be defined in terms of the citizenship of this or that city. As the first popular

[1] Often marked by *iste* and/or *ubi sunt. . .?*, cf. Fraenkel (1960) 136ff.

[2] For example, slaves claim a pedigree (*Amph.* 365), the right of *quiritatio* (*Amph.* 375), of making sacrifice (*Pseud.* 108), of owning property (*Pseud.* 108, cf. Ter. *H.T.* 86, Cic. *Rep.* 2.59, *Att.* 9.6.3 for the amusing anticlimax), of mancipation (*Men.* 1077), of making *sponsiones* (*Pseud.* 114–18). They and others pun (*Mil.* 611), joke (*Trin.* 267 – the divorce formula, applied to Love), and develop conceits (*Tru.* 141ff., *Trin.* 1037ff.) in ways that show Plautus' audiences were well acquainted with quite technical aspects of the law. See Watson (1971) *passim*.

[3] *Persa* 474ff., *Poen.* 372, where the promise that Adelphasium will become a *ciuis Attica atque libera* is merely a fancy way of saying that on manumission she will be a *ciuis libertina*.

writer to represent the idea of free birth as a practically enforcible legal universal, Plautus deserves a modest note in the history of ideas in the immediately post-Eratosthenic world. These uses of Roman assumption, custom, and law are means by which Plautus focuses his plays in the *hic et nunc* of his audience. On the other hand he avoids identifying the scene too explicitly as the *real* Rome, except in prologues and *entr'actes*. We are not to think of his *ciuitas* as fluctuating between Greek and Italian poles. It is homogeneous. A festival takes place in honour of Venus, but its occasion is not the native Vinalia but exotic Aphrodisia. *Praetores, comitia, senatus* may be mentioned alongside *dicae, agoranomi, strategi* because in contemporary usage they also denoted Greek institutions as well as Roman; not, however, consuls, censors, quaestors, flamens or the like. There are contemporary allusions in Plautus, probably more than we can detect, for those that can be grasped are always fleeting (*Cas.* 980), indirect (*Tru.* 75), and even deliberately garbled (*Men.* 407–12, *Poen.* 663–5).

The plot, typology, musical presentation, diction, and dramatic illusion of Plautine comedy are designed to subvert the regularities and realism of New Comedy. The real substance of Plautine drama is the 'play' which he constantly maintains with us as to whether we are unseen observers of real life or not. Many a scene, especially in senarii, is set up to invite us to suppose a Menandrian or Terentian mode of presentation, in which a glass wall separates us from the characters, who act, suffer, and discuss as if we were not there. Plautus delights in breaking this illusion in different ways. Here the characteristic presentation of lover, slave, and *leno* are important. Besides straightforward ruptures of the dramatic illusion there are confidential asides from characters who acknowledge our presence but seem to think we are Greeks (*Poen.* 597–9, contrast *Cur.* 288ff.). Plautus' most salient characteristic is his variety, an un-Hellenic trait picked up and sustained in satire. This is so marked that it should not be seen merely as a failure of Terentian art, but as a positive principle, alien to what was to become the main European tradition. Plautus deliberately commits all those errors which Hamlet condemns in bad actors.[1]

Hamlet's theory of comedy as a 'mirror of life' with paradigmatic value can be traced through Gellius, Quintilian, Horace, Cicero, and Terence to the practice of Menander, of whom Aristophanes of Byzantium, Plautus' contemporary, wrote 'O Menander and Life, which of you imitated the other?' The theory is implicit in the Hellenistic tags which call the *Odyssey* a fine mirror of human life and liken the *Iliad* to a tragedy, the *Odyssey* to a comedy. Plautus was not unaware of the view that comedy might have an educational as well as an entertaining function. At the end of the uniquely womanless *Captivi* he sententiously recommends the play to the audience on the ground that 'poets make few comedies like this, by which the good become better'.

---

[1] Shakespeare, *Hamlet* III ii *init*.

He lists several objectionable themes and *loci* which are absent from the play: the joke is that these are the normal material of his *œuvre* at large. The irony here and Plautus' disruptive treatment of New Comedy show that he put no weight on the alleged educational value of comedy: and if he needed an academic justification, he might have quoted Eratosthenes' view that the end of poetry was not moral improvement but the involvement of the audience in the entertainment.[1] From Plato's time we find in discussions of imaginative or fictional art the loaded terms ψεῦδος 'lie' and ἀπάτη 'deceit' which can imply that the artist's task is to trick or deceive his audience. Plautus might be said to apply this in a new way. The plots of his plays are not to be seen as coherent wholes, but as series of episodes of unpredictably various pace, mode, and tone and ambiguous presentation. His characters are not intended to deceive us uniformly into imagining that they are real or credible. There is a constant 'play' between the author and his audience on this point. The characters – or is it the actors? – know that we know that they are not real. As double and triple deceivers, they take pleasure in pretending to be what they seem, ever and again catching us out by reminding us that they are not, but never quite frankly admitting in the course of the action that they are really Romans like you and me.

Caecilius Statius

Caecilius (d. 168 B.C.) dominated the comic theatre between the ages of Plautus and Terence. His first efforts, perhaps put on around 190 B.C., had been failures, but success came through the support and persistence of L. Ambivius Turpio, who proudly recalls this when speaking on behalf of Terence's *Hecyra*. Caecilius was also a friend of Ennius, and these two playwrights were the first to benefit from the activities of literary scholars: there was no doubt about the number and authenticity of their productions; earlier playwrights, especially Plautus, were less fortunate. The scripts of Caecilius and Ennius soon found a place in the school syllabus; Cicero assumes that his jurors and correspondents have read them as well as seen them on the stage (cf. *Opt. gen. orat.* 6.18).

Volcacius Sedigitus (*c.* 100 B.C.) counted Caecilius as the funniest Roman playwright; yet he is also praised for his *grauitas*, moral earnestness (Hor. *Epist.* 2.1.59), his emotional power (Varro *ap.* Charis. in *GLK* I 241.28), and the quality of his plots (Varro, *Sat.* 399). Cicero criticizes his Latinity (*Att.* 7.3.10, *Brut.* 258); Gellius compares several passages of his *Plocium* with the corresponding passages of Menander in an important and carefully thought out essay (*N.A.* 2.23), much to Caecilius' discredit. The fragments are too brief to enable us to recognize, let alone to reconcile, the various points for which Caecilius is praised; and they are certainly not characteristic of the *Plocium-*

---

[1] Pfeiffer (1968) 166f.

fragments. These are thoroughly Plautine. A Menandrian monologue has been converted into a farcical canticum, while other exchanges quoted by Gellius have been vulgarized with jokes that recall the tone of Plautus' *Asinaria*. Unfortunately we have no means of knowing whether the *Plocium* was an early or late work, or whether it is representative, or whether and in what directions Caecilius' style developed over the years. Nevertheless, and with all due caution, one can point to a number of features of his work taken as a whole which suggest an intermediary position between Plautus and Terence, not only in time, but also in technique.

At least a third of his output – probably upwards of fifty plays in about twenty-five years – represents Menander. The titles of his plays fall more easily into the well-defined categories of New Comedy than Naevius' or Plautus'; most are simply the Greek title retained, or simply Latinized. Terence, Turpilius, and others followed this example. It is an aesthetically significant change, for it implies the identity of the Latin play and its model, and invites comparisons of the kind made by Gellius in a way avoided by Plautus. The slave appears to have been demoted from the prominent status with which Plautus and Naevius had endowed him. None of the plays is named after him (*Davos* is a corrupt title). Caecilius also gave up Plautus' freedom in naming his characters and apparently kept exclusively to the main stock names of New Comedy. While in most points, e.g. word-formation and articulation of the verse, Caecilius is like his seniors, he favours the line-cadence ... ⏑⏑⏑ ᗡ significantly more often than they. In these points he anticipates Terentian traits. Terence omits Caecilius' name when he appeals to others' example to defend his own interference with the dramatic structure of a model (*An.* 18), but it would he hazardous to combine this with Varro's praise of Caecilian plots, or the trimmed role of the slave, to infer that Caecilius kept specially close to his models. To judge from the fragments in general, even the late Caecilius can have contributed little to the revolution in style represented by Terence's *Andria*, which, according to a dubious story, was read and approved by the aged Caecilius.

This revolution was abortive. The old, full-blooded style represented by Caecilius was at least as influential as Terence's in the work of Sextus Turpilius, the last important writer of *palliatae*, and in the *togatae* of Afranius; and this exuberant style was still the only one favoured in the scripted mimes and Atellane farces of the first century B.C.

Terence

(i) *Terence's aims and models.* Terence regarded Plautus, Caecilius, and his own adversary Luscius Lanuvinus as old-fashioned; it was a fault that they did not even try to imitate the direct, accurate, and charming qualities of

Menander, but distorted the mirror of life by indulging on the one hand in any old comic business, and on the other in tragic bombast (cf. Gellius on Caecilius, Gell. 2.23.12). Terence cites from Luscius the case of a rumbustious running slave as an example of the one, and an overdone mad scene for the other.[1] Terence did not wish to eliminate such things, but to tame them (*An.* 338ff., a running slave; *Ad.* 789f., anger). He wanted to make plays without 'faults' (*H.T.* 29), and he probably would have approved of Hamlet's advice to the Players in respect of technique, theory, and the distinction of the judicious and the vulgar spectator.

Terence's first play, the *Andria* of 166 B.C., is conventional in theme – pregnancy, recognition, marriage – but strikingly new in treatment and ambition. That Terence should have interfered extensively with the plot of Menander's *Andria* was not in itself new. As he pointed out he was following Naevius, Plautus, and Ennius. Luscius Lanuvinus had evidently given up the freedom of older writers to add themes, scenes, and characters; *contaminari non decere fabulas*, one ought not to 'spoil' plays (*An.* 9–21). Otherwise, Terence could have retorted *tu quoque*. In fact, he criticizes Luscius (and, implicitly, Menander) for not changing the legally (but not necessarily dramatically) illogical order of a pair of speeches in Menander's *Thesaurus* (*Eun.* 10ff.). The term *contaminatio* has been coined from this passage and *H.T.* 17 and used by modern scholars as if it had been a current technical term for the addition of alien material from a particular Greek source to a main original, or even the joining of two whole Greek plays.[2] We have direct evidence that Plautus did sometimes write in the former manner (see p. 101), but there is no proof external or internal that comedians welded whole plays. In fact, *contaminare* is merely the quotation of Luscius' abusive description of Terence's particular procedure. If *contaminatio* as a technical term is to be used in future, it should be redefined to denote all those ways in which a Roman playwright might 'mess about' with his model.

Terence's arguments were not intended to be fair, but successful. Half-truths were adequate material. While there are superficial similarities between Plautus' and Terence's procedures, the motives and execution of the two playwrights differed fundamentally, and Terence (though he does not admit it) disliked what he called the negligence of a Plautus.

The first scene of the *Andria* is a dialogue between a father and a trusted freedman. This relationship, unique in comedy, is depicted in a humane and liberal manner as interesting in itself. The dramatic function of the freedman, however, is merely to listen to the suspicions and intentions of the father. In

[1] Ter. *H.T.* 31ff., cf. Plaut. *Amph.* 984ff., *Cur.* 280ff., *Mer.* 111ff.; Ter. *Pho.* 6ff., cf. *Men.* 835ff.
[2] See Ludwig (1968) 169ff.; Beare (1964) 96–108, 310–12.

the original *Andria* the father was alone and narrated all this in a long monologue. But in the *Perinthia*, a play of Menander which Terence alleges was
virtually identical in plot but different in 'style', the first scene was a conversation between mother and father. Terence says that he has taken 'what suited'
from the *Perinthia*, and he makes it sound as though this was the source of all
the alterations which Luscius criticized. Terence's commentator Donatus was
hard put to it to find any material or ideas specifically from the *Perinthia*, and
attributes to it the idea of a dialogue. Even so Terence's substitution of a freedman for the wife is a substantial independent change. The scene as a whole,
although the first, is among the best of all those where Terence can be seen to
differ from his models; and yet, even here, the integration is not quite perfect.
The father wants Sosia to counteract his slave Davus' influence on his son
(50, 168f.), but nothing comes of this; and the integration of the scene with its
sequel is not quite right.[1]

The other major change in the *Andria* was the introduction of a young man
Charinus and his slave Byrria. In Menander the man called Simo by Terence
(he rings the changes quite pointlessly on Menander's names) tried to force
Pamphilus' hand with respect to his unadmitted liaison with the girl next door
by pretending that Pamphilus shall marry a friend's daughter 'today'. The girl
next door, who was delivered of Pamphilus' baby during the play, was in fact
an Athenian citizen, and so could marry Pamphilus; the friend's daughter was
left unmarried at the end of the original. Neither girl actually appeared on stage.
Charinus' role is to be the friend's daughter's suitor and to marry her at the
end, after misapprehension as to Pamphilus' intentions. Thus a considerable
sub-plot is added to the action. It is Menandrian in character – Charinus'
misapprehensions are like those of Sostratos in the *Dis exapaton* (see p. 107) –
but the material in question cannot derive from the *Perinthia* in any simple
sense, unless Terence's allegation about the similarity of the plays is wholly
misleading. Terence's main reason for the addition was 'that there should not
be an element of sadness in the rejection of the girl without a husband and
Pamphilus' marriage to another' (Don. *ad An.* 301); that is an aesthetic reason,
and as such interesting: Terence thought that he could improve on Menander
in Menander's own terms – ethos and structure – and this is the earliest known
straightforward case in Roman literature of *aemulatio*, competition with Greeks
on their own terms. A secondary reason may have been a certain lack of confidence on Terence's part in the simple and unadorned plot of Menander's
Andria. We may question Terence's success in both taste and execution. His
main motive reveals some sentimentality and the confusion of artificiality with
structural neatness. Again, although we never see Glycerium, she matters to
us because of what we are told about her, because she has her baby in our hear-

---

[1] *sequor* or *sequar* at 171? cf. 204, 404.

ing, and because of the faithful Mysis' concern; it was dramatically right in Menander that the other girl and her father should have been relegated to an address 'down the road', for out of sight is out of mind, and if the girl had any real emotional presence, Terence's point might have been valid. In fact, her Menandrian function was simply as a threat to Pamphilus and Glycerium. Terence has kept this arrangement, but by giving the girl an admirer he has complicated matters. Something must be done to make us take an interest in the girl; the rather empty exclamations of the colourless Charinus are not good enough. A single appearance would have sufficed. The additions can be isolated from the main composition fairly easily, and their technical execution falls short of the Menandrian excellence emulated here by Terence. One example must suffice. Charinus and Byrria enter at 301, Pamphilus being 'left over' from the previous scene. He is given no proper reason for failing to observe the new-comers, and his integration into the conversation at 318 is unmotivated and arbitrary.[1] Menander did not compose thus – but Plautus did.

There are no substantial Terentian additions to the plays turned from origi-nals by Menander's admirer Apollodorus of Carystus, *Hecyra*, 'The mother in law', Terence's second play, unsuccessfully staged in 165 B.C., and only given a fair hearing at its third showing, in 160 B.C., and *Phormio*, his fifth, a version of *Epidikazomenos*, 'The suitor' (161 B.C.). The complex and tightly-knit *Heauton timorumenus*, 'The self-tormentor', his third play (163 B.C.) is the only Menander-original which has not been filled out. The *Eunuchus*, staged very successfully in 161 B.C., is from a Menandrian original in which a sympathetic *hetaira* Chrysis was obliged to accept the unwelcome attentions of an admirer – much to her lover Chairestratos' chagrin – because he was in possession of a young girl who had been brought up by Chrysis' deceased mother and who, as Chrysis believed, was really an Athenian citizen. Her problems were to play along with the suitor until she might gain custody of the girl; to restrain Chairestratos' consequent jealousy; and to find the girl's relatives. Chrysis having achieved the first two objects and nearly accomplished the third, the girl is raped in Chrysis' house by Chairestratos' nasty young brother, who has gained access by disguising himself as a eunuch; this débâcle was resolved by the marriage of the two on the establishment of the girl's identity. It may be conjectured that Chairestratos' rival was not a wholly unsympathetic figure. Menander would have been characteristically economical and subtle if he had made the rival the mysteriously deceased merchant of Terence's play; he brought Chrysis from Samos to Athens and set her up there in luxury (*Eun.* 119ff.). If he had some claim on our sympathy, the arrangement at the end of the play by which the courtesan shares her favours between the two lovers would be less unsatisfactory than it appears in Terence. For Terence has

---

[1] The dramaturgy at 404–31 is again rather crude.

substituted for Menander's rival a vainglorious soldier Thraso and his parasite Gnatho; this is not only an addition but also a substitution of alien material, and is more firmly integrated than the Charinus-theme of *Andria*. Terence claims as his only alteration that he has taken these characters from Menander's *Colax*, 'The toady' (*Eun.* 30ff.), but this is a gross oversimplification. His purpose was to enliven the action, and he has exploited perceptibly more various features of the traditional stage-language and business than in his previous work.[1]

These features represent a successful concession to the public which had rejected *Hecyra*, for his soldier and parasite are quite strongly drawn. However there is no technical improvement; for example, the advice which Gnatho gives Thraso at 439ff. would be strictly logical only if the girl were still in their possession, and the entry at 454 of Thais (Menander's Chrysis) is poorly motivated.[2] Terence's addition of a scene from Diphilus' *Synapothneskontes*, 'Companions in death', to his version of Menander's second *Adelphoi*, his last play (161 B.C.), is similar in intention and execution, though less ambitious; the scene in question represents the forcible abduction of a girl from a protesting *leno*, another stock-figure evidently beloved of the public. All the same, Terence does not represent him in a farcical Plautine manner, dedicated to *lucrum*, but as the victim of a robbery for which he is duly and justly compensated. Again the scene is not perfectly integrated; it represents as happening 'now' the consequence of what at 88ff. was represented (as in Menander) as having happened some time since; Sannio is 'spare' in ii.3–4; the theme of the girl's alleged freedom at 191ff. is dramatically irrelevant and illogically handled; we ought to be made aware earlier that Aeschinus is seizing the girl not for himself but for his brother. Evidently such things did not worry the Roman public. The end of the play has been rendered more farcical than in Menander, as in the *Eunuchus*: the liberal Micio is represented as a comic butt and unwilling bridegroom, as if good sense were on the side of the neurotic and authoritarian Demea.[3]

Thus a certain development may be discerned in Terence's treatment of plot. He began with ambitious notions of presenting and improving on Menander in his own terms by making alien additions for aesthetic reasons (*Andria*), and changing the emphasis of the *palliata* in the direction of psychological realism (*Hecyra*). He never gave up these ideals, but was obliged to make compromises with the groundlings. The *Heauton* was to be a play without aesthetic faults, and was, like the failed *Hecyra*, a quiet play (*stataria*) without parasites, soldiers, and *lenones*; but its plot was much more various and complex,

[1] E.g. *Eun.* 270f., cf. Plaut. *Pseud.* 457, *Epid.* 126f.

[2] It would be better if she entered wondering 'Where can Chremes be?', cf. 204f. The 'asides' in the siege-scene are awkward by Menandrian standards (1053–60).

[3] Rieth (1964), Martin (1976) 26–9.

and even spectacular – Bacchis' entrance is excellent theatre. Nevertheless this was not enough; those who deserted the *Hecyra* may have yawned at *Heauton*. The *Phormio* is taken from a sparkling and lively piece, and, unlike Terence's other plays, is dominated by a single strong character.[1] It is noteworthy that Terence felt the need to justify his change of the title of the original by pointing this out; the play could be seen in the Roman tradition of a *motoria* like *Pseudolus*, where the dominion of the slave was due to the Roman dramatist. In his *Eunuchus* and *Adelphoe* his alien additions and his adjustments of the final scenes show no technical improvement. This did not matter, for his purpose was to strengthen the variety and farcical element to please a conservative public unconcerned with niceties of structure.

(ii) *Techniques and tone.* Plautus had sometimes dropped an expository prologue (*Trinummus*), even in recognition plays (*Epidicus, Curculio*); Terence made this a rule, for the models of all five of his recognition plays as well as the *Adelphoe* had expository prologues identifying persons to be found, and explaining circumstances: thus the audience was able to appreciate ironies arising from their superior knowledge. Terence's departure from Greek practice has imposed re-casting of material in all the plays, particularly in the early scenes, and while it affords Terence the opportunity for some clever foreshadowing (*An.* 220ff.), it also introduces surprises of questionable dramatic merit – the arrival of Crito in *Andria*, Phormio's knowledge of Demipho's double life, the discovery that Ctesipho is the lover in *Adelphoe*. The omissions also lead to un-Menandrian obscurities, for example the unexplained detective-work by which Thais (Menander's Chrysis) had found Chremes and identified him as the likely brother of her protégée in the *Eunuchus*. Again, Terence follows Roman practice in running together and adjusting the act-divisions of his originals, and though Terence is more careful about this than Plautus, here too he fails to hide his traces (*H.T.* 170f., *Ad.* 511ff.). Terence has only a very small amount of non-iambo-trochaic canticum (*An.* 481ff., 625ff., *Eun.* 560, *Ad.* 610ff.), a significant shift towards the more prosaic voice of New Comedy away from the styles of Plautus and Caecilius; but the fact that there is any canticum at all, that only half the dialogue is in spoken iambic senarii, that the rest is in longer iambo-trochaic metres, often used in a new way and certainly 'sung' – these contrast Terence as strongly with New Comedy practice as with his Roman predecessors, within whose firmly established tradition he remains. He evidently followed his predecessors in regularly working up a good deal of trimeter-dialogue into longer, musically-presented Roman metres. These exhibit a somewhat more prolix and decorated manner than his senarii, and this too is an inheritance. On the other hand, he could be far more faithful over

---

[1] Arnott (1970) 32–57.

longer passages than any that can be confidently cited from Plautus. Thais'
discovery that Chaerea has raped Pamphila is such a passage.[1] Sometimes he
would implicitly Romanize a detail for the sake of comprehensibility or
immediacy,[2] but never with the gusto of Plautus. Sometimes he remodelled
a passage with a rather pusillanimous eye to Roman *decorum*: a dialogue between
a respectable wife and a prostitute is reported, not presented; a disappointed
lover contemplates not suicide but flight.[3] Terence avoids themes involving
aged or middle-aged lovers, and none of his Syruses or Parmenos steals even
those two or three *minae* which Plautus' Chrysalus regarded as such small beer.
From the few brief lines that can be compared directly with their originals and
from general comparison, it is clear that Terence often enfeebled the specific
quality of Menander by generalization, even where this was unnecessary: the
midwife at *An.* 483–5 gives her instructions in general and rhetorical form,
whereas her Menandrian counterpart spoke with a properly crone-like intimacy
and recommended the new mother to take 'the yolk of four eggs' (*Men.*
fr. 37 K–Th). At *H.T.* 64, on the other hand, it was essential to give up the
allusion to the setting of the play in Halai; but it is a weakness of all Terence's
plays that they take place nominally '*in his regionibus*', i.e. an undefined
'Athens'. Terence avoids the means which Plautus used to specify his plays
and actually goes beyond Menander in isolating his cast from contact with the
audience. He never solved the problem which his rejection of the older style
involved: Afranius, who greatly admired Terence (Macrob. 6.1.4), may have
done better here. An epigram of Julius Caesar praises Terence as *puri sermonis
amator* 'a lover of refined diction', but criticizes him as 'half-Menander' (*o
dimidiate Menander*) because of his lack of drive (*uis*, not *uis comica*).[4] This is
a fair point. Terence's alterations do not compensate for his failure to focus and
particularize adequately.

It is certainly mistaken, in the present writer's opinion, to interpret any of
the alterations reviewed as having deep spiritual significance, or to credit
Terence with the communication, even the invention, of a new conception of
reason, reasonability, and relationships (*humanitas*) that differed essentially
from ideas already present in Menander and widely diffused in the post-
Eratosthenic *oecumene*.[5] Plautus and Ennius do not use *homo*, *humanus* in the

[1] *Eun.* 817–922, cf. Men. *Dysk.* 233–81 for the dramaturgy.

[2] *Eun.* 255ff., an Italian market complete with butchers (cf. p. 109, n. 2); 319, the praetorian
edict.

[3] Ter. *Hec.* 816–40, *Ad.* 275, Don. *ad loc.*; Ludwig (1968) 176.

[4] Suet. *Vita Terenti* 7. The tag *vis comica* 'comic strength' is a mistake deriving from false punctu-
ation: *lenibus atque utinam scriptis adiuncta foret uis,* | *comica ut aequato uirtus polleret honore* | *cum Graecis
neue hac despectus parte iaceres*; as if Caesar meant that Terence failed in *uirtus* compared with the
Greeks rather than *uirtus comica*.

[5] Too much has been made of this alleged aspect of Terence, especially by Italian writers since
Croce. See Ludwig (1968) 169f., 175, 178.

loaded sense which we find in Terence, but that does not mean that they were unaware of the concept of the community of the wise and good; indeed that is an essential aspect of their cosmopolitan outlook. The inference to be made is rather that the usage had become fashionable in the 170s and 160s in the upper-class philhellene circles in which Terence grew up, and that it was a loan-translation of ἄνθρωπος, ἀνθρώπινος 'human(e)' as long since used in Greek, not least in Menander, whom the Roman pupils of such teachers as Chilon (Plut. *Cat. Maj.* 20.5) will no doubt have been reading as part of their syllabus. Since the nearest Latin translation of φιλανθρωπία would have to be something clumsy like *studium hominum*, the abstract corresponding to *humanus* came to be used instead, *humanitas*. Terence was not leading but reflecting contemporary polite usage and the most that could be attributed to him is the popularization of the usage.

We have used the terms 'upper-class philhellene circles' and 'polite usage' advisedly. Scholars have questioned the existence of the so-called 'Scipionic Circle' and pointed out that that phrase was only coined by Bernhardy in 1850 to denote Scipio Aemilianus' cultured friends (cf. Cic. *Amic.* 69).[1] There is some danger here of over-emphasis. Of course there never was an exclusive club or *salon* called the 'Scipionic Circle' (if anyone should think that), but nevertheless Scipio Aemilianus did count C. Laelius and C. Lucilius, who were his social equals, and the philosopher Panaetius and the historian Polybius, his inferiors, as personal friends on an equal footing. Polybius describes his relationship as respected teacher and friend of Aemilianus in a moving passage (Polyb. 32.9). From the intellectual point of view *humanitas* cut across social divisions and required that all of merit should be equal citizens in the Republic of Letters. Terence himself had friends in high places who took this view; whether these included or centred on Scipio is unimportant. *Humanitas*, of which a Greek education was an essential part, was admired by young Romans destined for high things in Terence's time, and, after Pydna, the practical advantages to the ruling class of a cosmopolitan education were becoming more than ever obvious.

(iii) *Language and style: Terence's achievement.* Luscius criticized Terence for having a 'thin' style, from which it may be inferred that he himself composed in the full-blooded traditional manner. This 'thin' style was, however, Terence's most remarkable and important achievement, for it was, together with his new and less insistently varied musical presentation, the essential medium for realistic characterization. Even Plautus' most consistent characters, Euclio (*Aul.*) and Hegio (*Capt.*), fail to convince us that they are real because they are writ too large, and thoroughly enjoy all their emotions indiscriminately.

[1] See Astin (1967) 295–306.

The noisy prolixity of the older style is such that there is no scope for fleeting and ironic retrospective verbal allusion as there is in Terence (e.g. Ter. *H.T.* 919/70; *An.* 586/503; *Ad.* 934/107). Terence's achievement is the more remarkable, as his medium is fashioned by numerous small adjustments, some in this direction, some in that, within a traditional and homogeneous stage-language which had been developed for different purposes.

Terence preserves this homogeneity and even emphasizes it, so that slaves do not speak with an accent different from that of their betters. Rhythm is still used as a component of the meaning of a verse (e.g. *Pho.* 429f., *An.* 767, *Eun.* 190), but generally Terence seeks to make his medium more Menandrian by under-emphasizing its movement. This is achieved in a number of ways; there is a significant overall reduction in clash of ictus and accent, and such clashes are distributed more evenly inside the verse than in Plautus; enjambement of sense from line to line and change of speaker are exploited more freely and variously. Some forms archaic already for Plautus, e.g. *-ĕrunt* as a line-end, are given up in the diction of the plays, but others, e.g. the line-end type *. . .nullu' sum*, are relatively commoner in Terence, and, what is significant and characteristic, are exploited with greater internal variety. Consequently the texture of his verse is more complex than his predecessors'.

> SIMO Íbi tum fílius
> cum illís qui amárant Chrýsidem úna aderạt fréquens;
> curábat úna fúnus; trístis ínterịm;
> nonnúmquam cónlacrumábat. plácuit tum ịd mihị;
> síc cọgitạbam: 'hic páruae cónsuetúdinịs 110
> causa húius mọrtém fẹrt[1] tam fámiliárițer:
> quid si ípse amạsset? quịd hic míhị faciẹt pátrị?'
> háec ẹgo putábam esse ómnia humáni íngenị
> mansuẹtíque ánimi offícia. quid múltịs mórọr?
> egomẹ́t quoque éius cáusa in fúnus pródẹọ, 115
> níl sụspicạns etiam máli. SOSIA. Hẹm quíd id ẹst? SIMO scíẹs:
> ecfértur; ímus. ịntérea ịnter múlierẹs

---

[1] Only verbs are freely admitted as monosyllabic forms at line-end not involving elision in Plautus and Terence; so Ter. *H.T.* 461 *. . .ómnẹs sollícitos hạbui – ạtque haec úna nọ́x!* 'I distributed *all* (my wines) – and that was just *one* night!' is intentionally and effectively anomalous in this (and its hiatus), expressing Chremes' horror at Bacchis' effects on his cellar. It follows that full coincidence of ictus and accent in the last place was strongly avoided, and that monosyllabic verb-forms were sentence-enclitic, as once all verb-forms in Latin had been, acquiring an accent only at sentence-head. In the above presentation word-accents have been also omitted in certain verb-collocations where dramatic emphasis suggests that the phrase-accent was stronger than the word-accent which, at least in later Latin, would be the verb's prerogative – *úna aderạt fréquens, síc cọgitạbam, si ípse amạsset, quịd hic míhị faciẹt pátrị, níl sụspicạns etiam máli, únam ạspicio ádulescẹ́ntulam, sorọ́rem essẹ aiunt Chrýsidịs*, perhaps *quịd multịs mọrọr, práeter cẹ́terạs/uisạst, ad sepúlchrum uẹnimụs, in ígnem impọsitast*. The phenomenon is so common that an interesting question arises as to the accentual status of verb-forms in general in pre-Classical Latin; was the old rule about verbal accent still operative to the extent that verbs tended to stand, as it were, in the accentual shade?

quae ibi áderant fórte únam aspicio ádulescéntulam
fórma – sos. Bóna, fortásse? simo Et uóltu, Sósia,
ádeo modésto, ádeo uenústo, ut níl supra.   120
quía tum mihi lámentári práeter céteras
uísast, et quía erat fórma práeter céteras
honésta ac líberáli, accédo ad pédisequas,
quáe sit rógo: sorórem esse aiunt – Chrýsidis!
percússit ílico ánimum: attát hóc íllud est,   125
hínc illae lácrumae, háec illast míséricórdia!
sos. Quam tímeo quórsum euádas! simo fúnus ínterim
procédit; séquimur; ad sepúlchrum uénimus;
in ígnem impósitast; flétur. ínterea haec sóror . . .   (*Andria* 101–29)

---

simo *Then my son began spending a great deal of time with those who had been
Chrysis' lovers; he organized the funeral with them. He was gloomy all the while,
and sometimes he would burst into tears. 'Good', I thought.* (110) *'He's taking
the death of this slight acquaintance very personally: what if he had fallen in love
with her himself? How deeply he will feel for me, his father!' I thought these were
all the proper manifestations of a warm disposition and a well-trained character.
Well, to be brief, I myself also went to pay my respects at her funeral,* (115)
not yet suspecting any trouble.
sosia *Trouble? What?*
simo *I'll tell you. The body was brought out, and the procession set off. As we went
along, among the women who were assisting I happened to spot a particular young
lady. Her figure –*
sosia *– was good, perhaps?*
simo *– and her features, Sosia,* (120) *were so classic, so lovely that it was perfection.
As her grief seemed to be deeper than the others', and as she looked more decent and
lady-like than the others, I went up to the servant-women and asked who she was.
'The sister', they said, 'of – Chrysis!'* (125) *It hit me at once. Aha, that's what it
meant, this was the cause of those tears, the cause of that 'compassion'.*
sosia *I don't like the way your story is going!*
simo *Meanwhile the funeral-procession went ahead; we followed; we came to the
tomb; she was placed on the pyre; general weeping. Meanwhile the sister . . .*

Simo had thought, rightly, that there was nothing between his son Pamphilus
and the deceased Chrysis; this was the more fortunate, since Simo had plans
for a good match for his son, and these were well advanced – without
Pamphilus' knowledge. Simo claims somewhat rhetorically – note the *prosopopoeia* and argument *a fortiori*, 110ff. – that it was a father's sympathy for his
son's feelings that brought him, an embarrassed outsider, to attend the funeral
of the socially dubious Chrysis; and so it was, but Simo does not add that he
was concealing something from Pamphilus. The sequel is described with
freshness, irony, economy, and considerable unobtrusive art. It is fresh, for
this is a real death and a real funeral such as one never finds in Plautus. It is

ironical in the presentation of Simo's character. He likes to think of himself as enlightened in his relationship to his son, yet as soon as he learns the truth

attặt hóc ịllud ẹst

that his own inferences have been mistaken, and, worse, that his plans are threatened anew and more seriously than by Chrysis, the understanding sympathy which he has claimed for himself runs out. Autumn was himself attracted by Spring, and he can understand all too well why his son should be in love with her. It is economical, for Simo says more about himself than he intends. These traits are Menandrian, and Terence has successfully conveyed them by adapting the traditional language and rhythms of Roman comedy. His originality and art lie here. The first spectators of this scene, the first of Terence's first play, were familiar only with the full-blooded manner of Plautus and Caecilius and Luscius. Whether they approved or not, they must have been struck by the lightness, rapidity, naturalism, and complexity of writing such as this. The alliteration, neologism, and prolixity of the 'full' style have gone. Terence makes Simo quote his own and others' words for vividness, and favours pungent and economical strings of verbs for rapid narrative. At the same time he freely admits very long words, not (as in Plautus) in order to increase the weight of a particular line, but simply as they occur as the *mots justes*; elision is very frequent; and he is much less insistent than his predecessors on the line as a sense-unit. These traits have the effect of complicating considerably the relation of word-accent and the flow of the verse. The passage above begins with familiar movement, but from 111 to 114 it is more complex; at 115 it is simple, in 116 complex, in 117 simple, in 118–20 complex, and from there to 125 essentially simple, effectively highlighting the famous couplet 125f.; normality of movement is restored in 127–9. However Roman actors delivered 'difficult' lines where elision across changes of speaker and breathpause was involved, or where the natural pattern of word-accents did not coincide with the flow of the verse, we may be certain that there was a contrast between them and 'easy' verses, and the *poeta* Terence was well aware of the importance of this aspect of composition. The reader may easily check for himself how effectively Terence varies the rhythms of this passage, and in particular, how 'difficult' rhythms correspond to emphasis and emotion in Simo's speech.

Terence's diction in longer metres is somewhat more ornate than in senarii, but here too he aims at a more various, naturalistic tone than his predecessors. It is precisely because of this that some inherited features of his language seem awkward when compared with Menander's more fluid usage, for example Terence's rather wooden use of what had become in the *palliata* fixed formulae of intention and entrance (e.g. *An.* 796–800, Crito's arrival).[1]

[1] See Gomme (1937) 255f.

Terence had a difficult theatrical career, not only because of Luscius Lanuvinus, but also because of his trouble in reconciling the tastes of a discriminating minority and a conservative majority. His reforms of theatrical technique all lie within the tradition of the *palliata*, but were mostly centripetal and negative. In particular, he eschewed the means by which older writers had established *rapport* with the audience without being able to focus his 'Athens' satisfactorily. He concentrated on a narrower spectrum of experience than Menander or his own seniors, but, on the other hand, he did this well: for example, his interest in the relationship of parents and children and in education, and his realistic, consistent, and sympathetic representation of character, particularly female, which were new to Roman audiences. He inadvertently damaged the *palliata* as a dramatic form, for the logical setting for such realistic characters as he presented was not his colourless 'Athens', but the real Italy; with him there opens a permanent rift between 'higher' and 'lower' literary tastes. The broad public did not like Terence much, and he did not like them. The spirit of the older comedians survived in the mime and farce, while Terence's interest in character was maintained by Afranius in his *togatae*. *Ea tempestate flos poetarum fuit* 'that age was the flower of poets', said the reviver of Plautus' *Casina* with reference to the pre-Terentian period; he may well have included Terence and Luscius in his condemnation of the moderns. However, Terence's unique and most important success was to become *Menander Latinus* in the library and classroom rather than on the stage, and as such he was very important in establishing the taste and diction of the classical period.

3. SERIOUS DRAMA

Praetextae *and* crepidatae

Grammarians drew a distinction between *tragoediae* (*fabulae crepidatae* 'Buskin-plays'), modelled on Greek tragedy, and *fabulae praetextae* 'Hem-' or 'Robe-plays', on Roman themes, ancient and modern. This is parallel to the distinction of *comoediae* (*fabulae palliatae*) and *fabulae togatae* (*tabernariae*).[1] There is no certain evidence for *fabulae togatae* before the time of Terence and Afranius, and no light dramatist is known to have written both kinds of comedy. The case is different in serious drama. All the known dramatists except Andronicus wrote the occasional Roman play and they seem to have used the same style and form, chorus and all, as in their *tragoediae*. Aeschylus' *Persians* belongs to the genre tragedy no less than his other plays, and Naevius' *Clastidium*, cele-

---

[1] The grammarians' classifications are worthy of Polonius, but the use of such terms as *crepidata*, *praetext(at)a*, *togata*, *tabernaria*, *mimus*, *Rhinthonica*, *palliata*, *Atellana* was not altogether self-consistent. Only *tragoedia* and *comoedia* and *fabula* are attested for the creative perod. The definitions implied in the text may not be strictly correct, but the terms are commonly so used. See Beare (1964) 264–6.

brating M. Claudius Marcellus' winning of the *spolia opima* in 222 B.C., was not really different in genre from his other *tragoediae*. However, apart from the obvious matter of costume, there were two special aspects of the *praetexta*. The playwright had to organize his dramaturgy and plot wholly for himself, using motifs and ideas transferred from tragedy.[1] Again, the *praetextae* were distinguished by their obvious *utilitas*, their 'importance', their 'relevance'. Cicero defended the poet Archias in 62 B.C. before an aristocratic jury by making much of the argument that the poet's highest task was to celebrate the deeds of famous men. Of course, by then the argument was obsolescent; Catullus would have sniggered.[2] At the beginning of the Hannibalic War, however, the successful production of the *Clastidium* must have seemed an important demonstration to the nobility of the high seriousness and political utility of the theatre. A generation later Fulvius Nobilior took Ennius with him on campaign, as Hellenistic kings had taken poets to celebrate their deeds, and the result, the *Ambracia*, was probably a *praetexta* rather than a narrative poem, produced in 187 or 186 B.C.; Fulvius was the object of political attacks when he returned, and such propaganda was really useful. The long if intermittent survival of the tradition begun by Naevius – Accius was still writing *praetextae* in the 130s B.C., and perhaps later – suggests that noble patrons, if not the dramatists, found this form congenial. The real vigour and popularity of the serious theatre, however, was in its Greek mythological aspect.

A survey of the writers of tragedy

Varro dated Andronicus' first production, probably a tragedy, to 240 B.C., and Naevius' first, which was certainly a tragedy, to 235 B.C. Another tradition was that 'the Muse', whether tragic or epic is not clear, 'arrived' in Rome during the Second Punic War (223–202 B.C.; Porcius Licinus *ap.* Gell. *N.A.* 17.21.45); a third states that it was after the Second Punic War that Romans turned to tragedy (Hor. *Epist.* 2.1.161ff.). Both the latter views seem to follow the mistaken chronology propounded by the scholar-tragedian Accius in his *Didascalica*, that Andronicus was junior to Naevius; the third even ignores him, and regards Ennius (*fl.* 203–169 B.C.) as the first real Roman tragedian. Whatever the truth about Andronicus, the plays of Plautus strongly imply in various ways that tragedy was in fact a well-developed and popular genre well before the end of the Punic War. The work of the pioneers, particularly perhaps Naevius, was crucial in establishing the form, style, and emotional province of serious drama. The titles of Andronicus and Naevius (see Appendix) suggest an interest in the Trojan Cycle, and in the fortunes of suffering heroines.

---

[1] Jocelyn (1972) 1004f.; Leo (1913) 179f., 398f.
[2] G.W. Williams (1968) 31ff.

The Argonautic saga and those parts of the Theban Cycle involving Dionysus and Bacchantes were also used; Oedipus himself is a strikingly rare figure in Roman tragedy. Andronicus is known to have used Sophocles (*Aiax Mastigophorus* and *Hermiona* (?)), while Naevius may have used originals as different in character as Aeschylus' *Lycurgus* and Euripides' *Iphigenia in Tauris*.[1]

Even the names of the rivals and lesser imitators of Ennius (who wrote between *c.* 202 and 169 B.C.) are forgotten. It was he who made the composition of tragedy an unequivocally respectable activity for the leisure of gentlemen who did not depend on the theatre. Among these his nephew the painter Pacuvius (*fl.* 154 B.C., according to Jerome) and Accius (who wrote between *c.* 145 and *c.* 100 B.C.) stood out and all but monopolized the attention of subsequent generations. Ennius was particularly fond of Euripides, though he was far from faithful to the true spirit of his author. Pacuvius, whose *œuvre* was small, used all three of the classic Athenian dramatists, and also the imitators of Euripides. There are almost as many titles of plays by Accius as there are of all the others together. Like Pacuvius, he was eclectic in his choice of models. In his case, as we shall see, the question arises whether he did not sometimes compose tragedies 'from scratch', exactly as a contemporary Greek might; in exploring the by-ways and sequels of the famous stories of Troy, Thebes, and the Argonauts, the scholar-poet would know and study not only the Masters' versions and others', but also the remarks of the commentators, and might take things 'even from a Latin', as Afranius in the contemporary *togata* (*CRF* 28, Macrob. *Sat.* 6.1.4).

Accius' latest-known play was a *Tereus* of 104 B.C., and fresh tragedies were still being composed, apparently for stage-performance, in the 90s B.C.[2] Throughout Cicero's lifetime, there were revivals (as of comedy) of what were now regarded as the classics of Pacuvius, Accius, and Ennius (this seems to have been their order of esteem)[3] before large audiences, who might interpret passages with reference to contemporary politics[4]. The acting profession bade fair to win the social prestige which it enjoyed in Greece; orators admired, befriended, and learnt from great actors such as Aesopus and Roscius. It is likely that the composition of tragedy had become a literary exercise already

---

[1] On Andronicus, *TRF* 16 = *ROL* 16~Soph. *Aj.* 1266f., see Traina (1970) 22, 42. Of the others' work the Greek models exist in whole or part for: Ennius, *Eumenides* (Aesch.), *Hecuba, Iphigenia in Aulis, Medea exul* (all Eur.); Pacuvius, *Antiopa* (Eur.); Accius, *Bacchae, Phoenissae, Telephus* (all Eur.). See Mette (1964) 5–212.

[2] Marius Victorinus in *GLK* VI 8 implies that the *Tecmessa* of C. Julius Strabo (*fl.* 100–90 B.C.) was for stage-performance.

[3] Cic. *Opt. gen. orat.* 1.2, Hor. *Epist.* 2.1.55; later Accius was more favoured (Vell. 2.9.3, Quint. *Inst.* 10.1.97).

[4] *Eurysaces*, 57 B.C. (Cic. *Sest.* 120); *Clytemestra*, 55 B.C. (Cic. *Fam.* 7.1.2); *Tereus*, 44 B.C. (Cic. *Phil.* 1.15.36, *Att.* 16.2.3).

before 100 B.C. The three classic Roman authors were read in Cicero's time (Cic. *Fin.* 1.2.4), and probably figured in the school syllabus. Quintus Cicero wrote several tragedies, including four which he dashed off in sixteen days of leave while he was serving with the army in Gaul in 54 B.C. (Cic. *Qu. Fr.* 3.5(6).7).

The appeal and scope of Roman tragedy

The province of Roman tragedy was firstly the celebration of contemporary aristocratic ideals through myth, with concessions neither to the Athens of Pericles or Cleon, nor to the distant mythical past; next, the stimulation not of the intellect but of the emotions; thirdly, the cultivation of rhetoric; lastly, to a limited extent, the retailing of current philosophical-scientific views.

The 'Corinth' or 'Mycenae' of the setting was (as in comedy) a blend of Greek and Italian elements; though naturally Italian allusions were generally less quotidian and specific than they could be in comedy, the values and value-terms were quite frankly Roman.

> uirtus praemium est optumum
> uirtus omnibus rebus anteit profecto
> libertas, salus, uita, res et parentes,
> patria et prognati
> tutantur, seruantur;
> uirtus omnia in sese habet, omnia adsunt
> bona quem penest uirtus.
>
> (Plautus, *Amphitruo* 648–53)

Manliness is the best prize; manliness in truth precedes all things; (by it) are protected and kept freedom, safety, life, property and parents, fatherland and children; manliness has all things in itself, and he has at hand all good things, in whose charge is manliness.

So Alcumena ends a tragic aria, in which it is wrong to see any parody. The highest function of tragedy was the celebration of *uirtus* in war and counsel in terms which were essentially those of contemporary politics. *Virtus* denoted physical fitness, endurance, bravery, initiative, piety, versatility, even eloquence. From it come the stability of the community and personal honour and fame. Thus *uirtus* far from being a coherent moral virtue was a collection of competitive skills put to good use in the service of the community (cf. Ennius, *TRF* 160f. = *ROL* 200 f.). It was through Stoic philosophy that in the second century there was added but not substituted the notion of moral purity. The cardinal Greek virtue of moderation is subordinate in Roman tragedy, and appears as such only as a woman's '*uirtus*', or as the criterion to be respected when the individual's thirst for glory endangered the common interest. Thus the moral concern of Roman tragedy, and its conception of a tragic hero, was narrow and unsystematic, but very relevant to the political battles of the second century.

There was much ferment in the religious life of the Romans in the years following the Punic War. The Senate sanctioned some alien cults, e.g. Magna Mater, Venus of Eryx, Hercules and the Muses, and inaugurated others, e.g. Pietas, while private enthusiams as diverse as the cult of Bacchus and a sub-Platonic astral mysticism were fashionable, though curbed eventually by law. From at least the 180s the teachings of the Epicurean and Stoic schools were becoming known at Rome. For all that, traditional public and private Roman religion and rites were more deeply ingrained and valued than is sometimes suggested. Thus by the time of Pacuvius, there co-existed many different levels and kinds of religious sophistication. Polybius, one of the very many educated Greeks who settled at Rome in the 160s, was amazed at the super-stitious punctiliousness of the audiences of Ennius and Pacuvius (Polyb. 12.56.6), and suggested that the ruling classes deliberately fostered traditional religion to keep the lower orders in their place. It was nothing so Machiavel-lian. The theological and cosmological *loci* which one finds in Ennius and Pacuvius (not, it seems, in Accius) reflect contemporary teachings, particularly of the Stoics, and no doubt tragedy played some part in disseminating such ideas among the unlearned. Roman religion was not dogmatic; when Ennius makes Telamo express the Epicurean view that the gods exist, but take no interest in human affairs, for otherwise the good would prosper and the wicked suffer (Cic. *Div.* 2.104 = *TRF* 269–71 = *ROL* 328–30), no article of a creed was directly attacked; the Roman spectator was no doubt impressed, but he will not therefore have ceased his pious Roman observances. An Ennian Neoptolemus expressed what was and remained a typical Roman view, that one must philosophize, but briefly; for systematic philosophy was uncongenial.[1] Stoic opinions are reflected and introduced by the dramatists as and when they coincided with traditional aristocratic ideas about self-discipline and service to the state.

Non uentus fuit sed Alcumena Euripidi (Plaut. *Rud.* 86) 'That was no gale, it was the Alcmene of Euripides', says Plautus, alluding to the razmataz of a recent Roman production about 190 B.C. Storms, shipwreck, torture, riddles, augury, dreams, portents, snakes, solitude, want, exile, ghosts, battle-narratives, madness, bacchantes, martial heroes, and ladies in reduced circumstances are prominent in the remains of Roman tragedy, and Euripidean themes of recog-nition, deception, and revenge are particularly favoured. The musical presenta-tion and highly elaborate diction of tragedy were to stimulate the audience emotionally, not intellectually. The demotic realism, the social criticism, the

---

[1] *TRF* 340 = *ROL* 400. 'Briefly' probably restricts 'philosophy' to the wisdom of Delphi – 'know thyself', etc.

direct challenge to received opinion characteristic of Euripides have boiled away in the decoction.

The rhetorical aspects of tragedy were popular, and, as the second century progressed, increasingly prominent. There had always been divergent tendencies in Latin eloquence. The one was laconic and compressed, and derived from the nature of the language: a single word, a verb, may express a quite complicated sentence; a major part of the nouns and adjectives in Latin are formed from verbal stems; and words may readily be 'understood'. Different facets of this tendency may be seen, for example, in some epitaphs and *elogia* of the second century, in Cato's speeches and *De agri cultura*, and in Terence's plays (not his prologues). The other tendency was towards elaboration, a fullness and decoration effected by alliteration, anaphora, assonance, antithesis, and the like. This may be seen in the epitaphs of the Scipios, the fragments of some of the annalists such as Coelius Antipater, and in the prologues (not the plays) of Terence, as well as in the 'full-blooded' style of Plautus and, above all, in tragic diction. Very roughly, these inherent tendencies correspond to the divergences between the 'Attic' and the 'Asiatic' schools of Greek rhetoric. In the two generations following the Second Punic War the relations of Rome and Pergamum were close, and the leading exponent of the Asiatic style of oratory was the head of the school there, Crates of Mallos. He visited Rome and lectured there on rhetoric while recovering from an accident in 167 B.C.; Terence's prologues, written over the immediately following years, are striking proof of the popularity of this style, which for us is perhaps most familiar in the Epistles of St Paul, himself an 'Asiatic' writer. The Romans discovered, as it were, in the theories and systems and patterns of Greek rhetoric, particularly Asiatic, that they had been speaking prose all the while; the strained antitheses and the almost painfully correct partitioning of Terence's prologues reflect a popular taste for euphuistic excess in judicial rhetoric. This did not go unchallenged. Cato's famous remark *rem tene, uerba sequentur* 'hold to the subject, the words will follow' was directed against this artificiality, and the satirist Lucilius in the 120s B.C. scoffed not only at the contortions of Pacuvian *exordia* (*ROL* (29) 879) but also at the 'tessellation' (*ROL* (2) 84–6) and 'childishness' (*ROL* (5) 186–93) of the Pergamene style.

Accius visited 'Asia', i.e. Pergamum, in the 130s B.C., and he was an adherent of that school both in rhetoric and in scholarship. When asked why he did not plead cases in court, Accius is said to have replied that whereas he (not his Greek author!) controlled what his characters might say, he could not control what an opponent might (Quint. *Inst.* 5.13.43). The story is *bien trouvé*: Accius was of the same age and social class as Afranius, the writer of *togatae*, who did plead cases (Cic. *Brut.* 167).

For all its extreme elaboration, the grand manner of tragedy was directly related to the real-life practice of judicial and forensic rhetoric, especially, no doubt, in Euripidean debates and monologues. Unfortunately no really extensive fragment survives. The figure of thought called by the schoolmen the *dilemma* ('Whither now shall I turn? To *A*? No, because...; then to *B*? No, because...', etc.) occurs at Ennius, *Medea exul*, *TRF* 231f. = *ROL* 284f., translating Euripides, *Medea* 502–4. It occurs again in C. Gracchus fr. 58 Malcovati (Cic. *De or.* 3.214), a fragment of his famous and final speech on the Capitol before being murdered (121 B.C.). Cicero used it in the peroration of his *Pro Murena* (Nov. 63 B.C.), and not much later Catullus again used it (with Ennius in mind) in Ariadne's lament (Cat. 64.177ff.). This intimate relation between the rhetoric of political oratory and of elevated poetry, and the fact that such stylization appealed not to the few but to the many, is very hard for the modern sensibility: our assumptions about the art of persuasion, the place of rhetoric in poetry, sincerity, originality, spontaneity, and so on, are so very different.

Tragic style

The best evidence for the tone and style of early tragedy is in Plautus, who alludes to well-known productions and assumes a considerable knowledge of mythology which will have been disseminated most widely by tragedy. He himself is a master of what was already a fully developed tragic style. He uses this not only for parody and burlesque,[1] but as a normal medium for *cantica* and as a way of elevating the emotional temperature, e.g. the inquisition in *Captivi* (659–767, senarii), the shipwreck scene and presentation of Ptolemocratia in *Rudens* (185–289, lyric melodrama), the gnomic quality of such passages as *Bac.* 534ff. (septenarii), *Persa* 341ff. (senarii), and above all the *Amphitruo*, the 'tragicomoedia' with its messenger-speeches (186ff., 1053ff., monodies in iambic octonarii) and Alcumena's polymetric song in praise of *uirtus* (633ff.).

As in comedy, a playwright will often have modulated 'upwards' by changing from senarii (representing Greek trimeters) to recitative or canticum also representing trimeters of the original on the arrival of a new character: far less was presented in senarii in a Roman tragedy than in trimeters in a typical Euripidean model. About 70% of the *Iphigenia in Aulis* is in trimeters, but only 30% of Ennius' fragments are in senarii. With the increasing popularity of rhetoric, this spoken element made a considerable recovery in Pacuvius (45%) and Accius (55%), but even so it was never as prominent as in Greek tragedy. On the musical form of Roman drama, see pp. 84–6; in Ennius, all the certain cases of song are solo arias, while all the certain cases of what

---

[1] Plaut. *Pseud.* 702ff., a messenger; *Mer.* 842ff., departure; *Men.* 831ff., a mad scene. All these in trochaic septenarii.

had been strophic songs in the originals for the chorus have been rewritten as recitative in the long trochaic metres.

This radical change of form naturally affected presentation and character. Ennius makes Medea enter with an operatic libretto in which the subtleties and density of the corresponding trimeter-speech in Euripides are lost (*TRF* 219–21 = *ROL* 266–8 ~ Eur. *Med.* 214ff.). Instead the Roman dramatist makes Medea express sentiments and use language which evoke Roman ideas about honour and service in the *res publica*, with the result that we seem to be listening to a Roman magistrate rather than a Medea.[1] Earlier in the same play Ennius used senarii for the trimeters of the nurse's opening speech (*TRF* 205–13 = *ROL* 253–61 ~ Eur. *Med.* 1ff.), comparison of which is instructive,[2] and for the ensuing dialogue (also in trimeters in the original) between the paidagogos and the nurse:

> παλαιὸν οἴκων κτῆμα δεσποίνης ἐμῆς,
> τί πρὸς πύλαισι τήνδ᾽ ἄγουσ᾽ ἐρημίαν
> ἕστηκας αὐτή...;   (Euripides, *Medea* 49–51)

Ancient chattel of my mistress' house, why standest thou alone before the doors, keeping this solitude....?

> antiqu(a) erilis fida custos corporis,
> quid sic t(e) extr(a) aedes exanimat(a) eliminas?
>   (Ennius, *Medea exul, TRF* 214f. = *ROL* 262f.)

Ancient faithful guardian of the mistress' person, why dost thou breathless unthreshold thyself from out the palace...?

As in Euripides, Ennius has a heavy, five-word line, varied in vowels, for the formal address. *Erile corpus* is calqued from such expressions as μητρῷον δέμας 'maternum corpus', as it were, 'the lady my mother' (Aesch. *Eum.* 84), which is far from natural Latin, but which had been 'naturalized' by Naevius:

> uos qui regalis corporis custodias
> agitatis...   (Naevius, *Lycurgus, TRF* 21f. = *ROL* 27f.)

Ye who exercise guardianships of the royal person...

where the poetic plural is also a Grecism. One notes also the tragic compound *e-liminare*, literally 'to unthreshold', the contrived assonance and alliteration of the Latin, and the regrettable exaggeration (*exanimata*) absent from the original. All these traits are characteristic not only of Ennius but all the Roman

---

[1] G.W. Williams (1968) 359–61.
[2] Leo (1912) 98.

dramatists. Perhaps most striking of all, the address by itself might have seemed a more 'literal' version of another context in Euripides altogether:

γύναι γεραιά, βασιλίδος πιστὴ τροφέ...

(Euripides, *Hippolytus* 267)

Aged woman, faithful nurse of the queen...

Clearly it is a fruitless task to infer details of lost Greek texts from even what appear to be 'literal' Latin translation. Ennius had that line at the back of his mind when he was turning the *Medea*, and has promoted the 'ancient chattel' unnecessarily.

The establishment of a suitably elevated diction for tragedy was not an easy matter. There was a definite upper limit. Epic admitted certain very archaic forms drawn from the language of ritual and law which were avoided in tragedy, e.g. *indu-*, *endo* for *in*, and tragedy could exploit forms from the same sources avoided in comedy, e.g. *quaesendum* for *quaerendum* in *liberum quaesendum causa* 'for the begetting of offspring'.[1] Formulae of the law such as this were used as patterns for analogical extensions and revivals of obsolescent forms (the genitive *-um* for *-orum* is a case in point). Words like *ciuis*, *lex*, *ius*, *arx*, *pater*, *matrona*, *uxor*, *liberi*, *honos*, *gloria*, *laus* were often loaded with emotional Roman connotations. The solemnity and rich diversity of Attic tragic diction were also echoed by analogical formations within living Latin patterns. Thus *e-liminare*, *con-glomerare* were typical tragic inventions, of which a surprising number now lead prosaic lives in English derivatives. On the other hand a formation *ipsi-uentralis*, a 'literal' translation of αὐτάδελφον 'same-wombed' (Soph. *Ant.* 1) would have sounded too bizarre, as there are no *ipse*-compounds in Latin to correspond to the common αὐτο-compounds of Greek. Naturally neologisms attracted the attention of scoffers like Lucilius and grammarians, and for that reason may be over-represented among the fragments: words like *ampl-are* 'enlarge', *clar-ere* 'be famous', adverbs in *-im*, *-atim*, *-itus*, long adjectives (often negated with *in-*) formed with *-bilis*, *-ficus*, *-osus*, *-bundus*, compound adjectives like *alti-uolans*, *tardi-gradus*, *taurigenus*, *flex-animus*, which correspond to types much more freely formed in Greek. The same striving after variety within the morphology of spoken Latin is to be seen in the coining of abstract nouns in *-tudo* for *-tas*, *-tia* (and the reverse), and of verbal derivatives in *-men(tum)*, *-io*. These are often used as if they were personifications, as the subjects of the sentence, against the grain of the language. Alliteration, assonance, homoeoteleuton, and all the figures which tend to an expansive rather than a laconic eloquence were exploited – anaphora, polyptoton, *figura etymologica*, climax, tricolon, and the multiplication of synonyms. These artifices as well as antitheses, quibbles, etymological and

---

[1] Ennius, *TRF* 97, 120 = *ROL* 126, 136; see G.W. Williams (1968) 371.

epigrammatic points, the clothing rather than the substance of a sound rhetoric, were favoured, the more so when the influence of Pergamum lent them academic support; but their over-use sometimes detracted from sense and precision.

> tú m(e) amóris mágis qu(am) honóris séruauisti grátiạ.
>
> (Ennius, *Medea exul*, *TRF* 233 = *ROL* 286)

You saved me for love rather than for honour.

So Ennius' Jason to Medea; but it is clear from the context (Eur. *Med.* 530f.) that *honoris* is Ennius' addition, for the sake of a jingle; it is in fact illogical, for *honos*, the reward of the public man, is irrelevant here; at the back of Ennius' mind there is the axiom that *amor* is the province of comedy, the passive condition of an idle soul.[1] In his version of Euripides' *Bacchae* Accius made Tiresias allege that 'neither antiquity nor death nor "huge-agedness"' (*grandaeuitas*) was to prevent Thebans from dancing in honour of Dionysus. Euripides had more reasonably said that the god made no distinction between young and old (Accius, *TRF* 245 = *ROL* 210 ~ Eur. *Bacc.* 206f.), without absurdly mentioning 'death'.

Originality

Cicero was misleading when he alluded to *fabellas Latinas ad uerbum ex graecis expressis* 'entertainments in Latin literally translated from the Greek' (*Fin.* 1.2.4). He had in mind Ennius' *Medea exul* and Pacuvius' *Antiopa*, of which sufficient survives in Greek and Latin to show that *ad uerbum* is an exaggeration. He only meant that in these cases, to which may be added Accius' *Bacchae*, the adaptor had kept the same scenes in the same order as in his original. Elsewhere (*Acad.* 1.10) Cicero says that Roman tragedians expressed the 'feel', not the words (*non uerba sed uim*) of the originals. Not even that is true: the Euripides who appears in Ennian or Accian guise has been transmogrified, especially with respect to his intellectual 'bite'.

Dramatists not only interfered with the musical, metrical, and stylistic presentation of Greek plays, but also changed their emphases and substance in all sorts of ways. The soldier-chorus of Euripides' *Iphigenia in Aulis* become girls in Ennius' version. Pacuvius toned down Ulysses' lamentations in his version of Sophocles' *Niptra* (Cic. *Tusc.* 2.21.48). He introduced a philosophical *locus* inspired by a passage of Euripides' *Chrysippus*, quite un-Sophoclean in tone, into Sophocles' *Chryses*. As Cicero noted (*Div.* 1.131) it is imperfectly integrated, both logically and dramatically. Accius changed the arrangement in Euripides' *Phoenissae* by which Polynices and Eteocles were to share power, thus altering the balance of sympathies (Eur. *Phoen.* 69ff., cf. Accius,

[1] G.W. Williams (1968) 362f.

TRF 590, 591–3 = *ROL* 589, 594–6). If his *Antigone* represents Sophocles' play, Accius changed the guard's famous narrative into dramatic action.

These alterations are like those known in Roman comedy, where, as we know, they gave rise to a controversy in Terence's time about the role of the adaptor and his fidelity to an original. Whether something similar was argued over by tragedians is unknown. Perhaps not; for since Naevius, tragedians had appeared as original authors of *praetextae*, and anyway, it was open to them to take the line that they were not dealing with works of fiction in the same sense as a comic poet. The tragedian was a poetic historian, a scholar, the interpreter of a complex source-material which included not only the Attic drama but Homer and Pindar and the commentators. He was as entitled to reinterpret, to cut, and to add, as a contemporary Greek dramatist. Ennius might have written tragedies without any particular model, but did not go so far. Free addition and complete independence came later. It is hard to imagine any Greek original for the laboured, academic rhetoric of Pacuvius' lines on Hellenistic Fortune (*TRF* 366–75 = *ROL tr. inc.* 37–46, Auct. *ad Her.* 2.23.36),[1] and Accius' plays *Nyctegresia* 'The night-sortie' and *Epinausimache* 'The battle at the ships' sound like direct dramatizations of the corresponding episodes of the *Iliad*. If these had no originals in the Attic drama, it is possible that other plays of his with more conventional tragic titles were also free compositions, the result of much reading, not only of the texts of the Attic dramatists, but also Greek literature in general, the commentators too, and the handbooks of rhetorical theory.

Accius, the polemical scholar, the Pergamene rhetorician, the authority on orthography, the head of the college of poets, the historian of the Greek and Roman theatre, and the Hellenistic tragedian evinces a new self-confidence and artistic awareness.[2] He, Afranius, and Lucilius were children in Terence's time; all were Roman citizens by birth, and had no need to earn their living by the pen. In this generation we see a thorough blending of the Greek and the specifically Roman (as opposed to Italian) traditions. It is unfortunate that the Greek intellectual influences to which Accius and his contemporaries were most open were those of Pergamum, rather than of Alexandria; Roman scholarship got off to a bad start from which it never recovered; it was the poets of Alexandria, rather than the rhetoricians of Pergamum, who had most fruitfully stimulated Ennius, and who were to do the same again for the poets of the classical period.

[1] Pacuvius quotes, as a lecturer might, the tenets of various *philosophi* (among whom he counts artists, like himself). The image of Fortune standing on a ball was modern; it occurs first in Greek literature in Cebes, *Pinax* 7.

[2] Leo (1913) 384ff.

6

PROSE LITERATURE

1. THE RANGE OF OLD LATIN PROSE: CATO AND FLAMININUS

'Manios made me for Numasios'; 'Let no one violate this grove nor cart or carry away what is in the grove nor cut wood except on the day when the annual sacrifice takes place.' The oldest use of the alphabet had been to record particular facts and prohibitions like these; and we need not doubt that from a very early date people wrote lists, recipes, letters, etc. on more perishable surfaces than stone or bronze. Of these all trace is lost, as there is no Roman Oxyrhynchus. Prose literature, as opposed to mere writing, may be said to have begun when men began to exploit the fact that their views on important matters could be disseminated by means of the *liber* or *uolumen* which could be multiplied. That was in the Hellenistic period, after the Romans came into contact with the Greeks of southern Italy and Sicily. Before then the Romans had been like most ancient peoples – for example, the contemporary Spartans or Carthaginians, or the Athenians down to Socrates' time – in using the alphabet for specific, 'one-off' purposes in writing prose. While men knew that to speak well was a necessary *uirtus* in politics, the pen was not regarded as a potential source of authority or glory in the affairs of the city, or any other sphere of life. As to what is implied by the 'multiplication' of copies of a book, the very notions of 'publication', 'book-trade', and 'reading public', as well as of reading itself – for listening was just as important – the reader is referred to Chapter 1, 'Books and Readers': the points made there have an important bearing on the styles, the range, and the order of the expansion of Latin prose literature.

From at least the 130s B.C. the Romans themselves believed that the father of Latin prose was Appius Claudius Caecus, a contemporary of Philemon, Ptolemy I, and Pyrrhus. Cicero refers to a letter of Panaetius (resident at Rome in the 130s B.C.) in which the Stoic philosopher praised a *carmen* – the word does not necessarily imply a verse-form – which he took to be by Appius Claudius Caecus and which was of apparently Pythagorean character (Cic. *Tusc.* 4.2.4).[1]

[1] Other ancient references to this supposed work of Appius are given by Schanz–Hosius (1927) 41f. Cato's *Carmen de moribus* was a collection of moralizing reflections quite certainly in prose (Gell. *N.A.* 11.2). It should not be lightly assumed that Cato put it together at all, though it is clear that collections of Cato's real or alleged *dicta* were already circulating in Cicero's time (cf., e.g., Cic. *Off.* 2.25).

Cicero himself accepted as genuine a speech in which Appius opposed peace with Pyrrhus (*Sen.* 16, *Brut.* 61, cf. p. 62 n. 1), and in the second century A.D. the jurist Pomponius refers to an alleged work of Appius, *De usurpationibus*, which, however, was no longer extant (*Dig.* 1.2.2.36). Morals, oratory, the law: it is significant for our appreciation of the Roman attitude to prose that it should have been works of this kind that were attributed to the venerable elder states-man. It is, however, at best doubtful whether any of them were authentic.

In the generation before Cicero the kinds of writing which were either already flourishing as distinct genres or still acquiring 'their own nature' ranged down in grandeur from oratory – forensic, judicial, commemorative – through history, memoirs, letter-writing, to technical treatises on practical subjects such as farming, the law, or the calendar. Besides, now that a Hellenizing Latin poetry had existed for a century and more, there were the beginnings of a scholarly literature directed to its mapping and explanation. This was naturally the business of the poets themselves and of educated freedmen or freedmen's sons like Accius, Aelius Stilo, Octavius Lampadio, and Lutatius Daphnis (cf. Suet. *Gramm.* 1ff.). All other kinds of prose writing, however, were developed by Roman senators, not for art's sake, but as ever more carefully honed weapons directly or indirectly useful in their political lives. M. Porcius Cato the Elder was the most important of them all. In the preface to his *Origines* (see p. 149) he remarked that the great and famous should give an account not only of their public lives but also of their *otium*, their relaxation (fr. 2 Peter).[1] He wrote history not to thrill nor to philosophize, but to persuade the reader of the right-ness for the present and the future of certain moral and political values – Cato's own, of course – as he saw them in the *exempla* of the past, and so confirm what he saw as the true Roman identity in the minds of his readers.

Cato reached the consulship in 195 B.C. at the age of thirty-nine, a remarkable achievement in itself for a *nouus homo* at this time, but this was only the begin-ning of the eventful period in which his long literary career belongs (see Appendix). As consul he campaigned in Spain; in 191 B.C. he was sent on an important diplomatic mission to Athens, where he spoke in Latin through an interpreter, and served with distinction under M'. Acilius Glabrio (whom he later prosecuted) at Thermopylae. In 189 B.C. he was an unsuccessful competitor for the censorship when the liberal and philhellene aristocrats T. Quinctius Flamininus and Marcellus were successful: Flamininus' brother was also the victim of a prosecution by the litigious Cato.

Flamininus, some six years younger than Cato, had fiery ambition in common with him, but in most other respects of background and temperament was very different. His early career had brought him into close contact with the Greek

---

[1] We cite the *Origines* from Peter (1914), the speeches from Malcovati (1955), and the other fragments from Jordan (1860).

culture of Tarentum, and, thanks to military and diplomatic skill as well as to his excellent connexions, he reached the consulship three years before Cato, and received charge of the war against Philip of Macedon, which he duly won (197 B.C.).[1] The spirit of his and Marcellus' censorship was optimistic and liberal. Wars were ending, and at last there was the prospect of lasting peace. Armies and navies were returning with vast booty and new tastes. Rome was now the diplomatic focus of the *oecumene*. Five years later, however, the mood had changed entirely. The Scipios had been disgraced in a series of trials which Cato himself had promoted; the scandal of the Bacchanalian affair had shaken domestic confidence, and a consular army had been lost in Liguria. Cato was elected censor for 184/3 B.C. at a time when it seemed that every facet of Roman life was subject to momentous and uncontrolled forces which (Cato thought) threatened to destroy the character of the Roman institutions. His censorship was never forgotten for its severity.

He championed what he saw as the true *mores maiorum*, ancestral customs, in which a vision (perhaps even then romantic) of the simple life was central. He presented himself as the hard-headed, commonsensical peasant, with no time for Hellenistic fol-de-rol: Greek doctors are death, *poetae* and expert chefs are a sign of decadence (cf. *or. fr.* 217).[2] Cato's son Licinianus was born about 192 B.C., and Cato took his role as educator seriously, even preparing a book of improving stories 'written in big letters' to teach the boy to read (Plut. *Cat. Maj.* 20). From this time until his death in 149 B.C. Cato used his pen to attack, to defend, to judge, and to instruct with a verve, originality, and directness that would be remarkable in a man half his age and in any era. His blunt and contentious manner involved him in many prosecutions of leading men; he himself was prosecuted forty-four times, though he was never convicted of anything: that is at least as much a tribute to his own eloquence as to his honesty.[3]

It would be an over-simplification to suppose that Flamininus and Cato were respectively simply 'for' and 'against' the tide of Hellenistic culture. In particular one must beware of irrelevant modern ideas of cultural nationalism if one is to understand Cato, who was a great deal more versed in things Greek than, say, Marius two generations later, and whose very eclecticism was Hellenistic. He recommended that one should dip into Greek literature, not soak oneself in it; and the once widespread idea, that he did not learn the language until he was an old man, has been recognized as a mistake.[4] Like

[1] On Flamininus see Badian (1970).

[2] *Ad Marcum filium* fr. 1 Jordan (Pliny, *N.H.* 29.7.14, *Cat. Maj.* 23); *carmen de moribus* fr. 2 Jordan (Gell. *N.A.* 11.2).

[3] On Cato see Kienast (1954) *passim* with his bibliography, 167f.

[4] See Helm, *RE* xxii 145.33ff., Gelzer, ibid. 110.43ff., Fraenkel (1968) 130, against Leo (1913) 283.

Flamininus, whose interest in Greek literature as such may even have been exaggerated, he will have learnt the language as a young man in southern Italy. A fragment of his Athenian speech, *Antiochus epistulis bellum gerit, calamo et atramento militat* 'Antiochus wages war with letters, he fights with pen and ink' (fr. 20 Malcovati), has been identified as an echo of a disparaging remark of Demosthenes about Philip of Macedon, a clever ploy in a speech delivered through an interpreter.[1] As Plutarch noted (*Cat. Maj.* 12), Cato could have used Greek if he had wanted: he used Latin for a political reason (see p. 149). Although Cato made a point of praising the collectivism of the good old *res publica* (cf. e.g. frs. 18, 149, 206) and of ridiculing the adoption of Greek customs (frs. 95, 115), he himself was an example of the drive and individualism of Hellenistic *uomo universale* dedicated to the active life. The dictum from the preface of the *Origines* quoted above (p. 139) is an adaptation of the first sentence of Xenophon's *Symposium*. Xenophon was the kind of Greek that Cato could admire as a man of action and as a writer: for he if anyone among Greeks 'held to the subject and let the words follow' (see p. 143).

It may surprise the student of literature that the spectrum of prose-writing described above did not include the novel, the short story, or *belles lettres* of any kind. This would have seemed less strange to a Panaetius or a Polybius; for Greeks as for Romans, what we would call fiction and expect to find in prose was properly a lower part of poetry. At Rome this meant *saturae* (see pp. 156–71). Nor was there any prose philosophy, theology, or sociology. The theory that Ennius' *Euhemerus* was a prose work, although widely accepted today, is questionable on this and on more particular grounds (see pp. 157–8). In the age of the Gracchi, Latin prose was a medium for facts, instruction, argumentation, exhortation, persuasion, and propaganda, not merely for entertainment, artistic experiment, or speculation, which, nevertheless, might have their places as means to more serious ends.

Before we survey the prose of the second century more closely, three general points must be made. Firstly, it is appropriate enough at almost any other stage of Latin literature's development to adopt a strict approach by genre; but here if we were to confine our attention to that which is in Latin and in prose, we should seriously restrict and misrepresent the horizons of our subject. Latin prose of the second century B.C. is even worse represented by fragments than poetry; in historiography a quite false picture would emerge if we ignored the works of Fabius Pictor, Aulus Albinus, and Polybius and others, all written in Greek and belonging equally to the history of Hellenistic literature; in oratory, the prologues of Plautus and Terence and the Greek diplomatic correspondence of, for example, Flamininus are important evidence for the practice of the art of persuasion in the earlier second century B.C., while the fragments of tragedy,

---

[1] Fraenkel (1968) 130 compares fr. 20 with Dem. 4.30.

Ennius' *Annales*, and Lucilius' *Satires* are in various ways important for the theory and practice of rhetoric.

Next, the ancient theory of genres was teleological; modern critics following ancient often discuss early Roman writing on the implicit premiss that what came first was necessarily crude, but prepared the way for later developments, which culminate when the genre 'achieves its own nature', after which there is a decline. There are some dangers in this model; see p. 154. We have dismissed the ancient claim made for Appius Claudius Caecus that he was the father of Roman prose-literature; but we do not therefore imply that when he addressed the Senate all he could do was grunt. There were strong men before Agamemnon, and there were eloquent Romans before Cato: Ennius called M. Cornelius Cethegus 'choice flower of the People, the marrow of Persuasion' (*Ann.* (9) 303–8v = *ROL* 300–5), and he died in 196 B.C., before the consulship of Cato.

Thirdly, and most important of all, it was the same men, active politicians all, who practised all the as yet imperfectly differentiated kinds of prose enumerated earlier. Among these Cato is most important, and the tones of voice which he used in any writing, even sometimes the technical, were naturally those which he used in the Senate and the courts. Oratory therefore, the highest of our categories, was crucially important for the style of prose-writing on any but the most mundane topics.

2. TECHNICAL WRITING

Only the least pretentious kind of prose is represented by a more-or-less complete surviving work. Cato's *De agri cultura* was written about 160 B.C., when Italy as a whole was beginning to recover from the worst effects of the Punic War and when radical changes in land-use were taking place. In the brief preface we hear the didactic voice of Cato the statesman and orator; his purpose is protreptic, and he is addressing the man with money to invest. Having briefly compared the profitability and security of farming with those of banking and trade and commended the farming way of life, 'So much for eloquence', Cato seems to say; 'now down to business.' In what follows we have a pot-pourri of principles, notes, recipes, instructions, and advice salted with apophthegms. Cato does not attempt a systematic treatment. The work altogether lacks the kind of structural organization that we find even artificially imposed in, say, Varro's *Res rusticae* (37 B.C.) or the anonymous *Rhetorica ad Herennium* (*c.* 80 B.C.). It is a work to dip into, not to read as a continuous whole, and except superficially it lacks the character of a Greek technical manual, a humble but well-established genre to which Hellenistic mathematicians, philosophers, and *philologoi* had contributed. Cato can be very precise in giving quantities for a recipe or the exact magic formula for a ritual or spell, but when he attempts the description of an oil-press he is less successful; for although he gives precise dimensions for the parts, he omits to explain adequately all his technical terms, and he does not use (as he might) lettered diagrams in the manner of an Archimedes or a Philon Mechanicus. For us, and for later generations of Romans, a remarkable quality of the book is the vivid impression of its editor's personality – his provocative directness (e.g. his advice on how to pick and control a bailiff and what to do with an old slave, 2–3), his idiosyncratic enthusiasms (e.g. for cabbage as a panacea, 156), his blend of sharp worldliness and credulous superstition, his authoritarian outlook, and his respect for the *mores maiorum*. The lack of formal organization can only to a very limited extent be explained as due to the vicissitudes of transmission and interpolation, and in several ways one is reminded of the characteristics of the *satura* of the poets.

This was only one of several monographs or treatises on practical subjects of social relevance that Cato wrote (see Appendix). Some of these were addressed as more or less open letters to his son Cato Licinianus, born *c.* 192 B.C. One on rhetoric contained the definition *orator est, Marce fili, uir bonus dicendi peritus* 'The statesman, Marcus my boy, is a gentleman experienced in speaking' (fr. 14 Jordan, Sen. *Contr.* 1 *praef.* 9), and the famous precept *rem tene, uerba sequentur* 'Hold to the subject, the words will follow' (fr. 15, Julius Victor p. 374 Halm). It is probably misleading to think of these works as a collection, constituting a kind of encyclopaedia; apart from the fact that they were certainly unsystematic and eclectic and quirky, there is no evidence at all to suggest that Cato himself collected or edited them as a body, whatever their *fortuna* may have been.[1]

The one and only example of the Senate's patronage of 'literature' was the commission given to D. Silanus after the destruction of Carthage in 146 B.C. to translate into Latin the twenty-eight books of the farming manual of the Carthaginian Mago (Pliny, *N.H.* 18.22). Other researches of which we hear include the chronological and calendaric studies of M'. Acilius Glabrio and M. Fulvius Nobilior, *c.* 190 B.C. (see p. 63), and the astronomical work of C. Sulpicius Galus (cos. 166 B.C., Pliny, *N.H.* 2.53, 2.83, Livy 44.37.5), who, however, is unlikely to have known, let alone understood, the researches of his great contemporary, Hipparchus of Bithynia. As mentioned above, poets and freedmen-scholars inaugurated the study of the history of Latin literature in the Gracchan period; unfortunately for the quality of their work it was the school of Pergamum rather than the tradition of Alexandrian scholarship which most influenced them (see pp. 78, 137). Much more important was the study of Roman law, to which the methods of Peripatetic classification and definition were directly appropriate, and this suffered less from the dogmatism and speculation

---

[1] The important growth-point for *florilegia* which ultimately lie behind the collections of *dicta Catonis* so well known in the Middle Ages (cf. F. Skutsch, *RE* v 358–70) will have been in Imperial times, when the memory of Cato the Elder and Cato Minor, the Stoic sage, was confused.

characteristic of Crates of Mallos and his Pergamene followers. The earliest important work was the *Tripertita* of Sex. Aelius Paetus Catus (Pomp. *Dig.* 1.2.2.38), written probably in the 190s B.C.[1] This included a text of the Twelve Tables, a commentary on their interpretation, and an account of the appropriate procedures at law. It is noteworthy that Aelius was the first jurist who was not himself a *pontifex* or *augur*. Neither was Cato; he himself, or his son, wrote commentaries of some kind on the civil law (Festus p. 144 L, cf. Cic. *De or.* 3.135, 2.142), while Licinianus certainly wrote fifteen or more books identical with or including a *De legis disciplina*, in which theoretical propositions appeared (Gell. *N.A.* 13.20(19).9). C. Sempronius Tuditanus (cos. 129 B.C.) wrote thirteen or more *libri magistratuum*, a work combining historical research and legal interpretation. Pomponius (loc. cit.) describes P. Mucius Scaevola Pontifex (cos. 133), M. Junius Brutus, and Manius Manilius (a friend of Lucilius) as the 'founders' of civil law. He ascribes to them respectively ten, seven[2] and three books. P. Mucius Scaevola Pontifex in some sense also published the *annales* of the pontifical college; these filled eighty books (Cic. *De or.* 2.52, Serv. auct. *ad* Virg. *Aen.* 1.373). What exactly 'publication' implies is not clear; the records had certainly been available to earlier historians. His son Q. Mucius Scaevola Pontifex (cos. 95) composed eighteen authoritative books on civil law, as well as a monograph, the title of which, Ὅροι 'definitions', itself implies the Peripatetic nature of the treatment. M. Junius Brutus' three genuine works are of interest as they were the first in dialogue form in Latin, with dramatic settings at Privernum, Albanum, and Tibur; this of course is the literary form used with such grace and nostalgia by Cicero in the last years of the Republic. Although virtually nothing specific can be cited from these legal studies of the second century B.C. they collectively represent an important contribution to the history of ideas, for these jurists went far beyond Greek achievement in this area by combining empirical studies of precedent with theoretical abstraction; from which emerged such important legal concepts as the *ius gentium* and the *liber homo*.

3. THE PEN IN POLITICS

The intended readers of the kind of technical works reviewed above were influential Romans professionally interested in the subjects treated. The authors, themselves rich men, will have seen to the multiplication and circulation of copies in the first instance; there was no 'copyright', and the very idea that an author might make some money, let alone a living, by writing prose would have seemed odd to all and to many perhaps wrong (cf. pp. 19–22). These circumstances naturally hindered the development of a prose literature addressed to a

[1] See Watson (1971) 9.
[2] Cicero emphasizes that only three of these were authentic (*De or.* 2.224).

wider audience on topics less specialist in character or of more ambitious appeal than the technical. The subject of potentially greatest interest and widest appeal was Roman history and contemporary politics: the whole cast of Roman thought, the character of the constitution, and the kaleidoscopic nature of the history of the past century precluded for the generation of the Gracchi the neat separation of the study of the past and the present into distinct genres. Even by the end of the century, the various strands which make up the rope of Roman historiography were still only strands. While certain themes can be seen to have been shared by writers as different as Ennius and Cato, Fabius and Coelius Antipater, for example an emphasis on the individual and his proper relation through *uirtus* to the extended family which was the *res publica*, fundamental questions of approach, emphasis, and presentation remained open at the end of the second century B.C. Thus, in discussing 'History' (pp. 149–52), we shall in fact be dealing with strands; and in order that we should appreciate their texture, it will be necessary first to discuss some kinds of writing which are best described as political manifestos or memoirs.

In the Greek world it had long been the custom of authors to address poems, histories, and technical works to a patron or friend, so that the work might take on the appearance of a private letter of didactic character. In the later second century we find the same in Latin literature. Lucilius addressed several of his poems to friends as verse-epistles; Accius' *Didascalica* was nominally addressed to one Baebius, Coelius Antipater's History of the Second Punic War was addressed to Aelius Stilo. Written during the last decades of the second century, this was the first prose-history in which the author sought to sweeten his instruction with the charms of rhetorical presentation. He seems to have followed the example of the worse sort of Hellenistic historian, and his style involved the disruption of the natural order of words in order to achieve rhythmical effects later, and rightly, condemned (cf. Auct. *ad Her.* 4.12.18 *has res ad te scriptas Luci misimus Aeli*, with a hexameter-movement, cf. Cic. *Orat.* 229). Clearly Coelius had a wider audience in mind, and his dedication to Aelius Stilo is only a literary device. In other works, however, the use of the letter-form or dedication was not so simply a convention. As we have seen, several of Cato's shorter works were addressed to Cato Licinianus, among them 'letters' on rhetoric (see p. 143), on medicine (Pliny, *N.H.* 29.14), and even several books on agriculture (Serv. *ad* Virg. *Geo.* 2.412). A century later the *Commentariolum petitionis* attributed rightly or wrongly to Marcus' brother Quintus Cicero is in the form of a private letter giving Marcus Cicero advice on the occasion of his standing for the consulship of 63 B.C. From the 120s B.C. there are excerpts of a similarly political letter written by Cornelia to her son Gaius Gracchus dissuading him from his plan to stand for the Tribunate in 123 B.C. The authenticity of the document has been much disputed, for no good reason at all.[1] It is of special interest that, if genuine, this is the earliest extant prose-writing in *any* language by a woman:

Verbis conceptis deierare ausim, praeterquam qui Tiberium Gracchum necarunt, neminem inimicum tantum molestiae tantumque laboris quantum te ob has res mihi tradidisse, quem oportebat omnium eorum quos antehac habui liberos [eorum] partis tolerare, atque curare ut quam minimum sollicitudinis in senecta haberem, utique quaecumque ageres, ea uelles maxume mihi placere, atque uti nefas haberes rerum maiorum aduersum meam sententiam quicquam facere, praesertim mihi quoi parua pars uitae superest. ne id quidem tam breue spatium potest opitulari quin et mihi aduersere et rem publicam profliges? denique quae pausa erit? ecquando desinet familia nostra insanire? ecquando modus ei rei haberi poterit? ecquando desinemus et habentes et praebentes molestiis insistere? ecquando perpudescet miscenda atque perturbanda re publica? sed si omnino non id fieri potest, ubi ego mortua ero, petito tribunatum: per me facito quod lubebit, cum ego non sentiam. ubi ego mortua ero, parentabis mihi et inuocabis deum parentem. in eo tempore nonne pudebit te eorum deum preces expetere, quos uiuos atque praesentes relictos atque desertos habueris? ne ille sirit Iuppiter te ea perseuerare nec tibi tantam dementiam uenire in animum! et si perseueras, uereor ne in omnem uitam tantum laboris culpa tua recipias, uti nullo tempore tute tibi placere possis.

'uerba ex epistula Corneliae Gracchorum matris ex libro Corneli Nepotis de Latinis Historicis excerpta.' (Nepos, frag. 2 Winstedt)

> *I would take a solemn oath that apart from those who killed Tiberius Gracchus no one has given me so much trouble and so much pain as you in this matter, who ought to undertake the part of all the children I have ever had, and to make sure that I should have as little worry as possible in my old age, and that, whatever your schemes might be, you should wish them to be agreeable to me, and that you should count it a sin to take any major step against my wishes, especially considering I have only a little part of life left. Is it quite impossible to cooperate for even that short space of time without your opposing me and ruining our country? Where will it all end? Will our family ever cease from madness? Can a bound ever be put to it? Shall we ever cease to dwell on affronts, both causing and suffering them? Shall we ever begin to feel true shame for confounding and destroying the constitution? But if that is quite impossible, when I am dead, then seek the Tribunate. Do what you like as far as I am concerned, when I am not there to know it. When I am dead, you will sacrifice to me and invoke me as your hallowed parent. At that time will you not be ashamed to seek the intercession of those hallowed ones whom alive and present you treated with abandonment and desertion? May Jove above not let you persist in this nor let such lunacy enter your mind! But if you do persist, I fear that through your own fault you will encounter so much trouble throughout your whole life that at no time will you be able to rest content.*

Cornelia wrote from Misenum, whither she had retired from Rome after Tiberius' assassination (133 B.C.). It is precisely because she is in deadly earnest that she addresses Gaius as if he were a public meeting, and it is remarkable that

---

[1] Cicero knew a collection of her letters, *Brut.* 211; cf. Leo (1913) 304f.

she is able to write so forcefully in Gaius' own language: no Roman lady ever had the opportunity or occasion to practise public oratory. Cornelia was an exceptional character: Plutarch comments on her culture (*C. Gracchus* 19) and Cicero recognized in her letters the same pure Latin as he admired in her son's speeches (*Brut.* 211, cf. Quint. *Inst.* 1.1.6, Plut. *C. Gracchus* 13). The style is virile, and it is noteworthy that Cornelia avoids diminutives even where they might have been appropriate (*pars* not *particula uitae*, *breue* not *breuiculum spatium*). The grammarian might criticize the loosely strung clauses of the opening sentence and the change of construction at *praesertim mihi* as well as the superabundance of Cornelia's rhetorical questions starting *ecquando...?*. These features, however, show that we are dealing not with a carefully revised and elaborate composition but with a spontaneous outburst, and it is therefore the more striking to note how naturally come the figures of speech which Cornelia uses – antithesis (*quam minimum...maxume*, *mihi aduersere*, *rem publicam profliges*), anaphora (*quantum...quantum*), hendiadys (*quos uiuos atque praesentes relictos atque desertos habueris*). This is a good example of Cato's precept *rem tene, uerba sequentur* observed. In fact, he could not have done better himself, and the Latinity and directness are precisely his (see below, p. 152). Although this has the appearance of a private letter intended for Gaius' guilty eyes alone, Cornelia's forensic vigour suggests that she may have intended to 'play dirty' by circulating copies at Rome to embarrass Gaius. In this case the ostensibly private letter would, like the *Commentariolum petitionis*, also be a political broadsheet.

Gaius himself wrote a memoir addressed to one M. Pomponius (Cic. *Div.* 1.18.36, Plut. *Ti. Gracchus* 8) which was clearly intended as an 'open letter' and contained information about his own and Tiberius' experiences. The autobiographical memoir is well attested in the period 120–90 B.C. Aemilius Scaurus wrote three books *De vita sua* to L. Fufidius (Cic. *Brut.* 112), Rutilius Rufus wrote five, and Q. Catulus one *De consulatu et de rebus gestis suis*, addressing the work to the poet Furius and affecting Xenophon's style (Cic. *Brut.* 132). All these men were considerable orators, and the forensic manner will naturally have coloured their writings. One can judge by analogy with the popularity in our own times of politicians' memoirs how such compositions would find a reading public not only among senators but also among many of lower degree who would otherwise have little interest in 'literature'.

This kind of prose-work was the special product of the Roman nobility at a particularly contentious period. Among Hellenes, as far as we know, only King Pyrrhus (possibly) and Aratus of Sicyon had written political autobiographies intended for the public and posterity. The later books of Cato's *Origines* included lengthy quotations of the author's own speeches, and undoubtedly had some of the character of political autobiography (see p. 150). Scipio Africanus (father of Cornelia) wrote a policy statement in Greek and addressed it to Philip V of Macedon (Polyb. 10.9.3) – and, no doubt, the world; none of his Latin speeches were preserved (cf. Cic. *Brut.* 77, *Off.* 3.1.4; Livy 38.56.6 and Gell. *N.A.* 4.18 derive from someone's imaginative concoction, not from Scipio).[1] Scipio Nasica Corculum wrote a Greek account of the Pydna campaign of 167 B.C., giving his own version of events, and addressing it to a Hellenistic prince (Plut. *Aem.* 15), no doubt to influence Greek opinion in general.

There survive from the 190s and 180s a number of decrees in the form of letters drafted in Greek and addressed to Greek communities by the Senate or individual Roman commanders. One by Flamininus to the lords and citizenry of the small town of Chyretiae in Perrhaebia illustrates the eager thirst of a Roman noble for χάριτα καὶ φιλοδοξίαν, i.e. *gratiam atque gloriam*. It is plausibly supposed that Flamininus wrote this rather flowery piece himself (*Syll.*[3] 593 = Sherk (1969) no. 33); while criticism of Flamininus' Greek as Greek is certainly mistaken,[2] the letter may fairly be faulted as over-elaborate, as diplomatese so often was and is. Flamininus overdoes the intensifying adverbs, and used the same kind of strained antithesis as is characteristic of Terence in his prologues. Nevertheless it is interesting and significant that at this comparatively early date a Roman should be seen taking such pains over phrase-length and sentence-structure. The passage turns easily into Latin, and the result will look if not like Cicero, then like C. Gracchus. How then did Flamininus speak when he addressed the Senate? And what kind of oratorical style underlies the very long and complex sentence with which Plautus makes Mercury greet the audience of *Amphitruo* (c. 189 B.C.: ll. 1–16)? We must beware of too simple a teleological model in describing the development of style in Latin oratory.

A quite different impression is given by the laconic but legally precise note scribbled by Aemilius Paullus in Spain in September 190 B.C. (Julian):

L. Aimilius L. f. inpeirator decreiuit utei quei Hastensium seruei in turri Lascutana habitarent leiberei essent. agrum oppidumque quod ea tempestate posedisent, item possidere habereque iousit, dum poplus senatusque Romanus uellet. act. in castreis a. d. xii k. febr. (*CIL* I² 614)

> *L. Aemilius (Paullus) son of Lucius, victorious general, decreed that the slaves of the Hastenses who lived at* Turris Luscitana *should be free. The land and the township which they possessed at that time he ordered they should likewise possess and own as long as the Roman People and Senate wished. Transacted in camp twelve days before the kalends of February.*[3]

---

[1] See Malcovati (1955) 6–8.

[2] The criticisms made by Sherk (1969) 199 are mistaken, and Badian's verdict that Flamininus' Greek is 'harsh and unidiomatic' is unkind (1974: 54). Neither takes account of the sentence structure.

[3] The calendar was out of true at this time (see p. 81), and the date in fact denotes September. The inscription is usually assigned to 189 B.C., after Paullus' victory over the Lusitanians (Livy 37.57.5).

When Cato spoke in Latin at Athens in 191 B.C. (see above, p. 141) it struck the listeners how much longer the interpreter seemed to take than Cato in making a point; and Cato could have got by in Greek if he had chosen (Plut. *Cat. Maj.* 12). It looks as though Cato was making a deliberate point here. By using Latin in his own pithy way, Cato was asserting the new importance of the language in international diplomacy, and implicitly rejecting the attitude and the Greek rhetoric of a Flamininus.

4. HISTORY

The earliest prose-histories of Rome were written in Greek by Q. Fabius Maximus and L. Cincius Alimentus, probably in the 190s B.C.; their aim will have been to explain and publicize the history of their relatively obscure πόλις, city, to the Hellenistic world at large.[1] Naevius and Ennius addressed a domestic audience in verse with quite another aim (see pp. 59–76). The sources theoretically available to them all included the *annales* kept by the Pontifex Maximus, treaties (e.g. with Carthage, Polyb. 3.22.3), *elogia*, family records and traditions, funeral laudations, the Greek historians Hellanicus, Hieronymus of Cardia, Antigonus, Timaeus, Silenus, Chaerea, Sosylus, the chronographical and geographical studies of Eratosthenes, and last but not least, personal experience; for all of them played some part in the events which they describe. Greek continued to be a medium for history right through the second century. P. Cornelius Scipio (the adoptive father of Scipio Aemilianus, Cic. *Brut.* 77), A. Postumius Albinus (whom Polybius called a windbag (32.29.1) and whom Cato mocked for his apologizing in advance for any stylistic shortcomings in his Greek, Gell. *N.A.* 11.8.2), C. Acilius (Liv. *per.* 53 *ad ann.* 142 B.C.), and Rutilius Rufus (Ath. 168d) all wrote in this tradition. It was Cato who founded Latin historiography as such with his *Origines*.

This was a work of his old age begun not earlier than 170 B.C. when he was sixty-five (cf. fr. 49 Peter and Leo (1913) 291); its general character is summarized in Cornelius Nepos' *Life of Cato* (24.3.4). The first book dealt with the Greek *Aborigines* of Italy, Aeneas and his Trojans, Lavinium, Alba, the foundation of Rome (752/1 B.C. in Cato's reckoning, fr. 17), and the reigns of the kings. The second and third books described the origins, customs and characters of Italian cities and peoples; it is only to the first three books that the

---

This would conveniently explain *inpeirator*, but it seems not to have been noticed that Polybius says that the Commissioners for the Eastern Settlement (of whom Paullus was one) left Italy just as Regillus' fleet was returning to Brundisium (21.24.16–17); Regillus hurried to Rome and triumphed *kal. feb.* 189 B.C. (Livy 37.59), i.e. early in September. Either Paullus must have missed the boat, or in fact the inscription belongs to September 190 B.C.: the fact that Paullus had suffered a heavy reverse that year (Livy 37.46) is not incompatible with his also having won a victory in virtue of which he had been hailed as *imperator*.

[1] See Badian (1966) ch. 1.

title *Origines* (κτίσεις 'foundations') properly applies. Probably what later passed as Books 4 to 7 were only published after Cato's death; these were a separate work as regards content and approach, and Cato omitted altogether the early Republic. According to Nepos Books 4 and 5 dealt with the Punic Wars, and he adds that here and subsequently Cato described wars *capitulatim* 'in summary form', or 'by topics', not like, say, Thucydides, or Polybius. There must be some over-simplification here, since Cato included a long quotation from his own speech *Against the Rhodians* (167 B.C.) in Book 5, which might imply that Philip, Antiochus, and Perseus also came in these books.[1] Book 7 ended with the misbehaviour in Spain of the praetor Servius Galba (151 B.C.) and Cato's own prosecution of him (149 B.C.), this last only months before Cato's death. Whatever the precise interpretation of *capitulatim* and the content of Books 4 and 5, the narrative evidently became slower and denser in the last books. Nepos ends by noting that Cato did not name the leaders in these wars, but referred to them simply by their military titles ('the consul', 'the praetor', etc.), that he narrated the *admiranda*, marvellous or surprising phenomena, to be seen in Spain and Italy, and that in the whole work there was a great deal of careful research and no small learning.[2]

Cato's motives for writing history were moral, didactic, and political. The elder statesman who had served and saved his country from enemies external and internal 'had no desire to write what can be found in the records of the Pontifex, how often corn was dear, how often an eclipse or whatever had obscured the light of the sun or moon', but to teach useful lessons (cf. frs. 2, 3). This might imply an indifference to detail and complexities; in fact ancient sources are unanimous in their praise of Cato's careful research, and his critical sense seems to have been a great deal better than, say, Accius'. He used the *annales* as the basis of his chronology (frs. 17, 45, 49) along with Eratosthenes (fr. 17); he appreciated the importance of documentary evidence (fr. 58); he recognized the limits of possible knowledge (frs. 40, 45); he had a thoroughly Alexandrian interest in the characteristics of peoples (frs. 31, 34, 51, 73, 76) and geography (fr. 38) and the *admiranda* to which Nepos alludes as a special feature are also represented in the fragments (frs. 17, 69). Besides Fabius Pictor (frs. 15, 23) it is likely that Cato will have consulted Timaeus, and Greek political theory lies behind his account of the constitution of Carthage (fr. 80). It would be quite wrong to see Cato simply as an Italian chauvinist (see p. 140): his Aborigines are Greeks from Achaia (fr. 6), Latin is a Greek dialect, the Sabines are of Spartan stock (fr. 50), the Arcadian Catillus founded Tibur (fr. 56).

---

[1] So Leo (1913) 294f.; but there are other possibilities.

[2] Nep. *Vitae* 24.4 *ad fin. in quibus multa industria et diligentia comparet, nulla doctrina* is beyond reasonable defence: read *nonnulla doctrina*.

To be truly Roman was not a matter of race but of service rendered to the *res publica*, and Cato's practice of leaving commanders anonymous is an affirmation of a view of society quite unlike that implicit in, say, Ennius' *Annales*. Unfortunately it is not clear how Cato spoke of himself in episodes where he himself was involved. His quotations from his own speeches (frs. 95, 106) certainly imply that the later books will have had some of the characteristics of the memoirs and autobiographies which were an important feature of political life in the next generation. Cato did not follow the convention of Greek historiography by which speeches might be invented to summarize issues dramatically or for appropriate occasions such as a meeting of Hannibal and Scipio before Zama. It is also to to his credit that his account of ancient Italy is based without speculative elaboration on what he found to be current local traditions, and he avoided the enigma of what might be called Rome's 'medi-aeval history' by omitting the Early Republic altogether, beginning Book 4 with the First Punic War.

The quality of Cato's *Origines* is highlighted by comparison with the work of his immediate successors who seem, by and large, to have been less critical and reliable, and who were not above inventing where sound evidence was lacking. Cassius Hemina's five books of *Annales* attempted a more continuous account of Roman history than Cato's: Books 2 and 3 dealt with the period which Cato had 'skipped', the early Republic, and, as in Cato, Book 4 began with the First Punic War. Cassius' style is clearly influenced by Cato; he shows an interest in etymologies (frs. 2, 3, 4, 6), 'firsts' (frs. 15, 26), aetiology (frs. 11, 14, 15, 20), moral points (fr. 13), and, what is new, imaginative description – the image of Aeneas leaving Troy as described by Cassius may owe something to Naevius (fr. 5 *ad fin.*). The *Annales* of L. Calpurnius Frugi was in seven books; he too dealt with the early Republic in Books 2 and 3, and wrote in a more jejune and less idiosyncratic manner than Cato, possibly with a Greek model such as Xenophon in mind as well as the pontifical records themselves. He quotes a *bon mot* of Romulus (fr. 8) and had a penchant for anecdotes of no real historical import (frs. 27, 33). The *Annales* of Cn. Gellius were on a scale that can only have been achieved by massive invention: he only reached 389 B.C. in Book 15 (fr. 25) and 216 B.C. in a book numbered at least 30 (fr. 26). Charisius quotes from a ninety-seventh book, which is perhaps not quite beyond credibility considering the scale of the *Annales* as published by Scaevola pontifex (Serv. auct. *ad* Virg. *Aen.* 1.373). The retreat from Cato's original and critical if quirky style of historiography into the mainstream of second-rate Hellenistic rhetoricizing narrative seems to have been completed by L. Coelius Antipater, the first to write on a single theme (the Second Punic War) (see p. 145), and C. Fannius, cos. 122 B.C., who included fictitious speeches (Cic. *Brut.* 81). Lastly Sempronius Asellio shows the influence of Polybius in his reflections on the nature of true history (fr. 1), but seems in his large-scale work (at least fourteen books) to have dealt with a subject which he knew at first hand, the Numantine War (fr. 6), thus fulfilling in prose a role which the satirist Lucilius declined to fulfil in verse (see p. 169).

5. CATO ORATOR

The following is from a speech *De sumptu suo* made by Cato in his own defence: in the extract he is presenting himself and his secretary as preparing the defence which he is now making:

Iussi caudicem proferri ubi mea oratio scripta erat de ea re quod sponsionem feceram cum M. Cornelio. tabulae prolatae: maiorum benefacta perlecta: deinde quae ego pro re publica leguntur. ubi id utrumque perlectumst, deinde scriptum erat in oratione: 'numquam ego pecuniam neque meam neque sociorum per ambitionem dilargitus sum.' 'attat, noli noli scribere inquam istud: nolunt audire.' deinde recitauit: 'numquam ego praefectos per sociorum uestrorum oppida imposiui qui eorum bona liberos ⟨uxores⟩ diriperent.' 'istud quoque dele: nolunt audire, recita porro.' 'numquam ego praedam neque quod de hostibus captum esset neque manubias inter pauculos amicos meos diuisi ut illis eriperem qui cepissent.' 'istuc quoque dele: nihil eo minus uolunt dici; non opus est recitato.' 'numquam ego euectionem dataui quo amici mei per symbolos pecunias magnas caperent.' 'perge istuc quoque uti cum maxume delere.' 'numquam ego argentum pro uino congiario inter apparitores atque amicos meos disdidi neque eos malo publico diuites feci.' 'enimuero usque istuc ad lignum dele.' uide sis quo in loco res publica siet, uti quod rei publicae bene fecissem, unde gratiam capiebam, nunc idem illud memorare non audeo, ne inuidiae siet. ita inductum est male facere impoene, bene facere non impoene licere.

(Or. fr. 173 Malcovati (Fronto p. 92 N))

I called for the book to be produced in which was written my speech on the subject of the contract which I had made with M. Cornelius. The records were produced, my ancestors' services read through, then what I had done for the community was read out. When each reading was over, the next item written in my speech was this: 'Never did I hand out sums of money, neither my own nor the allies', in bribery.' 'Aha! No, no, don't write that', says I; 'they don't want to hear that.' Then he read out: 'Never did I billet officers on your Allies' townships to ravage their property, children, and their wives.' 'Score that out too: they don't want to hear that: read on.' 'Never did I divide plunder, neither what had been taken from the enemy nor the cash from its sale, among my little circle of friends, in order to defraud those who had taken it.' 'Score that out too; there is nothing they want said less; no need to read that out.' 'Never did I automatically dole out travel-vouchers so that my friends could get large sums of money with the seals.'[1] 'Go on, score that out too as hard as you can.' 'Never did I distribute cash instead of the wine-ration among my staff and friends, nor did I enrich them at the public expense.' 'Yes, score that out right down to the wood.'[2] Just see

---

[1] Precisely what racket is implied by *per symbolos* is not clear.

[2] We are to understand that Cato's *codicilli* were the kind in which the writing surface was a layer of beeswax on wood.

what a position our country is in: the service which I have rendered the community and from which I won favour is now the very thing that I dare not mention, lest it be the source of envious spite. So the new order is the freedom to do mischief and get away with it, and to render useful service but not get away with it.

Cato composed this remarkably lively, witty, and ironic piece when he was seventy, in 164 B.C., that is in Terence's heyday; and a comparison and contrast of their styles is instructive. Cato was among the first to keep *codicilli* recording the texts of his speeches; his reasons were of course professional, as this extract shows. By the 160s he will have had a considerable library. Cicero tells us that he revised some of his speeches in his old age (*Sen.* 38), and we have seen that he used some in his *Origines*. How, when, and in what sense Cato's speeches were published and circulated after his death is obscure, but they will have been of interest to a potentially wide public as a political testament, as a historical source, and as oratory. Thus without intending it Cato made oratory a literary genre, as Demosthenes had at Athens: his speeches might be closely conned as examples in the teaching of the art of rhetoric, and evaluated by connoisseurs, both politicians and professors. By the end of the second century B.C. it was unusual for a prominent statesman such as M. Antonius *not* to circulate copies of his major speeches or keep them with an eye to his memoirs and his reputation (Cic. *Cluent.* 140, Val. Max. 7.3.5).

The directness of Cato's manner survived into the Gracchan era. The fragments of Gaius Gracchus show as many similarities to Cato as differences; such passages as Cornelia's letter (p. 146) and the Hogarthian description of the behaviour of Roman *iudices* in a forceful passage of C. Titius cited by Macrobius (*Sat.* 3.16.4) are genuinely Catonian in tone and expression. However, perhaps already in Flamininus' time, and certainly by the 160s B.C., more self-consciously showy and formalized rhetoric was coming into favour; the prologues of Terence's plays are miniature specimens of the Asiatic style of Pergamum; see *The Late Republic*, pp. 59–62 on the whole question of this and the Attic manner in Roman rhetoric before Cicero. In Cicero's time Cato was little read by aspiring orators, an omission much regretted by Cicero, who had managed, apparently with some difficulty, to trace 150 speeches by the old master. His commendation of Cato's attitude and style (*Brut.* 63–5) shows some historical perspective rare in Roman literary criticism, and it is probable that an edition of the speeches was prepared by Atticus. Thanks to this Cato's speeches continued to be read and admired well into the second century A.D.

The conventional view of the development of Roman oratory is summed up by Tacitus (*Dial.* 18): *Catone sene C. Gracchus plenior et uberior, sic Graccho politior atque ornatior Crassus, sic utroque distinctior et urbanior et altior Cicero* 'Gaius Gracchus is proportionately as fuller and richer than Cato the Elder as Crassus is more polished and ornate than Gracchus and as Cicero is more harmonious and civilized and sublime than either.' There are dangers in such pat summaries. The individual's qualities will be over-simplified, and the first in such a series is almost bound to appear by implication as less sophisticated and various than he was. An Andronicus, an Ennius, or a Cato were naturally especially liable to this kind of treatment in Roman literary criticism, which was often quite crudely teleological. It puzzled and surprised Fronto, a frank admirer of Cato's work, that the extended example of the figure of παράλειψις (omission; our cliché 'not to mention. . . ') which he quotes from the *De sumptu suo* seemed unparalleled in his experience and better handled than in any writer that he knew, Greek or Latin. This is typical of Cato. His rhetoric could not be neatly pigeon-holed according to the rules of the manuals and *exempla* (Gell. *N.A.* 6.3.52) which made teleological criticism easy.

Cato's style,[1] both in his speeches and in his *Origines*, was essentially paratactic, reflecting the same speech-patterns as we hear in Terence's narrative and dialogue rather than in his prologues. Sentence-connexion is simple, and Cato shows no desire to avoid repetition of words in linking sentences. A Crassus or Antonius would probably have regarded the brief narration at the beginning of the passage cited as marred by the repetitions 'read through' (*perlecta. . . leguntur. . .perlectum*) and 'written in the speech' (*oratio scripta erat. . .deinde scriptum erat*). On the other hand Cato took more care over phrasing in his speeches than in his *De agri cultura*: *tabulae. . .leguntur* is a modestly rising tricolon, and some of the attention to the rhythmical cadences of phrases and sentences so characteristic of later Roman oratory is already apparent in Cato. A small but clear sign of the different levels of diction which Cato felt appropriate to his speeches and to his technical works is the fact that the weighty *atque* is the normal word for 'and' in the speeches (so too in Cornelia's letter), but the lightweight *et* in the *De agricultura*. When Cato is being self-consciously didactic, this becomes a noticeable mannerism, as in the beginning of the speech against the Rhodians (Gell. *N.A.* 6(7).3, fr. 95 Malcovati).

Cato's language is remarkably various. He would not have agreed with the precept of the purist Julius Caesar that one should avoid an unknown word as one would a reef. Cato enjoyed something of the freedom of the older Comedians in exploiting the resources of morphology to make a striking phrase or to find the *mot juste*, e.g. *pauculos amicos* in the *De sumptu suo*. The exclamation *attat* is borrowed not from life but from comedy, and aptly, for Cato is here presenting himself as a character in a tragicomedy, where true moral values have been stood on their heads. Frequentatives (*futare = fu-it-are = saepius fuisse*), analogical formations (*pulchralia = bellaria* 'desserts', fr. 107), new adjectives (*impudentiam praemiosam*, 241), expressions like *cloacale flumen* (126) 'a sewery stream', *uecticulariam uitam uiuere* (246) 'to live a crowbarious life', nouns like

---

[1] See Leo (1913) 273f., 286ff., 299f.; Till (1936) *passim*.

plebitas, duritudo (cf. Gell. *N.A.* 17.2.20), *pelliculatio* (243), from **pelliculare*
from *pellicere* 'enticement', a phrase such as . . . *ridibundum magistratum gerere,
pauculos homines, mediocriculum exercitum obuium duci* . . . (44) ' . . . to exercise a
laughful magistracy, that a handful of men, a standardlet army be led to face . . . '
(cf. *tuburcinabundus, lurcinabundus,* 253) – all these mark one who is not the
servant but the master of a language in which the kind of decorum observed by
Terence has not yet become the rule. Anaphora, tricolon and the multiplication
of synonyms are used to render a passage formidable (δείνωσις): *tuum nefarium
facinus peiore facinore operire postulas, succidias humanas facis, tantam trucida-
tionem facis, decem funera facis, decem capita libera interficis, decem hominibus
uitam eripis indicta causa, iniudicatis, incondemnatis* 'You expect to hide your
foul crime with a worse crime; you cause human butchery, you cause such
slaughter, ten pyres you cause, ten free persons you kill, ten men's lives you
steal, their case unstated, themselves untried and uncondemned' (fr. 59, *In Q.
Minucium Thermum de decem hominibus,* 190 B.C.); and paronomasia and
vigorous puns (*M. Fulvius Mobilior,* 151; *eam ego uiam pedetemptim temptabam,*
45) also have their place in a style characterized by Cicero (*Orat.* 152) as *horridula*
'rather hirsute', and more fully and paradoxically by Plutarch (*Cat. Maj.* 7) as
εὔχαρις ἅμα καὶ δεινός . . . καὶ ἡδὺς καὶ καταπληκτικός, φιλοσκώμμων καὶ αὐστη-
ρός, ἀποφθεγματικὸς καὶ ἀγωνιστικός 'charming and at the same time formidable, simple and surprising, jocular and dry, full of quotable passages and tight
argument': 'Now they say that there are fine crops in the meadows and the
fields. Don't put too much trust in that. I have often heard it said that a lot can
happen between the dish and the mouth. But between the dish and the field,
that really is a long way' (fr. 217); 'That man can be hired for a crust of bread
to keep quiet or to speak' (fr. 112); 'Thieves of private property spend their
lives in jails and in fetters: public thieves in gold and purple' (fr. 224); 'It is
difficult, citizens of Rome, to address bellies: they don't have ears' (fr. 254);
'I spent my whole life as a young man right from the start in thrift and in
toughness and in hard work, cultivating the farm – making meadow out of
Sabine stones and flint and sowing seed on them' (fr. 217, cf. Men. *Dysk.* 1ff.);
*iure lege libertate re publica communiter uti oportet: gloria atque honore quomodo
sibi quisque struxit* 'all should equally enjoy justice, law, liberty, and the constitution: glory and public office, as each has built for himself' (fr. 252).

7

THE SATIRES OF ENNIUS
AND LUCILIUS

1. THE MINOR WORKS OF ENNIUS

Ennius was not only a major dramatist and the author of the most ambitious Roman epic. He also extended the range of Latin poetry in a series of compositions in the *genus humile*, the low key, some based on Greek models, and others original. In these the poet had a prominent part, sometimes as himself, more pervasively as arbiter, editor, and commentator. Ennius' aim was sometimes to instruct, sometimes to amuse, and most often to do both. Right from the start, 'to tell the truth with a smile' and 'to mix the useful with the sweet' were characteristics of what fifty years later in Lucilius emerged as an important and specially Roman genre, satire. Let us review the content and tone of these minor works.

Ennius' *Sota* was a Latin version of a bawdy poem by Sotades, an Alexandrian of the third century B.C. It was written in the species of ionic tetrameter named after Sotades, a rhythm intended to call to mind the salacious dance-style of *cinaedi* and fit for comic treatment (cf. Plautus, *Pers.* 826, *Stich.* 769ff.; Petronius, *Sat.* 23):

> ille ictu' retro reccidit in natem supinus...
>
> (Sota 5 V = ROL 5)
> *Knocked backwards, he fell square down on his bum...*

This was a linguistic and metrical experiment on Ennius' part. Even the few fragments extant show that he admitted low language and themes carefully avoided in the *palliata*. *Nates*, 'bum', occurs only once in Plautus, in the mouth of a vulgarian (*Pers.* 847): and Ennius used dialect words, e.g. *tongent* 'they ken' (*ROL* fr. 4) where the normal *callent* 'they know' would have done.

The *Hedyphagetica* was also experimental. We have some fragments of its model, the *Gastronomia* of Archestratus of Gela, enough to show that this was not simply a translation but an adaptation like Plautus' or Ennius' plays. One addition to Archestratus' catalogue of succulent fish implies that the poem was not written until after Ennius' visit to Ambracia (189/8 B.C.).[1] As in the *Sota*,

---

[1] Skutsch (1968) 38f.

Ennius kept the metre of the original, the dactylic hexameter,[1] proper to martial and didactic themes:

> Surrenti tu elopem fac emas glaucumque ἀπὸ Κύμης.
> Quid scaru'? Praeterii, cerebrum Ioui' paene supremi!
> Nestoris ad patriam hic capitur magnusque bonusque...
>
> (*Hedyphagetica, ROL* 6ff. = Apul. *Apol.* 39)

See you get sturgeon at Surrentum and blue shark from Cumae. What about wrasse?
I missed that – nearly the brain of majestic Jove, it is! A good one and a big can be
taken in the land of Nestor...

Here the expressions *fac emas* and the 'neat' Greek ἀπὸ Κύμης[2] as well as the pretence of spontaneity in *praeterii* are colloquial and stand in absurd contrast to the tone of *Nestoris ad patriam* and the use of the connectives ...*que*...*que* which are traits of a much more pretentious diction.[3]

Others of Ennius' minor works were more serious. A work called *Scipio* praised Africanus and included separate poems in trochaic septenarii and in hexameters; the style of the extant fragments corresponds to that of the tragedies and of the *Annales*. Moral instruction and entertainment were mixed in the *Protrepticum* (perhaps identical with a work called *Praecepta*), the *Euhemerus* or *Historia sacra*, and *Epicharmus*. In the last Ennius is supposed to have translated or adapted a didactic work which passed as that of Epicharmus; in it Ennius recorded how he dreamt that he was dead, and how he learnt, presumably from Epicharmus himself, the theory of the four elements and related ideas referred to also in the Tragedies and the *Annales*.[4] The dream is likely to be an Ennian invention, and Cicero may have taken the setting of the *Somnium Scipionis* from here. The *Epicharmus* and the *Protrepticus* are thought, probably rightly, to have been all in trochaic septenarii. The *Historia sacra* was modelled on the Ἱερὰ ἀναγραφή of Euhemerus of Messene (b. *c.* 340 B.C.),[5] a philosophical 'novel' in which the gods and heroes were explained as mortals whose deeds had been magnified and distorted by the poets. Lactantius preserves quite lengthy extracts in a strikingly bald prose; he thought that he was quoting Ennius verbatim (cf. *Div. inst.* 1.14.1, where Ennius' words are opposed to those of 'the poets'). It has been the fashion to regard these fragments as our earliest extant literary Latin prose; Ennius, it is alleged, experimented here with a deliberately naive style intended to match the manner of logographers like

---

[1] On unusual features of the verse-technique, see Lindsay (1922) ch. 1.

[2] The text here is uncertain, however.

[3] Fraenkel (1960) 199f.

[4] The ideas of 'Epicharmus' and Empedocles of Acragas are not to be nicely distinguished in this connexion; cf. e.g. Ennius, *Thyestes TRF* 351, *Annales (lib. inc.)* 522 V = *ROL* (8) 261, Menander fr. 614.

[5] Note that Archestratus, Epicharmus, and possibly also Euhemerus were Sicilian.

Hecataeus of Miletus in his *Historiae* or *Heroologia*, whom it is supposed – there is no direct evidence at all – Euhemerus himself will have imitated.[1] This is an elaborate theory with an important link missing, and one may ask what was the point of a poet's choosing such a peculiar style for a first extensive essay in Latin prose. There is in fact more probability in the older theory that the *Historia sacra* was, like Ennius' other expository works, presented in iambo-trochaic verse. There are constant echoes of the rhythms and diction of septenarii in Lactantius' citations and these become specially obvious when one compares the prose-version of the fable of the Crested Lark and its Chicks quoted by Gellius at *N.A.* 2.29.3ff. This, from Ennius' *Saturae*, was certainly written in septenarii. The prose citations of the *Euhemerus* are best seen as belonging to the same class of paraphrase. The extreme simplicity of the phrasing and syntax suggest that Lactantius' immediate source was a prose version intended for use as a schoolbook.

Porphyrio (*ad Hor. Sat.* 1.10.46) states that Ennius left four books called *Saturae*;[2] the manuscripts of Donatus *ad* Ter. *Pho.* 339, where a passage is cited from a sixth book, are probably corrupt. While it is likely that the title *Saturae* does derive from Ennius, it does not follow that the book arrangement or even the contents of the edition known to Porphyrio were due to Ennius himself. Each book, one *Satura*, contained miscellaneous poems, mainly in the iambo-trochaic metres and diction of comedy, but also some in hexameters and perhaps Sotadeans.[3] The subject matter was very diverse: fables (the Crested Lark; the Piper and the Fish (*Sat.* 65 V = *ROL* 20, cf. Hdt. 1.141)), moral criticism of types (a glutton, *Sat.* 1 V = *ROL* 1; busybodies, 5 V = *ROL* 5; slanderers, 8f. V = *ROL* 8f.), exhortation (2 V = *ROL* 2), proverbs (70 V = *ROL* 27), quasi-dramatic encounters implying dialogue (6f. V = *ROL* 6f.), an etymological point (69 V = *ROL* 23, *simia/similis*), a parasite's monologue (14–19 V = *ROL* 14–19) in good comic style, and a debate between Life and Death (Quint. *Inst.* 9.2.36). The poet himself is never far away – 'I never poetize but when I'm gouty' (64 V = *ROL* 21); 'Ennius the maker, greetings, you who pass to mortal men a cup of flaming verses drawn from your marrow' (6f. V = *ROL* 6f., a particularly fine pair of lines); '...from there I contemplate the clear and columned shores of Aether' (3f. V = *ROL* 3f.). It is probable that the *Saturae* are the source of some of the anecdotal and personal details that we have about Ennius, for example, an amusing story at Ennius' expense about an encounter with Scipio Nasica (Cic. *De or.* 2.276), that he lived on the Aventine with only one servant to 'do' for him, that he was a *contubernalis*, close

---

[1] Laughton (1951) 35ff., Fraenkel (1951a) 50ff.; followed by Waszink (1972) 106, 351, and Jocelyn (1972) 1023.

[2] For the meaning of this term, 'Salad-dishes', see below, p. 161.

[3] *Sat.* 28–31 (an enthymeme involving much repetition of the word *frustrari*) is in a species of ionic tetrameter, certainly not Saturnians (so Warmington).

associate, of Caecilius Statius, that he was a neighbour of the Servilii Galbae (Cic. *Acad.* 2.51), and that he had three personalities (*tria corda*) because he could speak Greek, Latin, and Oscan (Gellius, *N.A.* 17.17.1).[1]

The *Saturae* thus had elements and themes moral, paraenetic, reflective, comic, narrative, and autobiographical, and were based mainly on the stage-medium. The low language and tone of *Sota*, the mixture of colloquial and elevated in the hexameters of *Hedyphagetica*, the use of different metres in a single work (*Scipio*), the evident importance of the poet's *ego* in *Epicharmus*, and the paraenetic and didactic character of the other minor works – these features complement and agree with the tone and content of the fragments transmitted as belonging to the *Saturae*, and are all to be found in later Satire. It has been maintained that some of the works known by individual titles are really part of the *Saturae*. *Scipio*, for example, has been claimed as part of *Satura* III (cf. 10f. V = *ROL* 10f.), and *Epicharmus* might be part of *Satura* II (cf. 3f. V = *ROL* 3f.). Now in view of the complexities which can arise in the transmission of *libelli* consisting of collections of short works – Lucilius and Catullus are examples – it is prudent not to be dogmatic about this in any way. Such arguments as have been adduced in recent studies for separating the *Saturae* from the named minor works are not conclusive, since we know too little about the early transmission of any of the works in question.[2] It is in any case a rather serious mistake in tracing the history of the genre satire to draw a qualitative distinction between those works of Ennius referred to as *Saturae* and all the rest, and to focus attention on the former; for, however and *sub quocumque nomine* they circulated there is no essential difference between the poems referred to as from the *Saturae* and the rest, and by attending mainly or exclusively to the *Saturae*, one may beg the question 'What is the nature and origin of Latin satire?'

One characteristic of later satire is definitely absent from Ennius. He has no personal invective or specific social criticism. On the contrary, when Ennius names someone, it is to praise him (Scipio), or to tell a pleasant tale (Galba, Nasica). *Non est meum*, says he (63 V = *ROL* 22), *ac si me canis memorderit* 'It's not my way, as if a dog had bitten me...'; an attitude quite unlike Lucilius': *inde canino ricto oculisque inuolem...* 'from there let me fly (at him/them) with a dog's grin and eyes' (Lucil. (30) 1095–6 M = *ROL* 1001).[3] The one rejects, the other accepts gladly the κυνικὸς τρόπος, the cynic role and the accusation of hydrophobia.

---

[1] See in general van Rooy (1965) 30–49; Waszink (1972) 99–147; Coffey (1976) 27–32; Badian (1971) 168ff.

[2] Waszink (1972) 101–7, Jocelyn (1972) 1023. Van Rooy (1965) 39 only mentions the minor works in passing and does not raise the issue; Coffey (1976) 31 over-simplifies it; none of them sufficiently recognizes the homogeneity of the *Saturae* and the named minor works.

[3] See below, p. 163 n. 1.

In fact, Ennius' minor works as a whole remind one of many features of low-key, unpretentious Alexandrian poetry and moralizing literature. A judicious modern account of fourth- and third-century Greek literature as it relates in style, intent, and variety to *all* of Ennius' minor works remains a *desideratum*.[1] It is clear that Ennius' *Saturae* cannot possibly have been intended as a new genre of *poetry* 'untouched by the Greeks' as Horace puts it (*Sat.* 1.10.66). The Σωρός 'Heap (of grain for winnowing)' by Posidippus offers an analogy for a *Satura*, a 'Salad-dish' of σύμμεικτα or ἄτακτα, 'miscellanies', 'bits and pieces' in a variety of metres. The *Chreiai* 'Exercises' of Machon are a collection of anecdotes about parasites, playwrights, and courtesans, written in the medium of New Comedy, and hitting the same note as Ennius with his stage-language and iambo-trochaics. The moralizing of Cercidas of Megalopolis, the *Silloi* of Timon, and the exoteric writings of the Cynics are all relevant to him; and the *Iamboi* of Callimachus, although not themselves a direct pattern for Ennius' *Saturae*, are perhaps the best-known example of the kind of Greek poetry to which Ennius' *Saturae* may be compared.[2]

2. SATURA BEFORE ENNIUS?

According to the unreliable source used by Livy at 7.2.4–10, the last stage in the development of Roman drama before Andronicus (see p. 78) had been a dramatic *satura*, a show with music and a libretto, but no consecutive plot; and it was a received opinion in Imperial times, possibly deriving from Varro, that satire was a specially Roman genre. 'Grant that Lucilius is more polished', says Horace (*Sat.* 1.10.66), *quam rudis et Graecis intacti carminis auctor* 'than the unsophisticated originator of a poetry untouched even by the Greeks...'; he means Ennius in his *Saturae*, and is alluding to, though not necessarily embracing, an evidently well-known view that Ennius was *primus inventor* of the genre literary satire, to which Greek example allegedly contributed nothing.[3] In the course of a discussion of the relative merits of Greek and Latin literature by genre Quintilian (*Inst.* 10.1.93) remarks *satura quidem tota nostra est* 'but satire is all ours'; he has just finished discussing elegy, where he reckons the honours even, and, after a characteristically sensible and pithy evaluation of Lucilius and his successors, he proceeds to the Greek *iambus*, since Archilochus the form *par excellence* for Greek invective. Two interpretations of Quintilian's

---

[1] Geffcken's articles (1911) are useful, but our knowledge of Hellenistic literature is now much extended.

[2] It misses the point to debate how closely Ennius' *Saturae* resembled the *Iamboi*: his *Medea* is hardly faithful to Euripides in letter or spirit. See Waszink (1972) 119ff. for some account of the gradual acceptance over the last thirty years of the influence of Callimachus' *Iamboi*; we should add *id genus omne*.

[3] See Rudd (1960) 36ff.; van Rooy (1965) 45 n. 6; Waszink (1972) 123.

remark are current. The minority view, first proposed by W. Rennie (1922) 21 is that he means 'but in satire we Romans win easily'; the older and alternative, that he means 'but satire is an exclusively Roman genre', has been reasserted in recent studies.[1] Rennie's basic point is that Quintilian's discussion is not about origins but evaluations; on the other hand, it is argued, the passage of Horace cited above can be taken to support the other view; and there is the consideration that alone among the genres listed by Quintilian, satire does not have a Greek name. The grammarian Diomedes (*GLK* I 485) defines *satyra* (*sic*) as *carmen apud Romanos, nunc quidem maledicum et ad carpenda hominum uitia Archaeae Comoediae charactere compositum, quale scripserunt Lucilius et Horatius et Persius; sed olim carmen quod ex uariis poematibus constabat satyra uocabatur, quale scripserunt Pacuuius et Ennius* 'poetry with the Romans, now vituperative and composed with the *timbre* of Old Comedy, such as Lucilius, Horace and Persius wrote; but once poetry which consisted of different (kinds of) poems was called *satyra*, such as Pacuvius and Ennius wrote'. Diomedes proceeds to list various suggested etymologies for the word, starting with the one which he himself thought (certainly wrongly) the most probable: *satyra autem dicta siue a Satyris, quod similiter in hoc carmine ridiculae res pudendaeque dicuntur, uelut quae a Satyris proferuntur et fiunt* 'satyra is so called either from Satyrs, because ridiculous and shameful things are likewise said in this poetry as are delivered and done by Satyrs...'. There lies behind this an allusion to the satyr plays of Attic and Hellenistic drama such as Sophocles' *Ichneutae*. Among other serious objections to this evidently popular and widespread theory there are the points that in that case the name should be *satyrica* (n. pl.), not *satura* (-*yra*, -*ira*) (f. sing.); and that since there is no feminine nominal suffix -*ŭra* (-*yra*, -*ĭra*) in Latin, we must be dealing with the adjective *satur* in the feminine, with a noun left understood. That is indeed Diomedes' second suggestion, ...*siue satyra a lance quae referta uariis multisque primitiis in sacro apud priscos dis inferebatur*... 'or *satyra* is named after a *lanx* (f.), dish, which filled with many different first-fruits was offered to the gods in a religious service in olden times'. This is generally agreed to be the right explanation.[2]

These passages have given rise to an enormous amount of speculation, and in particular to the theory that Ennius' *saturae* with their dramatic elements some-how represent a literary development of pre- or sub-literate dramatic perfor-mances by a *cantor* and *tibicen*, which, on the evidence of Livy, will have been called *saturae*; and support for this has been found in the passages cited from Horace and Quintilian as interpreted by the majority, not without the aid of certain unhistorical prejudices of the late Romantic period about popular

[1] In particular van Rooy (1965) 117–23, followed by Coffey (1976) 3.
[2] For Diomedes' other suggestions, and modern elaborations, see van Rooy (1965) 1–27, Coffey (1976) 12–18, Waszink (1972) 103.

culture and nationalism and the originality of Roman literature vis-à-vis Greek. However, as Ennius said (*Sat.* 70 V = *ROL* 27), *quaerunt in scirpo soliti quod dicere nodum* 'As the common saying is, they are looking for a knot in a bulrush.' Livy's dramatic *satura* is plausibly explained as a confused and confusing attempt by Livy's source to include in the pedigree of Roman comedy an equivalent to the satyr plays of Greek drama, just as we find a rough Italian counterpart earlier in his account for the Old Comedy of Athens.[1] He or some other cultural nationalist may have patriotically derived literary satire from that source. There is indeed something specially Roman in Lucilius' (not Ennius') satire: the combination of his caustic tone, his impudent disregard for the decorum of literary theory, his use of his own experiences and encounters, and his variety are unique, not but what each separate trait can be found somewhere in Greek literature. It does not follow, however, that critics in the first century B.C. or the earlier twentieth A.D. were justified in inferring the existence of a lively native Italian tradition of satirical character passing back through Ennius to a hypothetical form of popular drama.

The only evidence for Latin satire before Ennius is in fact a single quotation of 'Naeuius in Satyra' (Festus p. 306 L); the line is a Saturnian, and therefore cannot come from a play called *Satura* 'The Pregnant Woman' (cf. Plautus. *Amph.* 667 and the title of an *Atellana* by Pomponius and a *togata* by Atta). With all due caution one may reckon with the possibility that Naevius did write occasional poems; his supposed epitaph (Saturnians: Gell. *N.A.* 1.24.2, from Varro), the line *fato Metelli Romae fiunt consules* (ps.-Asconius *ad* Cic. *Verr.* 1.10.29) cited as a senarius, but possibly a saturnian matching the reply *malum dabunt Metelli Naeuio poetae*, and the naughty story in iambic septenarii about the young Scipio Africanus (Gell. *N.A.* 7.8.5) might belong here. However, even if Naevius did write and circulate occasional poems in various metres, it does not follow that he issued a collected 'edition', still less that he himself called the collection a 'Salad-dish' or 'Medley'.

3. LUCILIUS

Nothing is known of the *saturae* of Ennius' nephew Pacuvius, and it is only by chance that we hear of the letters written at Corinth in 146 B.C. by Sp. Mummius *uersiculis facetis*, in witty verse, and sent to his *familiares*, his private friends (Cic. *Att.* 13.6a). There may have been much more of this domestic *lusus*, verse-play, than we know: Lucilius himself refers to a comic verse-edict regulating behaviour at banquets, the *Lex Tappula* of one Valerius Valentinus ((*lib. inc.*) 1307, 1316 M = *ROL* 1239–40), and in an early poem Lucilius implies that if his were the most notorious occasional verses, they were not the only ones

---

[1] Waszink (1972) 107–9; Coffey (1976) 18–22. See p. 78.

((30) 1013 M = *ROL* 1091).[1] His earliest traceable works date from the late 130s B.C., when he had returned to Rome after war-service as a cavalryman in the entourage of Scipio Aemilianus at the siege of Numantia in Spain. Lucilius belonged to the Latin (not the Roman) aristocracy; a senator Manius Lucilius may have been his brother, and he was great-uncle to Pompeius Magnus. He was rich and independent, owning an important house in Rome and large estates in southern Italy and Sicily; the family seat was at Suessa Aurunca on the borders of Campania and Latium Adiecticium. Thus, like Sp. Mummius, he was a grandee, superior in status to his contemporaries in letters L. Accius and L. Afranius. He was a friend of Scipio Aemilianus ((6) 1132–42 M = *ROL* 254–8; (11) 394f. M = *ROL* 424f., Hor. *Sat.* 2.1.71 and schol. ad loc.), Decimus Laelius and the young Iunius Congus ((26) 595–6 M = *ROL* 632–4), Gaius Laelius, and probably C. Sempronius Tuditanus ((30) 1079–87 M = *ROL* 1008–15 may be addressed to him). The sceptic philosopher Clitomachus as head of the Academy at Athens dedicated a work to Lucilius (Cic. *Acad.* 2.102), and it is likely enough that he knew the Stoic Panaetius and Polybius, also friends of Aemilianus. A salient feature of Lucilius' work in the eyes of posterity was his outspoken criticism of famous men, and he was compared with Archilochus (whom he had himself read, (28) 698 M = *ROL* 786) and the writers of the Old Comedy. It was Lucilius' privileged position in society that made it possible for him to mount and to sustain such attacks. Even the fragments attest an impressive series of the great as his victims: Q. Caecilius Metellus Macedonicus (*RE* no. 94), cens. 131 B.C. (schol. *ad* Hor. *Sat.* 2.1.72, (26) 676ff. M = *ROL* 636ff.); L. Cornelius Lentulus Lupus (*RE* no. 224), cens. 147 B.C., *princeps senatus* 131–126 B.C. (Hor. *Sat.* 2.1.62ff., schol. *ad* 67 and 72, Persius 1.114, (28) 784–90 M = *ROL* 805–11 and *lib.* 1 *passim*, Serv. *ad Aen.* 10.104); Macedonicus' son C. Caecilius Metellus Caprarius (*RE* no. 84, Supplbd. III 222), praetor 117 B.C. ((5) 1130, 210–1 M = *ROL* 232–4, schol. *ad* Hor. *Sat.* 2.1.67); C. Papirius Carbo (*RE* no. 33), tr. pl. 131 B.C., pr. 130 B.C., cos. 120 B.C. (*lib. inc.* 1312–13 M = *ROL* 1138–41); L. Opimius (*RE* no. 4) cos. 121 B.C. ((11) 418–20 M = *ROL* 450–2); Q. Mucius Scaevola Augur (*RE* no. 21), pr. 121/120 B.C. (*lib.* 2 *passim*); and others. A rather muddily-written passage defining *uirtus* is addressed to one Albinus; this may have been intended ironically for the benefit of A. or Sp. Postumius Albinus after their disgraceful showing in the Jugurthan War (110/109 B.C.) (*lib. inc.* 1326–38 M = *ROL* 1196–1208). Although some of those mentioned had been *inimici*, personal enemies of Aemilianus (d. 129 B.C.), Lucilius, who may or may not have been a Roman citizen, was not a party politician. As a Latin and a landowner, he must have had views about the major questions of his time, the proper relation of Rome and the Italian cities, and the effects of

---

[1] Here and *passim* in references to Lucilius the bracketed figure denotes the book number. As to how it is that a fragment of *lib.* 30 can be called 'early', see below, p. 168.

capitalism and large-scale plantation and ranch-style farming on the traditional peasant society of the countryside; yet he only mentions these things, if at all, fleetingly. Neither do we hear anything for certain of the Gracchi or of Marius. Lucilius' *ludus ac sermones* 'playful chats', *schedia* 'improvisations' – the term *satura* is not directly attested for him – were not the satire of a social reformer with a consistent standpoint and a long-term plan. Prose was the medium for a manifesto, see pp. 144–7. His targets were what he claims as notorious examples of arrogance, folly, delusion, incompetence, inhumanity, pretension, unworthiness, or greed whether in high places or low – in politics, in the tragic theatre (Pacuvius, *lib.* 26 and 29; Accius, *lib.* 30, 9 and 10), in trade ((20) 1181f. M = *ROL* 609f., an auctioneer, Q. Granius, cf. Cic. *Brut.* 160–1), or in the bedroom whether with the girls (Cretaea (29) 817 M = *ROL* 897, Collyra, *lib.* 16, among others) or the boys (Gentius and Macedo (7) 273–5 M = *ROL* 308–10). In view of this explicitness, it is amusing to read that Lucilius himself lost a case which he brought against an unknown comedian (auctor *ad Her.* 2.19, cf. 1.24), who had named him on the stage.

Facit indignatio uersum: but Lucilius was not monotonously shrill or self-righteous. He had a stronger and broader sense of humour than any other Roman satirist, and he presents himself with ironic detachment, warts and all. His opponents have their say: for them, he is *improbus* 'unfair' and no gentleman ((30) 1026 M = *ROL* 1077 where *formonsi fortes* = καλοκάγαθοί), *improbus ille Lucilius* 'that bounder Lucilius' ((29) 821f. M = *ROL* 929f.); he consciously adopts the role of the cynic dog ((30) 1095f. M = *ROL* 1000–1), and accepts the part of the muck-raking σκατοφάγος: *hic in stercore humi stabulique fimo atque sucerdis* 'he (grubs about) in the dung on the ground, in the filth of the byre and the pig-shit' ((30) 1018 M = *ROL* 1081). Moreover, his voice is direct and intimate: he speaks to you and me, not to an audience of connoisseurs in a declamation hall. It is noteworthy that politicians in Lucilius' time were giving a new validity to the literary convention by which a Greek tract intended for the public at large would be addressed to an appropriate individual: Gracchus, Rutilius Rufus, and others of course intended to influence the public in their political memoirs, but by causing them to be circulated in the guise of letters addressed to a sympathetic friend, they created the impression that the reader was being admitted to an inner circle, and thus was getting a more authentic account of affairs (see p. 145). Lucilius seems to have made quite extensive use of the letter-form:

> Quo me habeam pacto, tam etsi non quaeri', docebo,
> quando in eo numero mansi quo in maxuma non est
> pars hominum...
> ut periisse uelis quem uisere nolueris cum
> debueris. hoc nolueris et debueris te

si minu' delectat, quod ἄτεχνον et 'Ἰσοκράτειον
ληρῶδέςque simul totum ac sit μειρακιῶδες,
non operam perdo, si tu hic... ((5) 181–8 M = *ROL* 186–93)

I shall tell you how I'm keeping, even though you don't ask, since I have remained in
the number in which the greatest part of mankind is not; (not that I think you dislike
me so much) that you would wish him dead whom you have not sought when seek him
you ought. If you don't much fancy that 'sought' and 'ought', as being sans art *and*
Isocratique *and* bavard *and altogether* puéril, *I'm not wasting my time on it, if you*
are...

In a relatively early satire Horace comments thus on that kind of
writing:

Nam fuit hoc uitiosus: in hora saepe ducentos
ut magnum uersus dictabat stans pede in uno;
cum flueret lutulentus, erat quod tollere uelles:
garrulus atque piger scribendi ferre laborem,
scribendi recte: nam ut multum nil moror... (*Sat.* 1.4.9ff.)

For Lucilius was faulty in this: he would often stand on one foot and dictate two
hundred verses an hour, as if that were something great; whenever he flowed muddy,
there was always something that you would want to cut: he was garrulous and un-
ready to bear the work of writing, I mean writing properly: for I've no time for it as
(mere) bulk...

Later, however, he came to appreciate qualities in Lucilius which are a
function of this unmannered style:

ille uelut fidis arcana sodalibus olim
credebat libris, neque si male cesserat usquam
decurrens alio, neque si bene: quo fit ut omnis
uotiua pateat ueluti descripta tabella
uita senis... (*Sat.* 2.1.30ff.)

Lucilius used to entrust his secrets to his books as to faithful friends, not swerving off
to another theme if he had come out of something badly or well: and the result is that
all his later life lies exposed as if written down on a votive tablet...

Lucilius is not confessional in the sense that St Augustine is: he expresses no
serious regrets and is too much of a jester.[1] His real subject was nevertheless
himself and his reactions and experiences and acquaintances, and this was something new in Latin literature, without which it is difficult, for example, to
imagine some of Catullus' characteristic poetry.

---

[1] Fraenkel's excellent appreciation (1957) 150–3 does not do full justice to the complex character
of Lucilius' self-portrait. He is at times not only himself, the bluff Roman with an eye for a horse or a
girl, but also the cynic preacher, the man of the world, and a buffoon. We meet a *persona*, as in Pliny's
or Seneca's letters, not a person, as in Cicero's.

In a very early work this individualism is expressed in the often-quoted lines:

> publicanus uero ut Asiae fiam, ut scripturarius
> pro Lucilio, id ego nolo, et uno hoc non muto omnia.
>
> ((26) 671f. M = *ROL* 650f.)

That I should become a tax-gatherer in Asia, an assessment-man instead of Lucilius, that I refuse, and I would not exchange everything merely for this.

On the other hand he does not mind being a damned nuisance:

> . . .at libertinus tricorius, Syrus ipse ac mastigias
> quicum uersipellis fio et quicum commuto omnia. . .
>
> ((26) 669f. M = *ROL* 652f.)

But a triple-hided freedman, a very Syrus and a whipping post with whom I swap my skin and with whom I exchange everything (e.g. *is mihi cordi est* 'he is congenial').[1]

The language here is redolent of comedy; and it is Plautus who provides the best commentary of what *uersipellis* implies:

> uorsipellem frugi   conuenit esse hominem
> pectus quoi sapit: bonus sit bonis, malus sit malis.
>
> (*Bacchides* 658f.)

A useful fellow with any sense will be a turnskin: let him be good to the good, and bad to the bad.

The philosophy of Chrysalus (Syrus in Menander's original, see p. 104) is an appropriate motto for the writer of σπουδογέλοια, enjoyable but thought-provoking tales and discourses.

Lucilius, who was probably born in 180 B.C.,[2] grew up in the generation when once and for all *Graecia capta ferum uictorem cepit et artes | intulit agresti Latio* 'captive Greece caught her fierce conqueror and introduced the arts to rustic Latium' (Hor. *Epist.* 2.1.156). Carneades (accompanied among others by the young Clitomachus) visited Rome in 155 B.C., when Lucilius will have been about twenty-five, and made a great impression in a series of lectures intended to show the inadequacies of traditional moral assumptions. He argued convincingly on both sides of ethical questions, for example, whether a cavalryman in a rout

---

[1] On 671f. M = *ROL* 650f., see Williams (1968) 449f. The interpretation offered here for 669f. M = 652f. is new: commentators suppose that 669 M = *ROL* 652 denotes someone whom Lucilius dislikes, e.g. a dishonest agent or taxman; how that is compatible with the next line I do not see and they do not explain.

[2] He died and was honoured with a public funeral at Naples 'at the age of 46' according to Jerome, *ad ann.* 1869 (? 1870) = 103 (? 102) B.C. There are no sufficient grounds for accepting the emendation in Jerome *LXVI* for *XLVI*, which would put his birth in 169/8 B.C. The consuls of 148 B.C. had names very similar to those of 180 B.C., and this is the probable cause of the confusion in Jerome.

should risk his own life to rescue a wounded comrade or abandon him to save himself (Lact. *Div. inst.* 5.16.10, quoting Cicero, *Rep.* 3 (Ziegler pp. 85–96)). Cicero describes Lucilius as *homo doctus et perurbanus* 'an educated and thoroughly civilized man' (*De or.* 3.171), and Lucilius himself said in an early programmatic poem that he wrote neither for the ignoramus nor the expert ((26) 592–3, 595–6 M = *ROL* 632–5). His writings constitute an important document of the thorough blending of Greek and Roman culture in Aemilianus' generation; for the fragments not only display but also assume a knowledge of Ennius' *Annales*, Roman drama, the main authors of the Greek *paideia* – Homer, of course, whom Aemilianus was apt to quote, New Comedy, Euripides, Plato, Xenophon, Demosthenes among others. Similarly it is assumed that although we may not be experts we have some knowledge of the Academy and its teachings, of Peripatetic doctrines, of Epicureanism, and of Stoicism, some comments on which point to Panaetius ((27) 738 M = *ROL* 749, cf. Cic. *Off.* 1.51); and that we can take the technical language of philosophy and still more of rhetoric 'neat', in the original Greek, or only half assimilated into Latin. It would be a mistake to identify Lucilius from his fragments as a Stoic, or as a serious adherent of any ism: Stoic ideas are parodied at (*lib. inc.*) 1225f. M = *ROL* 1189f., and terms comically misapplied at (28) 784–90 M = *ROL* 805–11, while the somewhat dourly Stoic Q. Mucius Scaevola Augur, whose trial for alleged peculation during his governorship of Asia was the subject of Book 2, seems to have come off little better than his Epicurean prosecutor T. Albucius, whose silly mannerisms of Asiatic rhetoric are held up to ridicule.

Lucilius' style (described as *gracilis*, 'thin', by Varro *ap.* Gell. *N.A.* 6.14.6, Fronto p. 113 N) is itself an affront to the elaborate theory and practice of Asiatic rhetoric. One sympathizes with his attitude to artificiality in prose oratory and in the tragic diction of Pacuvius and Accius. Lucilius *primus condidit stili nasum* 'was the first to establish a nose for style', i.e. to practise literary criticism (Pliny, *N.H. praef.* 7). A discussion of the distinction of *poesis* and a *poema* ((9) 338–47 M = *ROL* 401–10), and of the nature of the unity of large-scale examples of *poesis* like the *Annales* or the *Iliad* draws on some current ideas of Hellenistic theory; this possibly came in the course of a defence by Lucilius of his already considerable *œuvre* against the charge that it ignored blatantly the proprieties advocated by Accius (*Didascalica lib.* 9 *ap.* Charis., *GLK* I 141). In the same book he advocated a number of spelling rules. Some of these are sensible enough, but others so intrinsically absurd that it is hard to believe that we are meant to take them seriously. In particular, Lucilius' prescriptions for the 'correct' use of the spellings *ei* and *i* ((9) 358–61 M = *ROL* 384–7) are a ludicrous alternative to a quite practical proposal of Accius (Warmington, *ROL* II xxii–xxiv).

In 123 B.C. or later[1] Lucilius arranged a collection in five books of the poems which, privately circulated, had brought him notoriety over the last ten years. These were arranged in roughly chronological order; and he wrote an important programmatic poem to serve as preface to the earliest book. Thus when the 'edition' was launched some, though not all, of those with whom Lucilius had crossed swords were dead (Lentulus Lupus and Pacuvius). Whether Lucilius himself called these (or any) of his works *Libri saturarum* or *Saturae* cannot be shown, and it is noteworthy that our major source for these earliest works, Nonius Marcellus in his *De compendiosa doctrina*, regularly cites these books by their number alone, whereas he refers to later books in the typical form *Lucilius in sexto satyrarum* (*sic*). The five earliest books were known to grammarians not as 1–5, but as 26–30: they counted as a separate part of a large collected edition in which 1–21 were all hexameter-poems and 22–5 (of which hardly anything remains) were wholly or partly elegiac. This arrangement is at least as old as Varro (*Ling. Lat.* 5.17) and has been attributed to C. Valerius Cato (b. 100 B.C.), cf. Hor. *Sat.* 1.10.1ff. The metres of 26–30 are principally iambo-trochaic; the arrangement of the *œuvre* into three sections, hexameters, elegiacs, and iambo-trochaics reflects ineptly enough in Lucilius' case the standard doctrine about the relative grandeur of those metres. Horace deals with them in this order in *Ars poetica*. Books 1–21 were arranged chronologically, as far as we can tell. Book 1 was possibly written as early as 126/5 B.C., that is, before 26–30 were presented as a group. Books 1, 2, and 3 seem to have consisted of one long composition each, so that it is here for the first time that the term *satura* might be applied (whether by Lucilius or his editors) to a single poem. This in turn affected the denotation of the term: if one calls a *libellus* containing one poem a *satura*, one no longer has in mind the Ennian meaning 'medley'[2] but the qualitative characteristics of that poem. It is not until Horace (*Sat.* 1.1.1) that we find *satura* used generically to designate a certain kind of poetry, and what Horace means is the kind of poetry that Lucilius wrote.

Reconstruction of individual books of Lucilius is extraordinarily hard. There is no connected theme, and with Book 4 Lucilius reverted to his original practice of including several poems in a book. Lucilius' language is often difficult and obscure, and it is often a question whether a remark belongs in the mouth of the satirist or someone else. Horace is helpful: the programmatic poem of the earliest book, 26, can to some extent be elucidated from Hor. *Sat.* 2.1, where the poet meets the charge that his previous work is excessively

---

[1] Cichorius (1908) 72ff., 84ff. pointed out that (26) 671f. M = *ROL* 650f. (quoted above) alludes to a consequence of the *Lex Sempronia* of C. Gracchus (123 B.C.), that the right to farm taxes in the province of Asia would belong to Roman *equites*.

[2] It cannot be shown that Lucilius himself called any of his *ludus ac sermones* or *chartae* or *schedia* specifically *saturae* (cf. (30) 1039 M = *ROL* 1039, 1084 M = *ROL* 1014, (*lib. inc.*) 1279 M = *ROL* 1131).

cruel by asking a friend how then, and what, he should write; reasoned rejection of the friend's advice amounts to a positive assertion of the poet's stance against humbug. Lucilius seems to have done something similar, and this is the context of his definition of his ideal reader ((26) 592–3, 595–6 M = *ROL* 632–5), his assertion of his identity ((26) 671–2, 669–70 M = *ROL* 650–3, cf. 675 M = *ROL* 647), and his refusal of the suggestion that he should confine himself to the uncontroversial Ennian role of *praeco uirtutis*:

> hunc laborem sumas, laudem qui tibi ac fructum ferat:
> percrepa pugnam Popili, facta Corneli cane
>
> ((26) 620, 621 M = *ROL* 713, 714)

You should undertake this labour, which would bring you fame and profit: boom out the battle of Popilius Laenas [against the Numantians, 138 B.C.: Livy, *epit.* 55], *sing the deeds of Cornelius* [Scipio Aemilianus, again against the Numantians, 134/3 B.C.][1]

Book 3 of Lucilius, a verse-epistle (cf. (3) 94–5) in which he described a journey from Rome to his estates in Sicily, provided the framework of Horace's 'Journey to Brundisium' (*Sat.* 1.5), and an anecdote about Aemilianus and an unwelcome hanger-on in Book 6 was the model for 'Horace and the Bore', *Sat.* 1.9. In Book 1 Lucilius felicitously exploited the conjunction of the death of Lentulus Lupus and a disastrous storm which hit Rome in 126 B.C. (cf. Julius Obsequens 29 (89)). Lucilius reported a meeting of the gods at which the questions were debated whether Rome could be allowed to continue to exist and what was to be done with Lentulus Lupus, who though convicted of extortion had become censor and *princeps senatus*. In the end, a condign punishment was no doubt fixed for Lupus and it was decided to send the prodigious storm as a warning to Romans to mend their ways. Thus Lucilius could pose as didactic *uates*, explaining the cause of the gods' anger, and he modelled his council of the gods on a famous episode in the first book of Ennius' *Annales* at which the deification of Romulus was ratified. The vein of parody was rich. The gods were made to observe the etiquette and procedure of the Senate; in their speeches they used mannerisms and clichés of contemporary earthly rhetoric ((1) 33–5 M = *ROL* 30–2, an *enthymema*; (1) 26–9 M = *ROL* 19–22, the hackneyed exordium 'I wish that *X* was not the case; but since it is . . .'); a confused Neptune doubts whether even Carneades (d. 129 B.C.) could help on some baffling point if he were released from Hades ((1) 31 M = *ROL* 35). A god, probably Romulus, complains about the mercenary attitudes of modern Rome ((1) 10 M = *ROL* 10), contrasting the old simple ways with fashionable exquisiteness in diet and dress; why, says he, even our language is being destroyed; what we used to call 'bed-feet' and 'lights' are now *pieds de lit* and

---

[1] A task for which he would have been well qualified: he served with Scipio at Numantia, Vell. 2.9.3.

lumières. It is part of the joke that Romulus himself uses a bizarre Graeco-Latin *franglais* to express this ((1) 15f. M = *ROL* 15f.). Lucilius clearly enjoyed clothing his provocatively demotic language in the heroic hexameter. This was important, for he never reverted to the iambo-trochaics of his earliest work, in which the contrast of form and style was less preposterous and pointed; and consequently the slackly-written hexameter became the form *par excellence* in Latin satire.[1]

The language and form of those earliest works were those of drama, as was only natural, since Ennius had established the iambo-trochaic metres and diction of the form as the ordinary medium for any poetry of less than heroic pretensions; including in Lucilius' time even epitaphs (*CIL* I² 1529). The question to be asked is not why Lucilius should have used iambo-trochaics at first instead of hexameters, but why and how he came to use hexameters. The earliest hexameter-poem was in Book 28: only seven lines survive (794–801 M = *ROL* 844–51); Accius is mentioned and two lines (795 M = *ROL* 845; 799 M = *ROL* 848) have the characteristic rhythms and alliteration of the epic style. Book 29 also included one hexameter poem (851–67 M, 1297 M = *ROL* 910–28), a mock-didactic disquisition on sex and whores. Book 30 consisted entirely of hexameter poems on a variety of themes – a barrack-room story telling how one Troginus acquired the nickname 'Pintpot', a debate between Lucilius and his adversaries, a letter addressing a marshal (Tuditanus?) in honorific terms can be distinguished. The hexameter *a priori* excluded common word-configurations, e.g. *cīuĭtātēs, făcĭnŏră, ēxpōstŭlānt,* unlike the iambo-trochaic metres, to which most of the vocabulary could be accommodated; thus it was in itself less λεκτικόν, appropriate for ordinary speech. There was, then, in spite of Horace's stricture (see p. 165), a certain cleverness in the ability to rattle off prose which conforms to the metrical rules of the hexameter, and the comic possibilities even included the confession:

> seruorum est festus dies hic
> quem plane hexametro uersu non dicere possis
>
> ((6) 228f. M = *ROL* 252f.)

There is a slaves' holiday here which you cannot possibly name in hexameter verse

(cf. Hor. *Sat.* 1.5.87, Porph. ad loc.).

It was a noted feature of Lucilius' diction that he drew directly on 'the technical words in every art and business' (Fronto p. 62 N), and among these

---

[1] The best accounts of the contents of Lucilius' works are those of Leo (1913) 411ff., and Coffey (1976). It was a regrettable decision of Krenkel (1970) 63–103 to give a detailed reconstruction, for he provided the German public with no means of distinguishing in his reconstruction what is certain, probable, possible, and worse. His edition represents a retreat from the critical standards of Warmington's *ROL* (1957), an edition itself only the best available, not the best possible, of this very difficult author.

Greek words are very prominent (cf. Hor. *Sat.* 1.10.20). Rhetoric, philosophy and science, medicine, the *cuisine*, and the *boudoir* are the main sources. There is a contrast here with Plautus, whose Greek expressions are fewer in number, and sometimes drawn from sources in southern Italy so colloquial and sub-literary that his borrowings are not attested in written Greek at all (*graphicus* 'clever', *thermipolium* 'bistro', the combination ναὶ γάρ 'yes'); and with Terence, who was more selective than either. Lucilius' use of Homer represents another and often witty kind of Greek borrowing: in the satire in which Scipio was plagued by a hanger-on, someone, perhaps Scipio, wishes

> nil ut discrepet ac τὸν δ' ἐξήρπαξεν ᾽Απόλλων
> fiat   ((6) 231f. M = *ROL* 267f.)

that it be no different than if 'Apollo snatched him away' [*Il.* 20.443] *should happen*

(cf. Porph. *ad* Hor. *Sat.* 1.9.78 *sic me seruauit Apollo*, imitated from here). With such allusiveness, we are but a step from the world of Cicero's letters.

APPENDIX OF
AUTHORS AND WORKS

ANDRONICUS, LUCIUS LIVIUS

LIFE

(1) Name. Livius, L. Livius, or Livius Andronicus in extant sources. The name T. Livius (twice in Nonius, once in Jerome) is presumed to be an error due to confusion with the Augustan historian. That he was called L. Livius Andronicus is strictly an inference.

(2) Status and origin. Apparent implication of these *tria nomina* is that the poet was a Greek by birth, named Andronikos, that somehow he became a slave in the household of a Roman Livius, and that he was manumitted and became a *ciuis libertinus* with the *praenomen* Lucius; he might, however, be the son of such a person. Accius in his *Didascalica* (reported by Cic. *Brut.* 72 and Jerome, *Chron.* 187 B.C.) said that he was a native of Tarentum and came to Rome in 209 B.C. when the city was taken by the Romans (Livy 27.15–16; for problems in the Cicero passage see A. E. Douglas, *M. Tulli Ciceronis Brutus* (Oxford 1966) 62–4); further, that he was granted his freedom by M. Livius Salinator (he has in mind the victor of the battle at the Metaurus in 207 B.C., *RE* 33), as a reward for teaching his children (cf. Suet. *De gramm. et rhet.* 1 for A. as teacher).

(3) Career according to Accius. Most circumstantially documented fact in A.'s life is that in 207 B.C. he composed or re-used a ritual hymn to be sung by thrice nine girls in procession; during a rehearsal the temple of Juno Regina on the Aventine was struck by lightning; as an important part of the especially elaborate rite of expiation which the curule aediles ordered, the girls performed A.'s hymn in procession to Juno's temple (Livy 27.37, cf. 31.12). This happened shortly before Salinator's important victory at the Metaurus, and retrospectively this was seen as the time at which Juno had given up her hostility to the Trojans and their descendants (cf. Ennius, *Ann.* (8) 291 V = *ROL* 293). As a result the *scribae* and *histriones* were given the right to hold official meetings in the Temple of Minerva on the Aventine and make offerings (Festus p. 448 L; see p. 84). On Accius' view this would have been the beginning, not the end of A.'s public life; and Cicero (loc. cit.) makes it clear that Accius thought A.'s first play was not produced until the votive games of his patron Salinator at the *ludi Iuuentutis* in 197 B.C. (so Cicero; Livy dates the games to 191 B.C.,

36.36.5). Jerome unreliably puts A.'s *floruit* in 187 B.C. Other traces of this Accian account of A.'s career in Porcius Licinus fr. 1 *FPL* p. 44 (arrival of the Muse at Rome during Second Punic War), Hor. *Epist.* 2.1.162 (tragedy developed after Punic Wars), Valerius Antias *ap.* Livy 36.36.5 (first *ludi scaenici* those of 191 B.C.; untrue), and in failure of Volcacius Sedigitus to mention A. at all in his list of the best comic poets, not even *antiquitatis causa* (fr. 3 *FPL* pp. 46f.).

(4) View of Varro, Atticus and Cicero. Cicero (*Brut.* 72) refutes Accius' view on A.'s chronology by alleging that A. was the first to produce a play and did so in 240 B.C. the year before Ennius' birth (cf. *Tusc.* 1.1.3). For this he cites the authority of Atticus (in his *Liber annalis*), who was in turn following Varro in his *De poetis* (cf. Gell. 17.21.42), and 'old *commentarii*' which Cicero himself had seen, presumably documents like those which gave 204 B.C. as date of Naevius' death (*Brut.* 60). Status of these documents is important but indeterminable: it would be sanguine to suppose they were official contemporary records, but they must have been older than the Gracchan era, because Cicero commends them as old in order to imply that their authority was better than that of Accius. Other reflections of Varro's opinion in Cassiodorus *Chron.* who speaks of a tragedy and comedy put on at the Roman Games in 239, not 240 B.C., and the *Glossae Salomonis* (9–10th c., St Gall) 7 (*CGF* I Kaibel p. 72; H. Usener, 'Vergessenes', *Rh.M.* 28 (1973) 418 = *Kleine Schriften* III (Berlin 1914) 37), *tragoedias comoediasque primus egit idemque etiam composuit Liuius Andronicus duplici toga infulatus*, as well as in Gellius (loc. cit.: *primus omnium L. Liuius fabulas docere Romae coepit*), and in the unreliable source used by Livy in his account of the growth of Roman drama (7.2.4ff., see p. 78), who in passing also mentions A. as he *qui ab saturis ausus est primus argumento fabulam serere*. On Varro's fondness for *primi inuentores* see H. Dahlmann, *Abh. Akad. Mainz* 1970, 94f. Under this label it is easy to confuse 'earliest known' and 'ultimate originator', and it is not clear what Varro meant, for if it was his claim that A. was the first to adapt Greek plays for the Latin stage, or the earliest known, it is rather odd that none of the citations make this explicit by using some such expression as *uertit ex graeco*. Evidently it was not being claimed that he invented the iambo-trochaic metres of dialogue and recitative or the quantitative polymetry of *cantica* (to the performance of which, however, Livy (loc. cit.) would have it that he made changes of presentation, see p. 79).

(5) Modern interpretation of chronology. Accius alone is our authority for the Tarentine origin of A. and for his connexion with the Livii Salinatores in particular; for Cicero *Brut.* 72 does not attribute belief in either of these points to Atticus, and they appear nowhere in the remains of the Varronian account. As Cicero's sole concern was to demonstrate what he believed to be a gross error on Accius' part as regards chronology, his silence on these two points cannot be interpreted either as affirming or denying the claims that A. was a Tarentine and a slave of the Salinatores. Nevertheless scholars generally accept that A. did come from Tarentum and that Accius has confused the assault on Tarentum in 272 B.C. with its capture in 209 B.C. In this case A. would have been a slave of the grandfather of the Salinator whom Accius

had in mind. The superficial attraction of this would be that it allows one to reconcile and partly account for the widely discrepant sources; a difficulty which arises, however, is that in this case we must suppose that A. can hardly have been born later than 290 B.C., for otherwise he could not have acquired the education which he exploited at Rome, and therefore that he must have been a very old man in 207 B.C. when he composed his *carmen*. H. B. Mattingly (*C.Q.* n.s.7 (1957) 159–63) would see Livy 27.37 and 31.12 as confused, Festus p. 448 L as wrong, and Cic. *Sen.* 50 as implying that A. died *c.* 215 B.C., so that the *carmen* of 207 B.C. would be a revival of a work composed for an earlier occasion. However, even if A. had been born *c.* 300 B.C. (so Mattingly), it is not beyond belief that he should have still been alive and active (like Sophocles) in his nineties; nor is Mattingly's treatment of Livy and Festus satisfactory. G. Marconi (*M.A.L.* 8.12.2 (1966) 125–213) asserts the authenticity of Accius' account: A.'s arrival as a slave at Rome from Tarentum 209 B.C.; hymn, 207 B.C.; stage-début, 197 B.C.; *floruit* 187 B.C. See review by H. B. Mattingly, *Gnomon* 43 (1971) 680–7. If Accius is to be saved at all costs from a gross blunder in his dating – and Mattingly and Marconi overestimate his quality as a scholar – it would seem better to raise the question whether perhaps there were not two Livii Andronici, father and son, whose activity stretched from the middle of the third century into the second decade of the second and whom history has confused.

WORKS

(1) *Odusia* (*Odyssey*), an adaptation in saturnians of Homer; undated; *c.* forty-five fragmentary lines. (2) *Fabulae palliatae* (comedies). *Gladiolus* (from an *Enchiridion* 'The dagger'; Menander's was famous, cf. S. Charitonides, L. Kahil, R. Ginouvès, *Les mosaïques de la maison du Ménandre, Antike Kunst* VI (Bern 1970) pl. 4, though there were others by Philemon and Sophilus); *Ludius* ('The player'?); *Livius in* † *Virgo*. Half a dozen citations. (3) *Fabulae crepidatae* (tragedies). *Achilles, Aegisthus* (*TRF* 38 = *ROL* 38 ~ Aesch. *Choeph.* 897f.), *Aiax mastigophorus* (*TRF* 16f. = *ROL* 16f. ~ Soph. *Aj.* 1266f.), *Andromeda, Danae, Equos Troianus* (both also titles of plays by Naevius), *Hermiona, Tereus.* About 140 fragmentary lines. (4) Apotropaic hymn (sung in honour of Juno 207 B.C.). (5) *Ino* falsely attributed to A. by Terentianus Maurus, *GLK* VI 383 (line 1931); the four extant lines are by Laevius. (6) [Evanthius], *De comoedia* 5.1.4 (Donatus vol. I p. 23 Wessner) states that A. not only invented comedy and tragedy but also the *togata*. (7) *Carmen Nelei* 'Poem about Neleus', five fragmentary citations all in Festus except one from Charisius (*GLK* I 84) who quotes as if from A.; the work was regarded as ancient and anonymous in antiquity and it is not clear whether it was a play or a narrative poem.

BIBLIOGRAPHY

TEXTS: (1) COMPREHENSIVE: *ROL* II 2–43; M. Lenchantin de Gubernatis (Turin 1937). (2) 'ODUSIA': *FPL* 7–17; S. Mariotti (Milan 1952: with essay; text 93ff.), cf. O. Skutsch, *C.R.* n.s.4 (1954) 252–4. (3) TRAGEDIES: *TRF* 1–7. COMEDIES: *CRF* 3–5.

STUDIES: COMPREHENSIVE: Leo, *Gesch.* 55–75; E. Fraenkel, *RE* suppl. V (1931) 598–607 (valuable remarks on style). LIFE AND CHRONOLOGY: Mattingly and Marconi cited under *Life* (5) above; W. Beare, 'When did Livius Andronicus come to Rome?', *C.Q.* 34 (1940) 11–19, cf. *The Roman stage*, 3rd ed. (London 1964) 25–32; W. Suerbaum, *Untersuchungen zur Selbstdarstellung älterer römischen Dichter* (Hildesheim 1968) 1–12, 297–300 (full doxography); J.-H. Waszink, 'Zum Anfangsstadium der römischen Literatur', *ANRW* I.2 869–902 (important survey). 'ODYSSEY': S. Mariotti, under *Texts* above; G. Broccia, *Ricerche su Livio Andronico epico* (Padua 1974); A. Traina, 'Sulla Odyssia di Livio Andronico', *Paideia* 8 (1953) 185–92, rev. ed. in *Vortit barbare* (Rome 1970) 10–28. TRAGEDIES: H.-J. Mette, *Lustrum* 9 (1964) 41–50. COMEDIES: J. Wright, *Dancing in chains: the stylistic unity of the comoedia palliata* (Rome 1974) 15–32.

NAEVIUS, GNAEUS

LIFE

Served in First Punic War (Gell. 17.21.45, quoting N. himself) and was therefore born c. 285–260 B.C. Either a Capuan with Roman *ciuitas sine suffragio* by birth until city's disgrace in 211 B.C. (connexion severed because of Capua's having sided with Hannibal), or from area of Capua and belonging to a community *nominis Latini*, 'of the Latin name', allied to Rome (inference from Gell. 1.24). Varro had evidence of some sort that N. produced *fabulas* (for the first time) in 235 B.C. (Gell. 17.21.45). N. had a reputation for outspokenness, and in 1st c. B.C. there was an evidently widespread story that he had crossed verbal swords with the Metelli and had suffered punishment. Story apparently referred to the consulship of Q. Caecilius Metellus (*RE* 81) in 206 B.C., but its details are too ill-preserved for it to be reconstructed or evaluated; see Cic. *Verr.* 1.29 with ps.-Ascon. *ad loc.*; [Caesius Bassus], *GLK* VI 265; Gell. 3.3; Jerome, *Chron.* 201 B.C.; Plaut. *M.G.* 209–12 with Festus p. 32 L s.v. 'barbari'. Varro found it written in 'old *commentarii*' (see also under Andronicus) that N. died in 204 B.C., but regarded this as erroneous (perhaps because he saw that really this date was only the latest record of a new Naevius-play) and extended his life 'longius' (Cic. *Brut.* 60); Jerome (*Chron.* 201 B.C., of dubious value) put his death in that year at Utica, where he had gone into 'exile'.

WORKS

(1) *Bellum Poenicum* (*Punicum*) in saturnians represented by c. sixty fragments. Originally undivided, the work was presented in seven *libri* by Octavius Lampadio, a scholar of the mid-2nd c. B.C. (Suet. *De gramm. et rhet.* 2), and it is from this version

that the citations (almost all due to grammarians) come; third of total come from bk 1.

(2) *Fabulae palliatae* (c. 130 fragmentary verses, almost all in iambo-trochaic metres). Thirty-four titles known: *Tarentilla*, 'The girl from Tarentum', is easily the best represented (more than twenty fragmentary verses). Others: *Acontizomenos* 'Struck by a spear' (from Dionysius' play of that name?); *Agitatoria* 'The driver-play'; *Agrypnuntes* 'Sleepless nights'; *Apella* 'The Jew' (?); *Ariolus* 'The soothsayer' (not to be taken as an Italian *togata*); †*Assitogiola* (*CRF* 25 = Naevius *com. ROL* 103); *Asteiologia* 'The art of wit' (?): this citation is the only lyric fragment of a Naevian comedy, cf. E. Fraenkel, *Elementi plautini in Plauto* (Florence 1960) 327; *Carbonaria* 'The charcoal comedy' (Menander's *Epitrepontes?* Plautus is credited with this play too); *Clamidaria* 'The greatcoat comedy'; *Colax* 'The toady' (Menander; attributed to 'Plautus and Naevius' by Ter. *Eun.* 23–6); *Commotria* 'The beautician'; *Corollaria* 'The garland comedy'; *Dementes* 'The lunatics'; *Demetrius* (Alexis; also turned by Caecilius Statius); *Dolus* 'The trick'; *Figulus* 'The potter'; *Glaucoma* 'The cataract'; *Gymnasticus* 'The trainer'; *Lampadio*; *Leo(n)*; *Ludus* (?); *Nautae* (?) 'The sailors'; *Nervolaria* 'The prison play' (?), also attributed to Plautus; *Pellex* 'The temptress'; *Personata* 'The girl in the mask' (?), cf. Festus p. 268 L; *Proiectus* 'The outcast'; *Quadrigemini* 'The quadruplets'; *Stalagmus*; *Stigmatias* 'Black and blue'; *Technicus* 'The artful dodger'; *Testicularia* 'Balls'; *Tribacelus* 'Superqueer'; *Triphallus* 'His chopper's a whopper'; *Tunicularia* 'The underwear play'.

(3) *Fabulae crepidatae.* Six or seven titles known among which *Lycurgus* (thirty-five verses) is by far the best represented (only c. seventy verses altogether). Others: *Andromacha* (?); *Danae* (also title of play by Andronicus); *Danae TRF* 5 = *ROL* 10f. is in cretico-bacchiac metre, from a *canticum*; *Equos Troianus* (also title of play by Andronicus); *Hector proficiscens*; *Hesione*; *Iphigenia* (*in Tauris?*) (possibly from Euripides).

(4) *Fabulae praetextae. Clastidium*; *Romulus* or *Lupus* (?). Three lines.

(5) 'Naevius in Satyra', Festus p. 306 L; cf. Gell. 7.8.5 and see p. 162.

(6) Epitaph, Gell. 1.24; cf. H. Dahlmann, *Abh. Akad. Mainz* 1962, 65ff.

(7) There is no evidence that N. invented the *fabula togata*; *Ariolus* was a *palliata*. See p. 94.

BIBLIOGRAPHY

TEXTS AND COMMENTARIES: (1) 'BELLUM POENICUM': *FPL* 17–29; S. Mariotti (Rome 1955: with essay); Ł. Strzelecki (Warsaw 1959: two chapters of prolegomena); M. Barchiesi (Padua 1962: full examination of fortunes of N. through the ages); Ł. Strzelecki (BT, 1964: abbreviated version of 1959 ed. with minor changes to text; on both edd. see S. Mariotti, *Gnomon* 39 (1967) 242–8); A. Mazzarino (Messina 1966: 2nd ed. 1969). (2) 'BELLUM POENICUM' AND PLAYS: E. V. Marmorale, 3rd ed. (Florence 1953: with useful *introduzione biobibliografica* and commentary); *ROL* II 45–156. (3) PLAYS ONLY: *TRF* 7–16; *CRF* 6–35.

STUDIES: Leo, *Gesch.* 76–92; E. Fraenkel, *RE* suppl. VI (1935) 622–40, with important correction in *Elementi plautini in Plauto* (Florence 1960) 436; W. Beare, *The Roman stage*, 3rd ed. (London 1964) 33–44; H.-J. Mette, *Lustrum* 9 (1964) 50–4 (*Forschungsbericht* 1945–64); B. Snell, 'Ezechiels Moses-Drama', *A. & A.* 13 (1967) 150–64; W. Suerbaum, *Untersuchungen zur Selbstdarstellung älterer römischer Dichter* (Hildesheim 1968) 13–42 and *passim*; H. D. Jocelyn, 'The poet Cn. Naevius, P. Cornelius Scipio, and Q. Caecilius Metellus', *Antichthon* 3 (1969) 32–47; J.-H. Waszink, *ANRW* I.2 902–27 (critical *Forschungsbericht* 1953 and earlier to 1968); U. Hübner, 'Zu Naevius' Bellum Poenicum', *Philologus* 116 (1972) 261–76; J. F. Killeen, 'Plautus, Miles gloriosus 211', *C.Ph.* 88 (1973) 53–4; J. Wright, *Dancing in chains: the stylistic unity of the comoedia palliata* (Rome 1974) 33–59; G. Morelli, 'Il modello greco della Danae di Nevio', *Poesia latina in frammenti* (Genoa 1974) 85–101; M. von Albrecht, 'Zur Tarentilla des Naevius', *M.H.* 32 (1975) 230–9.

ENNIUS, QUINTUS

LIFE

b. 239 B.C. (Cic. *Brut.* 72, Varro *ap.* Gell. 17.21.43) at Rudiae (*Ann.* 377 V; Cic. *Arch.* 22, Strabo 6.281 *ad fin.*) in Calabria (hence *Calabrae Pierides* at Hor. *Odes* 4.8.20), a Messapian area; he claimed descent from King Messapus (Serv. *ad* Virg. *Aen.* 7.691, cf. Suda s.n. Ἔννιος) and said that he had *tria corda*, three personalities, because he spoke Greek, Latin and Oscan (Gell. 17.17). Suetonius (*De gramm. et rhet.* 1) calls him *semigraecus* (cf. Festus p. 374 L) and he evidently received a full Greek education, perhaps at Tarentum (Jerome, *Chron.* 240 B.C., wrongly dating his birth). Came to Rome in 204 B.C. having met the quaestor Cato in Sardinia (Nepos, *Cato* 1.4); what he was doing there is unclear (soldiering? Sil. Ital. 12.390ff. is fiction). At Rome he taught (Suet. loc. cit.); when he began writing for the stage is unclear, but he made his reputation in the tragic theatre in the 190s (he was less successful in comedy) and it will have been this which induced M. Fulvius Nobilior to take E. with him on campaign to celebrate his *gesta* (189–187 B.C.) in Ambracia (Cic. *Tusc.* 1.2, Livy 39.4); Choerilus of Iasos had accompanied Alexander (Curt. 8.5.8, Hor. *Epist.* 2.1. 233) as propagandist-poet, and more recently Simonides of Magnesia (Suda s.n.) and Leschides (Suda s.n.) had respectively celebrated the deeds of Antiochus III of Syria and one of the kings of Pergamum named Eumenes. The capture of Ambracia was celebrated in a work, probably a *fabula praetexta* rather than a narrative poem, which might appropriately have been staged at the votive games put on by Nobilior in 186 B.C. (Livy 39.22). Nobilior had celebrated his triumph a year earlier (August 187 B.C., Julian) and was severely criticized both for the liberality of his donatives to his soldiers (Livy 39.5 *ad fin.*, Gell. 5.6.24–6) and (by Cato) for taking *poetas* (i.e. Ennius; Cic. loc. cit.) on campaign. E. liked to put it about (in his *Satires*) that he lived in genteel but contented poverty (cf. Jerome, loc. cit., Cic. *Sen.* 14). A late source (Symm. *Epist.* 1.20.2), usually discounted, states that Nobilior merely awarded E. an old cloak after returning home; this is not beyond belief, because in the face of Cato's and others' criticisms in 188/187 B.C. it would have been impolitic to be seen to award a non-combatant with more than the least of the citizen soldiery. The real reward for the propaganda represented by the *Ambracia* was E.'s enrolment as a *ciuis Romanus* and *colonus* by Nobilior's son Quintus (*RE* Fulvius 93) when as *triumuir coloniae deducendae* in 184/183 B.C. he was in part-charge of the establishment of the settlements at Potentia and Pisaurum (Livy 39.44 with Cic. *Brut.* 79). Cato (now censor, and exercising a very strict review of the census-roll) must have given his tacit approval. Cicero (*Arch.* 22) is wrong in implying that the grant of citizenship was a reward for the (completed) *Annales*; it was only now that E. got seriously down to work on this his *magnum opus*. Besides Cato and the Fulvii Nobiliores, E. is associated in our sources with Scipio Africanus (Cic. *Arch.* 22), Scipio Nasica (Cic. *De or.* 2.276) and Ser. Sulpicius Galba (Cic. *Acad.* 2.51), his eminent neighbour on the Aventine where he lived modestly with only one servant-girl to 'do' for him. For a time he shared with Caecilius (q.v.) (Jerome, *Chron.* 240 and 179 B.C.). See E. Badian, 'Ennius and his friends', *Entretiens XVII* (Fondation Hardt 1972). He died in 169 B.C. (Cic. *Brut.* 78) during the *ludi Apollinares* at which his (new) *Thyestes* was being performed. He never married and his heir (legal as well as literary) appears to have been his nephew Pacuvius, who seems to have been a Roman citizen by birth, implying that E. had long been related by the marriage of some sister to a Roman of the *gens Pacuvia*.

WORKS

(1) DRAMATIC: (*a*) Tragedies. More than forty extant verses: *Alexander, Medea exul* (both from Euripides), *Hectoris lytra*. More than twenty: *Andromacha aechmalotis, Hecuba, Iphigenia (in Aulis)* (all from Euripides), *Telamo*. Other plays: *Achilles* (from Aristarchus; alluded to at Plaut. *Poen.* 1, produced 188/187 B.C., though the authenticity of the beginning of the prologue is problematic), *Aiax, Alcmeo* (possibly from Euripides), *Andromeda* (from Euripides), *Athamas, Cresphontes* (possibly from Euripides), *Erechtheus* (from Euripides), *Eumenides* (from Aeschylus), *Melanippa* (from Euripides), *Nemea, Phoenix, Telephus, Thyestes* (169 B.C.). *c.* 425 lines in all. (*b*) Comedies. A *Caupuncula, Pancratiastes* and *Telestis* are meagrely attested (five citations). Volcacius Sedigitus lists Ennius tenth and last in his list of the best comic poets (*ap.* Gell. 15.24) *antiquitatis causa* 'out of respect for his venerable age', which is faint praise indeed. (*c*) *Fabulae praetextae. Ambracia* (see above), *Sabinae* 'The Sabine Women' (seven citations).

(2) 'ANNALES' (*Romais*, Diomedes, *GLK* I 484, not inaptly) in eighteen books. Over 500 citations/allusions.

(3) MINOR WORKS: (*a*) *Hedyphagetica* 'Tit-bits', in mock-heroic hexameters, experimental in technique, based on the *Hedypatheia* ('Luxury') or *Gastronomia* ('Belly-rule') of Archestratus of Gela (*fl.* 350 B.C.). Apul. *Apol.* 39 cites eleven lines which may be compared with their model, cited by Ath. 3.92D. Composed after E.'s

return from Ambracia, i.e. 187 B.C. or later (O. Skutsch, *Studia Enniana* (London 1968) 38); texts and discussion, W. M. Lindsay, *Early Latin verse* (Oxford 1922) 1f. Possibly the earliest extant Latin hexameters. (*b*) *Sota*, i.e. Σωτᾶς, a hypocoristic form of Sotades, who wrote *c.* 280 B.C. and invented the Sotadean verse (E. uses this). Bawdy in character (fr. 1 σκατοφαγία; fr. 5 *natem*, a coarse synonym for *lumbum*). (*c*) *libri saturarum* IV (Porph. *ad* Hor. *Sat.* 1.10.46; VI, Donat. *ad* Ter. *Ph.* 339). (*d*) *Scipio*: a non-dramatic *laus* of Scipio Africanus, perhaps partly in trochaic septenarii (Gell. 4.7.3, Macr. *Sat.* 6.2.26) and hexameters (Lucil. 1190 M, cf. Suda s.n. Ἔννιος); relation to the preceding problematic. (*e*) *Epicharmus* in trochaic septenarii (Cic. *Acad.* 2.51, Prisc. *GLK* II 341.20, Varro, *Ling. Lat.* 5.59 and 68); fourteen surviving verses. (*f*) *Praecepta*, Priscian, *GLK* II 532.17, perhaps identical with *Protrepticum* (*-us?*), Charisius, *GLK* I 54.19; cf. Leo, *Gesch.* 204. (*g*) *Euhemerus* or *historia sacra*, a version of the philosophical 'novel' of Euhemerus (b. *c.* 340 B.C.). Lactantius (*Inst.* 1.11.33ff., cf. 1.14.1) quotes several paragraphs of what he took to be E.'s actual words, in decidedly jejune prose; it is, however, more probable (*pace* E. Laughton, 'The prose of Ennius', *Eranos* 49 (1951) 35f. and E. Fraenkel, 'Additional notes on the prose of Ennius', ibid. 50ff.) that this, like E.'s other didactic works, was written in iambo-trochaic verse, and that Lactantius is quoting a school paraphrase for children; see R. M. Ogilvie, *The library of Lactantius* (Oxford 1978) 56. (*h*) Epigrams. Three distichs on Scipio Africanus; one in the form of an epitaph (Cic. *Leg.* 2.57, Sen. *Epist.* 108.32), though in Livy's time it was uncertain where Scipio was buried, another (Lact. *Inst.* 1.18.10) makes Scipio claim the right to enter heaven (like Hercules or a Hellenistic king); a third comments that from West to East none could equal his *gesta*. Two other epigrams are on E. himself as public poet and private artist; cf. W. Suerbaum, *Untersuchungen zur Selbstdarstellung älterer römischer Dichter: Livius Andronicus, Naevius, Ennius* (Hildesheim 1968) 208–15, 332–6, who also presents literary evidence for iconography of Ennius (210–11); see G. Hafner, *Das Bildnis des Q. Ennius* (Baden Baden 1968), cf. D. E. Strong, *C.R.* n.s.20 (1970) 254. An acrostic 'signature' *Q. Ennius fecit* is mentioned by Cicero (*Div.* 2.111) as occurring in *quibusdam Ennianis*; Diog. Laert. 8.78 says that 'Epicharmus' similarly signed most of his ὑπομνήματα with an acrostic (see Suerbaum above 11, 135f., 261f.). (*i*) Orthographical precepts attributed to E.: regular gemination of consonants (Festus p. 372 L s.v. 'solitaurilia') (though it appears sporadically in earlier inscriptions); the change of the spelling of some words to suit etymological fancies (Varro, *Ling. Lat.* 5.86, Charisius, *GLK* I 98.12); two books *de litteris syllabisque* and *de metris* attributed by some to E. the poet are mentioned by Suetonius (*De gramm. et rhet.* 1), who, however, agreed with the view of one L. Cotta that these and some *libri de augurandi disciplina* were the work of another Ennius. Tenuous evidence for a S. Ennius the inventor of scholarly symbols and shorthand signs is offered by the *anecdotum parisinum* (*GLK* VII 534.4), *in adnotationibus Ennii Lucilii et historicorum usi sunt Varrôs hennius* (sic) *haelius . . .* , and by the quotation of Isid. *Orig.* 1.22.1 in the *tractatus grammaticus de V nominum declinationum* of *codex Bernensis* 611 fol. 72 verso (s.VIII) (W. Arndt, *Schrifttafeln zur Erlernung der lateinischen Palaeographie* I, 4th ed.

M. Tangl (Berlin 1904) 26 (transcription), Tafel 35 (reproduction); H. Hagen, *Catalogus codicum Bernensium* (*Bibliotheca Bongarsiana*) (Bern 1875) 479–83), *de uulgaribus notis: uulgares notas sennius primus mille et centum inuenit . . .*

BIBLIOGRAPHY

TEXTS: (1) COMPREHENSIVE: J. Vahlen (Leipzig 1903; repr. Leipzig 1928, Amsterdan 1963), cf. O. Seyffert, *B.Ph.W.* 1904, 1322–6, C. Bailey, *C.R.* 18 (1904) 169–72, J. Paulson, *Eranos* 6 (1905) 55–65; *ROL* I 2–465, cf. C. J. Fordyce, *C.R.* 49 (1935) 188, A. Klotz, *Ph.W.* (1938) 645–9. Vahlen's numeration (*Ann.* 356 V, *Sat.* 15 V) is standard for all E.'s works except the plays (cited from *TRF* pp. 17ff., pp. 323f. and *CRF* pp. 5f.); in this book we follow this convention, with cross-references to numeration in *ROL*, adding in brackets the book-number where appropriate, e.g. *Ann.* (17) 443–5 V = *ROL* 430–2; *Medea exul TRF* 231f. = *ROL* 284f. (2) TRAGEDIES: H. D. Jocelyn (Cambridge 1967: with commentary), cf. S. Timpanaro, *Gnomon* 40 (1968) 666–71. (3) 'ANNALES': E. M. Steuart (Cambridge 1925: with commentary); L. Valmaggi (Turin 1900, repr. 1947, 1962: with commentary). (4) MINOR WORKS: E. Bolisani (Padua 1935: with commentary and tr.). (5) SELECTIONS: J. Heurgon, *Ennius I: Les Annales; II: Fragments tragiques* (Paris 1960) has a running commentary on the Ennius-fragments in A. Ernout, *Recueil de textes latins archaïques*, 2nd ed. (Paris 1957).

STUDIES: FUNDAMENTAL: F. Skutsch, *RE* V (1905) 2589–2628 and introductions to edd. of Vahlen and Jocelyn; Leo, *Gesch.* 150–211; E. Norden, *Ennius und Vergilius: Kriegsbilder aus Roms grosser Zeit* (Leipzig 1915); for *c.* 1940–52 see S. Timpanaro, *A.A.O.H.G.* 5 (1952) 195–212; H.-J. Mette, *Lustrum* 9 (1964) 14–16, 55–78 (tragedies); papers on various topics by O. Skutsch, collected in his *Studia Enniana* (London 1968); J.-H. Waszink, 'The proem of the Annales of Ennius', *Mnemosyne* 4.3 (1950) 215–40, revised version 'Il proemio degli Annales di Ennio', *Maia* 16 (1964) 327–40; idem, 'Retractatio Enniana', *Mnemosyne* 4.15 (1962) 113–32; S. Mariotti, *Lezioni su Ennio* (Pesaro 1951; repr. Turin 1963), cf. O. Skutsch, *C.R.* n.s.4 (1954) 254–5; K. Ziegler, *Das hellenistische Epos*, 2nd ed. (Leipzig 1966) 53–77 (E. as a Hellenistic poet); W. Suerbaum, *Untersuchungen zur Selbstdarstellung älterer römischer Dichter* (Hildesheim 1968) 43–295 (mainly on *Annales*; exhaustive bibliography, supplementing Timpanaro up to *c.* 1967); Williams, *TORP* 359ff., 691ff., *passim*; (ed.) O. Skutsch, *Ennius. Sept exposés suivis de discussion, Entretiens XVII* (Fondation Hardt 1972); H. D. Jocelyn, 'The poems of Quintus Ennius', *ANRW* I.2 987–1026; J. Wright, *Dancing in chains: the stylistic unity of the comoedia palliata* (Rome 1974) 61–7 (comic fragments).

PLAUTUS, TITUS MACCIUS

LIFE

(1) Fragments of speciously biographical information deriving ultimately from Varro, *De poetis* and *De comoediis plautinis libri* (?) *tres*: the comic playwright Maccius, an Umbrian from Sarsina, acquired the *cognomen* Plotus, later Plautus (urban form) because he had flat feet (Pauli Festus s.v. 'ploti'; Jerome, *Chron.* 200 B.C.); there was, according to Varro, another playwright Plautius, which added to the confusion after P.'s death as to which were his plays, for both names have genitive *Plauti* (Gell. 3.3.10). On coming to Rome P. worked *in operis artificum scaenicorum*, 'in the service of the stage-artists (i.e. actors)' (for the expression cf. Cic. *Fam.* 13.9.3), which should mean 'as a stage-hand' (Gell. 3.3.14, quoting Varro from memory). Varro *may* also have said that P. later became an *histrio*, actor; cf. Livy 7.2, in the old days all poets *agebant*, produced and acted in their own plays. P. was supposed to have made money through this employment (cf. Hor. *Epist.* 2.1.170) and left Rome on an abortive business venture; returning to Rome he hired his services (*addicere*) to a miller. During this time he allegedly wrote three comedies, *Saturio*, *Addictus*, and a third whose name Gellius (loc. cit.) could not remember. Jerome (*Chron.*) wrongly states that P. died in 200 B.C.; Gellius rightly implies that his *floruit* agreed with that of Cato in politics, i.e. c. 195–184 B.C. (17.21.47). Cicero, indirectly following Varro on this, implies that P. was an old man when he produced the *Truculentus* (c. 188 B.C.) and the *Pseudolus* (Megalensian Games and inauguration of the Great Mother's temple, Nov. 192 B.C. (Julian); not April 191 B.C. as usually stated (the Roman calendar was four months adrift at the time)), and he does not merely mean *senex* in the technical sense that so defined anyone over 40½ years of age. Elsewhere (*Brut.* 60) he says that P. died in the censorship of Cato (184/183 B.C.). Gellius quotes an epigram in rough hexameters from Varro's *De poetis* (1.24) praising P. retrospectively as the irreplaceable master of *risus ludus iocusque et numeri innumeri* (referring to his metrical virtuosity), and is rightly sceptical of Varro's apparently unqualified assertion that P. actually wrote this himself and intended it to be incised on his tomb. No tradition as to his resting-place, nor even the pretence of an iconographical tradition.

(2) Evaluation of Varronian account. Varro himself was drawing on the 'researches' of scholars of the Gracchan era such as Accius and Aelius Stilo (c. 154–90 B.C.). Neither they nor he had access to documentary evidence about P. other than the scripts which passed under his name or combinations of his names (*Plautus* and various cases but not the genitive, *Maccus*, *Macci Titi* are attested in prologues; *T. Macci Plauti Casina* *explicit* only in Ambrosian palimpsest); some at least of these scripts included production-notices giving details of the first performance. Only two of these survive (*Stichus*, Plebeian Games 200 B.C.; *Pseudolus*, see above) and it is hypercritical to entertain suspicions about these particular notices. The critical standards set by the example of Pergamene scholarship were low (see R. Pfeiffer, *History of classical*

scholarship (Oxford 1968) 1 241f.) and Accius and others were guilty of passing off dubious inferences and combinations as fact within the limits of what seemed *a priori* likely, for example, that P. should have been an alien of low standing whose livelihood was precarious and depended on the theatre. The romantic tale of his vicissitudes in business and of his working and writing in a mill has no authority and is probably fabricated from well-known themes of P.'s *oeuvre* – changes in material fortune, slaves' remarks such as *Per.* 21f. and fathers' complaints such as *Trin.* 820ff. The statement that P. came from Sarsina looks like an inept construction on the joke at *Most.* 770, and the dogmatic allegation that he died in 184 B.C. probably represents an inference from the absence of later production-notices; maybe P. simply retired, or was invited to retire by the censor Cato. Although Cicero (*Sen.* 50) certainly implies that he and Varro thought that P. was born earlier than 250 B.C., there is no antique authority for the frequently repeated statement that P. was born either in 254 or 259/258 B.C. The first date is arrived at by counting back three score years and ten from 184 B.C., while the second depends upon an absurd combination: at *M.G.* 629 Periplectomenus mentions that he is fifty-four years of age; since antiquity it has been supposed (not necessarily rightly) that *M.G.* 211f. contains an allusion to the imprisonment of Naevius in 205/204 B.C.; *ergo*, P. was born in 259/258 B.C. Either or both of these arguments is worthy of Accius, but seem to have been worked out in post-Renaissance times by scholars as yet unidentified (P. Crinitus, *De poetis latinis* (Florence 1505) is exonerated). On the available evidence, P. could have been ten years younger than Cato (b. 234 B.C.). We do not even know his real name: Varro apparently assumed that Maccius was the real *nomen gentile* and took Plautus to be a *cognomen* which had nothing to do with the writer's profession. T. Maccius Plautus, however, appears to be a jocose pseudonym connoting 'Phallus the son of Clown (Maccus of Atellane Farce), the Entertainer (*plautus* 'flatfoot' = *planipes* 'mime')', i.e., as it were, 'Dick Dopeson Prancer'; see A. S. Gratwick, *C.Q.* n.s.23 (1973) 78–84, W. Beare, *The Roman stage*, 3rd ed. (London 1964) 47f., F. Leo, *Plautinische Forschungen*, 2nd ed. (Berlin 1912) 81ff. On the positive side: all the surviving plays are essentially the work of one hand, and date, in so far as they can be dated, from between the last years of the Second Punic War and the mid-180s; the author was associated over a long period with T. Publilius Pellio (an important actor-impressario); he may have acted in his own productions, though the only possible direct evidence for this depends upon the interpretation of the joke at *Bacch.* 211ff., which is wittiest if Pellio is playing Pistoclerus and P. himself Chrysalus; the occasion at which the *Pseudolus* was produced was a particularly special celebration for which greater funds than usual were available, and the play calls for unusually though not uniquely extravagant resources, which implies that P.'s reputation already stood very high as a successful dramatist; and he was the first to specialize in a single genre of drama, as had been the standard practice of Greek dramatists.

WORKS

(1) DUBIOUS AND SPURIOUS WORKS: No authentic canon of P.'s plays existed in or near his own time (contrast the case of Caecilius), and his scripts were the property of such as Publilius Pellio, stage-managers who contracted for plays individually. In the Gracchan era some 130 scripts passed under P.'s name(s), not as reading-editions, but as actors' copies. Not only were there several species of authentic 'signatures' (see above) – Varro's Plautius may be one of these – but also a large number of patently spurious works had been staged as 'rediscovered' comedies. Aelius Stilo thought only twenty-five genuine (Gell. 3.3.11), which should mean our surviving plays and four others; someone else, probably Varro, counted forty as genuine (Serv. *praef. Aen.* p. 4 15 Th). We know that Varro listed twenty-one plays as genuine *consensu omnium*, meaning that none of his predecessors had impugned the authenticity of any of these, and that he acquiesced in that view. These twenty-one are rather inappropriately named the *fabulae Varronianae* by Gellius (3.3.3), and it is virtually certain that it is they that survive to us. The name *fabulae Varronianae* would more properly be applied to the second group of plays segregated by Varro, namely those which he himself regarded as genuine on stylistic grounds against the doubts or denials of one or more scholars; if Varro thought forty in all genuine, there were nineteen of these, and he recognized a third group of ninety forgeries. It seems certain that at least several genuine works have been lost. Accius denied the authenticity of a *Commorientes* 'Partners in death', which Terence in 160 B.C. had thought genuine (Ter. *Ad.* prol.); Gellius may well have been right in asserting with Varro the authenticity of a *Boeotia* also attributed by some to one Aquilius and again damned by Accius (see A. S. Gratwick, *C.Q.* n.s.29 (1979) 308–23). The issue was further complicated by the possibility of revision and joint authorship, as in the case of a *Colax* which Terence assigns to 'Plautus and Naevius' (*Eun.* prol.). Citations amounting to about 110 fragmentary lines from thirty-two named plays not among the canon of twenty-one and about sixty non-canonical citations simply of 'Plautus' are preserved, almost all made by grammarians.

(2) THE FABULAE VARRONIANAE: *Amphitruo*, the only mythological comedy. *Asinaria* 'Horse-play', from the *Onagos* 'Muleteer' of one Demophilus. Later than *Menaechmi* (*Asin.* 879–930 repeats ideas from *Men.* 563ff. and 621ff.). *Aulularia* 'The pot of gold', possibly from Menander. *Bacchides* 'Bacchis and Bacchis', from Menander's *Dis exapaton* 'The double deceiver', of which important fragments exist. One of P.'s latest surviving works; beginning lost. *Captivi* 'The prisoners'. *Casina* 'Miss Godot', from the *Kleroumenoi* 'The lot-takers' of Diphilus. After 186 B.C. *Cistellaria* 'The little casket', from Menander's *Synaristosai* 'The ladies at elevenses'. Shortly before 201 B.C.; badly damaged. *Curculio* 'Weevil'. Seriously cut. *Epidicus* 'Mr Legally Liable'. Before *Bacchides*, cf. *Bacch.* 211ff. *Menaechmi* 'Standspeare and twin'. Not necessarily an early work. *Mercator* 'The merchant', from Philemon's *Emporos* 'The merchant'. *Miles gloriosus* 'The braggart warrior', from an *Alazon* 'Braggart'.

Mostellaria 'Whigmaleerie', possibly from a *Phasma* 'Apparition'. *Persa* 'The man from Persia' (not 'woman', as often translated). *Poenulus* 'The wretch from Carthage', from Alexis' *Karchedonios* 'The Carthaginian'. 188/187 B.C. Heavily interpolated. *Pseudolus* 'What, me lie?'. *Rudens* 'The rope', from Diphilus. *Stichus* 'Sketch', from Menander's first *Adelphoi* 'The brothers'. 200 B.C. *Trinummus* 'Threepence', from Philemon's *Thesauros* 'The treasure'. Later than *Curculio*, cf. *Trin.* 1016, where read *Curculiost. Truculentus* 'The grumpy fellow'. *c.* 188 B.C. *Vidularia* 'The wallet', from a *Schedia* 'The raft', possibly of Diphilus; all but lost.

BIBLIOGRAPHY

TEXTS AND COMMENTARIES: TEXTS: F. Leo (Berlin 1895–6); W. M. Lindsay (OCT, 1903). TEXTS WITH TRANSLATIONS: P. Nixon (Loeb, 1916–38, rev. ed. 1952–62: with Leo's text); A. Ernout (Budé, 1932: best *apparatus criticus*). COMMENTARIES: (1) Complete. A. Turnebus (Paris 1587); F. Taubmann (Wittenberg 1605); M. Z. Boxhorn (Leiden 1645); J. F. Gronovius (Amsterdam 1684); J. L. Ussing, 5 vols. in 7 parts (Copenhagen 1875–86). (2) Individual plays. *Amphitruo*: A. Palmer (London 1890); W. B. Sedgwick (Manchester 1950). *Asinaria*: F. Bertini, 2 vols. (Genoa 1968). *Aulularia*: C. Questa (Milan 1972). *Bacchides*: C. Questa, 2nd ed. (Florence 1975: with fragments of Menander's *Dis exapaton*). *Captivi*: W. M. Lindsay, 2nd ed. (Oxford 1930); J. Brix, O. Niemeyer, O. Köhler, 7th ed. (Leipzig–Berlin 1930). *Casina*: W. T. MacCary and M. M. Willcock (Cambridge 1976). *Cistellaria*: none; cf. G. Thamm, *Zur Cistellaria des Plautus* (diss. Freiburg 1971). *Curculio*: J. Collart (Paris 1962); G. Monaco (Palermo 1969). *Epidicus*: G. E. Duckworth (Princeton 1940). *Menaechmi*: J. Brix, O. Niemeyer, F. Conrad, 6th ed. (Leipzig–Berlin 1929). *Mercator*: P. J. Enk, 2 vols., 2nd ed. (Leiden 1966). *Miles gloriosus*: A. O. F. Lorenz, 2nd ed. (Berlin 1886). *Mostellaria*: A. O. F. Lorenz, 2nd ed. (Berlin 1883); E. A. Sonnenschein, 2nd ed. (Oxford 1927); J. Collart (Paris 1970). *Persa*: none; cf. G. L. Müller, *Das Original des plautinischen Persa* (diss. Frankfurt 1957). *Poenulus*: G. Maurach (Heidelberg 1975), cf. A. S. Gratwick, *The Poenulus of Plautus and its Attic original* (diss. Oxford 1968). *Pseudolus*: A. O. F. Lorenz (Berlin 1876). *Rudens*: E. A. Sonnenschein (Oxford 1891); F. Marx (Leipzig 1928); A. Thierfelder, 2nd ed. (Heidelberg 1962); H. C. Fay (London 1969). *Stichus*: H. Petersmann (Heidelberg 1973). *Trinummus*: J. Brix, O. Niemeyer, 5th ed. (Leipzig–Berlin 1907). *Truculentus*: P. J. Enk, 2 vols. (Leiden 1953), cf. K.-H. Kruse, *Kommentar zu Plautus' Truculentus* (diss. Heidelberg 1974). Fragments: F. Winter (diss. Bonn 1885).

TRANSLATIONS: W. Warner (London 1595: *Menaechmi*); H. T. Riley (London 1852); B. B. Rogers (Oxford 1907: *Menaechmi*); (ed.) G. Duckworth, *The complete Roman drama*, 2 vols. (New York 1942); A. Thierfelder (Stuttgart 1962–5: *Miles gloriosus, Curculio, Captivi*); L. Casson (New York 1963: *Amphitruo, Aulularia, Casina, Menaechmi, Pseudolus, Rudens*); E. F. Watling (Penguin, 1964–5: *Rudens,*

Mostellaria, Trinummus, Amphitruo, Aulularia, Captivi, Menaechmi, Miles gloriosus, Pseudolus); E. Segal (New York 1965: *Miles gloriosus*); S. Allot (London 1967: adapted from *Mostellaria, Miles gloriosus, Rudens*); A. G. Gillingham (Andover, Mass. 1968: *Captivi, Curculio, Mostellaria*, five scenes from other plays); P. Grimal (Paris 1971: with Terence).

SURVEYS: A. O. F. Lorenz, *J.A.W.* 1 (1873) 341–428; 3 (1877) 606–71; 18 (1880) 1–90; 22 (1880) 1–89; O. Seyffert, *J.A.W.* 31 (1882) 33–111; 47 (1886) 1–138; 63 (1890) 1–94; 80 (1894) 227–351; 84 (1895) 1–60; W. M. Lindsay, *J.A.W.* 130 (1906) 116–282; 167 (1912) 1–58; O. Köhler, *J.A.W.* 192 (1922) 1–45; 217 (1928) 57–81; F. Conrad, *J.A.W.* 247 (1935) 63–90; J. A. Hanson, *C.W.* 59 (1966) 103–7, 141–8 (for 1950–66); J. D. Hughes, *A bibliography of scholarship on Plautus* (Amsterdam 1975); D. Fogazza, *Lustrum* 19 (1976) 79–284 (for 1935–75).

STUDIES: (1) GENERAL: E. Fraenkel, *Plautinisches im Plautus* (Berlin 1922), Italian tr. with additional notes *Elementi plautini in Plauto* (Florence 1960); P. Lejay, *Plaute* (Paris 1925); G. E. Duckworth, *The nature of Roman comedy* (Princeton 1952); E. Paratore, *Plauto* (Florence 1961); W. Beare, *The Roman stage*, 3rd ed. (London 1964); E. Segal, *Roman laughter* (Harvard 1968); W. G. Arnott, *Menander, Plautus, and Terence* (Oxford 1968); F. H. Sandbach, *The comic theatre of Greece and Rome* (London 1977) 118–34; J. Blänsdorf, 'Plautus', in (ed.) E. Lefèvre, *Das römische Drama* (Darmstadt 1978) 135–222. (2) PARTICULAR TOPICS: Transmission: F. Leo, *Plautinische Forschungen*, 2nd ed. (Berlin 1912) ch. 1 *passim*. Usage: W. M. Lindsay, *The syntax of Plautus* (Oxford 1907). Metre: W. M. Lindsay, *Early Latin verse* (Oxford 1922); L. Braun, *Die Cantica des Plautus* (Göttingen 1970); H. Drexler, *Die Iambenkürzung* (Hildesheim 1969); C. Questa, *Introduzione alla metrica di Plauto* (Bologna 1967). Dating: K. H. E. Schutter, *Quibus annis comoediae plautinae primum actae sint quaeritur* (Groningen 1952). Interpolations: A. Thierfelder, *De rationibus interpolationum plautinarum* (Leipzig 1929). Lexicons: G. Lodge (Leipzig 1914–33); A. Maniet (Hildesheim 1969). Dramaturgy: H. Marti, *Untersuchungen zur dramatischen Technik bei Plautus und Terenz* (Zurich 1959). Law: U. E. Paoli, *Comici latini e diritto attico* (Milan 1962); A. Watson, *Roman private law around 200 B.C.* (Edinburgh 1971). Prologues: K.-H. Abel, *Die Plautusprologe* (Mülheim-Ruhr 1955). Relation to Greek originals: E. W. Handley, *Menander and Plautus: a study in comparison* (*London* 1968); K. Gaiser, 'Zur Eigenart der römischen Komödie: Plautus und Terenz gegenüber ihre griechische Vorbildern', *ANRW* 1.2 1027–1113; V. Pöschl, *Die neuen Menanderpapyri und die Originalität des Plautus* (Heidelberg 1973), French version in *Association Guillaume Budé, Actes du IXe Congrès, Rome 13–18 avril 1973* vol. 1 (Paris 1975) 306–21. See further under Terence.

CAECILIUS STATIUS

LIFE

Jerome (*Chron.*) makes 179 B.C. his *floruit* as a comic dramatist, adding that he was by birth an Insubrian Gaul, and that some said he came from Milan. It is inferred from this that he was captured and brought to Rome as a slave *c.* 223/222 B.C. after the battle of Clastidium. Statius appears to be the Latinized form of his Celtic name, which became his *cognomen* on manumission by the Caecilii; his Roman *praenomen* is unknown (Gell. 4.20.13 is confused). Thus he was an alien freedman like Andronicus and Terence. Jerome says that he was 'at first a close associate' (*primum contubernalis*) of Ennius and that he died the year after Ennius, i.e. 168 B.C., and was buried next to the *mons Janiculus*. This information derives at several removes from Varro's *De poetis* and sounds more circumstantial than his account of the life of Plautus. The story that the young Terence met C. and read him some of his *Andria* is hard to reconcile with this (Suet. *Vita Ter.* 3, Jerome, *Chron.* 159 B.C.); the *Andria* was put on in 166 B.C. The size of C.'s oeuvre and the date of his *floruit* imply that he had begun writing in Plautus' heyday. At first he had difficulty in gaining a name, but succeeded thanks to the persistence of the actor-impressario Ambivius Turpio (Ter. *Hec.* 9–27). Volcacius Sedigitus (*ap.* Gell. 15.24) judged C. the best of all the comic poets (above Naevius and Plautus), and it is evident from the way that Cicero cites him and expects others to know his text that he was, like Terence but unlike Plautus, a school-author in the 1st c. B.C. There is no explicit reference to revival-productions, but this is no doubt an accident. Ancient judgements: Varro, *Sat. Men.* 399 Buecheler; idem, *ap.* Charisius, *GLK* I 241.28; Cic. *De opt. gen. orat.* 1.2; Hor. *Epist.* 2.1.59; Vell. Pat. 1.17.1; Quint. 10.1.99; Gell. 2.23 *passim* (Gellius' adverse judgement, together with Cic. *Att.* 7.3.10, may in part account for C.'s failure to survive).

WORKS

Forty-two titles known, represented by *c.* 280 fragmentary verses. The *Plocium* is by far the best represented (forty-five verses) (next best *Synephebi*, seventeen verses). It is of importance as Gellius cites the Menandrian original for comparison; passages of Plautus' *Bacchides* corresponding to papyrus fragments of Menander's *Dis exapaton* provide the only other opportunity for direct, extensive examination of the techniques of adaptation used by Roman comedians.

(1) Probably or certainly from Menander. *Andria* 'The girl from Andros', *Androgynos* 'Epicene', *Chalcia* 'The coppersmiths' holiday', *Dardanus*, *Ephesio* (?), *Epiclerus* 'The heiress', *Hymnis*, *Hypobolimaeus* (*subditivos*, *Chaerestratus*, *rastraria*) 'The changeling' (probably only two and possibly one play), *Imbrii* 'The Imbrians', *Karine* 'The wailing-woman', *Nauclerus* 'The captain', *Plocium* 'The necklace', *Polumenoe* 'The men for sale', *Progamos* (?), *Synaristosai* 'The ladies at elevenses'

(also the original of Plautus' *Cistellaria*), *Synephebi* 'The likely lads', *Titthe* 'The nurse'.

(2) From other Greek authors. *Aethrio*, *Chrysion*, *Davos* (corrupt title), *Demandati* 'The boys in care', *Epistathmos* 'The quartermaster' (?), *Epistula* 'The letter', *Ex hautou hestos* 'Standing on his own two feet', *Exul* 'The exile', *Fallacia* 'The trick', *Gamos* 'The wedding', *Harpaʒomene* 'The girl who gets seized', *Hypobolimaeus Aeschinus* 'Aeschinus the changeling' (relation to other *Hypobolimaei* problematic), *Meretrix* 'The courtesan', *Nothus Nicasio* 'The bastard [or 'fake'?] Nicasio', *Obolo-states / Faenerator* 'The moneylender', *Pausimachus*, *Philumena*, *Portitor* 'The janitor', *Pugil* 'The boxer', *Symbolum* 'The token', *Syracusii* 'The Syracusans', *Triumphus* 'The triumph'.

BIBLIOGRAPHY

TEXTS: *CRF* 2.40–94; *ROL* III 468–561; T. Guardi (Palermo 1974).

STUDIES: P. Faider, 'Le poète comique Caecilius: sa vie et son oeuvre', *Mus. Belge* 12 (1908) 269–341, 13 (1909) 5–35; Leo, *Gesch.* 217–26; H. Haffter, *M.H.* 10 (1953) 5ff.; W. Beare, *The Roman stage*, 3rd ed. (London 1964) 76–80; Williams, *TORP* 363–6; A. Traina, *Vortit barbare* (Rome 1970) 41–53; J. Wright, *Dancing in chains: the stylistic unity of the comoedia palliata* (Rome 1974) 86–126.

TERENTIUS AFER, PUBLIUS

LIFE

Main source is Suetonius' *Vita Terenti*, written *c.* A.D. 100 and preserved in preface of Donatus' commentary. Although Suetonius quotes Volcacius Sedigitus and Porcius Licinus (writing later-2nd c. B.C.), and probably (though without acknowledgement) used Varro's *De poetis* (mid-1st c. B.C.), it is evident that they knew very little for certain.

Suetonius reports (*Vita* 5) that T. died in 159 B.C. (Jerome, *Chron.* says 158 B.C.) when he had not yet completed his twenty-fifth, or thirty-fifth year (MSS divide evenly). The younger age would make T. a contemporary of Scipio Aemilianus and Laelius, and, with suspicious neatness, would put his birth in 184 B.C., supposed year of Plautus' death. Cornelius Nepos claimed that Scipio, Laelius and Terence were 'of an age' (Suet. *Vita* 2), and this seems to have been assumed also by those who alleged that Scipio's real interest in Terence was sexual (Suet. *Vita* 1, 2) and who told the story of his meeting with Caecilius (see below). On the other hand Fenestella (late-1st c. B.C.) argued that T. was older than Scipio and Laelius, but not so old as to have been captured in the Hannibalic War 'as some think' (Suet. *Vita* 1–2), and this fits well with the alternative birth-date in 194 B.C. Suetonius says that T. was born at Carthage and was a slave at Rome of the senator Terentius Lucanus (otherwise unknown) (Oros. 4.19.6 mentions a Terentius Culleo (*RE* Terentius 43), an expert in

Carthaginian affairs); he was educated and manumitted early 'because of his brains and good looks' (Suet. *Vita* 1). This may merely be based on inference from the form of T.'s name, but is not conclusive; he could be the descendant, for example, of someone captured and manumitted after the First Punic War. On offering his first play, the *Andria*, to the aediles he was told to read it to the doyen of the comic stage Caecilius Statius, who was filled with admiration for it. The story (Suet. *Vita* 3) has added point if Caecilius' own *Andria* had also been a version of Menander's play, but is suspicious as a 'succession-tale', and also on chronological grounds: Caecilius died in 168 B.C., and the *Andria* was put on first in 166 B.C. (production-notice).

Suetonius (*Vita* 4 and 6) reports anecdotes and rumours that T. was helped in composition by his noble friends Scipio Aemilianus, C. Laelius and L. Furius Philus; not so much friends as sexually motivated exploiters, according to the pathetic and hostile imagination of Porcius Licinus (Suet. *Vita* 2 = *FPL* fr. 3). These speculations have their origin in the allusions which T. makes at *H.T.* 23–6 and at *Ad.* 15ff. to charges that he received aid from *amici* and *homines nobiles*, charges which T. does not refute, but mentions with some pride; cf. Cic. *Att.* 7.3.10, Quint. 10.1.99. A C. Memmius, more probably the Gracchan orator and *inimicus* of Scipio Aemilianus (*ORF* pp. 214–17) than the orator and poet of mid-1st c. B.C. (so *ORF* p. 404), mentioned in a speech *pro se* that 'Aemilianus, borrowing the mask from Terence, presented on stage what he had scribbled himself at home' (cf. Volcacius Sedigitus *ap.* Suet. *Vita* 9 = *FPL* fr. 3). Cornelius Nepos had what he thought was unimpeachable evidence for a story that Laelius, on being told by his wife to hurry up and come to dinner, asked not to be disturbed; at last, coming in late, he remarked that his writing had gone particularly well that day and read out the passage of *H.T.* beginning *satis pol proterue me Syri promissa huc induxerunt . . .* (723ff.); the point of this story is that it took place on the first of March, the feast of the Matronalia, the Roman 'Mothers' Day', and, apart from the fact that *mutatis mutandis* the passage was wittily appropriate to the occasion, the speaker is the formidable and mercenary courtesan Bacchis (Suet. *Vita* 4). T.'s relationship to Scipio Aemilianus, if any, remains entirely obscure.

T. travelled to Greece 'on holiday, or to avoid the charge of publishing others' work as his own, or to acquire a better grasp of Greek life and manners, which he had not perfectly expressed in his writings' (Suet. *Vita* 5). If true, this would be the earliest recorded example of the 'cultural tour' which became common among the wealthy in the next generation. Volcacius Sedigitus said that he was going to Asia, i.e. Pergamum, and was never seen again (Suet. *Vita* 5 = *FPL* fr. 2); Q. Cosconius said that he perished on the return journey at sea with 108 plays turned from Menander's Greek; others, that he died at Stymphalus in Arcadia or at Leucas (cf. Auson. *Epist.* 13.16; Ambracia, schol. *ad* Luc. 5.652), having fallen ill, or through grief at the loss at sea of his baggage, which had been sent on ahead and included a number of fresh plays (Suet. *Vita* 5). In assessing the credibility of this it should be remembered that Menander was supposed to have drowned in the Piraeus (schol. *ad* Ovid, *Ibis* 591f., Pfeiffer on Call. fr. 396), and that according to one count Menander wrote 108 plays

(Gell. 17.4.4). Fenestella wisely left the matter open, stating merely that T. lived and died between the Second and Third Punic Wars (Suet. *Vita* 1).

T. supposedly left a daughter, who later married a man of equestrian rank, and a small but comfortable estate of twenty iugera. His description (Suet. *Vita* 6) is merely the stock appearance of any Carthaginian (cf. Plaut. *Poen.* 112). For the iconographical tradition (spurious) see: Schanz–Hosius I 104; S. Charitonides, L. Kahil, R. Ginouvès, *Les mosaïques de la maison du Ménandre* (Bern 1970) 28–31, 103, and pl. 2 (relationship to iconography of Menander).

WORKS

(1) *Andria* 'The girl from Andros', from Menander with ideas or elements also from his *Perinthia* 'The girl from Perinthos' according to T. (9ff.), though this is a quite inadequate account of all the changes he made. Criticized by Luscius Lanuvinus (contemporary writer of *fabulae palliatae*) on the ground that *contaminari non decere fabulas* (16). Produced at Megalensian Games 166 B.C. with moderate success (Donat. *praef. An.* 7). Curule aediles M'. Acilius Glabrio (*RE* 36) and M. Fulvius Nobilior (*RE* 93); principal players L. Ambivius Turpio and L. Atilius Praenestinus (see C. Garton, *Personal aspects of the Roman theater* (Toronto 1972) 245).

(2) *Hecyra* 'The mother-in-law', from Apollodorus of Carystus without substantial changes. A failure at its first trial, Megalensian Games (so the production notice in the *codex Bembinus* and Donat. *praef. Hec.* 6; Roman Games, Calliopian MSS) 165 B.C. Curule aediles Cn. Cornelius Dolabella (*RE* 132) and Sex. Iulius Caesar (*RE* 148/9). Principal player L. Ambivius Turpio (prol. *passim*, Donat. loc. cit.).

(3) *Heauton timorumenos* 'The self-tormentor', from Menander. T. says it is a fresh (i.e. previously untried Latin) version of a fresh (i.e. previously unexploited) Greek model, and that it is a play *duplex quae ex argumento factast simplici* – whatever that may mean (4–6). He alludes to Luscius' charge *multas (se) contaminasse graecas dum facit paucas latinas* (17f., cf. *An.* 16) and to the accusation that he depended on his friends' brains, not his own talent (24). Performed successfully at the Megalensian Games 163 B.C.; curule aediles L. Cornelius Lentulus Lupus (*RE* 224, later *princeps senatus* and *bête noire* of Lucilius) and L. Valerius Flaccus (*RE* 174). Principal players as in *Andria*.

(4) *Eunuchus* 'The eunuch', from Menander with two characters taken from his *Colax* 'The flatterer' (20ff.), though that is in no way an adequate explanation of the manifold alterations T. has made to his model. He was accused in this case of plagiarism by Luscius, for there had been a previous version of *Colax* 'by Plautus and Menander' about which T. says he had known nothing. Performed with great success at the Megalensian Games 161 B.C., it was sold a second time, as if a new play, for 8,000 sesterces, a record price (Donat. *praef. Eun.* 6, Suet. *Vita Ter.* 10). Curule aediles L. Cornelius Merula (*RE* 271) and L. Postumius Albinus (*RE* 42). Principal players as in *Andria* (so the production-notice; Ambivius and L. Minucius Prothymus, Donat. *praef. Eun.* 6, on which see Garton, under *Andria* above, 257).

(5) *Phormio*, from Apollodorus of Carystus' 'The rival suitor', with little substantial alteration. Performed successfully at the *ludi Romani* (so the production-notices in Calliopian MSS; Megalensian Games, *codex Bembinus* and Donat. *praef. Ph.* 6) 161 B.C. with same presiding magistrates as for *Eunuchus*; actors as in *Andria* (*L. Cassio Atilio* (sic) *et L. Ambivio*, Donat. loc. cit.). The charge laid here by Luscius was that T.'s previous plays *tenui esse oratione et scriptura leui* (5).

(6) *Adelphoe* 'The brothers', Menander's second play of that name, with a scene (154–96) taken from the *Synapothnescontes* 'Partners in death' of Diphilus; Plautus had turned this play, but omitted the material in question, so that no charge of plagiarism from a Latin source could arise. Again this is not an adequate account of all the substantial changes T. has made (6ff.). T. here returns to the charge that he received more than encouragement from *homines nobiles* (15ff., cf. *H.T.* 24). Performed at funeral games of L. Aemilius Paullus (*RE* 114) 160 B.C., financed and put on by his sons by blood Q. Fabius Maxumus Aemilianus (*RE* 109) and P. Cornelius Scipio Aemilianus. Principal actors uncertain: L. Ambivius Turpio and L. Atilius Praenestinus (production-notice in *codex Bembinus*); L. Atilius Praenestinus and Q. Minucius Prothynus (production-notice in Calliopian MSS); L. Ambivio et L. [vac.] (Donat. *praef. Ad.* 6).

A second attempt to produce the *Hecyra* failed at this festival (*Hec.* prol. 1). It was finally produced successfully at one of the regular festivals run by curule aediles of 160 B.C. (Donat. *praef. Hec.* 6 is confused) Q. Fulvius Nobilior (*RE* 95; in honour of whom Ennius had taken his *praenomen* Quintus) and L. Marcius Censorinus (*RE* 46, dedicatee of a work by the philosopher Clitomachus, Cic. *Acad.* 2.102). These philhellenes must have been sympathetic to Terence's ideas to have backed such a loser.

BIBLIOGRAPHY

TEXTS AND COMMENTARIES: TEXTS: F. Umpfenbach (Berlin 1870: still fullest source of information as to MSS); K. Dziatzko (Leipzig 1884); R. Y. Tyrrell (Oxford 1902); R. Kauer, W. M. Lindsay (OCT, 1926; slightly revised O. Skutsch 1958); S. Prete (Heidelberg 1954), but cf. O. Skutsch, *C.R.* n.s.6 (1956) 129–33. TEXTS WITH TRANSLATION: Sir J. Sargeaunt (Loeb, 1912); J. Marouzeau (Budé, 1942–9; vol. 1 rev. 1963); R. Ranzato, R. Cantarella, vol. 1: *Andria, Heauton timorumenos* (Milan 1971: in progress). COMMENTARIES: (1) Complete. M. Antonius Muretus, 2 vols. (Venice 1555); G. Faernus, 2 vols. (Florence 1565); F. Lindenbruchius (Paris 1602: with Donatus' comm.); N. Camus (Paris 1675); R. Bentley (Cambridge 1726, Amsterdam 1727: includes Bentley's *De metris terentianis* σχεδίασμα, fundamental work on relation of ictus and word-accent in iambo-trochaic verse, i–xix); W. Wagner (Cambridge 1869); S. G. Ashmore (New York 1908). (2) Individual plays. *Andria*: G. P. Shipp, 2nd ed. (Oxford 1960). *Hecyra*: T. F. Carney (Pretoria 1968). *Heauton timorumenos*: K. I. Lietzmann, 2 vols. (Münster 1974). *Eunuchus*: P. Fabia (Paris

1895); ed. by P. McG. Brown (Oxford) in preparation. *Phormio*: R. H. Martin (London 1959). *Adelphoe*: idem (Cambridge 1976). K. Dziatzko's edition of *Phormio* rev. E. Hauler (Berlin 1913), of *Adelphoe* rev. R. Kauer (Berlin 1921).

TRANSLATIONS: H. T. Riley (London 1853); (ed.) G. Duckworth, *The complete Roman drama* II (New York 1942) 141–452 (anonymous except *Phormio*, tr. B. H. Clark); L. Echard (1689), ed. R. Graves (London 1963); F. O. Copley (Indianapolis 1967); B. Radice, 2nd ed. (Penguin, 1976).

BIBLIOGRAPHICAL AIDS AND SURVEYS: W. Wagner, *J.A.W.* 1 (1873) 443; 4 (1874–5) 798; A. Spengel, *J.A.W.* 6 (1876) 356–94; 27 (1881) 177–200; 39 (1884) 74–90; 68 (1891) 171–209; F. Schlee, *J.A.W.* 84 (1897) 116–64; R. Kauer, *J.A.W.* 143 (1909) 176–270; H. Marti, *Lustrum* 6 (1961) 114–238 (for 1909–59), 8 (1963) 5–101 and 244–64 (exceptionally useful); S. Prete, *C.W.* 54 (1961) 112–22. See also: P. W. Harsh, 'Early Latin metre and prosody 1904–55', *Lustrum* 3 (1958) 215ff.; H.-J. Mette, 'Der heutige Menander', *Lustrum* 10 (1965) 5ff.; G. Duckworth, *The nature of Roman comedy* (Princeton 1952) 447–64.

STUDIES. (1) COMPREHENSIVE: P. E. Legrand, *Daos, Tableau de la comédie grecque...dite nouvelle* (Paris 1910: English tr. by J. Loeb, *The Greek New Comedy* (London 1917)); Leo, *Gesch.* 232–58; G. Norwood, *Plautus and Terence* (New York 1932: good on T., bad on Plautus); G. Jachmann, *RE* VA.1 (1934) 598–650; B. Croce, 'Intorno alle commedie di Terenzio', *La Critica* 34 (1936) 401–23 (illuminates certain traits of much subsequent Italian scholarship); E. Reitzenstein, *Terenz als Dichter* (Amsterdam-Leipzig 1940); G. Duckworth, *The nature of Roman comedy* (Princeton 1952); W. Beare, *The Roman stage*, 3rd ed. (London 1964: good on *contaminatio*); H. Marti, *Untersuchungen zur dramatischen Technik bei Plautus und Terenz* (Zurich 1959); M. R. Posani, 'Aspetti del comico in Terenzio', *A. & R.* 7 (1962) 65–76; O. Bianco, *Terenzio: problemi e aspetti dell'originalità* (Rome 1962), cf. W. Ludwig, *Gnomon* 36 (1964) 152ff.; D. Klose, *Die Didaskalien und Prologe des Terenz* (Freiburg 1966); H.-J. Gluecklich, *Aussparung und Antithese: Studien zur terenzischen Komödie* (Frankfurt 1966), cf. H. Marti, *Gnomon* 43 (1971) 354–9; H. Haffter, *Terenz und seine künstlerische Eigenart* (Darmstadt 1967) = *M.H.* 10 (1953) 1–20, 73–102, Italian tr. by D. Nardo, *Terenzio e la sua personalità artistica* (Rome 1969); B. Denzler, *Der Monolog bei Terenz* (Zurich 1968), cf. E. Fantham, *Phoenix* 23 (1969) 406–8; P. Flury, *Liebe und Liebessprache bei Menander, Plautus, und Terenz* (Heidelberg 1968); W. Ludwig, 'The originality of Terence and his Greek models', *G.R.B.S.* 9 (1968) 169–92; Williams, *TORP* 289–94, al.; E. Lefèvre, *Die Expositionstechnik in den Komödien des Terenz* (Darmstadt 1969); K. Gaiser, 'Plautus und Terenz gegenüber ihren griechischen Vorbildern', *ANRW* 1.2 1027–1113; W. Goerler, 'Doppelhandlung, Intrige, und Anagnorismos bei Terenz', *Poetica* 5 (1972) 241–55; H. Gelhaus, *Die Prologe des Terenz: eine Erklärung nach den Lehren von der inventio et dispositio* (Heidelberg 1972);

B. Taladoire, *Térence, un théâtre de la jeunesse* (Paris 1972), cf. E. Segal, *A.J.Ph.* 96 (1975) 203–5, E. Lefèvre, *Gnomon* 48 (1976) 78–80; *Association Guillaume Budé, Actes du IXe Congrès, Rome 13–18 avril* 1973 vol. 1 (Paris 1975: papers on Plautus and T.); (ed.) E. Lefèvre, *Die römische Komödie: Plautus und Terenz*, Wege der Forschung 236 (Darmstadt 1973), cf. P. McG. Brown, *Gnomon* 48 (1976) 244–9; L. Perelli, *Il teatro rivoluzionario di Terenzio* (Florence 1973); K. Büchner, *Das Theater des Terenz* (Heidelberg 1974); W. G. Arnott, *Menander, Plautus, and Terence* (Oxford 1965); F. H. Sandbach, *The comic theatre of Greece and Rome* (Oxford 1977); H. Juhnke, 'Terenz', in (ed.) E. Lefèvre, *Das römische Drama* (Darmstadt 1978) 223–307.

(2) LEXICON: P. McGlynn, 2 vols. (Glasgow–London 1963–7), cf. J.-H. Waszink, *Mnemosyne* 20 (1967) 88–98, 23 (1970) 214.

(3) INDIVIDUAL PLAYS (since Marti's *Lustrum*-survey): *Heauton timorumenos*: A Primmer, 'Zum Prolog des Heautontimorumenos', *W.S.* 77 (1964) 61–75; idem, 'Die homo-sum-Szene im Heautontimorumenos', *W.S.* 79 (1966) 293–8; E. Fantham, 'Hautontimorumenos and Adelphoe. A study of fatherhood in Terence and Menander', *Latomus* 30 (1971) 970–98; H. D. Jocelyn, 'Homo sum: humani nil a me alienum puto', *Antichthon* 7 (1973) 14–46; E. Lefèvre, 'Der "Heautontimorumenos" des Terenz', *Die römische Komödie: Plautus und Terenz*, Wege der Forschung 236 (Darmstadt 1973) 443–62. *Eunuchus*: B. Bader, 'Terenz, Eunuchus 46–57', *Rh.M.* 116 (1973) 54–9; K. Gilmartin, 'The Thraso-subplot in Terence's Eunuchus', *C.W.* 69 (1975) 263–7; C. F. Saylor, 'The theme of planlessness in Terence's Eunuchus', *T.A.Ph.A.* 105 (1975) 297–311. *Phormio*: W. G. Arnott, 'Phormio Parasitus', *G.&R.* 17 (1970) 32–57. *Adelphoe*: W. G. Arnott, 'The end of Terence's Adelphoe: a postscript', *G.&R.* 10 (1963) 140–4; O. Rieth, *Die Kunst Menanders in den 'Adelphen' des Terenz* (Hildesheim 1964: ed. with Appendix by K. Gaiser); W. R. Johnston, 'Micio and the perils of perfection', *C.S.C.A.* 1 (1968) 171–86; E. Fantham, 'Terence, Adelphoe Act II', *Philologus* 112 (1968) 196–216; H. Tränkle, 'Micio und Demea in den terenzischen Adelphen' *M.H.* 29 (1972) 241–55; H. Lloyd-Jones, 'Terentian technique in the Adelphi and the Eunuchus', *C.Q.* n.s.23 (1973) 279–84; J. N. Grant, 'The ending of Terence's Adelphoe and the Menandrian original', *A.J.Ph.* 96 (1975) 42–60; V. Pöschl, 'Das Problem der Adelphen des Terenz', *S.H.A.W.* 1975, 4, cf. C. Garton, *C.W.* 70 (1976) 203–7.

(4) STYLE: J. B. Hoffman, *Die lateinische Umgangssprache* (Heidelberg 1926: 3rd ed. 1951); J. T. Allardice, *The syntax of Terence* (Oxford 1929); H. Haffter, *Untersuchungen zur altlateinischen Dichtersprache* (Berlin 1934); J. Straus, *Terenz und Menander: Beitrag zu einer Stilvergleichung* (diss. Bern 1955); G. Luck, *Rh. M.* 108 (1965) 269–77.

(5) TRANSMISSION: G. Jachmann, *Die Geschichte des Terenztextes im Altertum* (Basel 1924); L. W. Jones, C. R. Morey, *The miniatures of the MSS of Terence prior to the thirteenth century*, 2 vols. (Princeton 1932); S. Prete, *Il codice di Terenzio Vaticano 3226: saggio critico e riproduzione del manoscritto*, Studi e testi 262 (Vatican City 1970: full photographic reproduction of *codex Bembinus*); J. N. Grant, 'Contamination in the mixed MSS of Terence: a partial solution?', *T.A.Ph.A.* 105 (1975) 123–53.

(6) DONATUS' COMMENTARY: Text: P. Wessner (BT, 1902–8; repr. Stuttgart 1963); H. T. Karsten (Leiden 1912–13). Cf. J. N. Grant, 'Notes on Donatus' commentary on Adelphoe', *G.R.B.S.* 12 (1971) 197ff.

AFRANIUS, LUCIUS

LIFE

Active *c.* 160–120 B.C. as a writer of *fabulae togatae* (Vell. Pat. 1.17.1, 2.9.3) and possibly also as an orator in the lawcourts (Cic. *Brut.* 167 *homo perargutus*; Leo, *Gesch.* 375 n.4).

WORKS

Forty-two titles represented by *c.* 430 fragmentary verses, almost all cited by grammarians, are known. More than fifty verses: *Vopiscus* 'The surviving twin'. More than twenty verses: *Divortium* 'The divorce'; *Emancipatus* 'Free from father' (?); *Epistula* 'The letter'; *Exceptus* 'Rescued from shipwreck' (?); *Fratriae* 'Sisters-in-law'; *Privignus* 'The stepson'. Others: *Abducta* 'The kidnapped girl'; *Aequales* 'The friends'; *Auctio* 'The auction'; *Augur* 'The augur'; *Brundisinae* 'The ladies from Brindisi'; *Cinerarius* 'The hairdresser'; *Compitalia* 'The Crossroads Festival'; *Consobrini* 'The cousins'; *Crimen* 'Calumny'; *Deditio* 'Capitulation'; *Depositum* 'The sum set aside'; *Ida* (corrupt title); *Incendium* 'The fire'; *Inimici* 'The rivals'; *Libertas* 'Freedom'; *Mariti* 'The husbands'; *Materterae* 'Mother's sisters'; *Megalesia* 'The Feast of the Great Mother'; *Omen* 'The sign'; *Pantaleo* (personal name, or corrupt); *Pompa* 'The procession'; *Prodigus* 'The wastrel'; *Proditus* 'Betrayed'; *Promus* 'The steward'; *Purgamentum* 'The expiation'; *Repudiati* 'The rejected lovers' (?); *Sella* 'The seat'; *Simulans* 'The feigner'; *Sorores* 'The sisters'; *Suspecta* 'The girl under suspicion'; *Talio* 'Tit for tat'; *Temerarius* 'Jumping to conclusions'; *Thais*; *Titulus* 'The notice'; *Virgo* 'The girl'.

The character and categories of these titles closely match those of New Comedy playwrights such as Menander as opposed to those of the older *palliata*-writers. Afranius was evidently a self-conscious and well-educated artist, borrowing a good deal in technique and themes from Menander (Cic. *Fin.* 1.3.7, Hor. *Epist.* 2.1.57) and 'even from the Latins' (Macr. *Sat.* 6.1.4. (25–30 Ribbeck, *Compitalia*), cf. Suet. *Vita Terenti* p. 8) – Terence, whom he greatly admired (for his Menandrian aspirations?) (Macr. loc. cit.), the tragedian C. Titius (Cic. *Brut.* 167), and Pacuvius (a quotation, fr. 7 Ribbeck). The prologue of the *Compitalia* included or consisted of a defence of his eclectic approach in the same argumentative manner as in a Terentian prologue; elsewhere (277, 298f., 403f.) there are fragments of prologues spoken by divinities and abstractions, which implies that Menandrian ironies arising from the superior knowledge of the audience were a feature of his plays. Quintilian qualifies his praise of Afranius as an excellent all-round author for school-use like Menander because of the explicitly homosexual themes of some of the plays (Quint. 10.1.100). This boldness must be set against what appears to have been a relatively pusillanimous if realistic treatment of slave-roles, if Donatus' comment at Ter. *Eun.* 57, that clever slaves were not permissible in the explicitly Italian ambience of the *fabula togata*, is to be taken literally. It is important to note that although he wrote after Terence's time the musical and metrical presentation and the diction of Afranius' plays is essentially a direct continuation of the manner of the older *fabula palliata*: anapaests, bacchiacs, other lyric metres, and the jaunty iambic septenarius are well represented among the fragments. His verbal inventiveness and use of alliteration is like that of Caecilius and Plautus.

Afranius was well known in later times: Cicero refers to a performance of *Simulans* (*Sest.* 118); there was an extravagantly realistic performance of *Incendium* in Nero's reign (Suet. *Nero* 11); Quintilian thought highly of him except in one respect; and one Paulus wrote a commentary on some of his plays in the Hadrianic period (Charis. *GLK* I 241.1f.). The suggestion, however, that *P. Hamb.* 167, a fragment of prose mime, is from an Afranius-play must be rejected (J. Dingel, 'Bruchstück einer römischen Komödie auf einem Hamburger Papyrus (Afranius?)', *Z.P.E.* 10 (1973) 29–44; B. Bader, 'Ein Afraniuspapyrus?', ibid. 12 (1973) 270–6; J. Dingel, 'Zum Komödienfragment *P. Hamb.* 167 (Afranius?)', ibid. 14 (1974) 168).

BIBLIOGRAPHY

TEXTS: *CRF* 193ff. (not in *ROL*). A selection of the fragments is given by E. Diehl, *Poetarum Romanorum veterum reliquiae*, 6th ed. (Berlin 1967) 95–102.

STUDIES: Leo, *Gesch.* 374ff.; W. Beare, 'The fabula togata', *Hermathena* 55 (1940) 35–55; idem, *The Roman stage*, 3rd ed. (London 1964) 128ff.; M. Cacciaglia, 'Ricerche sulla fabula togata', *R.C.C.M.* 14 (1972) 207–45.

PACUVIUS, MARCUS

LIFE

b. 220 B.C. (Cic. *Brut.* 229 with Jerome, *Chron.* 139 B.C.); nephew of Ennius (Pliny, *N.H.* 35.19; Jerome wrongly says grandson). Jerome puts his *floruit* in 154 B.C. and says he came from Brundisium (Pacuvius an Oscan name). Varro quotes an epigram by one Pompilius who claims to have been a 'pupil' of P. as he was in turn of Ennius and Ennius of the Muses (*Sat. Men.* 356); cf. traditions that Menander was nephew and pupil of Alexis (Suda s.n. Ἄλεξις Θούριος κωμικός, anon. *De comoedia* (*CGF* ed. Kaibel I p. 9) 17). This implies that P. was a *ciuis ingenuus* and not necessarily *libertino patre natus* like, say, Horace: Ennius' family claimed descent from king Messapus. P. was, after Ennius, the first unequivocally 'respectable' poet. It is evident from the facts that he was the first to specialize exclusively in serious drama, and that his output was relatively small for one who lived so long, that he did not depend upon the pen for his livelihood. Pliny (loc. cit.) says he was the painter of a picture still to be seen in the Temple of Hercules in the *forum Boarium* and was the first to lend prestige (through his theatrical fame) to the art of painting in Rome; cf. Jerome, *Chron.* 154 B.C. Cicero makes Laelius mention P. as his *hospes et amicus* (*Amic.* 24), implying that he was one of the 'Scipionic circle'. Both P. and Accius staged plays at festival of 140 B.C. (Cic. *Brut.* 229). Gellius (13.2.2; cf. Jerome, loc. cit.) says that P. retired to Tarentum owing to illness and tells a *traditio*-story according to which Accius, on his way to Asia, stopped at Pacuvius' and read him his *Atreus c.* 135 B.C. d. *c.* 131 B.C. (Gell. loc. cit.). Varro quoted his epitaph in *De poetis* (*ap.* Gell. 1.24.4); this, unlike the epitaphs which he quotes for Naevius and Plautus, is probably genuine in the sense that it appeared on his tombstone, but it is far from certain that he wrote it himself as Varro claims: essentially the same epitaph is attested for two others of this period (*CIL* I² 1209–10; *CLE* 848, 53), and though the poet's name is accommodated to the metre better than in these other cases, it is still awkwardly fitted in (... *Pacuui Marci sita | ossa. hoc uole-bam* ...); there is no difficulty in the inversion of *nomen* and *praenomen*, but the enjambment with hiatus followed by elision across a strong breath-pause is suspiciously artificial. It is probable that in all three cases we have a standard epitaph from the copy-book of a mason of the Gracchan era. Reputation: Favourable comment: Cic. *Opt. gen. orat.* 1.2; Hor. *Epist.* 2.1.55; Vell. Pat. 2.9.3; Quint. 10.1.97; Gell. 6.14.6. Adverse: Lucilius bks 26–9 *passim* (early 120s, not long after P.'s death: word-formation, gloom, pretentiousness, contorted diction); Cic. *Brut.* 258 (his and Caecilius' *latinitas* unfavourably contrasted with that of Laelius and Aemilianus), cf. *Or.* 152; Quint. 1.5.67 (word-formation); Pers. 1.77 (cf. Lucilius).

WORKS

(1) TRAGEDIES: Twelve or thirteen titles, of which *c.* 380 assigned and *c.* 55 unassigned verses survive. More than thirty-five extant lines: *Chryses* (from Sophocles), *Dulo-restes, Medus, Periboea, Teucer*. More than twenty: *Antiopa* (from Euripides), *Atalanta, Hermiona, Iliona, Niptra* (from Sophocles: the earliest known Odysseus-drama on the Roman stage). Others: *Armorum iudicium* (Aeschylus), *Pentheus*, perhaps *Protesilaus* (but see R. Helm, *RE* XVIII (1942) 2172; the only evidence is in Antonius Volscus' introduction to Ovid, *Her.* 13 (*Epistulae Heroidum*, Venice 1497)). (2) FABULA PRAETEXTA: *Paullus*, after 168 B.C.; in honour of L. Aemilius Paullus, the victor at Pydna (four citations). (3) SATURA mentioned by Diomedes, *GLK* I 485.32, Porph. *ad* Hor. *Sat.* 1.10.46. No fragments.

BIBLIOGRAPHY

TEXTS: *TRF* 86–157; *ROL* II 158–322; (ed.) A. Klotz, with O. Seel, L. Voit, *Scaenicorum Romanorum fragmenta* vol. I: *Tragicorum fragmenta* (Oldenbourg 1953), cf. O. Skutsch, *Gnomon* 26 (1954) 465–70 (review more important textually than the edition, which had been intended to replace *TRF*; both examined with special reference to P.); R. Argenio (Turin 1959); G. d'Anna (Rome 1967), cf. C. Garton, *A.J.Ph.* 91 (1970) 228–33.

STUDIES: FUNDAMENTAL: Leo, *Gesch.* 226–32; R. Helm, *RE* XVIII (1942) 2156–74 (excellent survey of post-Leo scholarship and accounts of individual plays); I. Mariotti, *Introduzione a Pacuvio* (Urbino 1960: complementary to Helm), cf. H. Haffter, *Gnomon* 40 (1968) 206; M. Valsa, *Marcus Pacuvius, Poète tragique* (Paris 1957). SEE ALSO: H.-J. Mette, *Lustrum* 9 (1964) 78–107, al. (Roman tragic poets 1945–64); B. Bilinski, *Contrastanti ideali di cultura sulla scena di Pacuvio* (Warsaw 1962), cf. J.-H. Waszink, *Mnemosyne* 19 (1966) 82–4; W. Beare, *The Roman stage*, 3rd ed. (London 1964) 79–84.

ACCIUS, LUCIUS

LIFE

b. 170 B. C. at Pisaurum; his family freedmen *coloni*. Put on a tragedy at same festival as the aged Pacuvius in 140 or 139 B.C. (Jerome, *Chron.* 139 B.C., given as his *floruit*). Wrote his *Brutus* and a triumphal saturnian inscription (*Works* 2 and 5) for D. Junius Brutus Callaicus (*RE* Iunius 57, cos. 138 B.C.); cf. Cic. *Arch.* 27, schol. Bob. *ad loc.*, Val. Max. 8.14.2, Cic. *Leg.* 2.54, Plut. *Q. Rom.* 34, Cic. *Brut.* 107 and 229. *c.* 135 B.C. travelled to 'Asia' (Gell. 13.2), i.e. Pergamum; before embarking is supposed to have met and stayed with Pacuvius at Tarentum and read him his *Atreus* (Gell. loc. cit.). In 120s was object of repeated attacks by Lucilius and became official head of the College of Poets, on which he had erected a gigantic statue of himself (Pliny, *N.H.* 34.19, cf. Lucilius (28) 794 M = *ROL* 844: he himself was very short); cf. Serv. *ad Aen.* 1.8, B. Tamm, *Opusc. Rom.* III (1961) 157–67, H. Cancik, *M.D.A.I.(R)* 76 (1969) 323, E. Badian, 'Ennius and his friends', *Entretiens XVII* (Fondation Hardt 1971) 151–95. It was noted that A. would not rise in honour of the senatorial poet Julius Caesar Strabo *in collegium poetarum uenienti*, an anecdote referring to *c.* 95–87 B.C. (Val. Max. 3.7.11); Cicero heard him lecturing in early 80s B.C. His latest known tragedy was *Tereus* (104 B.C., Cic. *Phil.* 1.15.36). The freedman scholar Lutatius Daphnis was educated as a slave by A. and he sold him for a record price to the *princeps senatus* M. Aemilius Scaurus (Pliny, *N.H.* 7.128). He successfully prosecuted an actor who named him on the stage (auct. *Ad Her.* 1.24, cf. 2.19). Reputation: Cic. *Planc.* 24, *Sest.* 56; Ovid, *Am.* 1.15.19; Vitr. 9 *praef.* 16; Vell. Pat. 1.17.1. Comparisons with Pacuvius: Hor. *Epist.* 2.1.55; Vell. Pat. 2.9.3; Quint. 10.1.97.

WORKS

(1) FABULAE CREPIDATAE (*c.* 700 verses): (*a*) more than forty verses: *Epigoni, Eurysaces, Philocteta Lemnius*; (*b*) more than twenty verses: *Armorum iudicium, Astyanax,*

Atreus (c. 135 B.C.), *Bacchae, Epinausimache, Medea* or *Argonautae, Phoenissae, Telephus*; (c) fewer than twenty verses: *Achilles, Aegisthus, Agamemnonidae, Alcestis, Alcmeo, Alphesiboea, Amphitryo, Andromeda, Antenoridae, Antigona, Athamas, Chrysippus, Clytaemestra, Deiphobus, Diomedes, Hecuba, Hellenes, Io, Melanippus, Meleager, Minos* or *Minotaurus, Myrmidones* (= *Achilles?*), *Neoptolemus, Nyctegresia, Oenomaus, Pelopidae, Persidae, Phinidae, Prometheus, Stasiastae* or *Tropaeum liberi, Tereus* (104 B.C.), *Thebais, Troades.*

(2) FABULAE PRAETEXTAE: *Aeneadae* or *Decius, Brutus.*

(3) SCHOLARLY WORKS: (a) *Didascalicon libri ix*, partly in Sotadic metre and partly in prose (so Leo, *Gesch.* 389, n.3, rightly; Warmington, *ROL* II 578 is wrong), on the history of the Greek and Roman theatre and other literary questions (e.g. the priority of Homer and Hesiod, lib. i *ap.* Gell. 3.11.4, contradicting Eratosthenes (R. Pfeiffer, *History of classical scholarship* I (Oxford 1968) 164)). (b) *Pragmatica*, two or more books in trochaic verse on literary themes. (c) *Annales* in hexameters: the only long fragment (Macr. *Sat.* 1.7.36) is aetiological, explaining the Roman Saturnalia as an imitation of the Athenian Kronia. (d) *Parerga*, two or more books: the one citation (senarii) is about ploughing. (e) *Praxidica* twice mentioned as by 'Attius' (Pliny, *N.H.* praef. 18 and 18.200). (f) *Sotadicon libri* assumed to be identical with *Didascalica* (Gell. 6.9.16), but perhaps erotic in theme and to be identified with

(4) AMATORY VERSE (Pliny, *Epist.* 5.3): but this might be elegiac epigrams like those of Q. Catulus and Valerius Aedituus (Gell. 19.9.11, Apul. *Apol.* 9).

(5) SATURNIANS on the temple of Mars dedicated in later 130s by A.'s patron D. Junius Brutus Callaicus (Cic. *Arch.* 27, schol. Bob. *ad loc.*).

(6) ORTHOGRAPHICAL PRECEPTS: write *-gg-* for *-ng-*; use *u* and *s* not *y* and *ʒ*; distinguish long vowels by writing, e.g., *-aa-* not *-a-*; but in the case of long *-i-* write *-ei-*; use *-i-* for the short vowel; do not Latinize the oblique cases of Greek names (*Hectora* not *Hectorem*). See Mar. Vict. *GLK* VI 8.11, Prisc. *GLK* II 30.12, Vel. gramm. *GLK* VII 55.25, Scaur. gramm. *GLK* VII 18.12, Varro, *Ling. Lat.* 7.96, 10.70; cf. Lucilius (9) 351ff. M = *ROL* 368ff.

BIBLIOGRAPHY

TEXTS: (1) COMPLETE: *ROL* pp. 326–606; A. Resta Barrile (Bologna 1969). (2) PLAYS ONLY: *TRF* pp. 157–263; O. Seel, L. Voit (ed. A. Klotz), *Scaenicorum Romanorum fragmenta* vol. I: *Tragicorum fragmenta* (Oldenbourg 1953); Q. Franchella (Bologna 1968). (3) OTHER WORKS: *GrRF* I. (4) SELECTIONS: *Poetarum Romanorum veterum reliquiae* selegit Ernestus Diehl, 6th ed. (Berlin 1967) 73–92; R. Argenio, *Frammenti tragici scelte* (Rome 1962) with 'Tragedie acciane', *R.S.C.* 14 (1966) 5–53.

STUDIES: Leo, *Gesch.* 384–405; J. Glaser, 'Bericht über Accius 1926–1930', *J.A.W.* 224 (1934) 70f.; H.-J. Mette, 'Die römische Tragödie und die Neufunde zur griechischen Tragödie für die Jahre 1945–64', *Lustrum* 9 (1964) 17f., 107–60;

I. Mariotti, 'Tragédie romaine et tragédie grecque: Accius et Euripide', *M.H.* 22 (1965) 206–16; E. Dobroiou, 'A propos des oeuvres d'érudition d'Accius', *Analele Univ. Bucureşti*, St. Soc. fil. 15 (1966) 13–35; R. Argenio, 'Tragedie acciane', *R.S.C.* 14 (1966) 5–53; H. D. Jocelyn, 'The quotations of Republican dramatists in Priscian's treatise De metris fabularum Terenti', *Antichthon* 1 (1967) 60–9 (appendix on the *Medea* or *Argonautae*); E. Gabba, 'Il Brutus di Accio', *Dioniso* 43 (1969) 377–83; H. Cancik, 'Die Statue des L. Accius im Tempel der Camenen', *Silvae: Festschrift für E. Zinn ẓum 60. Geburtstag*, ed. M. von Albrecht, E. Heck (Tübingen 1970) 7–17; idem, *M.D.A.I.(R)* 76 (1969) 323; A. Traina, *Vortit barbare* (Rome 1970) 181–203; A. de Rosalia, 'L'alliterazione in L. Accio', *A.L.G.P.* 7–8 (1970–1) 139–215; V. d'Anto, 'L'Athamas di Ennio e di Accio', *B. Stud. Lat.* 1 (1971) 371–8; D. Ferrin Sutton, 'Aeschylus' Edonians' (and the *Stasiastae* of Accius), *Saggi in onore di V. d'Agostino* (Turin 1971) 387–411; S. Sconocchie, 'L'Antigona di Accio e l'Antigone di Sofocle', *R.F.I.C.* 100 (1972) 273–82; A. di Benedetto-Zimbone, 'L'Atreus di Accio', *Sic. Gymn.* 26 (1973) 266–85; G. Paduano, 'Sul prologo delle Fenicie di Accio', *A.S.N.P.* 3 (1973) 827–35; G. B. Pighi, 'Gli annali di Accio', *Scritti in onore di C. Vassalani raccolta da L. Barbesi* (Verona 1974) 373–80; M. R. Ruiz de Elvira y Serra, 'Los Pelópidas en la literatura clásica', *C.F.C.* 7 (1974) 249–302.

CATO, MARCUS PORCIUS

LIFE

b. at Tusculum 234 B.C. of peasant stock; served in Hannibalic War (217/216 B.C., Campania; 214 B.C., military tribune in Sicily; 207 B.C., distinguished conduct at battle of Sena). Impressed the aristocratic L. Valerius Flaccus with whose help he embarked on a political career. Quaestor in Sicily 204 B.C., C. is supposed to have been responsible for bringing Ennius to Rome in 203/202 B.C. from Sardinia. Plebeian aedile 199 B.C., praetor 198 B.C. in charge of Sardinia; reputation as a just and strict governor, expelling usurers and cutting the 'perks' which as praetor he could have exploited (*leges Porciae de prouocatione* and *de sumptu prouinciali* may be dated to this year). Consul 195 B.C. (with Valerius Flaccus) he opposed the repeal of the *Lex Oppia* which limited the public display by women of family wealth, and took charge of Spain, where he behaved with severity towards the Spanish tribes and cultivated his reputation for frugality and efficiency. In 191 B.C. as military tribune with Valerius Flaccus under Acilius Glabrio the consul he fought at Thermopylae and conducted an important diplomatic mission to Athens and other Greek cities. In 190 B.C. prosecuted Q. Minucius Thermus, the first known in a long succession of prosecutions aimed at the then dominant Scipionic faction, and supported charges of peculation against Acilius Glabrio who, as C. himself, was a candidate for the censorship of 189 B.C. This time he failed, but in the sequel he was a central figure in the now obscure manoeuvres which led to the downfall of the Scipios in politics (188 B.C.). Exploiting this and other shocks to public confidence, he became censor (again with L. Valerius Flaccus) in 184 B.C., presenting himself as the champion of the good old Roman virtues at a time of unprecedented social, economic and moral upheaval; see Plut. *Cato maj.* 17–19. Most of C.'s writings date from this time or later, and for the rest of his life he continued to advocate the *mores maiorum*, presenting himself as a bluff and canny peasant, with the self-made man's contempt for those born to wealth and power. He made many enemies and was constantly involved in prosecutions both as prosecutor and defendant, though he himself was never convicted. He was the enemy and mocker not of Hellenism as such, but of pretentiousness, as he saw it, humbug, and vice in philhellenes of noble houses (e.g. the Quinctii Flaminini, the Fulvii Nobiliores) who paid scant attention to the 'ways of their ancestors' – as C. defined them: for what was *noua res* to one generation was *mos maiorum* to the next. He was himself, paradoxically, an outstanding example of the versatility and individualism of the Hellenistic period. He opposed the repeal of a sumptuary law, the *Lex Orchia* (181 B.C.), supported the *Lex Voconia* which limited women's rights of inheritance (169 B.C.), opposed war with Rhodes (167 B.C.) and favoured independence for Macedonia; in 155 B.C. he spoke against the Athenian ambassadors, all three of them philosophers, who caused a stir at Rome, especially the sceptic Carneades. In 153 B.C. he visited Carthage and became convinced then if not earlier that Rome to survive must destroy her old enemy. His overriding political concern was to restore and preserve social cohesion in Rome and Italy, which he saw as a question of morals and moral education; Greece and the East could be left to themselves. On the other hand the government of Spain, still at the end of his life far from settled, concerned him closely from the time of his consulship; in 171 B.C. he prosecuted P. Furius Philus for extortion and in the last year of his life (149 B.C.) Sulpicius Galba on behalf of the Lusitanians. He was survived by two sons, Cato Licinianus by his first wife and Cato Salonianus (grandfather to Cato Uticensis) by a second. Sources: Plut. *Cat. maj.*; Livy 29.25, 32.27, 34, 36, 38–9 *passim*, 43.2, 45.25; Cic. *Sen. passim*; Nepos, *Cato*; and C.'s fragments, see below.

WORKS

(1) Speeches. Cicero found and read more than 150 (*Brut.* 65) and seems to have been responsible for a revival of interest. Today the titles or occasions of some eighty are known (list, *ORF* pp. 553–6), among which twenty belong to the year of his censorship. Best represented or most notable are the following: (*a*) From his consulship (195 B.C.) to his censorship (184 B.C.). (i) Against repeal of *Lex Oppia* (195 B.C.), arguing against relaxation of sumptuary regulations relating to women's expenditure and ornament. Only known from Livy's extensive paraphrase (34.2–4); not in *ORF* (but see *ORF* p. 14). (ii) To cavalry at Numantia (195 B.C.), *ORF* fr. 17–18. (iii) In defence of his actions as consul (191/190 B.C.?), *ORF* fr. 21–55. (iv) To Athenians (191 B.C.), *ORF* fr. 20; important as the earliest known assertion of Latin as a language of international diplomacy on a par with Greek. (v) Against Q. Minucius Thermus *De falsis pugnis*

(190 B.C.), *ORF* fr. 58. (*b*) From his censorship (184/183 B.C.). (vi) Against L. Quinctius Flamininus, *ORF* fr. 69–71. (vii) Against L. Veturius, *ORF* fr. 72–82. (viii) Anticipating a prosecution threatened by tribune of plebs M. Caelius, *ORF* fr. 111–20. (*c*) From his censorship to his death (149 B.C.). (ix) On his Own Fine Qualities, against L. Minucius Thermus after his censorship (183 B.C.), *ORF* fr. 128–35. (x) Against repeal of *Lex Orchia* (181 B.C. or later), *ORF* fr. 139–46; the *Lex Orchia* (182 B.C.) had fixed sumptuary regulations relating to banqueting. As in the case of the *Lex Oppia* C.'s opposition was unsuccessful. (xi) On behalf of the Rhodians (167 B.C.), *ORF* fr. 163–71; the best represented speech, together with (xii) *De sumptu suo* (164 B.C.), *ORF* fr. 173–5. (xiii) Against Ser. Sulpicius Galba on behalf of the plundered Lusitanians (149 B.C.), *ORF* fr. 196–9, delivered by C. aged 85.

(2) *Origines*, a title which properly applies only to the first three of seven books of historical, geographical and political studies, didactic in character, composed during 160s and 150s B.C. in C.'s old age. Bk 1: the Kings of Rome; thirty citations or allusions. Bk 2 (thirty-seven citations) and bk 3 (nine): *origines* of towns, cities and peoples of Italy other than the Roman. Bk 4: First Punic War (fifteen citations). Bk 5: Second Punic War (thirteen citations, including a lengthy passage of the speech *For the Rhodians* (*ORF* fr. 163). Bk 6 (one citation) and bk 7 (twelve): recent and contemporary history, right up to year of C.'s death (149 B.C.), including citation of his speech against Ser. Sulpicius Galba (*ORF* fr. 198). A further twenty-eight citations or allusions of uncertain or ambiguous attribution are preserved.

(3) *De agri cultura*, one book lacking formal structure, the only 'complete' surviving work of C. Extent of interpolation indeterminable.

(4) A book *De disciplina militari* (fifteen citations, pp. 80–2 Jordan) probably not to be distinguished from

(5) A series of pamphlets or letters addressed to his son Marcus (Porcius Cato Licinianus, b. *c.* 192 B.C.): a story-book 'written in big letters' (Plut. *Cato maj.* 20.7); *libri ad filium de agri cultura* (Serv. *ad* Virg. *G.* 2.412), eight citations; *De medicina* (five citations); on rhetoric (three citations including the famous *rem tene, uerba sequentur*, Julius Victor in K. Halm, *Rhetores Latini minores* I (Leipzig 1863) 374.17). Also allusions to a letter of C. to his son (notably Cic. *Off.* 1.10, Plut. *Cat. maj.* 20) written during his service in the army in Macedonia 168 B.C. Relation of these works to each other and manner in which they came to be 'published' is problematic. It goes beyond the evidence and probability to suppose that C. himself published them as a collection which constituted a kind of encyclopaedia.

(6) *Carmen de moribus*, a book of saws attributed to C., only known from Gell. 11.2: no reason to suppose that *carmen* here implies a verse-form, and the three fragments are all prose; cf. *OLD* s.v. *carmen* 'sacred utterance'.

(7) A collection of C.'s 'sayings' and witty remarks was already current in Cicero's day (cf., e.g., *De or.* 2.256, Hor. *Sat.* 1.2.31), the source of some ten anecdotes or examples in Cicero and more in Plutarch's *Life of Cato*. While some of these may be traced to speeches of C., much of this material will have been adventitious. The

versified *Dicta Catonis* which enjoyed a wide circulation in the middle ages derives from a source hardly earlier than the 3rd c. A.D.

(8) The popular belief that C. ended all his speeches by saying *Carthago delenda est* or *ceterum censeo Carthaginem esse delendam* is an overinterpretation of Plut. *Cat. maj.* 27 (cf. Diod. Sic. 34/35.33.3): in the first place, this would only apply to speeches by C. delivered in the senate, and in the second there is no Latin source for the quoted formulations which have been current since only the early 19th c. See S. Thürlemann, *Gymnasium* 81 (1974) 465–75.

BIBLIOGRAPHY

TEXTS AND COMMENTARIES: Speeches: *ORF* 12–97, cf. E. Badian, *J.R.S.* 46 (1956) 218–21, 58 (1968) 256. *Origines*: *HRR* cxxvii–clxiv, 55–97; W. A. Schroeder (Meisenheim 1971: bk 1, with commentary). *De agri cultura*: H. Keil (Leipzig 1882–1902); G. Goetz (Leipzig 1922); E. Bréhaut (New York 1933, repr. 1966: tr. and notes); W. D. Hooper and H. B. Ash (Loeb, 1934); A. Mazzarino (BT, 1962); P. Thielscher (Berlin 1963: with tr.); R. Goujard (Budé, 1975). Remaining works are conventionally cited from H. Jordan, *M. Catonis praeter librum De re rustica quae extant* (Leipzig 1860).

STUDIES: (1) COMPREHENSIVE: M. Gelzer, *RE* XXII (1953) 108–45; Leo, *Gesch.* 265–300; P. Fraccaro, *Opuscula* vol. 1: *Scritti di carattere generale, Studi Catoniani* (Pavia 1956) 43–386; E. V. Marmorale, *Cato maior* (Bari 1949); F. della Corte, *Catone censore: la vita e la fortuna* (Florence 1949; 2nd ed. 1969); H. H. Scullard, *Roman politics 220–150 B.C.* (Oxford 1951; 2nd ed. 1973); D. Kienast, *Cato der Zensor: seine Persönlichkeit und seine Zeit mit einem durchgesehenen Neuabdruck/der Redenfragmente Catos* (Heidelberg 1954). (2) STYLE: R. Till, *Die Sprache Catos, Philologus* suppl. 28.2 (1936), Italian tr. by C. de Meo, *La lingua di Catone* (Rome 1968: with supplementary observations); Leo under (1) above; E. Fraenkel, *Leseproben aus den Reden Ciceros und Catos* (Rome 1968). (3) HISTORICAL WORK: B. Janzer, *Historische Untersuchungen zu den Redenfragmenten des M. Porcius Cato. Beiträge zur Lebensgeschichte und Politik Catos* (diss. Würzburg 1936); D. Timpe, 'Le origine di Catone e la storiografia latina', *Atti e Mem. dell'Accademia Patavina* (Classe di Sc. mor., Lett., ed Arti) 83 (1970) 1–33. (4) MINOR WORKS: P. L. Schmidt, 'Catos Epistula ad M. filium und die Anfänge der römischen Briefliteratur', *Hermes* 100 (1972) 568–76.

LUCILIUS, GAIUS

LIFE

(1) DATES: Jerome (*Chron.* 102 B.C.) says L. was honoured with a public funeral at Naples when he died there that year aged 46. This implies he was born in 148 B.C. (coss. Sp. Postumius Albinus and L. Calpurnius Piso), that he was on Aemilianus' staff

at Numantia (Vell. Pat. 2.9.3) at the age of only fifteen, and began writing his Satires before he was twenty. This is not intrinsically impossible but is ruled out by Horace's allusion to L.'s oeuvre as a whole as giving a comprehensive *uita senis* (Hor. *Sat.* 2.1.34); it is generally accepted that Jerome confused the consuls of 148 B.C. with those of 180 B.C. (A. Postumius Albinus and C. Calpurnius Piso); for a compromise (168/167 B.C.), see I. Mariotti, F. della Corte, W. Krenkel, *Maia* 20 (1968) 254–70; W. Krenkel, *ANRW* 1.2 1240–59. (2) FAMILY: Came from distinguished family of the Latin aristocracy whose seat was at Suessa Aurunca on the borders of Campania (Juv. 1.20, schol. *ad loc.*). Horace calls him *auus* (ps.-Acron *ad* Hor. *Sat.* 2.1.29) and *auunculus* (Porph. *ad* Hor. *Sat.* 2.1.75) to Pompey the Great through his sister; Pompey's mother was herself another Lucilia. This makes L. great-uncle of Pompey. His precise relationship to Lucilius Hirrus, pr. 134 B.C. and to M'. Lucilius M.f. Pomptina, a senator who visited Pergamum as ambassador in 129 B.C., is obscure (C. Cichorius, *Untersuchungen zu Lucilius* (Berlin 1908) 2f.; *RE* XIII (1927) 1638–40, 1642–3, 1647; M. Coffey, *Roman satire* (London 1976) 35f., and nn. 6 and 8). L. owned estates in Campania and Sicily (*Sat.* 3 *passim*, Cic. *Fin.* 1.3.7) and the house at Rome which had been built to accommodate Demetrius, son of Antiochus III, while he was a hostage at Rome (Asconius, *Pis.* p. 12.9 K.–S.), and L. or a relative was among those accused of ranching illegally on *ager publicus c.* 114–111 B.C. (Cic. *De or.* 284). It is not clear whether he ever became a *ciuis Romanus* himself or whether he married.

WORKS

Thirty books of Satires: some 1,300 citations, all but a handful very brief. On order of composition, arrangement, 'publication', and character of these books, the earliest of which are those numbered 26–30 (iambo-trochaic metres with a small element of hexameter-writing), see pp. 168–70.

BIBLIOGRAPHY

TEXTS: F. Marx, vol. I (Leipzig 1904), vol. II, commentary (Leipzig 1905), cf. A. E. Housman, *C.Q.* 1 (1907) 53–74, 148–59, F. Leo, *G.G.A.* 168 (1906) 837–61; E. Bolisani (Padua 1932); N. Terzaghi (Florence 1934, 1944: rev. I. Mariotti, 1964); *ROL* III (with brief notes); J. Heurgon (*Les cours de Sorbonne*: Paris 1959); W. Krenkel, 2 vols. (Leiden 1970: with German tr. and commentary), cf. A. S. Gratwick, *J.R.S.* 63 (1973) 302–4; F. Charpin (Budé, 1978–9).

SURVEYS: E. Lommatzsch, *J.A.W.* 139 (1908) 213–16; 175 (1919) 91–8; 204 (1925) 211–15; 235 (1932) 139–42; 260 (1938) 89–94; R. Helm, *J.A.W.* 282 (1943) 1–37; K. Büchner, *Gymnasium* 62 (1955) 220–5; W. S. Anderson, *C.W.* 50 (1956) 33–40; 57 (1964) 293–301; 63 (1970) 181–99; J. Christes, *ANRW* 1.2 1182–1239, and W. Krenkel, ibid. 1240–59.

STUDIES: C. Cichorius, *Untersuchungen zu Lucilius* (Berlin 1908) and *Römische Studien* (Berlin 1922); Leo, *Gesch.* 405–29; G. C. Fiske, *Lucilius and Horace: a study in the classical art of imitation* (Madison 1920); A. Kappelmacher, *RE* XIII (1927) 1617–37 (Lucilius 4); U. Knoche, *Die römische Satire* (Berlin 1949); M. Puelma-Piwonka, *Lucilius und Kallimachos. Zur Geschichte einer Gattung der hellenistisch-römischen Poesie* (Frankfurt 1949); H. Bardon, 'Catulle et ses modèles poétiques de langue latine', *Latomus* 16 (1957) 614–27; I. Mariotti, *Studi Luciliani* (Florence 1960: helpful as to style); M. Coffey, *Roman satire* (London–New York 1976); J. Christes, *Der frühe Lucilius. Rekonstruktion und Interpretation des XXVI. Buches sowie von Teilen des XXX. Buches* (Heidelberg 1971).

SENECA, LUCIUS ANNAEUS

LIFE AND WORKS

LIFE: b. of equestrian family at Corduba in Spain, probably in 50s B.C. Divided his time between Rome and Spain (dates uncertain). *Condiscipulus* and lifelong friend of Porcius Latro, but not a rhetorician himself. Three sons: Novatus (later Junius Gallio), Seneca (the philosopher), and Mela (Lucan's father). d. before A.D. 41. See Fairweather, under *Studies* below, 3–26. WORKS: (1) Extant: *Oratorum et rhetorum sententiae divisiones colores* (completed after A.D. 34 (*Suas.* 2.22), possibly in Caligula's reign): one book of seven *Suasoriae* (more were planned, *Contr.* 2.4.8), and ten, each with preface, of *Controversiae* (only bks 1–2, 7, 9–10 survive; 4th–5th c. abridgement supplies two missing prefaces and excerpts from lost books). (2) Lost: History from beginning of civil wars to his own times; see younger Seneca fr. 98 Haase.

BIBLIOGRAPHY

TEXTS AND COMMENTARY: TEXTS: A. Kiessling (BT, 1872); H. J. Müller (Vienna 1887); M. Winterbottom (Loeb, 1974). COMMENTARY: *Suas.*: W. A. Edward (Cambridge 1928).

STUDIES: H. Bardon, *Le vocabulaire de la critique littéraire chez Sénèque le Rhéteur* (Paris 1940); L. A. Sussman, *The elder Seneca* (Leiden 1978); J. A. Fairweather, *Seneca the elder* (Cambridge 1981).

SURVEYS: J. E. G. Whitehorne, *Prudentia* 1 (1969) 14ff.; forthcoming articles by Sussman and Fairweather in *ANRW*.

METRICAL APPENDIX

(1) BASIC PRINCIPLES

(A) STRESSED AND QUANTITATIVE VERSE

In metres familiar to speakers of English, rhythm is measured by the predictable alternation of one or more stressed syllables with one or more unstressed syllables (distinguished by the notation – and ∪, or ′ and ×). Consequently, it is word-accent that determines whether or not a word or sequence of words may stand in a certain part of the verse. Thus the word *classical* may occupy the metrical unit represented by the notation –∪∪ by virtue of the stress imparted to its first syllable in everyday pronunciation. In contrast, the rhythms of classical Latin metres are measured by the predictable alternation of one or more 'heavy' syllables with one or more 'light' syllables (defined below, and distinguished by the notation – and ∪), so that in the construction of Latin verse the factor of primary importance is not word-accent but syllabic 'weight'. Thus the word *facerent*, although accented in normal speech on the first syllable, consists for metrical purposes of two light syllables followed by one heavy syllable, and for this reason can only occupy the metrical unit ∪∪–. Verse constructed upon this principle is conventionally designated *quantitative*: it should be emphasized that this term refers to the quantity (or 'weight') of syllables, and that throughout this account such quantity is described by the terms 'heavy' and 'light' to distinguish it from the intrinsic length of vowels; unfortunately, both syllabic weight and vowel-length are still generally denoted by the same symbols, – and ∪.

(B) SYLLABIFICATION

A syllable containing a long vowel or diphthong is heavy (e.g. the first syllables of *pacem* and *laudo*).

A syllable containing a short vowel is light if it ends with that vowel (e.g. the first syllable of *pecus*), but heavy if it ends with a consonant (e.g. the first syllable of *pectus*).

To decide whether or not a short-vowelled syllable ends with a consonant (and thus to establish its quantity), the following rules should be observed:[1] (i) word-division

---

[1] The resulting division is practical only; for the difficulties involved in an absolute definition of the syllabic unit see Allen (1973) under (4) below, esp. 27–40.

should be disregarded; (ii) a single consonant between two vowels or diphthongs belongs to the succeeding syllable (thus *pecus →pe–cus*; *genus omne →ge–nu–som–ne*); (iii) of two or more successive consonants, at least one belongs to the preceding syllable (thus *pectus →pec–tus*; also *nulla spes →nul–las–pes*, though short final vowels are normally avoided in this position), except as allowed for below.

Note: for this purpose *h* is disregarded; *x* and *z* count as double consonants, 'semi-consonantal' *i* and *u* as consonants (except in the combination *qu*, regarded as a single consonant).

To (iii) there is an important exception. In the case of the combination of a plosive and liquid consonant (*p*, *t*, *c*, *b*, *d*, *g* followed by *r* or *l*), the syllabic division may be made either between the consonants (e.g. *pat–ris*) or before them (e.g. *pa–tris*), resulting in *either* a heavy *or* a light preceding syllable. However, when two such consonants belong to different parts of a compound or to two different words, the division is always made between them, giving a heavy preceding syllable (e.g. *ablego →* *ab–lego*, not *a–blego*; *at rabidae →at–rabidae*, not *a–trabidae*). Lastly, when, after a short final vowel, these consonants begin the next word, the division is nearly always made before them, giving a light preceding syllable (e.g. *plumbea glans →plum–be–a–glans*).

(C) ACCENT

The nature of the Latin word-accent (whether one of pitch or stress) and its importance in the construction of verse are both matters of controversy: for a clear discussion of the basic problems see Wilkinson under (4) below, 89–96, 221–36. By way of practical guidance in reading Latin verse, all that may be said is that for the present-day English speaker, accustomed to a naturalistic manner of reading poetry, it will sound as strange (and monotonous) to emphasize the heavy syllables of a metrical structure ('Quális Théseá iacuít cedénte carína') as it does to read Shakespearian verse with attention only to its iambic structure ('Now ís the wínter óf our díscontént'); furthermore that, even in giving stress to the word-accent in Latin verse, heavy syllables will generally coincide with accented syllables with sufficient frequency to ensure that the metre is not forgotten – particularly at the beginning and end of many metres, as in the hexameter quoted above. It should be remembered, however, that what sounds natural is not thereby authentic, and that poetic delivery is highly susceptible to whims of fashion, idiosyncrasy and affectation. Even now it is not uncommon criticism of a Shakespearian actor that he 'mutilates' the shape of the verse by reading it as prose, while recordings of Tennyson and Eliot reading their poetry already sound bizarre (in different ways) to the modern ear.

(2) TECHNICAL TERMS

Anceps ('unfixed'): term used to describe a metrical element which may be represented by either a heavy or a light syllable. The final element of many Latin metres is regularly of this nature, but not in certain lyric metres in which there is metrical continuity (*synaphea*) between as well as within lines.

Brevis brevians, or *the law of iambic shortening*: in comedy and other early Latin verse a heavy syllable may be lightened if it directly follows a light syllable and is adjacent to an accented syllable. See p. 87.

Caesura ('cutting') and *diaeresis*: division between words within a verse is termed *caesura* when occurring inside a metrical foot, or *diaeresis* when occurring at the end of a foot. The varied distribution of these plays an important part in avoiding monotony in the structure of verse; in particular, the caesura prevents a succession of words co-extensive with the feet of a metre (as found in Ennius' hexameter, 'sparsis hastis longis campus splendet et horret').

Elision and *hiatus*: a vowel (or vowel + *m*) ending a word is generally suppressed or *elided* when immediately preceding another vowel or *h*. When it is not elided in these circumstances (a phenomenon most frequently found in comedy), it is said to be in *hiatus*; by the rare process of *correption* a long vowel or diphthong in hiatus may be scanned short to make a light syllable. *Prodelision* (or *aphaeresis*) signifies the suppression of *e* in *est* after a final vowel or *m*, *hypermetric elision* the suppression of a vowel between lines (nearly always that of *–que*).

Resolution: the substitution of two light syllables for a heavy one.

(3) COMMON METRES

For the sake of simplicity only the most basic characteristics of each metre are given here. For the numerous divergencies regarding anceps, resolution, position of caesura etc., see Raven under (4) below.

(a) Stichic verse (constructed by repetition of the same metrical line)
Iambic senarius (or trimeter):

$$\underline{\smile}-\smile-\,|\,\underline{\smile}-\smile-\,|\,\underline{\smile}-\smile\underline{\smile}$$

(commonest dialogue metre in early Roman drama; also used in Seneca's tragedies, Phaedrus' *Fables*, and, in alternation with an iambic dimeter ($=\underline{\smile}-\smile-\,|\,\underline{\smile}-\smile-$), Horace's *Epodes* 1–10)
Iambic septenarius (or tetrameter catalectic):

$$\underline{\smile}-\smile-\,|\,\underline{\smile}-\smile-\,|\,\underline{\smile}-\smile-\,|\,\smile-\underline{\smile}$$

(common dialogue metre of comedy)

Trochaic septenarius (or tetrameter catalectic):

$$-\cup-\underline{\cup}\,|-\cup-\underline{\cup}\,|-\cup-\underline{\cup}\,|-\cup\underline{\cup}$$

(very common dialogue metre in early Roman drama)

Hexameter:

$$-\cup\cup\,|-\cup\cup\,|-\cup\cup\,|-\cup\cup\,|-\cup\cup\,|-\underline{\cup}$$

(regular metre for epic, satiric, pastoral and didactic poetry)

Pentameter:

$$-\cup\cup-\cup\cup-\,|-\cup\cup-\cup\cup\underline{\cup}$$

(following the hexameter this forms the elegiac couplet, which is regarded as an entity and hence as stichic; regular metre for love-poetry and epigram)

Phalaecean hendecasyllables:

$$\underline{\cup\cup}\,|-\cup\cup-\,|\cup-\cup-\underline{\cup}$$

(i.e. first foot may be a spondee, iamb or trochee; used by Catullus, Martial and Statius)

(b) Non-stichic verse (constructed by combination of different metrical lines)

Alcaic stanza:	$--\cup--\,|-\cup\cup-\,|\cup\underline{\cup}$	(twice)
	$--\cup---\cup\underline{\cup}$	
	$-\cup\cup-\cup\cup-\,|\cup-\underline{\cup}$	
Sapphic stanza:	$-\cup--\,|-\cup\cup-\,|\cup-\underline{\cup}$	(three times)
	$-\cup\cup-\,|\underline{\cup}$	(adonean)
Third asclepiad:	$--\,|-\cup\cup-\,|\cup\underline{\cup}$	(glyconic)
	$--\,|-\cup\cup--\cup\cup-\,|\cup\underline{\cup}$	(lesser asclepiad)
Fourth asclepiad:	$--\,|-\cup\cup--\cup\cup-\,|\cup\underline{\cup}$	(lesser asclepiad, three times)
	$--\,|-\cup\cup-\,|\cup\underline{\cup}$	(glyconic)
Fifth asclepiad	$--\,|-\cup\cup--\cup\cup-\,|\cup\underline{\cup}$	(lesser asclepiad, twice)
	$--\,|-\cup\cup-\,|\underline{\cup}$	(pherecratean)
	$--\,|-\cup\cup-\,|\cup\underline{\cup}$	(glyconic)

(the First and Second asclepiad consist, respectively, of the lesser and greater asclepiad only; the latter $=--\,|-\cup\cup--\cup\cup--\cup\cup-\,|\cup\underline{\cup}$)

All the above found in Horace's *Odes*; some in Catullus and Statius.

(4) BIBLIOGRAPHY

Allen, W. S., *Vox Latina*, 2nd ed. (Cambridge 1978).

idem, *Accent and rhythm* (Cambridge 1973).

Raven, D. S., *Latin metre* (London 1965).

Wilkinson, L. P., *Golden Latin artistry* (Cambridge 1963) 89–134 and *passim*

ABBREVIATIONS

Anth. Lat.	A. Riese–F. Bücheler–E. Lommatzsch, *Anthologia Latina Latina* (Leipzig, 1894–1926). (Cf. *CLE*)
ANRW	H. Temporini, *Aufstieg und Niedergang der römischen Welt* (Berlin, 1972–)
Bardon	H. Bardon, *La littérature latine inconnue* (Paris 1951–6)
BT	Bibliotheca Scriptorum Graecorum et Romanorum Teubneriana (Leipzig & Stuttgart)
Budé	Collection des Universités de France, publiée sous le patronage de l'Association Guillaume Budé (Paris)
Bursian	Bursian's *Jahresbericht über die Fortschritte der klassischen Altertumswissenschaft* (Berlin, 1873–1945)
CAF	T. Kock, *Comicorum Atticorum Fragmenta* (Leipzig, 1880–8)
CAH	*The Cambridge Ancient History* (Cambridge, 1923–39)
CAH²	2nd ed. (Cambridge, 1961–)
CC	*Corpus Christianorum.* Series Latina (Turnholt, 1953–)
CGF	G. Kaibel, *Comicorum Graecorum Fragmenta* (Berlin, 1899)
CGFPap.	C. F. L. Austin, *Comicorum Graecorum Fragmenta in papyris reperta* (Berlin, 1973)
CIL	*Corpus Inscriptionum Latinarum* (Berlin, 1863–)
CLE	F. Bücheler–E. Lommatzsch, *Carmina Latina Epigraphica* (Leipzig, 1897–1930). (= *Anth. Lat.* Pars II)
CRF	O. Ribbeck, *Comicorum Romanorum Fragmenta*, 3rd. ed. (Leipzig, 1897)
CSEL	*Corpus Scriptorum Ecclesiasticorum Latinorum* (Vienna, 1866–)
CVA	*Corpus Vasorum Antiquorum* (Paris & elsewhere, 1925–)
Christ–Schmid–Stählin	W. von Christ, *Geschichte der griechischen Literatur*, rev. W. Schmid and O. Stählin (Munich, 1920–1924) 6th ed. (Cf. Schmid–Stählin)
DTC	A. W. Pickard-Cambridge, *Dithyramb, tragedy and comedy.* 2nd ed., rev. T. B. L. Webster (Oxford, 1962)
DFA	A. W. Pickard-Cambridge, *The dramatic festivals of Athens.* 2nd ed., rev. J. Gould–D. M. Lewis (Oxford, 1968)

DK	H. Diels–W. Kranz, *Die Fragmente der Vorsokratiker*. 6th ed. (Berlin, 1951)
EGF	G. Kinkel, *Epicorum Graecorum Fragmenta* (Leipzig, 1877)
FGrH	F. Jacoby, *Fragmente der griechischen Historiker* (Berlin, 1923–)
FHG	C. Müller, *Fragmenta Historicorum Graecorum* (Berlin, 1841–70)
FPL	W. Morel, *Fragmenta Poetarum Latinorum* (Leipzig, 1927)
FPR	E. Baehrens, *Fragmenta Poetarum Romanorum* (Leipzig, 1886)
FYAT	(ed.) M. Platnauer, *Fifty years (and twelve) of classical scholarship* (Oxford, 1968)
GLK	H. Keil, *Grammatici Latini* (Leipzig, 1855–1923)
GLP	D. L. Page, *Greek Literary Papyri* (Cambridge, Mass. & London, 1942–)
Gow–Page, *Hell. Ep.*	A. S. F. Gow–D. L. Page, *The Greek Anthology: Hellenistic Epigrams* (Cambridge, 1965)
Gow–Page, *Garland*	A. S. F. Gow–D. L. Page, *The Greek Anthology: The Garland of Philip* (Cambridge, 1968)
Guthrie	W. K. C. Guthrie, *A History of Greek Philosophy* (Cambridge, 1965–81)
HRR	H. Peter, *Historicorum Romanorum reliquiae* (Leipzig, 1906–14)
HS	J. B. Hofmann, *Lateinische Syntax und Stilistik*, rev. A. Szantyr (Munich, 1965)
IEG	M. L. West, *Iambi et Elegi Graeci* (Oxford, 1971–2)
IG	*Inscriptiones Graecae* (Berlin, 1873–)
ILS	H. Dessau, *Inscriptiones Latinae Selectae* (Berlin, 1892–1916)
KG	R. Kühner–B. Gerth, *Ausführliche Grammatik der griechischen Sprache: Satzlehre*. 4th ed. (Hannover, 1955)
KS	R. Kühner–C. Stegmann, *Ausführliche Grammatik der lateinischen sprache: Satzlehre*. 3rd ed., rev. A. Thierfelder (Hannover, 1955)
Leo, *Gesch.*	F. Leo, *Geschichte der romischen Literatur*. I *Die archaische Literatur* (all pubd) (Berlin, 1913; repr. Darmstadt, 1967, w. *Die römische Poesie in der sullanischen Zeit*)
Lesky	A. Lesky, *A History of Greek Literature*, tr. J. Willis–C. de Heer (London, 1966)
Lesky, *TDH*	A. Lesky, *Die tragische Dichtung der Hellenen*, 3rd ed. (Göttingen, 1972)
LSJ	Liddell–Scott–Jones, *Greek–English Lexicon*, 9th ed. (Oxford, 1925–40)
Loeb	Loeb Classical Library (Cambridge, Mass. & London)
MGH	*Monumenta Germaniae Historica* (Berlin, 1877–91)
OCD²	*Oxford Classical Dictionary*, 2nd ed. (Oxford, 1970)

OCT	Scriptorum Classicorum Bibliotheca Oxoniensis (Oxford)
Paravia	Corpus Scriptorum Latinorum Paravianum (Turin)
PIR	E. Klebs–H. Dessau, *Prosopographia Imperii Romani Saeculi I, II, III* (Berlin, 1897–8), 2nd ed. E. Groag–A. Stein (Berlin & Leipzig, 1933–)
PL	J.-P. Migne, *Patrologiae cursus completus* Series Latina (Paris, 1844–)
PLF	E. Lobel–D. Page, *Poetarum Lesbiorum Fragmenta* (Oxford, 1963)
PLM	E. Baehrens, *Poetae Latini Minores* (Leipzig, 1879–83), rev. F. Vollmer (incomplete) (1911–35)
PLRE	A. H. M. Jones–J. R. Martindale–J. Morris, *The prosopography of the later Roman Empire* (Cambridge, 1971–)
PMG	D. L. Page, *Poetae Melici Graeci* (Oxford, 1962)
PPF	H. Diels, *Poetarum Philosophorum Graecorum Fragmenta* (Berlin, 1901)
Pfeiffer	R. Pfeiffer, *A history of classical scholarship* (Oxford, 1968)
Powell	J. U. Powell, *Collectanea Alexandrina* (Oxford, 1925)
Powell–Barber	J. U. Powell–E. A. Barber, *New chapters in the history of Greek Literature* (Oxford, 1921), 2nd ser. (1929), 3rd ser. (Powell alone) (1933)
Preller–Robert	L. Preller, *Griechische Mythologie*, 4th ed., rev. C. Robert (Berlin, 1894)
RAC	*Reallexicon für Antike und Christentum* (Stuttgart, 1941–)
RE	A. Pauly–G. Wissowa–W. Kroll, *Real-Encyclopädie der klassischen Altertumswissenschaft* (Stuttgart, 1893–)
ROL	E. H. Warmington, *Remains of old Latin* (Cambridge, Mass. & London, 1935–40)
Roscher	W. H. Roscher, *Ausführliches Lexicon der griechischen und römischen Mythologie* (Leipzig, 1884–)
SEG	*Supplementum Epigraphicum Graecum* (Leyden, 1923–71; Alphen aan den Rijn, 1979–)
SVF	H. von Arnim, *Stoicorum Veterum Fragmenta* (Leipzig, 1903–)
Snell	B. Snell, *Tragicorum Graecorum Fragmenta* (Göttingen, 1971–)
Schanz–Hosius	M. Schanz–C. Hosius, *Geschichte der römischen Literatur* (Munich, 1914–1935)
Schmid–Stählin	W. Schmid–O. Stählin, *Geschichte der griechischen Literatur* (Munich, 1929–1948)
Spengel	L. Spengel, *Rhetores Graeci* (1853–6); I ii rev. C. Hammer (Leipzig, 1894)
Teuffel	W. S. Teuffel, *Geschichte der römischen Literatur* (Leipzig & Berlin, 1913–1920)

TGF	A. Nauck, *Tragicorum Graecorum Fragmenta*, 2nd ed. (Leipzig, 1889)
TLL	*Thesaurus Linguae Latinae* (Leipzig, 1900–)
TRF	O. Ribbeck, *Tragicorum Romanorum Fragmenta*, 3rd ed. (Leipzig, 1897)
Walz	C. Walz, *Rhetores Graeci* (Stuttgart, 1832–6)
Williams, *TORP*	G. Williams, *Tradition and originality in Roman Poetry* (Oxford, 1968)

WORKS CITED IN THE TEXT

Allen, W. (1972). 'Ovid's *cantare* and Cicero's *Cantores Euphorionis*', *T.A.Ph.A.* 103: 1–14.

Allen, W. S. (1973). *Accent and rhythm: prosodic features of Latin and Greek.* Cambridge.

Anderson, R. D., Parsons, P. J. and Nisbet, R. G. M. (1979). 'Elegiacs by Gallus from Qaṣr Ibrîm', *J.R.S.* 69: 125–55.

André, J. (1949). *Étude sur les termes de couleur dans la langue latine.* Paris.

André, J.-M. (1967). *Mécène. Essai de biographie spirituelle.* Paris.

Arnott, W. G. (1970). 'Phormio Parasitus', *G. & R.* n.s. 17: 32–57.

(1972). 'Targets, techniques, and tradition in Plautus' Stichus', *B.I.C.S.* 19: 54–79.

(1975). *Menander, Plautus, and Terence. Greece & Rome* New Surveys in the Classics IX. Oxford.

Arns, E. (1953). *La technique du livre d'après Saint Jérôme.* Paris.

Astin, A. E. (1967). *Scipio Aemilianus.* Oxford.

Badian, E. (1966). 'The early historians', in T. A. Dorey (ed.), *Latin historians* 1–38. London.

(1970). *Titus Quinctius Flamininus: Philhellenism and Realpolitik.* Lectures in Memory of Louisa Taft Semple, Second Series. Cincinnati.

(1971). 'Ennius and his Friends', in *Ennius*, Entretiens Hardt XVII 149–208. Geneva.

Barchiesi, M. (1962). *Nevio epico.* Turin.

Bardon, H. (1940). *Les empereurs et les lettres latines d'Auguste à Hadrien.* Paris.

(1956). *La littérature latine inconnue.* II. *L'époque impériale.* Paris.

Beare, W. (1964). *The Roman stage.* 3rd edn. London.

Bentley, R. (1726). 'De metris Terentianis schediasma', in *P. Terenti Afri Comoediae* i–xix. Cambridge.

Besslich, S. (1973). 'Die "Hörner" des Buches. Zur Bedeutung von cornua im antiken Buchwesen', *Gutenberg-Jahrbuch* 44–50.

Birt, T. (1882). *Das antike Buchwesen in seinem Verhältniss zur Litteratur mit Beiträgen zur Textgeschichte des Theokrit, Catull, Properz und anderer Autoren.* Berlin.

(1913). *Kritik und Hermeneutik nebst Abriss des antiken Buchwesens.* Munich.

Bonner, S. F. (1949). *Roman declamation in the late Republic and early Empire.* Liverpool.

(1977). *Education in ancient Rome from the elder Cato to the younger Pliny.* London.

Boyancé, P. (1955). 'M. Fulvius Nobilior et le dieu ineffable', *R.Ph.* 29: 172–92.

(1970). *Études sur l'humanisme cicéronien*. Collection Latomus CXXI. Brussels.

Büchner, K. (1961). 'Überlieferungsgeschichte der lateinischen Literatur des Altertums', in *Geschichte der Textüberlieferung* I. Zürich.

Burr, V. (1959). 'Editionstechnik', *RAC* IV 597–610.

Callmer, C. (1944). 'Antike Bibliotheken', *Acta Inst. Rom. regni Sueciae* 10: 145–93.

Cameron, A. (1964). 'Literary allusions in the Historia Augusta', *Hermes* 92: 363–77.

(1970). *Claudian: poetry and propaganda at the court of Honorius*. Oxford.

Cancik, H. (1969). 'Zur Geschichte des Aedes (Herculis) Musarum auf dem Marsfeld', *M.D.A.I.(R.)* 76: 323–8.

(1970). 'Die Statue des L. Accius im Tempel der Camenen', in M. von Albrecht and E. Heck (eds.), *Silvae: Festschrift für E. Zinn zum 60. Geburtstag* 7–17. Tübingen.

Caplan, H. (1970). *On eloquence*. Cornell.

Cavenaile, R. (1958). (ed.). *Corpus papyrorum Latinorum*. Wiesbaden.

Cèbe, J.-P. (1960). 'Le niveau culturel du public plautinien', *R.E.L.* 38: 101–6.

Cichorius, C. (1908). *Studien zu Lucilius*. Leipzig.

Clarke, M. L. (1953). *Rhetoric at Rome: a historical survey*. London.

Clausen, W. V. (1964). 'Callimachus and Latin poetry', *G.R.B.S.* 5: 181–96.

Clift, E. H. (1945). *Latin pseudepigrapha*. Baltimore.

Coffey, M. (1976). *Roman satire*. London & New York.

Cole, A. T. (1972). 'The Saturnian verse', *Y.Cl.S.* 21: 3–73.

Crowther, N. B. (1971). 'Valerius Cato, Furius Bibaculus, and Ticidas', *C.Ph.* 66: 108–9.

Dahlmann, H. (1951). 'Zur Überlieferung über die "altrömischen Tafellieder"', *A.A.M.* 17: 1191ff.

D'Alton, J. F. (1931). *Roman literary theory and criticism*. London.

Derow, P. S. (1973). 'The Roman calendar, 190–168 B.C.', *Phoenix* 27: 345–56.

Devoto, J. (1954). *Tabulae Iguvinae*. Rome.

Douglas, A. E. (1973). 'The intellectual background of Cicero's Rhetorica: a study in method' in *ANRW* 1.3 95–138. Berlin & New York.

Drexler, H. (1932/3). *Plautinische Akzentstudien*. 2 vols. Breslau.

(1967). *Einführung in die römische Metrik*. Darmstadt.

(1969). *Die Iambenkürzung*. Hildesheim.

Duckworth, G. E. (1952). *The nature of Roman comedy*. Princeton.

Dziatzko, K. (1899*a*). 'Buch', *RE* III 939–71.

(1899*b*). 'Buchhandel', *RE* III 973–85.

Enk, P. J. (1953). 'The Latin accent', *Mnemosyne* 4.6: 93–109.

Erath, W. (1971). *Die Dichtung des Lygdamus*. Diss. Erlangen.

Fraenkel, E. (1922). *Plautinisches im Plautus*. Berlin.

(1927). 'Zur Vorgeschichte des *versus quadratus*', *Hermes* 62: 357–70.

(1928). *Iktus und Akzent im lateinischen Sprechvers*. Berlin.

(1937). Review of Pasquali (1936), in *J.R.S.* 27: 262ff.

(1951*a*). 'Additional notes on the prose of Ennius', *Eranos* 49: 50ff.

(1951*b*). 'The pedigree of the Saturnian metre', *Eranos* 49: 170f.

(1957). *Horace*. Oxford.

(1960). *Elementi plautini in Plauto*, tr. F. Munari. Florence. (Rev. version of *Plautinisches im Plautus*. Berlin 1922.)

(1964). *Kleine Beiträge zur klassischen Philologie*. 2 vols. Rome.

(1968). *Leseproben aus Reden Ciceros und Catos*. Sussidi eruditi XXII. Rome.

Fraser, P. M. (1972). *Ptolemaic Alexandria*. 3 vols. Oxford.

Friedländer, L. (1908–28). *Roman life and manners under the early Empire*, tr. L. A. Magnus, J. H. Freese, A. B. Gough. 4 vols. London.

Gaiser, K. (1970). 'Die plautinischen *Bacchides* und Menanders *Dis exapaton*', *Philologus* 114: 51–87.

(1972). 'Zur Eigenart der römischen Komödie: Plautus und Terenz gegenüber ihren griechischen Vorbildern', *ANRW* 1.2 1027–1113.

Geffcken, J. (1911). 'Studien zur griechischen Satire', *Neue Jahrbücher für das klassiche Altertum* 27: 393–411, 469–93.

Georgii, H. (1891). *Die antike Äneiskritik*. Stuttgart.

Getty, R. J. (1955). (ed.). *M. Annaei Lucani De bello ciuili Liber I*. Corr. repr. Cambridge.

Gomme, A. W. (1937). 'Menander', in *Essays in Greek history and literature* 249–95. Oxford.

Grube, G. M. A. (1965). *The Greek and Roman critics*. London.

Guillemin, A.-M. (1937). *Le public et la vie littéraire à Rome*. Paris.

Gwynn, A. (1926). *Roman education from Cicero to Quintilian*. Oxford.

Haffter, H. (1934). *Untersuchungen zur altlateinischen Dichtersprache*. Berlin.

(1935). *Die altlateinische Dichtersprache*. Problemata X. Leipzig.

Hafner, G. (1968). *Das Bildnis von Q. Ennius*. Baden-Baden.

Handley, E. W. (1968). *Menander and Plautus*. London.

Horsfall, N. M. (1976). 'The *Collegium Poetarum*', *B.I.C.S.* 23: 79–95.

Ihm, M. (1893). Die Bibliotheken im alten Rom', *Centralbl. für Bibliothekswesen* 10: 513–32.

Immisch, O. (1923). 'Zur Frage der plautinischen *Cantica*', *Sitzungsberichte der Heidelberger Akademie* (Phil.-Hist. Kl.) 14: 7. Abhandlung 41.

Jahn, O. (1851). 'Über die Subscriptionen in den Handschriften römischer Classiker', *Ber. d. sächs. Ges. d. Wiss. zu Leipzig* (Phil.-Hist. Kl.) 3: 327–72.

Jellicoe, S. (1968). *The Septuagint and modern study*. Oxford.

Jocelyn, H. D. (1969). 'The poet Cn. Naevius, P. Cornelius Scipio, and Q. Caecilius Metellus', *Antichthon* 3: 32–47.

(1972). 'The poems of Quintus Ennius', *ANRW* 1.2 987–1026.

(1973). 'Greek poetry in Cicero's prose writings', *Y.Cl.S.* 23: 61–111.

Jordan, H. (1860). *M. Catonis praeter librum de re rustica quae extant*. Leipzig.

Kenyon, F. G. (1951). *Books and readers in ancient Greece and Rome*. 2nd edn. Oxford.

Kienast, D. (1954). *Cato der Zensor*. Heidelberg.

Kleberg, T. (1967). *Buchhandel und Verlagswesen in der Antike.* Darmstadt.

Klotz, A. (1947). 'Zur Verskunst des römischen Dramas', *Würzburger Jahrbücher für die Altertumswissenschaft* 2: 301–57.

Knowles, M. D. (1958). 'The preservation of the classics', in *The English library before 1700.* London.

Knox, B. M. W. (1968). 'Silent reading in antiquity', *G.R.B.S.* 9: 421–35.

Koep, L. (1954). 'Buch I (technisch)', *RAC* II 664–88.

Krenkel, W. (1970). *Lucilius, Satiren.* Leiden.

Latte, K. (1960). *Römische Religionsgeschichte.* Munich.

Laughton, E. (1951). 'The prose of Ennius', *Eranos* 2: 35ff.

(1960). 'Observations on the style of Varro', *C.Q.* n.s. 10: 1–28.

Lejay, P. (1925). *Plaute.* Paris.

Leo, F. (1897). *Die plautinischen Cantica und die hellenistische Lyrik.* Berlin.

(1906). 'Diogenes bei Plautus', *Hermes* 41: 441–6 (= *Ausgewählte Kleine Schriften* I, Rome 1960, 185–90).

(1912). *Plautinische Forschungen.* 2nd edn. Berlin.

(1913). *Geschichte der römischen Literatur* I: *Die archaische Literatur.* Berlin.

Lewis, N. (1974). *Papyrus in classical antiquity.* Oxford.

Lindsay, W. M. (1904). *Ancient editions of Plautus.* Oxford & St Andrews.

(1907). *Syntax of Plautus.* Oxford.

(1922). *Early Latin verse.* Oxford.

Luck, G. (1968). (ed.). *P. Ovidius Naso. Tristia. II. Kommentar.* Heidelberg.

Ludwig, W. (1968). 'The originality of Terence and his Greek models', *G.R.B.S.* 9: 169–82.

Maas, P. and Lloyd-Jones, H. (tr.) (1962). *Greek metre.* Oxford.

MacCary, W. T. and Willcock, M. M. (1976). (eds.). *Plautus, Casina.* Cambridge.

Malcovati, H. (1955). *Oratorum Romanorum fragmenta liberae rei publicae.* 2nd edn. (1st edn. 1930). 3 vols. Turin.

Mariotti, S. (1952). *Livio Andronico e la traduzione artistica.* Milan.

(1955). *Il 'Bellum Poenicum' e l'arte di Nevio.* Rome.

Marrou, H. I. (1956). *A history of education in antiquity,* tr. G. Lamb. London.

(1958). *Saint Augustin et la fin de la culture antique.* 4th edn. Paris.

Martin, R. H. (1976). (ed.). *Terence, Adelphoe.* Cambridge.

Marx, F. (1904). *C. Lucilii carminum reliquiae.* 2 vols. Leipzig.

Mette, H.-J. (1964). Die römische Tragödie', *Lustrum* 9: 5–212.

Meyer, W. (1886). 'Ueber die Beobachtung des Wortaccentes in der altlateinischen Poesie', *Abhandlungen der bayerischen Akademie der Wissenschaften* (Phil.-Hist. Kl.) 17: 3–120.

Michels, A. K. (1967). *The calendar of the Roman Republic.* Princeton.

Momigliano, A. (1957). 'Perizonius, Niebuhr and the character of early Roman tradition', *J.R.S.* 47: 104–14.

(1975). *Alien wisdom: the limits of Hellenization.* Cambridge.

Mountford, J. F. and Schultz, J. T. (1930). *Index rerum et nominum in scholiis Servii et Aelii Donati tractatorum*. Ithaca, New York.

Nachmanson, E. (1941). *Der griechische Buchtitel. Einige Beobachtungen*. Gothenburg.

Nash, E. (1961–2). *A pictorial dictionary of ancient Rome*. London.

Nettleship, H. (1890). 'Literary criticism in Latin antiquity', *Journal of Philology* 18: 225–70.

Neumeister, C. (1964). *Grundsätze der forensischen Rhetorik*. Munich.

Norden, E. (1915). *Ennius und Vergilius. Kriegsbilder aus Roms grosser Zeit*. Leipzig & Berlin.

(1926). (ed.). *P. Vergilius Maro, Aeneis Buch VI*. 3rd edn. Leipzig & Berlin.

(1939). *Aus altrömischen Priesterbüchern*. Lund.

Nougaret, L. (1943). 'La métrique de Plaute et de Térence', *Mémorial des études latines ... offert ... à J. Marouzeau* 123–48. Paris.

(1948). *Traité de métrique latine classique*. Paris.

Pasquali, G. (1936). *Preistoria della poesia romana*. Florence.

Patzer, H. (1955). 'Zum Sprachstil des neoterischen Hexameters', *Mus. Helv.* 12: 77–95.

Pearce, T. E. V. (1966). 'The enclosing word-order in the Latin hexameter', *C.Q.* n.s. 16: 140–71, 298–320.

(1968). 'A pattern of word-order in Latin poetry', *C.Q.* n.s. 18: 334–54.

Peter, H. (1914). *Historicorum Romanorum fragmenta*. 2nd edn. Leipzig.

Peterson, W. (1891). (ed.). *M. Fabi Quintiliani Institutionis oratoriae Liber decimus*. Oxford.

Pfeiffer, R. (1968). *History of classical scholarship from the beginnings to the end of the Hellenistic age*. Oxford.

Poultney, J. W. (1959). *The Bronze Tables of Iguvium*. A.P.A. Monograph XVIII.

Questa, C. (1967). *Introduzione alla metrica di Plauto*. Rome.

(1970). 'Alcune strutture sceniche di Plauto e Menandro', in *Ménandre*, Entretiens Hardt XVI 181–228. Geneva.

Raven, D. S. (1965). *Latin metre*. London.

Rennie, W. (1921). 'Satira tota nostra est', *C.R.* 35: 21.

Reynolds, L. D. (1965). *The medieval tradition of Seneca's letters*. Oxford.

Reynolds, L. D. and Wilson, N. G. (1974). *Scribes and scholars. A guide to the transmission of Greek and Latin literature*. 2nd edn. Oxford.

Ribbeck, O. (1866). *Prolegomena critica ad P. Vergili Maronis opera maiora*. Leipzig.

Rieth, C. (1964). *Die Kunst Menanders in den Adelphen des Terenz*. Hildesheim.

Roberts, C. H. (1954). 'The Codex', *P.B.A.* 40: 169–204.

(1956). *Greek literary hands 350 B.C.–A.D. 400*. Corr. repr. Oxford.

Robinson, R. P. (1923). 'Valerius Cato', *T.A.Ph.A.* 54: 98–116.

Ross, D. O. jr. (1969). 'Nine epigrams from Pompeii (*CIL* 4.4966–73)', *Y.Cl.S.* 21: 127–42.

Rowell, H. T. (1947). 'The original form of Naevius' *Bellum Poenicum*', *A.J.Ph.* 68: 35ff.

Rudd, N. (1960). 'Horace on the origins of Satire', *Phoenix* 14: 36–44.

Schanz, M. and Hosius, C. (1927). *Geschichte der römischen Literatur* 1: *Die römische Literatur in der Zeit der Republik.* 4th edn. Munich.

Schubart, W. (1921). *Das Buch bei den Griechen und Römern.* 2nd edn. Berlin & Leipzig.

Schutter, K. H. E. (1952). *Quibus annis comoediae Plautinae primum actae sint quaeritur.* Groningen.

Scivoletto, N. (1966). 'Quando nacque Seneca?', *G.I.F.* 19: 21–31.

Shackleton Bailey, D. R. (1965–70). (ed.). *Cicero's Letters to Atticus.* 7 vols. Cambridge.

Sherk, R. K. (1969). *Roman documents from the Greek East: Senatus consulta and Epistulae to the age of Augustus.* Baltimore.

Sherwin-White, A. N. (1966). *The Letters of Pliny: a historical and social commentary.* Oxford.

Shipp, G. P. (1953). 'Greek in Plautus', *W.S.* 66: 105–12.

(1955). 'Plautine terms for Greek and Roman things', *Glotta* 34: 139–52.

Sifakis, G. M. (1967). *Studies in the history of Hellenistic drama.* London.

Skutsch, O. (1968). *Studia Enniana.* London.

Smith, K. F. (1913). (ed.). *The Elegies of Albius Tibullus.* New York.

Sommer, R. (1926). 'T. Pomponius Atticus und Ciceros Werke', *Hermes* 61: 389–422.

Speyer, W. (1971). *Die literarische Fälschung im heidnischen und christlichen Altertum. Ein Versuch ihrer Deutung.* Munich.

Strzelecki, L. (1935). *De Naeviano 'Belli Punici' carmine quaestiones selectae.* Krakow.

Suerbaum, W. (1968). *Untersuchungen zur Selbstdarstellung älterer römischer Dichter, Livius Andronicus, Naevius, Ennius.* Hildesheim.

Syme, R. (1958). *Tacitus.* 2 vols. Oxford.

Taylor, L. R. (1937). 'The opportunities for dramatic performances in the time of Plautus and Terence', *T.A.Ph.A.* 68: 284–304.

Thulin, C. (1906). *Italische sakrale Poesie und Prosa.* Berlin.

Till, R. (1936). *Die Sprache Catos. Philologus* Suppl.-Band XXVIII, Heft 2.

Townend, G. B. (1969). 'Some problems of punctuation in the Latin hexameter', *C.Q.* n.s. 19: 330–44.

Traina, A. (1970). *Vortit barbare. Le traduzioni poetiche da Livio Andronico a Cicerone.* Rome.

Trendall, A. D. (1967). *Phlyax vases. B.I.C.S.* Suppl. XIX. 2nd edn. London.

Turner, E. G. (1968). *Greek papyri: an introduction.* Oxford.

(1971). *Greek manuscripts of the ancient world.* Oxford.

van Groningen, B. A. (1963). '"Εκδοσις', *Mnemosyne* 4.16: 1–17.

Van Rooy, C. A. (1965). *Studies in classical satire and related literary theory.* Leiden.

Vessey, D. W. T. C. (1973). *Statius and the Thebaid.* Cambridge.

Waszink, J.-H. (1950). 'The Proem of the *Annales* of Ennius', *Mnemosyne* 3. 3: 215–40.

(1972). 'Zum Anfangsstadium der römischen Literatur', *ANRW* 1.2, 869–927.

Watson, A. (1971). *Roman private law around 200 B.C.* Edinburgh.

Watts, W. J. (1971). 'The birthplaces of Latin writers', *G. & R.* n.s. 18: 91–101.

Wendel, C. (1949). *Die griechisch-römische Buchbeschreibung verglichen mit der des Vorderen Orients.* Halle.

(1954). 'Bibliothek', *RAC* II 664–88.

Wessner, P. (1929). 'Lucan, Statius und Juvenal bei den römischen Grammatikern', *P.Ph.W.* 49: 296–303, 328–35.

West, D. A. (1969). 'Multiple-correspondence similes in the *Aeneid*', *J.R.S.* 59: 40–9.

White, P. (1974). 'The presentation and dedication of the *Silvae* and the *Epigrams*', *J.R.S.* 64: 40–61.

Williams, G. W. (1956). 'Some problems in the construction of Plautus' *Pseudolus*', *Hermes* 84: 424–55.

(1958). 'Evidence for Plautus' workmanship in the *Miles Gloriosus*', *Hermes* 86: 79–105.

(1968). *Tradition and originality in Roman poetry.* Oxford.

Williams, R. D. (1961). 'The function and structure of Virgil's Catalogue in *Aeneid* 7', *C.Q.* n.s. 11: 146–53.

Wingo, E. O. (1972). *Latin punctuation in the classical age.* The Hague & Paris.

Winterbottom, M. (1974). (ed.). *The Elder Seneca. Declamations.* 2 vols. Loeb. London & Cambridge, Mass.

Wright, J. (1974). *Dancing in chains: the stylistic unity of the comoedia palliata.* Papers and monographs of the American Academy in Rome xxv. Rome.

Zetzel, J. E. G. (1972). *Latin textual criticism in antiquity.* Unpubd diss. Harvard. [Now pubd New York 1981.]

INDEX

Main references are distinguished by figures in bold type. References to the Appendix (which should normally be consulted for basic details of authors' lives and works, and for bibliographies) are given in italic figures.